BRAVE NEW HUMANS

For Sam, and the comedy trio

BRAVE NEW HUMANS

THE DIRTY REALITY OF DONOR CONCEPTION

Sarah Dingle

Hardie Grant
BOOKS

Published in 2021 by Hardie Grant Books, an imprint of Hardie Grant Publishing

Hardie Grant Books (Melbourne)
Wurundjeri Country
Building 1, 658 Church Street
Richmond, Victoria 3121

Hardie Grant Books (London)
5th & 6th Floors
52–54 Southwark Street
London SE1 1UN

hardiegrantbooks.com

A catalogue record for this book is available from the National Library of Australia

Brave New Humans
ISBN 978 1 74379 638 2

10 9 8 7 6 5 4 3 2 1

Cover design by Josh Durham, Design by Committee
Cover image courtesy of bigstockphoto.com
Typeset in 11/15 pt Adobe Caslon Pro by Cannon Typesetting

Printed in Australia by Griffin Press, part of Ovato, an Accredited ISO AS/NZS 14001 Environmental Management System printer.

The paper this book is printed on is certified against the Forest Stewardship Council® Standards. Griffin Press holds FSC® chain of custody certification SGS-COC-005088. FSC® promotes environmentally responsible, socially beneficial and economically viable management of the world's forests.

Hardie Grant acknowledges the Traditional Owners of the country on which we work, the Wurundjeri people of the Kulin nation and the Gadigal people of the Eora nation, and recognises their continuing connection to the land, waters and culture. We pay our respects to their Elders past, present and emerging.

PROLOGUE

IT WAS EASTER. I'd brought her flowers, and we were sitting in a Vietnamese restaurant, metres from Oxford Street, on a Saturday night.

At twenty-seven, I was vaguely aware that there was no longer infinite time. I loved my job. I didn't want children any time soon. But I didn't want all options to vanish while I filed stories. My mother's not always my first port of call for advice, but she's lived a lot longer. And she had me.

'Mum, you know how you had me late,' I said cautiously. 'Did you have any problems conceiving me?'

Her eyes flickered. My mother was in her sixties. She is Malaysian Chinese, with short salt-and-pepper hair.

'Why do you ask, Sarah?'

'Because,' I explained, aware it was an unusually personal question between us, 'because I don't know if I want to have children now, or at all, and I was wondering how late to leave it. If there was a deadline I should know about.' (Such a journalist.)

She moved in her seat. 'Maybe this isn't the right time to tell you.' Shrug. 'But your father is not your father.'

What?

'You're joking, aren't you?' I said.

'No. We had … we had problems conceiving, and it turned out your father couldn't. So we used a donor.'

WHAT?

'You're joking! Mum – are you joking?'

'No, no.'

Half a beat —

'But the only difference it makes,' she said quickly, a burst to finish what she had to say, 'the only difference it would make to you at all is your medical history. Knowing your medical history, that's all. Because your father is your father. He loved you like his own daughter. You couldn't ask for a better father. He was a fantastic father to you.'

My mother now looked anxious. 'It doesn't make a difference, does it, Sarah?' she said.

I felt like the pressure in the room had dropped. The lights and walls were very yellow, and other sounds had faded. My brain danced around what she'd just told me, refusing to engage.

In that pause, something happened. It's hard to be completely in the moment when you're a journalist: some external self is always standing at a distance, noting, nodding. And so, despite my shock, I'd automatically picked up the flow of power in the conversation.

This was a moment when her guard was down. She wasn't actually asking me. She wanted reassurance. And she needed to hear it straightaway.

I wanted to scream, to rip the tablecloth off, to smash something, to go to the bathrooms and cry.

'No,' I said. 'It doesn't.'

That was my first lesson in what it's like to be donor conceived: your feelings about the whole business come last.

CHAPTER 1

BEFORE THAT NIGHT – before the lights turned yellow and the background noise dropped and the world shattered into many pieces – this is what I knew about myself: I grew up in Sydney in the 1980s. I had no siblings. It was just me, my dad and my mum.

We travelled a lot. We went to Malaysia, every year, to see my mother's side of the family in Kuala Lumpur. My father was a travel agent, which was a hell of a lot more important before the internet. Before I was born, he ran tours through the USSR, driving a tour bus and telling clients to bring extra pairs of American-style jeans they could sell to the locals. Later, after the breakdown of the Soviet Union, my father mostly concentrated his business on Eastern Europe. We lived in Moscow for a month while he set up an office there. We went to China, to my uncle's home, and on the Silk Road, road testing potential guesthouses.

I'm not sure why Dad became fixed on Eastern Europe and Central Asia, but it was definitely a world apart from where he grew up. Dad came from white middle-class Adelaide. In his childhood, he had a horse in the Adelaide Hills. He was a Boy Scout. He was from a generation where the ability to play tennis and squash was an important social currency. My dad's family are all still in South Australia. Every year, at Christmas, we drove from Sydney to Adelaide to see them, which for me meant fourteen hours in the back seat with the dog at my feet.

My dad was good looking. He was tall, with wavy brown hair and blue eyes, and a loud juddering laugh like a lawnmower starting.

He liked to look smart. He impressed on me the near-unassailable merits of wearing navy blue. My dad and I, we didn't look alike. But this never rang any alarm bells for me. I can only say to you: mixed-race children, we never quite fit. We never look like our parents. We never fully belong to anyone, except, occasionally, to one another.

One reason, perhaps, that the physical disconnect between my father and me never bothered me was because, temperamentally, we were so similar. We understood each other. We could make each other laugh. When I was too young to go to school, he woke up early and left me drawing exercises. He took me to sport and to work with him on weekends. And when I started high school, he was very strict. I get annoyed every time someone raises the (racist) stereotype of the tiger mother, because it was my white father, not my Chinese mother, who decided that success was not optional.

Dad never went to university. He left high school early. He regretted both, I think, and consequently he was obsessed with my education. He was something of a helicopter parent, in pre–helicopter parent times. He made sure I played hockey and basketball. He made sure I learned piano. He even found me a piano teacher while we stayed in Moscow so I could keep it up.

Dad monitored all my school results. He argued with me about my subject choices. He bought me novels at the drop of a hat and wrote in each one, noting the date and the place and the pretext for the gift.

When I was fifteen, and studying German in high school, I asked to go on a three-month student exchange to Germany. I was pretty blasé about the enormity of it until the last minute.

But at the airport, I suddenly felt a lurch at the thought of leaving my parents and all that familiarity: all that family.

'I'm afraid,' I blurted.

My dad hugged me. 'Don't be afraid. Never be afraid.'

That was the last thing he said to me, face to face.

On a white Christmas day in Germany, I got a phone call. Apparently my father had fallen off a ladder and broken his arm. But my mother's voice shook on the phone. I was to come home.

I was angry, an extremely unhelpful adolescent response, at having to cut short my exchange. I packed up all my stuff and my host parents took me to the airport.

We made it to the departure gates, and my German host mother, who until then had been extremely no-nonsense, squashed me in a hug and started to cry. I put the tears down to her being an unexpected softie. In Singapore, I had a seven-hour stopover to try to work out what on earth had just happened. My exchange was over almost before it had begun. How would I explain this to my friends? Teenagers: chronically self-absorbed.

I flew into baking hot Adelaide. My mother and my godfather picked me up from the airport. My mother didn't recognise me until I stood right in front of her, saying her name: it seemed I'd grown.

In the car, I told them I had a present for Dad. A huge twist of boiled aniseed lollies, bought at the airport in Germany. Dad loved liquorice with the fever of an addict.

'When can I give it to him?' I asked.

I saw my godfather, driving, and my mother in the front passenger seat exchange a glance.

'Maybe later,' one of them said.

We pulled up at the hospital.

As usual, my parents were staying at my grandfather's place for Christmas. My grandfather was in his nineties and still living at home. Something had gone wrong with the electricity in the house. My father was asked to go up on the roof and take a look.

My father was electrocuted. He fell off the ladder. (There were, as it turned out, broken bones.) He was rushed to hospital. When I arrived from the other side of the world, a day or so later, he was still in a coma.

I think he hung on for me.

His skin had a sick mustard tinge, and there was a strange smell to it. He kept sweating, and my mother kept wiping his brow: a painfully silent loop of activity. Other than that, he looked more or less normal. I think I found out later that, under the blankets, on his body, there were entry and exit burns where the current had passed through, but I don't know: those days were a haze.

I went to his bedside, feeling self-conscious, and started to speak to him. At some point I promised him that I'd do well in my final year of school. I had the distinct impression that was what he really wanted to hear.

He never woke up. The machine monitoring his vital signs flatlined that evening.

My father died when I was fifteen. I have no siblings. Only my mother is left in my immediate family. Or so I thought.

CHAPTER 2

WHAT HAPPENED IN that hospital room would mark me indelibly for years. Everything there was alive and remarkable in some way – the sounds too loud, the colours off – except, in the end, my father. But there was another layer to everything too, one which I couldn't see.

Despite the evidence of all my senses, what happened there that day was not the full story. That would take another twelve years to emerge, in that restaurant on a Saturday night.

After that Easter dinner revelation, I went home in a daze. I don't know how I got there. In my flat, I curled up on the couch and bawled. There's no other word for it.

Somewhere in the middle of it, I rang my then-boyfriend, who was overseas, and choked out what had happened.

'She said he's not my father,' I mumbled.

'She WHAT?'

'He's not my, my father.'

'What does she mean? Did she have an affair?'

'They used [*hiccup*], used a donor.'

'WHAT?'

On the line, my boyfriend fell silent.

'I don't know what to say,' he said eventually.

I wailed some more. He comforted me. Then I said what was really on my mind: 'He's not my father,' I hiccupped. 'Dad, he's not … he's not mine.'

I'm no shrink, but I now know that when you find out you're donor conceived, there are a number of common emotional stages. As with all processes, it depends on the individual. You may skip some or linger in others.

My first stage was grief. The man I thought was my father had died when I was fifteen. Now, twelve years later, I was back at the funeral, in baking hot Adelaide, with cicadas screaming. The scene was the same, but I was different. I was an interloper, because: *he was never mine in the first place.*

I'd always believed that when someone dies, if you love them, they are yours forever. Until now, it had been a comforting thought.

I had been tricked. I felt like a fool. I had lost even that.

OVER THE NEXT few months, I carried on as normal. I went to work. I was then a reporter with the ABC's *7.30*, a national TV current affairs show. It was a job I'd wanted for years. It was also a demanding job at the best of times. This was not the best of times. I tried to keep my shit together. I told a select few people. Mostly, I didn't tell people.

I was a mess.

In the mornings, I looked at myself in the mirror and I didn't know what I saw. I didn't recognise myself. When you grow up Asian in Australia, it's easy to forget how different you look to those around you. Most of my friends are white. My partner is white. Advertisements, magazines, newspapers, everything on Australian television – from the news to the trashiest reality TV show – is overwhelmingly white. Even my workplace, the public broadcaster, is still an extremely white institution. In photos or TV footage from work, surrounded by mostly white people, I'm sometimes surprised by how much I stand out. But there had always been a magnetic connection to my own face: *I am different, but I am who I am.*

Now that connection was broken.

The mirror was different: it was worse. I now didn't understand what I saw, as if my brain couldn't decode it. My face had become just colours and mass. Its shape was meaningless. It was not a face: it was a thing. I knew nothing about myself.

Standing in front of the mirror and struggling, I thought: maybe being only half Chinese can help me work my way back to some sort of solid ground. Because it's obvious that my biological father was not Chinese. Maybe he was Anglo-Saxon, like I'd always believed. Maybe he wasn't.

I studied my face again. I tried to separate the Chinese (the known) from the other (the unknown). It was impossible.

A whole is greater than the sum of its parts. Unfortunately, the flipside of that is: a whole cannot be broken down into those parts and still retain its meaning. With only one known biological parent, trying to work out *what* came from *whom* is like trying to reduce a cake to its original ingredients after the whole mess has already been baked.

Some mornings, I thought about it in mathematical terms: if I have the answer, can I work out what the equation is? Of course I couldn't. The equation could be anything. I could be almost all my mother's child, or virtually none. I have dark hair. I have dark brown eyes. I have light skin which can tan quite dark. I am of medium height. I have a straight nose. All of those traits could have come from either my mother or my father.

How do you take something away from a face and expect to understand what's left?

All of these thoughts would scream their way through my head every morning in front of the mirror, and then I'd go to work, where I was supposed to make stories about the big issues facing our nation. It wasn't ideal. On top of all that, I was managing a chronic pain condition.

Six months before I'd learned about my conception, I'd been vacuuming at home in the flat with the music cranked up loud. Suddenly, there was a bolt of extreme pain across my hips, like an iron bar. Black came down over my eyes. When it passed, I staggered to the bench where my phone was. I called my mother and told her something was wrong, that she had to come and find me. Then I passed out.

I woke up on the floor. The music was still going. I tried to get up, but I couldn't raise a single limb without a giant wave of pain and fear going off in my brain. It made me pass out again, and when I came to, I just lay there. I knew I wasn't paralysed because I could move my fingers and my toes. After what I think was a couple of hours, my mother and some paramedics broke in. They got me up, and into bed.

Over the next weeks, months, years, from MRIs, CTs, physio, osteo, chiro, acupuncture, massage, neurosurgery and pain clinics I learned that I had a herniated disc. It's a common injury, although less common among people in their twenties. The disc which had 'slipped' (such an awful term) was also desiccated – it had lost its sponginess. The muscles around it had gone into spasm, and this was something that I'd have to manage ongoing.

Unfortunately, chronic pain is not purely physical; to a certain extent, it's inextricably linked to your state of mind. Finding out that my father was not my father, and failing to recognise my own face in the mirror, meant that I was in a lot of mental and therefore physical pain. I was extremely depressed. The pain was coalescing with all the grief I still felt for my dad. When Dad died, I thought maybe that was the worst thing that would ever happen to me in my life.

It seemed ridiculously unfair that someone could die twice.

I had to leave *7.30*. Every few months, it seemed, I would be back on the floor again, paralysed, immobile for a week or more. When I was mobile and able to work, I couldn't do more than four hours a day without crippling pain. I moved to radio current affairs, trudging home early each day to spend my afternoons in agony, feeling useless. I wasn't even thirty and my life was over.

But a few things saved me. For a start, I did new things. Working only half days, I was bored out of my mind, so I enrolled in a creative writing course at night, making things up (which, after years of journalism, felt like a holiday). I dealt with the pain by lying on top of a row of desks at the back of the lecture room, while the rest of the group sat at the front. It was weird, but they bore it admirably; writers are very forgiving of idiosyncrasies.

I had heaps of leave, so I terrified myself by abandoning my support structures and went on a six-week trip to Italy to get away. If I couldn't have my dream job ever again, I was definitely going to eat good food, and if my life was over, I decided I'd rather spend the rest of my cash in euros than on miserable things like MRIs. To get around the pain, I planned wacky short flights to get there, with many stopovers. I did stretches on the ground in airports, train stations and car parks. I spent a lot of time in various Italian Airbnbs, flat on my back in the room, either resting or meditating. Back in Sydney, I ended my relationship of around seven years. I moved out on my own, into share housing with strangers. I had decided that being afraid and exhilarated was better than being stuck in the wheel of sameness and sadness.

And, behind it all, I was still thinking about what my mother had told me.

My thirtieth birthday was approaching. I'd changed a lot of stuff, ended a lot of stuff, but what did I need to put in place?

In a classic Type A personality moment, I drew up a list. (It was titled 'Fuck My Life: Things to Do'.) All items on the list were in caps, with boxes to be ticked. There were short-term goals (roll over super) and very, very long-term ones (buy house). At the bottom of the list was: find biological father. I stuck the list on the wall.

Journalism is the first draft of history, as the cliché goes, but maybe a better way of putting it would be: journalism is a running update on society. Anything that happens to a journalist is grist for the mill. I didn't know who I was; I didn't know anything about my life or my future anymore. So, I decided, I would *journalism* my way out of his hole.

I would investigate.

THIS IS A book about the maelstrom of donor conception – stranger than you thought and more widespread than you probably realise. It is not a book about the desires of would-be parents. It is not a book about couples engaging in fertility treatment using their own biological material. This is a book about the human beings born of *third-party* material. This is a book about creating life from collected human tissue, not social relationships.

This is a book about breeding humans.

CHAPTER 3

Even if you've never set foot in a fertility clinic – or thought about doing so – you've probably seen the billboards, heard the radio ads, or been served the promotions online. Fertility treatment is marketed as something shiny, delivered to middle-class couples in white-walled clinics by calm, smiling professionals. But conception is never guaranteed. Pregnancy is not calm and controlled. Birth is messy as hell. And human fertility treatment is pure animal husbandry – at least, the part that involves selective, mechanical breeding. Ongoing care for the resulting animal is absent.

The first documented case of human artificial insemination occurred not in the 1970s, as you might assume, but in fact the 1770s. In London, there lived and worked a certain Dr John Hunter. He would become one of the most famous British surgeons of his age, if not all time.

John Hunter lacked the proper schooling to become a medical student himself, so his first job was to procure human corpses for students to dissect. At the time, the only lawful way for Hunter to do that was by cutting down a murderer after a public execution, because murderers' bodies were the only corpses allowed to be dissected for science. This restriction was supposed to be an extra deterrent to any would-be murderers. But as anatomy schools grew, this hung-murderers-only rule really throttled the supply of cadavers. There just weren't enough bodies to meet scientific demand. What to do?

A disturbing trade in body parts arose. The practice of digging up fresh graves, stealing the bodies, and selling them to anatomy schools flourished. Until the UK passed the *Anatomy Act* in 1832, which allowed the bodies of those who had died in other circumstances to be dissected, some say the majority of corpses in anatomy schools were from grave robbers.[1]

Hunter was eventually allowed to become a student at the anatomy school and then a teacher. Strange rumours of his conduct persisted long after his death. One was that Hunter deliberately infected himself with a sexually transmitted disease, more recently revised to have likely been someone else that he deliberately infected (well, that makes it all right).[2]

Here is John Hunter: probable body-snatcher, STD-curious, and in 1776, doctor to a linen draper who came to him for help. The draper had hypospadias, a condition where the opening of the urethra is on the underside of the penis. It's a common birth defect which affects about 1 in 150 male babies and can be associated with infertility.

Hunter had previously successfully fertilised the eggs of moths – yes, moths – and decided he could therefore assist this human couple to conceive. Semen from the draper was collected in a syringe, which was then injected into the woman's vaginal canal, after which she became pregnant. This technique may sound alarmingly basic. In fact, it is still used by practitioners of animal husbandry today, as well as by fertility specialists for humans, although the latter now inject directly into the uterus.

It's widely recorded that Hunter's artificial insemination procedure on the draper's wife resulted in conception – but it's not similarly confirmed that the draper's wife then gave birth to a live child. The distinction is worth noting. Here, the story of Hunter illustrates another fundamental aspect of fertility treatment, which still holds true: treatment does not mean baby, and not all results are equal. To the scientist, a pregnancy is a result to be counted. Many clinics will advertise their pregnancy rates. To the customer, the only real measure, in such a business transaction, is the rate of live births, not pregnancies. The only outcome which matters is the birth of a living child.

But the first instance of AI creating just such a child, documented beyond all doubt, wasn't far off. Shortly after Hunter and the linen draper, a Catholic priest achieved a live mammalian birth. The priest, Italian Lazzaro Spallanzani, was also a natural scientist, and in 1784, he successfully artificially inseminated a female dog. A couple of months later, that bitch had three live puppies. The first live AI litter had been born. The race was on.

In 1868, a paper was published reporting a successful human artificial insemination on a couple in France. According to the paper, the insemination had in fact been performed decades earlier, in 1838, by a Dr Girault on a young countess, who gave birth to a son the following year.

But it was in the 1880s that a key milestone was reached, one which would have profound consequences for millions of people around the world. In 1884, an American doctor successfully treated a woman with artificial insemination resulting in a live birth. The woman was married. But crucially, the sperm used was not her husband's. It was sperm from another man – a donor. It is likely that this was the first documented instance of successful donor conception and the birth of the first donor-conceived child.

With this birth, human reproduction entered the age of third-party material, more than one hundred years before I was born.

The circumstances of this first donor-conceived baby set the tone of what was to come. For the doctor in question, it was a career triumph. For professional medical ethics, it was an ill-fated start. The first donor conception featured disturbing doctor–patient dynamics and a whole bunch of lies.

In 1884, Professor William Pancoast was working in the Sansom Street Hospital of Philadelphia. He had as two new patients a married Quaker couple – the wife thirty-one years old, the husband forty-one, and both apparently healthy, yet unable to conceive. What happened next was revealed years later in a 1909 letter to the editor of *Medical World* by a former student of Pancoast's, the unfortunately named Addison Davis Hard.[3]

Professor Pancoast invited a select group of students from his senior class to attend his consultation with the couple. The professor assumed the problem was the woman's. However, after a group examination which was 'very complete', no issue was discovered. The student Addison Davis Hard says of the procedure: 'During this examination was discovered for the first time, as far as I know, the suction function of the uterus, which takes place during orgasm.' (I note here it is possible for rape victims to orgasm; orgasm alone is not an indicator of consent.) Having ruled out the woman as the problem, by whatever method, the professor discovered her husband had an extremely low sperm count, probably due to gonorrhoea. The professor believed he could treat the husband. But after two months of unspecified 'careful attention', nothing had changed.

In a scene more reminiscent of a men's locker room, one of Pancoast's class joked, 'The only solution of this problem is to call in the hired man.' In the words of Addison Hard:

'The woman was chloroformed, and with a hard rubber syringe some fresh semen from the best-looking member of the class was deposited in the uterus, and the cervix was slightly plugged with gauze. Neither the man nor the woman knew the nature of what had been done at the time.'

'Subsequently,' Addison Hard writes, 'the Professor repented of his action and explained the whole matter to the husband.' Not to the wife, whose body it was. 'Strange as it may seem,' Addison Hard continues, 'the man was delighted with the idea, and conspired with the Professor in keeping from the lady the actual way by which her impregnation was brought about.'

The wife gave birth to a boy, who, like his mother, presumably never knew the truth of his biological parentage.

Not much has changed.

CHAPTER 4

AT THE SAME time as the race to artificially breed humans, the race to artificially breed farm animals continued apace or even faster. Often the two paths crossed.

In 1898, Russian scientist Ilya Ivanovich Ivanov established his Moscow laboratories. Ten years later, he'd studied artificial insemination in farm animals, dogs, foxes, rabbits and poultry, developing an AI procedure which could be used across all livestock.[1] His ideas spread. A Japanese scientist who studied with Ivanov, Dr Ishikawa, returned to Japan and began an AI program in horses, which led to Japanese scientists using AI in cattle, sheep, goats, pigs and poultry. Eduard Sørensen, a Danish scientist also familiar with Ivanov's work, organised the first dairy AI cooperative in Denmark in the mid-1930s. Sørensen's results would lead to AI in dairy cattle in other Western nations.

Sørensen was the one who came up with the idea of packaging semen in straws – inspired by, of all things, the cellophane straws at his young daughter's birthday party. To this day, human donor sperm is divided, packaged and sold by the straw at fertility clinics.[2]

The use of AI to breed dairy cattle in the US grew rapidly in the 1940s. After WWII, the new technique of freezing semen opened up a world of distribution.[3]

And the ability to bring about fertilisation outside the body, either animal or human – what Aldous Huxley called 'exogenesis' in *Brave New World* – wasn't far off. Huxley published *Brave New World* in 1932. That same decade, Harvard scientists were trying to develop in-vitro fertilisation using rabbits. In-vitro fertilisation or IVF: literally, fertilisation in glass, the components of life fusing in a Petri dish. But their goal eluded them. It would take until 1959 before a young Chinese scientist, MC Chang, working at the Worcester Foundation in the US, finally proved that fertilisation in-vitro could result in the birth of a real, live rabbit. This was a game changer. If it could be done in rabbits, it could be done in other mammals. It could be done in humans.

Chang was a pioneer twice over: to create this first live IVF birth, it was reported he'd also used a donor egg from a different rabbit. Not only had he achieved the first mammalian live birth from IVF, but the first mammalian donor egg offspring.[4]

THROUGHOUT THE TWENTIETH century, the use of human donor material also became more common. There are no hard numbers, because nobody counts all the people like me – the products. There is, to this day, no national record kept in Australia, the US or the UK, for example, of all donor-conceived humans born there. Meanwhile, breeders of animals like dairy cows have kept meticulous notes on all sorts of things, including bloodlines, health, numbers of offspring and individual identification.

Many people think donor conception – particularly its mass provision in a clinical setting – is recent, but I have met Australian donor-conceived people who were made as long ago as the 1960s. The first fertility clinic in this country was set up in Sydney in 1938.[5] In 1940, the UK's Barton Clinic began operations, going on to create hundreds of donor-conceived people.[6] And in the Australian state of Victoria at least, doctors have provided donor conception since the 1940s. Soon Australia will hit a centenary of people being made by doctors, of families across society becoming vastly more complicated. The donor-conceived people born in those first decades have their own children. Their children now have children. Yet nowhere has any government, state or federal, recorded the full story of what was done to make us, and by whom. No government in Australia has a truthful record of its own citizens, despite Australia having a leading reputation in this space.

During the latter decades of the twentieth century – the crucial years in which human fertility treatment exploded – Australia was a global frontrunner in assisted reproductive technology, and Australian scientists recorded some of the earliest key milestones.

It began in the '70s. Although sperm donation already existed around the world, it was at this time that the slide towards commercialisation began. In 1972, Australia's first bank for frozen sperm was set up in Adelaide. However, such an approach was far from universal. More than a decade later, the biggest clinics on Australia's east coast were still treating women using fresh, not frozen, sperm donations – essentially walk in, walk out.

By the mid-seventies, mere human baby-making using third-party material wasn't the biggest prize. Doctors in Australia, and around the world, were competing for a new crown, something impossibly futuristic. They wanted to create human life in the lab.

It was a clinic in Melbourne which reported the world's first human IVF pregnancy. In 1971, Dr Alex Lopata at Queen Victoria Medical Centre began collecting eggs from women and attempting to fertilise them in the laboratory. By the end of 1973, there was 'an encouraging early pregnancy', after a number of failed embryo transfers to different patients. The patient in question was already in the Queen Victoria Medical Centre for surgical repair of her blocked fallopian tubes. The doctors removed her eggs, grew an embryo in the lab, then came back and implanted it successfully in the still-recovering patient three days later.

'Unfortunately, a few days later her surgical wound burst open, she went into shock and had to be returned to the operating theatre to repair her abdomen,' Lopata would recall. 'The patient recovered well but unfortunately her pregnancy was lost after the second surgery.'[7] Talk about doubling down on medical trauma. The scientists kept going.

To the chagrin of the Melbourne team, five years later British scientists beat them to the finish line. On 25 July 1978, the world's first 'test tube baby' was born: Louise Brown.[8] Two years later, in June 1980, the Melbourne team finally reported a successful IVF live birth – an Australian first, and only the third in the world.

Today, everyone's heard of IVF, and you probably know someone who's used it. That someone might even be you. IVF has become shorthand for 'fertility treatment', but IVF is far from being the only form of fertility treatment. There's a bunch of other techniques that were, and are, used. Mostly, they involve things done to the bodies of women.

There's injecting sperm into a woman's body. There's taking drugs to boost a woman's egg release. There's even the hopefully named GIFT process, where a collected egg and sperm are placed in a woman's fallopian tubes and everyone essentially crosses their fingers that they do the right thing. (GIFT has a low success rate and is often used for religious reasons.) IVF is, if you like, the full-service option.

With the introduction of IVF in the late '70s, doctors could create life outside the human body. They already had one of the components of life being delivered to their door: donor sperm. It could be used fresh, or frozen for later. And pretty soon, they worked out how to extract and successfully use the other half.

It was that same Melbourne team who would achieve the world's first human pregnancy using a donor egg. (Rightly, the women who became pregnant for each of these 'firsts' should also share these titles, but history for the most part does not record their names.) However, once again, there was no live birth. And then they were beaten for the second time, not by British specialists, but by a team in the US, who in 1984 recorded the first live birth from donor eggs.[9]

Now both donor eggs and donor sperm could be used to make the beginnings of life outside the human body – a creation utterly divorced from human relationships.

Then, in 1992, a doctor in Belgium pushed the science one step further. He inadvertently developed the technique of injecting a single sperm directly into an egg – thereby forcing fertilisation itself.[10]

This is the classic procedure usually depicted on TV shows as visual shorthand for all fertility treatment. You've probably watched it happen: an egg under the microscope, prodded and then punctured by a sharp needle, after which a single sperm travels down the neck of the needle right into the centre of the egg itself. It's known as ICSI, which stands for intracytoplasmic sperm injection. With ICSI, the egg is fertilised with a sperm chosen by a lab technician. As such, ICSI does something fairly massive: it replaces natural selection. The implications of that are enormous.

Since its accidental invention, ICSI has been practised by the fertility industry for decades – without randomised control trials.

'ICSI is a huge experiment, which was not trialled in animals, and to some extent we've gotten away with it,' says veteran fertility specialist Professor Rob Norman. He's the Professor for Reproductive and Periconceptual Medicine at the University of Adelaide. In the early '90s, Norman was deputy head of the first team in Australia to use ICSI – a team which reported some of the first ICSI pregnancies in the world. 'And then, of course, once we started getting a lot of pregnancies around the world [with ICSI], people say there's no need for randomised controlled trials, because it works.'

The technique, therefore, was unleashed. But ICSI is another aspect of fertility treatment where, as a society, we've never had the discussion prior to its introduction: should we actually be doing this?

In natural fertilisation, the egg is fertilised by a sperm which has successfully made it all the way through the female reproductive tract to its goal, while most of its fellows have perished or fallen behind. In 2017, a landmark American study found that the egg, rather than just waiting around for the sperm, also plays a role in selecting which sperm might win the race, disproving the long-held notion of the egg as a docile cell, and proving its active role in reproduction. Principal scientist Joe Nadeau called it 'the gamete equivalent of choosing a partner'.[11]

But with ICSI, the sperm is chosen by a lab tech, not by the egg, and their judgement is subjective. Professor Norman says sperm are generally selected on the basis of two major characteristics: motility – how many sperm in a sample are actually moving – and morphology, or how many 'look normal'. Replacing the egg's role with what 'looks normal' to a lab tech is a potential issue. After decades of practice, Norman says the DNA is what really matters. In other words, it's not looks: it's what's on the inside that counts.

Today, ICSI is often offered as an add-on service (and cost) to IVF cycles. And it is everywhere. If you're already paying thousands of dollars for a single round of IVF, who wouldn't shell out extra cash to make sure the egg and sperm do as they're told? Who wouldn't want to shore up their chances of fertilisation?

For heterosexual couples who cannot conceive, Rob Norman says there's a rough causal rule of thumb: one-third will be male factor infertility, one-third female and one-third unknown. He says ICSI has a place in helping couples who cannot conceive due to male-factor infertility – it forces fertilisation where sperm may fail. But for the other two-thirds, it's a different story. Once again, the only outcome that matters is having a living child.[12]

Despite findings over the years that ICSI doesn't increase the likelihood of either female-factor or unknown-factor infertility patients having a live birth, ICSI rates have soared around the world. In some countries, ICSI rates are now at 100 per cent. Rob Norman has long been concerned about this overuse of ICSI. He puts it down to clinician fear.

'[Clinics] are very scared of fronting up to a patient and saying there's been no fertilisation, but we can do it next time,' Norman says. 'Well, why didn't you do it the first time? … The competitive nature is, if you won't give me this treatment I'll go down the road and find someone else.' The fact that such a threat works points undeniably to a culture of consumerism, not responsible medicine.

ICSI definitely means revenue. According to a report on the fertility industry by market researchers IBISWorld, total Australian fertility industry revenue for the financial year 2019–20 was $568 million. And ICSI alone made up 47 per cent of that figure – an incredible statistic for a procedure which doesn't improve the chances for a lot of patients.

It's not just Professor Norman who's worried about the overuse of ICSI. In 2018, a group of researchers in *Human Reproduction* summed up the emerging unease around ICSI. A large Australian study, they noted, reported a 'significantly higher' rate of congenital malformations in ICSI babies than among IVF-only babies. They were concerned that other studies comparing ICSI babies to IVF-only babies had also reported that ICSI was associated with increased risks of congenital heart disease, autism and intellectual disability, and higher rates of admission to newborn intensive care units. The authors took care to note that such findings were not universal: some studies had found no difference between the two groups, or even reported lower risks of adverse outcomes in ICSI babies.[13]

And whether fertility customers are heterosexual or not, today ICSI is big in donor conception. 'Almost universally, ICSI is used for donor sperm these days,' Rob Norman says. 'Few clinics are willing to do intrauterine insemination [an injection of sperm into the body] for eggs with donor sperm because it uses much more sperm.' The less donor sperm clinics use in a single procedure, the more donor sperm they can sell. 'So some clinics are doing 100 per cent ICSI for women who have donor sperm. And with donor eggs, you'll also find ICSI is used,' he says. 'I think once again it's because donor eggs are so "precious" they don't want to take a risk. And with frozen eggs, there is no doubt you need to use ICSI there.'

ICSI was loosed in the world of human fertility treatment with no trials, and less than three decades later, it is rampant. It is expensive. Its purchase delivers something akin to a dopamine hit to satisfy anxious consumers, but in many cases, it may not improve your chances of a live birth whatsoever. Its risks are still being documented. Its long-term impacts are unknown. For donor-conceived people, who are much more likely than the general population to be born of ICSI, those answers must be found. Yet the full size and scale of any problems with ICSI will only be known in retrospect.

In that, it's rather like donor conception itself.

TODAY, THE FERTILITY industry has an ever-increasing array of tools at its disposal. IVF and ICSI abound. Both eggs and sperm can be obtained from third parties, and embryos too. All three can be frozen for later retrieval at a convenient time. With the rise of surrogacy, wombs can be either borrowed or rented. The techniques can be mixed and matched. Surrogacy-born people are often also donor-conceived people. Donor-conceived people born, like me, in the early '80s or before tend to be a product of donor insemination, where the sperm is injected into a woman's uterus. But increasingly, donor-conceived people born from the early '80s on are IVF babies. Sometimes surrogacy-born people are donor-conceived people and also babies born of IVF with ICSI.

IVF and IVF with ICSI are merely techniques: a means to an end. They can be used by people to create their own children. Or they can be used by people to create children biologically not their own. And the rise of IVF, ICSI and donor material in recent decades has coincided with a huge spike in demand for fertility treatment, and in particular donor conception.

There are a lot of reasons for this rise in donor conception: numbers of children available for domestic adoption dropped dramatically last century as single parenthood became less taboo and contraception use increased; increased access to and take-up of fertility treatment among LGBTIQ+ couples; more single women who wish to parent alone; and mature-aged/older would-be parents. More people are leaving it until later to have their first child. With that delay can come anxiety about a fertility decline, and this perceived or actual chronology: impatience, stress, despair, fertility treatment, possible failure. Then, for some, a so-called lifeline: donated human material, usually collected from younger and more fertile bodies.

If that sounds like something out of *A Handmaid's Tale*, that's because it is. Donor conception means extremely mechanical acts with the building blocks of life to engineer children for some parts of society.

CHAPTER 5

MEDICINE MADE ME, and medicine was also a part of my childhood. My mother has worked as a nurse, in the public system, since the 1970s. She first came to Australia aged eighteen on a nursing scholarship. There was nothing much for her in Malaysia, she told me.

She was one of six children, and she was a girl in a culture that has a long history of prizing boys. During her childhood, her family – my grandparents – were very poor. At one point, the whole family lived in a single room divided by a sheet, above a cobbler and a tailor. Without good marks in the right areas at school, without the right ethnicity or gender to make it in 1960s Malaysia, there was nothing on the horizon.

So my mother applied for a scholarship to study nursing in Adelaide. I don't think she even wanted to be a nurse at that point – it was just a good opportunity. My mother told me the one thing that she thinks set her apart: at the end of the interview, she asked questions. She asked what it would be like. She showed interest and curiosity. She won a place.

Towards the end of the '60s, my mother moved to Australia for the scholarship and never moved home again. There was a bunch of young Malaysian women who came to Adelaide to train as nurses, and my mother made lifelong friends. She wore flares and striped turtleneck tops. She met my father at a party. He noticed the shape of her mouth, he told me once: the bow-shaped lips. That was it.

My mother and father settled in Sydney a few years before I was born, and Mum began nursing at the Royal North Shore Hospital.

I went to the staff creche there, and as a kid I remember trying out my swim strokes in the pool they had for employees. Mum would take home disposable gowns from work and cook stir fries in scrubs, to protect her clothes from the oil splatter. The hospital was always a part of our lives.

So when my parents wanted to have a baby, and found that they couldn't, they'd naturally turned to the experts at my mother's workplace.

MY PARENTS WENT to the Human Reproduction Unit at the public Royal North Shore Hospital – one of the major fertility clinics in the country at the time. The unit was known by the sinister-sounding name 'Clinic 20'. It was 1982. That year, Clinic 20 achieved the first IVF pregnancy in the state of New South Wales. Australia was in the grip of a severe drought. Argentina and Britain were at war in the Falklands, and Michael Jackson released *Thriller*. In the US and Europe, young men were already dying from a new disease: AIDS. That same year, the first HIV-positive case was diagnosed in Australia.

To find out how I was made, and by whom, my first thought was to get in touch with Clinic 20. I was after records of treatment, or maybe there would be a register, or staff who could set me on the path: anything that would tell me who I was. And here I came across the first problem.

By the time I started looking, in 2011, the RNSH's Clinic 20 no longer existed. In fact, it seemed to have disappeared.

One of the leading fertility clinics in Australia, funded by public money in one of New South Wales' largest and most prestigious hospitals, had vanished into the private sector after seventeen years of operation, during the most groundbreaking years in the history of fertility treatment.

Clinic 20 was set up in 1977 at the RNSH under Professor Douglas Saunders. It operated as such until 1994. It treated heterosexual couples who couldn't conceive, using donor material. The NSW Government couldn't tell me how many donor-conceived children it made at Clinic 20; they said, if I wanted, I could pay to lodge a freedom of information request to find out. There was no guarantee the information actually existed.[1]

In 1994, the public Clinic 20 suddenly became an exempt proprietary company called North Shore A.R.T. or NSART. NSART was owned by Douglas Saunders, who'd run Clinic 20, and a partner.[2] Saunders and his partner had somehow taken the whole taxpayer-funded operation private. NSART apparently remained on site at the public hospital for the next two years. It also appeared to operate at a private hospital in Hunters Hill.[3] Then it moved to private premises in Chatswood in 1996.

I asked the NSW Ministry of Health a number of basic questions about this key public operation becoming private, and after two months, I got a reply. 'The Ministry of Health has not able [sic] to locate any electronic records referring to the sale of the ART clinic or lease arrangements. However, a paper file has been identified relating to the ART clinic and this has been requested.' Nearly two weeks later, I had an update: the paper file 'had no further information about the lease or sale of the ART Clinic'.

No-one in the Health Ministry could tell me why the public Clinic 20 was sold. Or for how much. Or even confirm to whom.

I don't know how NSART, and its co-owner and leading specialist, Douglas Saunders, managed to do this. But in what would seem to be a highly questionable move, the new private company NSART copied all the treatment files of the public clinic's patients and took them along to set up shop: intimate details of the women treated and of their husbands. These contained notes on health conditions, vaginas, ovaries, sperm counts, test results, babies born, intimate inspections of those babies – all copied and kept as part of this new, private company's property. And NSART also took with it some of the only records of the men who were sperm donors to this public clinic – notes on each man's semen, how many straws it was divided into, when it was used. The public hospital – a government service – was left with nothing of these sperm donor records, not even copies.

In 2002, it appears that NSART and its operations were subsumed, along with three other clinics, into a bigger company, IVF Australia.[4] In 2008, IVF Australia became part of Quadrant's IVF Holdings Group, which then acquired one of the biggest clinics in Melbourne, Melbourne IVF, along with others in Queensland, New South Wales and Victoria. IVF Holdings Group renamed itself Virtus Health.[5] In 2013, Virtus Health listed on the Australian Stock Exchange.[6]

Today, Virtus Health is by far the biggest fertility operator in the country. According to an industry report by market researchers IBISWorld, published in March 2020, Virtus Health had revenue worth nearly a quarter of a billion dollars ($219.8 million) – or 38 per cent of the total revenue of Australia's fertility industry.[7]

All three of Australia's largest fertility operators – Virtus, Monash and Genea – also play on an international stage, where the baby business is booming and attracting the notice of investors. Virtus has operations in the UK, Singapore, Denmark and Ireland. Monash IVF is in Malaysia and China. Genea is in New Zealand, Thailand, Hong Kong, the UK and the US. Australia has exported fertility to the world, and the world is responding with interest. In 2019, the *Economist* reported that globally, the fertility industry was raking in USD$25 billion annually in sales – a figure predicted to hit USD$41 billion within seven years.[8]

My early search for Clinic 20 and my origins had ended in a behemoth. Virtus Health, I realised, owns the entity that owns the entity that, somehow, owns the public clinic that made me. It was to Virtus Health that I would have to put in a request for the truth of my own humble existence.

I RANG IVF Australia's office. I was put on to a woman who handles people like me, the babies who actually come back to ask questions. I'll call her Mary. Mary took my details, then said I probably wouldn't be able to find out my donor's name, because when I was conceived in 1982, 'the law was different'.

She then told me a story I couldn't quite believe. It was about how the clinic operated when it was the publicly owned Clinic 20.

In 1982, New South Wales had yet to enact any laws around donor conception, but that didn't stop its practice, including by taxpayer-funded hospitals. At Clinic 20, men donated sperm under a promise of anonymity. The deal was, said Mary, that their future offspring would never be able to find them.

At Clinic 20, donor anonymity was achieved by assigning each sperm donor a donor code. Lots of Australian fertility clinics did this, but there was no single system they all used. Codes could contain letters and numbers. Some had a connection to the donor's actual name, like T4, where the donor's surname began with a T. Others were just random. My clinic, at Royal North Shore Hospital, favoured three-letter codes: BXQ, LMD.

Over the phone, Mary from IVF Australia said she'd be able to find my donor code, but that code would only yield the barest details about my biological father. This was the whole point of the code system. In the records of my mother's treatment – that is, any files I might be able to recover – the donor's identity would be represented by a code. The clinic could then look up that code separately and find corresponding, non-identifying family medical history from my donor. There would be no name of my biological father, no picture, no inkling of whether he shares my weakness for olives.

Mary said I had to understand that I would only be given my biological father's name if that donor had, at some point, come back to the clinic and specifically consented, which was extremely unlikely. I wasn't surprised, but it was disappointing. Still, I wanted any information they had, particularly medical history.

Mary said she would call in a fortnight with my information. I waited on edge. Everything I knew about myself had been blown apart since that Easter dinner. This was a small glimmer of hope: I wanted to stop feeling so awful and move on to my new reality. From the little information she could find, I would slowly reconstruct who I was.

But a fortnight went by, and nothing. I controlled myself. A whole month went by without a word. I rang IVF Australia. The fortnight up, Mary had made zero effort to contact me and had then gone on leave overseas. No-one else from the slick offices of IVF Australia had followed up.

This was the first warning sign that I was dealing with an entity entirely uninterested in the life it was paid to create.

Eventually, Mary returned and gave me a call. She said that she'd found my file – and the information it contained about my donor had been deliberately cut out and destroyed by the clinic.

I can't properly explain how I felt hearing that.

What was destroyed was not the record of my donor's name – because that was never in my mother's treatment file in the first place. What was destroyed was any mention of the three-letter donor code.

Without any donor code in the file of my conception, I was adrift. I had zero chance of ever finding my biological father or my half-siblings. This deliberate destruction took place in a public hospital.

Mary said (in a singsong: she'd clearly had to do this before) that destroying donor codes happened sometimes with the older files, because 'things were different back then'.

This was a phrase I would hear many, many times in coming weeks, months and years. People still trot it out to me. It is a phrase which is repeated everywhere you turn for answers, by the health system, by parents, by clinics and by medical practitioners, said as if it abrogates them of any responsibility. It's also completely ridiculous. This was the 1980s, not the Dark Ages. Medical records are a matter of statutory responsibility, and deliberately mutilating them to hide what has been done to a patient is not, nor ever has been, conscionable conduct by any medical practitioner, clinic or hospital, let alone a public one.

On the phone, Mary from IVF Australia was still talking. The file had been tampered with and the donor code destroyed. On top of that, Mary said I had no right to see the file without my mother's permission, because it 'belonged' to my mother. Legally, my mother was the patient.

I was nothing. I had no right to any information whatsoever relating to my own conception, and they would not be giving me access. Despite creating me, they did not recognise my existence.

I went back to my mother and asked her for access to the file. She refused.

CHAPTER 6

When I was conceived, and indeed for many years, clinics told parents to never, ever tell anyone what they had done. They told them to pretend that the child was theirs, that they had fallen pregnant naturally.

In the '80s, at Clinic 20 and many others, parents did not choose a sperm donor. Often, doctors matched donors to couples based on the physical characteristics of the woman's partner (height, eye colour, etc.) to minimise the chance of 'embarrassing' revelations and to enhance the lie. My mother had only told a handful of people in her life the truth. Almost all of them have been dead for years.

From my research, I know that many other donor-conceived people both in Australia and around the world have been denied medical information to which that person has a literal birthright, even though they are adults, because their parent does not consent. Compare this to the situation for Australian adoptees: they have the legal right to identifying information about their biological parents – a change to law which was recognition of decades of heartbreak.

By destroying donor codes, public hospital staff at Clinic 20 appear to have been breaking the minimum standards set out by the NSW Health Department itself. In August 1976, the department issued a Circular (a way of communicating department-wide policy) on Medical Records in Hospitals. It set out the following minimum standards for medical records, saying they existed 'to protect the legal interest of the patient', 'to enable a practitioner to give effective continuing care to the patient and any other practitioner to assume the care of the patient at any time by inclusion of all significant information in sufficient detail' and that 'the record must contain sufficient information … to justify the diagnosis and treatment and document the results accurately'. It also added: 'It is the responsibility of the hospital to safeguard the information in the record against loss and use by unauthorised persons. Written consent of the patient or a Court Subpoena is required to release medical information to persons other than the attending physician.'[1]

The NSW Health Ministry told me: 'This particular Circular only transferred to become a NSW Health Policy Directive in January 2005.' So before that, all of those important-sounding standards were apparently optional. Which seems strange.

And by destroying donor codes, it appears Clinic 20 wasn't breaking a specific law. I can't find any law, then or now, which criminalises what was done: the deliberate destruction of their donor conception records, which denies me even non-identifying information like basic family medical history.[2]

IN FACT, WHEN it comes to donor conception, there are very few laws at all.

When I was conceived, New South Wales clinics had been making children from donor material for years before there was any actual legislation on whether that should be allowed – let alone how it should be done. In 1982, no Australian state or territory had any legislation in place regarding donor conception, either by artificial insemination or by IVF. Meanwhile, Australian doctors had been practising donor conception for decades, artificially creating babies, and publishing on it in medical journals.

You might be thinking that maybe the states and territories had failed, but surely there was something nationally? Some sort of law on third-party babies? Some rules? Or oversight of all this?

There was nothing.

There had been some calls for action by the national Australian Law Reform Commission in 1977, but more than forty years on, at the time of writing, the Australian Government still has not enacted any national laws on the donor conception – the for-profit manufacture – of its own citizens. There is, to this day, also no national legislation on fertility treatment itself.

A federal government leaving regulation of the fertility industry to its states and territories creates a massive inconsistency – an inconsistency in fundamental human rights – which is inherently unfair. Why are you allowed your biological father's name if you're from Melbourne, but not if you're from Hobart?

But inconsistency isn't the biggest problem. The Australian Constitution gives the power to regulate health to the states. At the time of writing, only half of all Australian states and territories have any laws on assisted reproductive technology. None of those legal regimes are perfect. The other half have no laws on assisted reproductive technology at all. (For the record, that's the Australian Capital Territory, the Northern Territory, Queensland and Tasmania.) I don't just mean zero laws on donor conception: they have zero laws on fertility treatment full stop.

In 2010, there was a moment of hope. The Australian Senate conducted an eight-month inquiry examining donor conception, the industry, and the rights of donor-conceived individuals. It made some good recommendations: create nationally consistent donor conception regulation, a national register of donors and of donor-conceived individuals, and that donor-conceived people should be able to know who their donor is. Some expert advice to the inquiry even contained suggestions on how the federal government could act – for instance by using its external affairs power, which has been held to extend to areas traditionally the domain of the states.[3]

In 2012, the Australian Government responded. Its sixteen-page response can be largely summarised by the word 'no'.

In essence, the Australian Government's position is that it does not have the constitutional power to legislate in this area; therefore, it kicks all of this back to the states and territories.

To me, the stock-standard response of 'it's not our responsibility' is appalling. To me, it says, in short, that the Australian Government does not recognise a duty of care towards its own people – people deliberately produced by a for-profit industry on Australian shores. Surely a federal government has a moral obligation to act, particularly when half its states and territories fail to do so. And particularly when that federal government does provide the fertility industry with a significant amount of federal cash – one of the few developed countries in the world to supply 'substantial government funding' to this sector, according to IBISWorld market research. The latest data, from 2017–18, shows that $249 million went to the industry as Medicare rebates for fertility treatment.[4]

Handing out the money is fine. Regulating its use, apparently, is not.

FROM WHAT I'VE observed in my research, the vast majority of people who are donor conceived will try to find out what they can about their biological family. The desire to know where you come from, to know something about your tribe, is all too human.

For most, the logical first step is to contact the clinic where you were made. It's pretty unlikely you'll then get a straightforward answer. Clinics have been sold, shut down and amalgamated, and the in-house knowledge about the donor-conceived people they produced gets lost or destroyed, or was simply never kept in the first place.

Most people assume these days that donor-conceived people must have a legal right to access identifying information about their donor. In fact, legal regimes vary by country – and within countries. Today, for the majority of us around the world, that legal right to know your biological parent(s) is still non-existent. Whether you're an adult, or a child, or born yesterday.

In Australia, Victoria is the most enlightened state, but it's still far from perfect. All donor-conceived people there over the age of eighteen may access identifying information about their donor – if it exists. There's no accompanying right to identifying information about siblings.

In New South Wales, only donor-conceived people born after 1 January 2010 may have access to identifying information about their donor, and only after they turn eighteen. In Western Australia, those born after 2004 may have access to identifying information about their donor after they turn sixteen. In South Australia, those born after 1 July 2010 may have access after their eighteenth birthday – or earlier if they're deemed sufficiently 'mature' by persons unknown, according to one state government document.[5] It is discriminatory, not a little patronising and unfair. And what of the states and territories where there are no laws at all? If, to this day, only half of Australia has (patchy) laws on the fertility industry, what happens to the other half? Are there any constraints, or are we looking at some kind of gamete free-for-all?

If you are a fertility specialist in those jurisdictions where fertility laws are absent, you're apparently kept in line by national 'Ethical Guidelines' and your own peers. The enormously profitable fertility industry self-regulates, through the Fertility Society of Australia. The Fertility Society of Australia, the national association of fertility industry professionals, has a sub-committee, the Reproductive Technology Accreditation Committee, which sets out certain standards for fertility clinics. The RTAC audits the fertility clinics for compliance. All fertility clinics pay a licence fee to the Fertility Society of Australia. The conflict of interest is clear.

The national *Ethical Guidelines on the Use of Assisted Reproductive Technology in Clinical Practice and Research* are set out by Australia's National Health and Medical Research Council. These NHMRC Ethical Guidelines were first issued in 1996 and have never incorporated any formal consultation with people made by assisted reproductive technology. It's a bit like forming Indigenous policy without ever consulting with Indigenous Australians or passing adoption legislation without actually trying to get adoptees' views. And boy, does it show.

For a foundation document, governments and authorities should have looked no further than the United Nations' International Convention on the Rights of the Child.[6] It's the most widely ratified human rights treaty in history, taken up by almost every country on earth. And in it, there are not one, but several articles which *should* guarantee donor-conceived people's right to know biological parents and siblings. For instance: Article 7 says that every child has, as far as possible, the right to know and be cared for by their parents. In more recent years, the UN's powerful Committee on the Rights of the Child has objected to laws which stop adopted children from finding their biological parents – with specific reference to Article 7.

Article 8 says that every child has the right to preserve their identity, nationality and family relations, to not be deprived of any elements of their identity, and to seek state assistance to re-establish their identity.

Article 9 says every child has the right to maintain personal relations and direct contact with both parents on a regular basis. Article 35 says all children have the fundamental right not to be bought or sold. And above all, Article 3 of the Convention states that the best interests of the child shall be a primary consideration in all actions concerning children. The UN Committee on the Rights of the Child has warned: 'If the interests of children are not highlighted, they tend to be overlooked' and that 'a larger weight must be attached to what serves the child best.'

So what happens in the fertility industry?

The NHMRC Ethical Guidelines say the interests and wellbeing of the child born of ART are not a primary consideration, but 'an important consideration'. And they say: 'Those who require ART do not want to face unnecessary obstacles.'

Instead of putting the best interests of the child first and foremost, the ethical guidelines say there's a whole bunch of competing interests to look after – like the interests of commissioning parents, any gamete or embryo donors, and potential surrogates – as well as the actual child produced. This is not such a big issue when would-be parents are using fertility treatment to conceive children born of their own biological material. But once third-party material comes into play, the shortcomings are stark. From the outset, Australia's so-called ethical guidelines for the fertility industry do not meet the minimum standards in the Convention on the Rights of the Child.

In terms of knowing who your biological parents are, for anyone conceived before 2004, the ethical guidelines say the clinic must provide identifying details about your donor to you – if the donor has consented. There are a number of issues with that. Maybe he or she didn't. Maybe he or she would have if they'd been asked a second time, after they'd come up with the goods. Maybe he or she changed their address and the clinic couldn't find them. Maybe, as in my situation, the clinic itself decided to deliberately destroy the records of what donor was used for whom so that no second chances could be given, and no questions could ever be asked.

And post 2004? The ethical guidelines do say that post 2004, clinics must not use donors unless those donors have consented to their offspring being given identifying information about them. Do we really trust that simply saying this in an ethical guideline guarantees that it will always be so? What happens when a fertility clinic breaks these ethical guidelines? Who would know? Unfortunately, the body that issues these guidelines does not police them: 'NHMRC is not responsible for monitoring fertility clinics for compliance with the ART Guidelines', the NHMRC told me. Instead, it leaves that to the fertility industry's system of self-regulation.

The ethical guidelines also say that 'persons born from donated gametes' – that is, donated sperm and eggs – 'are entitled to know the details of their genetic origins'. It sounds good, but read it again more closely. That's not a right to know biological family. It's not really a right to know anything much. What 'details', precisely, are you entitled to? And from whom?

Don't get me wrong: merely knowing that you are donor conceived is hugely important, and it's a key piece of information that many, if not the majority of donor-conceived people lack. Australia's ethical guidelines say the recipients of donated material – in other words, the customers in donor conception, the commissioning would-be parents – 'cannot be forced to disclose' to their children the fact that those children are donor conceived. That is, although children are 'entitled' to know 'details' about their genetic origins, if commissioning parents don't want to give their own kids the truth, well, there's nothing any fertility clinic can do. The guidelines say that clinics should 'encourage gamete recipients to disclose to children their genetic origins'. What does 'encourage' mean? Have some pamphlets at reception?

Yet the ethical guidelines do set out other things clinics must get commissioning parents to agree to – if they want to receive any donor material. Once again, the focus is on the adults. Clinics must ensure that commissioning parents specifically consent to tell the donor (not the child) non-identifying things about their biological children like age, sex and number. They must agree to acknowledge their responsibility to the donor (not the child).[7] The adults, therefore, must acknowledge their responsibility to the adults, while being free to lie to the children produced about who they really are.

Let's be clear: if you are donor conceived, and your commissioning parents do not tell you the truth, you may never realise it. The clinic will not tell you. The government will not tell you. Your donor – your biological parent – doesn't have the right to your name. You will walk through your entire life with this lie. Or perhaps you'll find out in some deeply inappropriate and unpleasant way, like during a parental argument – a relatively common experience – or in a high school genetics class, or by being casually informed by a neighbour. All of these are real-life examples.

Only your social parents – the commissioning parents, the parents who raised you – are on your birth certificate. All Australian adoptees now have an original birth certificate and then may have a second birth certificate of adoptive parents, or a single integrated document. There is no such truthful record for all Australian donor-conceived people.

The thing is, when you're donor conceived, parented by either a heterosexual or same-sex couple, you have more than two parents. Some are social parents, some are biological parents, and one may be both. Similarly, donor-conceived people raised by single people (usually women) have more than one parent. They may have a biological father out there, or biological mother, or a biological father and mother, if the person raising them used a donor embryo. Donor-conceived people may choose not to call the biological parent(s) a 'father', or a 'mother', or a 'parent' at all: that's their decision. But you should not be able to deny any donor-conceived person the *knowledge* of biological parent(s), nor their identit(ies).

This notion of extra parents is not a difficult or new concept. Children in stepfamilies have more than two parents. Many adoptees, with the right to biological family, feel they have more than two parents. I don't know why, when it comes to donor conception, society is so complicit in this erasure. Society insists we are immaculate, miraculous conceptions. Why is everyone so quick to decide for us that we do not need our biological family?

IT'S NOT ONLY important to know who your biological parents are; there is also a fundamental need to know your biological siblings. All of them. This may be a bigger undertaking than it seems.

Today, in Australia, there are some attempts at limiting the numbers of donor-conceived siblings. But these legal limits only exist in the four out of eight states and territories that have fertility industry laws.

And there's a lot of us.

In 1982, it was estimated there were about 10,000 children under the age of fifteen who had been born by donor insemination in Australia. (To say nothing of the donor-conceived people *over* fifteen in 1982.) In 2010, the Senate Inquiry reported 'some estimates suggest that there are in excess of 60,000 donor conceived individuals in Australia'.[8]

That was more than a decade ago. Perhaps there are 80,000 in Australia today. Perhaps 100,000. Perhaps more. And population-wise, Australia is a small country.

I am in contact with hundreds of donor-conceived people across Australia and hundreds more overseas. I have never come across a single donor-conceived person made by a donor to a fertility clinic who says, with confidence, that they know who all of their brothers and sisters are. And some of them have dozens of siblings. Some have hundreds. Think about that. Think about the terror and the enormity of that. If you don't know who your brothers and sisters are, how can you know if you have ever kissed one of them? Have you ever slept with one of them? Have you kissed, or slept with, *more* than one of them? Have you had a child with them?

But how can one end up with so many siblings that incest is a real risk? Easily. It's because no-one knows, from clinic to clinic, from state to state, who has fathered and who has mothered whom.

Despite calls from donor offspring all the way up to members of the Senate, there is no national register of sperm, egg and embryo donors in Australia. One would have thought that this, at least, would be a policy issue for the *Ethical Guidelines on Assisted Reproductive Technology*. The clinics are supposed to be collecting all this data from now on anyway, as per those same national ethical guidelines. Why not make them send all that information to a central entity?

Unfortunately, when faced with this policy proposal of national importance, the NHMRC Ethical Guidelines take a leaf out of the Australian Government's playbook, stating: 'It is outside the remit of these Ethical Guidelines to establish a national registry.'[9]

Without a national central registry of donors, what you have is a baked-in social disaster. Donors can donate many, many times at different clinics across the country. In addition, clinics send sperm interstate. There will be no total sum of how many times someone has donated. Their activities will never be documented. This is not a hypothetical concern.

Let's take Victoria as a case study. In Victoria, the limit is: a donor may create children with no more than ten women. That's not ten children. That's ten women, who may have multiple children each. Say the commissioning parents – the commissioning woman and any partner of hers – want all their kids to be full siblings. So they want to keep using the same donor. Fine, great, a nice idea in itself. But say each of those ten commissioning women has two children. Or three. Suddenly you're looking at thirty brothers and sisters. Will they all know of each other? No. This is because even if identifying records are preserved, and held in a central register, and some of the kids know about the register, and formally give the register their consent to be known to each other, there is this: any commissioning parent can lie to their own children about the very fact of their being donor conceived. So the kids who are lied to will never contact the register in the first place.

In Victoria, this ten-woman rule also includes the donor's current and/or former partners they may have had children with; they are counted among the ten. Okay. But what if, after donating, the donor breaks up with their partner? And that donor goes on to have another relationship producing children? Or two? Or more? Suddenly you're looking at maybe twelve families of brothers and sisters, and even less guarantees that the ones raised by the donor will know the other ones who aren't. And what if the donor donates interstate? Without a national donor register, will anyone know if they've already hit that ten-woman limit?

We are told that all will be well. But when it comes to the truth, and the rights of the child, everyone passes the buck. The federal government leaves it to the states and territories. States and territories leave it to the fertility industry. Fertility specialists leave it to the commissioning parents. Commissioning parents do what they do, and no-one is the wiser. Money changes hands. We are made, born, grown in secret, even vast batches of us. The state recognises a degree of care and responsibility for adoptees, but none to anyone like me.

CHAPTER 7

On a sunny day, I was driving around the wide, calm backstreets of Sydney's beachy Bondi. Bondi always crawls with tourists, but for good reason. The curving golden slice of sand is spectacular. The surf is reliable. The historic ocean pool at one end of the beach is stunning. The rocks at the other end are good for snorkelling or jumping off, when you don't want to mix with the beautiful people lazily tanning themselves on their towels.

Today, I was in a different part of Bondi, and I was on edge.

Set back from the beach, in a wide street lined with big Moreton Bay fig trees, is Scarba House, a heritage-listed Victorian mansion set in generous grounds.

The Benevolent Society charity used Scarba House as a babies' and children's home for nearly seven decades – most of the twentieth century. Between 30,000 and 40,000 children passed through Scarba. Many of their experiences were not good ones.

By the time I visited, in an extremely strange about-face, Scarba House had become a site for the Benevolent Society's Post Adoption Resource Centre. PARC is a counselling service specifically for those grappling with trauma related to adoption. In this building, where so many children suffered, counsellors now aimed to help people with ongoing issues from their childhoods around loss, grief, trauma and identity.

I knew, by that time, that losing my father and gaining another one was too big for me to handle alone. The crippling physical pain told me so. The spaced-out blankness when I looked in the mirror was another massive warning sign. The deliberate destruction of records clinched it.

I also knew I wasn't the only donor-conceived person on earth, but there was nothing by way of specialised support. There were few active groups for this cohort, and none at that time in New South Wales. For years, there had been a very dynamic organisation called the Donor Conception Support Group, run by the parents of donor-conceived people – in particular, two indefatigable women: Caroline Lorbach and Leonie Hewitt. This group firmly believed that their children deserved the right to know their biological parents as well as their social parents, to have information about their siblings, and also deserved access to any medical information. They lobbied politicians, made submissions to governments around the country, and functioned as an information point and support service for donor-conceived families, and even donors who wanted to trace their kids. They did all this as volunteers, and they went hard.

Unfortunately, when I started searching, the group had burned out. I found a phone number for Caroline and gave her a call. After all my rollercoaster months and fruitless conversations, Caroline was the first person I'd ever spoken to about donor conception who was both kind *and* knew what she was talking about. She gave me what advice she could, while emphasising the DCSG was at least in hiatus, if not over for good.

I appreciated it. But I still needed help. It was 2011, and seemingly very few donor-conceived people were 'out'. There was, I think, a single online forum that I found, where a handful of donor-conceived people from around the world had posted occasionally over the years. It was nice to hear from other people like me, but this forum had the digital equivalent of dust and spiderwebs.

I needed something in my town, delivered face-to-face. So I went to Scarba House, and the Post Adoption Resource Centre. PARC was for adoptees, yes; but, I reasoned – at least that would mean they specialised in this stuff?

My counsellor was nice. She was British. I'll call her Kate. I'm sure Kate had spent years hearing utterly heartbreaking stories from adoptees. But Kate had literally never met anyone like me in her life. She did not know what I meant by donor conception.

Our sessions let me vent but provided absolutely nothing by way of solutions. Expert in adoption, Kate had no idea what the system was for donor conception. She asked me to walk her through it. I explained there was, in fact, no system. I had no rights.

Ultimately, I think it *was* useful to see Kate, although not for the reasons I'd hoped. A pattern emerged. I'd find out something outrageous about donor conception, then I'd tell Kate. It became rolling updates on how, at every turn, donor conception was completely messed up. In fact, it became a series of reports – reporting to Kate. And because – like all journalists – I enjoy telling stories, it became occasionally amusing. Eventually, it was funny. The jokes were definitely the sick kind. 'You'll never guess what I found out last week,' I'd start, and Kate would make a face of mock horror.

After a while, I stopped seeing Kate, because I was more myself. The dark humour helped. I was starting to gather myself and wonder: why is donor conception like this? And can I change it?

The odds were bad. Ranged against me were: the fertility industry, the public health system, the law, more than a century of secrecy and lies about donor conception, society (inasmuch as society even *thought* about donor conception), and my own personal distaste for the fact that in order to do anything about this, I was going to have to talk about sperm. A lot.

It seemed pretty unlikely, then, that I could change anything. But I was certain, on the other hand, that doctors should not be paid to mass produce children in the absence of law, particularly when they then destroyed the evidence of what they'd done. And in terms of fighting for a complete reversal of societal attitudes, well – there was an enormous precedent, one with many parallels. It was the story of adoption.

THROUGHOUT THE TWENTIETH century, around the world, adoptees and their biological families – mainly mothers – waged war on 'closed adoption': where an adopted child's original birth certificate is sealed forever and a new replacement birth certificate issued, with only the child's adoptive parents on it.

In many places, they won huge victories. Today, the records of adoption have been opened in countries like Australia, the UK and the US – to name just a few – allowing adoptees to know their biological family. Across Australia, domestic adoptees, no matter when they were born, have achieved a major turnaround: 'All state and territory legislation provides adopted people with the right to identifying information about their biological parents, including their original birth certificate,' writes health law expert Dr Sonia Allan.[1] Controversial caveats still exist in some jurisdictions, including blocking access if it's deemed that a threat to personal safety may result, but the laws are there.[2] In England and Wales, the first laws to open adoption records were passed in 1975. In Scotland, all adoptees aged seventeen and older have had full access to their adoption records and original birth certificates since the 1930s. In the US, legislation varies by state: most have conditional or full access. In a minority of jurisdictions, original birth certificates remain sealed, but can be opened following an individual's appeal to a court.[3]

Adoption, like donor conception, is still complex and very far from problem free.

But there has been a fundamental shift in how we view adoption. Thanks to all the decades of speaking up, it is now far more widely accepted – both in social attitudes and in legislation – that in adoption, biological families matter. They should not be simply discarded, erased, obliterated. Moreover, we understand that to do so causes huge damage. Those still stubbornly practising closed adoption around the world are on the wrong side of history. And slowly, slowly, the dominoes fall and are falling: the opening of records, the removal of caveats around the opening of those records, the provision of support services to adoptees and biological families wishing to reconnect.

Strange, then, that as societies belatedly, and grudgingly, undo some of the damage done to adoptees, they hurt hundreds, thousands, millions of donor-conceived children in the same way.

UNTIL THE 1970S, adoption was the go-to option for many infertile couples in Australia. The demands of that market created some extremely disturbing realities. According to academics Denise Cuthbert and Patricia Fronek, the wants of would-be parents led to normalising 'the exploitive and abusive treatment of mostly single mothers and their children in the service of an adoption industry geared to serve the interests of adoptive families.' The emphasis was on recipients and satisfying their desires. It was not on the adopted child or their biological parents.[4]

After the social changes of the 1970s, including the rise of feminism and greater social acceptance of single mothers, the local supply of adoptees slowed dramatically. Cuthbert and Fronek say that in 1971–2, up to 10,000 babies alone were placed for adoption. Australian Institute for Health and Welfare figures show that by 1994–5, the total number of all Australian children adopted had declined to 631. In 2018–19, that number had dropped to just 253.[5]

So domestic supply dried up – but demand did not. In 2001, Alan Trounson – an internationally recognised member of the Melbourne IVF pioneers' crew – reminisced on the ABC: 'Abortion was made available to women, and so suddenly there were no babies, or relatively few babies, for adoption. We had to develop something different, because the physicians who were then treating women for infertility were being pressured much more to get a solution, and so IVF was born out of that particular need.' If one source of supply ceases, the market just switches to another.[6]

As the numbers of Australian babies for adoption dwindled, Australia's fertility industry was booting up. New horizons beckoned. Yet this potential new 'solution' for infertility – donor conception – was developed disregarding the learnings of adoption, even as such learnings were taking place in the spotlight. While human rights activists, politicians, those expert in the social sciences, and adoptees and birth parents themselves were turning the debate around closed adoption on its head, proving that such a practice was detrimental, fertility doctors were explicitly practising and advocating anonymous donor conception.

Ironically, the very same year that Victoria opened records to adoptees, next door New South Wales passed laws erasing the biological parents of donor-conceived people: the *Artificial Conception Act 1984*. Despite its name, the *Artificial Conception Act 1984* is concerned with just one aspect of the vast complexity of donor conception: shielding men from any offspring. Remarkably, the Act states that, where a woman becomes pregnant by artificial insemination, or by using an embryo fertilised with donor sperm, any man who produced the semen used shall 'be presumed not to have caused the pregnancy and not to be the father of any child born as a result of the pregnancy'. You can pass a law stating my eyes are blue, but they will remain brown.

Some may say that adoption is different to donor conception because with adoption a child is separated from both their biological parents, while in donor conception there is still usually a genetic connection to one parent. Yet in donor conception, both your biological parents can be donors. Your social parents may have used a sperm donor and an egg donor. Or they may have used a (pre-existing) donated embryo. Or they may have done either of those things and also used a surrogate to carry you. In all those scenarios, you are a donor-conceived person. If you were born using the human tissue of only one donor, you are a donor-conceived person. And having just one donor, not two, doesn't make anonymous donor conception okay.

Even back then, some in the adoption reform space could see history repeating. Chris Sidoti was the foundation director of the Australian Human Rights and Equal Opportunity Commission from 1987 to 1992, after which he became Australian Law Reform Commissioner from 1992 to 1995, and thereafter Australian Human Rights Commissioner from 1995 to 2000. 'A number of people, including me, who were involved in the adoption information debate, were also very concerned about donor conception information,' he told me. 'The issue was alive at the same time, no doubt about that. But there wasn't very much of it. And as I say, the doctors who were involved in fertility clinics were completely opposed.'

'And did anyone question their motives?' I asked.

'Yep,' he said. 'There were discussions about [their opposition] being primarily economic.'

'And what was the response?' I asked.

'Well,' he said, with a small laugh. 'People didn't move. You know, part of the response was, "There is a demand for donor insemination, it's legal. So we should not be deterring it. We should not be restricting it." The response was about the role of the state.'

In 1997, Chris Sidoti told Queensland newspaper the *Courier-Mail* that the use of anonymous sperm donors was creating a 'social time bomb'. In 1999, he wrote to the Donor Conception Support Group:

'One of the most fundamental of all human rights is the right to an identity. Without a sense of their identity – who they are and where they come from – people cannot achieve their true potential as human beings ... Denial of this right can lead to inestimable suffering, distress and alienation. Australia's stolen generations of Indigenous children illustrated the enormous destruction that results when people are refused access to knowledge about their roots, their background and their heritage. Yet there are many other children who have also been forced to grow to adulthood not knowing who they are. The plight of donor offspring has not been given the attention it deserves by governments, the media, and society as a whole.'[7]

These days, Chris Sidoti is an international human rights consultant. And his position on donor conception hasn't changed.

'What does the Convention [on the Rights of the Child] say?' he asks. 'The Convention says the child has a right to know his or her parents. And I don't think we can define away the concept of parenthood. We can expand the concept to say that adoptive parents, for example, or parents who have conceived through artificial conception are also parents. But I don't think you can define away the actual factual state, and it's a factual determination rather than a legal determination.'

Chris Sidoti says, again, adoption laws provide a parallel: 'To all intents and purposes, the adoptive parents acquire not only the rights, but also the responsibilities that the birth parents had in relation to the child. But that doesn't define away the *existence* of the birth parents. And as we discussed previously, adoption law now recognises very much the continued existence of those people. And the child's right to have information about those people.'

Biological fact, then, cannot be erased by human law.

THERE ARE A few key differences between donor-conceived people and adoptees. But they have enormous consequences.

Adoption, in cold terms, is what you do after the fact: a child exists, and the practice follows. As IVF pioneer Alan Trounson noted, it's no coincidence that the increased availability of abortion was one factor leading to far fewer babies to adopt.

Donor-conceived people are not just what you deal with after the fact of childbirth: we begin, oddly enough, before that. Crucially – unlike adoption – there is always an intended child. The steps towards our existence are extremely deliberate and – if they're clinic-based, and often even if they're not – transactional in nature. We are commissioned. Money changes hands with the express intent of creating us, either through engaging the services of the fertility industry, or even paying a stranger on Facebook for donor material. In the clinic setting, where the main opportunity for regulation arises, human tissue is solicited, traded, screened, washed, manipulated and implanted with the objective of creating us. Written legal agreements are drawn up governing the forever-use of that money, and that tissue, without us. Only after all these acts – which all have the same goal – are we finally born. The intent is always there. The preliminary acts are all of enormous consequence and deserve intense scrutiny – and regulation.

In any agreements on donor conception, particularly written agreements, I believe the 'best interests of the child' principle should come first. That goes for before they are born – but it also goes further back than the hotly fought abortion debate: it includes *before conception* itself. It must be the primary concern of doctors, clinics, commissioning parents, donors and surrogates, not just one woman. It must be upheld in all pre-conception written agreements on sperm, egg and embryo donation. That approach should also cover measures to prevent trafficking and exploitation. It should put the highest value on the welfare of the intended child, their right to know their biological family and their right to be as healthy and safe as possible.

IN AUSTRALIA, ABORTION is legal in all jurisdictions. Let me be clear: I have no desire to impinge on any woman's right to a safe, affordable, accessible and legal termination of pregnancy.

But co-existing with the legality of abortion, there are already a number of ways in which the law has also recognised the best interests of the child who will be born.

In New South Wales, for instance, a court has held that a living child may recover damages for any pre-conception or in-utero harm caused by negligence, or omission, on the part of a doctor.

And in Victoria, the law covering the fertility industry – the state's *Assisted Reproductive Treatment Act 2008* – already states that 'in the carrying out of activities regulated by this Act, the welfare and interests of persons born or to be born as a result of treatment procedures are paramount'.

They're good words. They're the right words. But a nod to those words alone is not enough.

CHAPTER 8

I DIDN'T EVER SUSPECT that I was donor conceived, and I think for a long time after my mother told me the truth, she regretted it. Why upset the apple cart?

'Do you wish I'd never told you? Is that it?' she said once, in one of our rare exchanges on the subject. But that wasn't it at all. I know that tantalising, frustrating thought occupied her mind: *What if I'd never said any of it, what if I'd just held it inside, would it all have been fine?*

To me, though, that's the wrong question, starting from the wrong angle. To me, the issue is not *why bother with the truth at twenty-seven,* but *why not tell the truth from the beginning.* The question is not what produces the happier twenty-seven-year-old. It is what makes for a better life. And to a child, whatever you grow up with is normal.

My mother and father had been advised by Clinic 20, all those years ago, to pretend the donor conception had never happened, to pretend that I was my father's child. God knows how many times each of them thought about it, separately or together, for fifteen years while I grew and changed, oblivious to any of these currents. When my father died, my mother shouldered his share of the secret too.

IF YOU DON'T tell your kid they're donor conceived, it's unlikely anyone else will. But if the truth does emerge from a third source, it will probably happen in a problematic and hurtful way for your child.

In adoption, a child can become an adoptee at birth, or when they're a few months old, or five years old, or at any point until they reach legal maturity (and even afterwards, as adults). But donor-conceived babies are always with their commissioning parents from the very first. Commissioning mothers can give birth to children that have a sperm donor as their father; children that have an egg donor, a different woman, as their biological mother; or, in the case of donated embryos, commissioning mothers can give birth to children wholly genetically unrelated to her and/or whatever partner she may have. If a surrogate is used, commissioning parents can take a child newly born from a surrogate that has not been carried by either commissioning parent, nor is genetically related to either commissioning parent. The separation from biological and gestational roots is instantaneous and total.

And commissioning parents can lie from the start.

For donor-conceived people, there will be no original birth certificate of biological (or gestational) parents. In some states and territories of Australia, for donor-conceived people produced through fertility clinics, there is a central register of donor conception status and record of biological parents. However, apart from in Victoria, this central register only includes those born in recent years. Those children can only access this identifying information once they turn eighteen. And the catch is, if you don't know you're donor conceived, you won't apply to any register. You probably haven't even thought about donor conception. You might not even know what it is. There is no intervention by any authority to automatically notify you, at age eighteen or any other, that you are donor conceived.[1] Without such mechanisms, from birth we are left in a situation highly conducive to others' lies.

The biggest liars in donor conception are heterosexuals. They lie because they can. In contrast, if you are a single mother or in a same-sex relationship and you have a child through donor conception, you can't pretend to that child that they are exclusively yours, or yours and your partner's. Logically, there must also be another biological parent somewhere. You might still lie, of course, and say it was a one-night stand or whatever. But a certain low level of truth is inbuilt – and that's a good thing.

Heterosexual couples, on the other hand, have no such nudge to tell the truth. They can lie with abandon, and they do. And the result is damage.

In 2013, there was a fascinating Finnish study published in the Oxford journal *Human Reproduction*.[2] It drew on research from countries around the world. Rates varied, but this article said that in general, 10 to 35 per cent of donor insemination parents were willing to tell their donor-conceived child about their conception. That means up to 90 per cent of those donor-conceived children were going to be deceived. In Finland itself, the study found 16.5 per cent of children of heterosexual couples aged one to twenty-two years had been told the truth. In New Zealand, clinics have encouraged disclosure since 1985, and donors have been required to be identifiable since 2004. Even with both these supposedly protective factors, a 2009 study found only about one-third of New Zealand donor insemination offspring aged seventeen to twenty-one years had been told the truth by their heterosexual parents.

A 2016 article in *Human Reproduction* maintained that heterosexuals who initially said they would tell the truth failed to do so: 'The majority of heterosexual couples who have conceived through anonymous sperm or oocyte donation decide against disclosure or are uncertain about whether or not to do so, or report intentions to tell which are generally not borne out in practice.'[3]

In other words, even if they say they won't lie, they do.

WHY IS IT so important to know you are donor conceived?

Firstly, there's the fundamental human right to family and identity. It's hard to overstate the importance of this right.

Secondly, for reasons of mental health.

A number of studies have shown that the earlier you tell donor-conceived people the truth about how they came to be, the better it is for them. These studies, it must be said, are unavoidably self-limiting. If you don't know you're donor conceived, how can you participate in a survey on your feelings about it? And if governments around the world fail to keep track of all the donor-conceived people created within their borders, how can we ever know just how large this community is, let alone survey them?

In 2009, a study published in *Human Reproduction* surveyed 165 donor-conceived people, mostly American, aged between thirteen and sixty-one years old. All knew they were donor conceived.[4]

The study asked donor-conceived people at what age they had been told the truth about their origins, and how they felt about it. Approximately half the respondents had been told at age seventeen or under, and the other half were aged eighteen or older. Fifty-eight per cent said they had been raised by heterosexual couples, 23 per cent by single mothers and 15 per cent by lesbian couples.

The study found that of those raised by heterosexual couples, one-third had only been told the truth at age nineteen or older. By contrast, all the donor-conceived people raised by single mothers or lesbian couples had been told that they were donor conceived, at the latest, by the time they were fifteen – and most of them significantly younger. 'Only 9 per cent (9) of offspring from heterosexual-couple families were told about their conception before the age of three, compared with 63 and 56 per cent of offspring from single mother and lesbian-couple families, respectively,' the authors found.

To work out what, if any, difference the age of disclosure made, the authors decided to exclude those told very young (under the age of three). If you were told the truth in adulthood, you were about three times more likely (44 per cent) to be upset than those told in childhood (16 per cent). If you were told the truth in adulthood, you were three times more likely to be angry (38 per cent) than those told in childhood (12 per cent). And interestingly, 38 per cent of those told the truth in adulthood were relieved, compared to just 6 per cent of those told in childhood. A sixfold increase, suggesting, perhaps, that the secret of donor conception in a family is one that grows in complications.

The study asked all participants how they felt towards their disclosing parent – usually a mother – at the time of disclosure. 'Significant associations were found between age of disclosure and offspring feeling angry about being lied to and feeling a sense of betrayal, with offspring told during childhood less likely to report these feelings,' the authors found.

In recent years, another intriguing survey of donor-conceived people has grown online. It's an annual project which also skews towards the US and Canada but includes the views of those born outside North America, including Australia, South Africa, Belgium, Norway and the UK.

The survey is the brainchild of Erin Jackson, a donor-conceived person from the US. Erin found out she was donor conceived at age thirty-five – late in anyone's book.

'My mom told me,' says Erin. 'And one of the first things I said – like it just came out of my mouth without me even thinking about it – I said, "I knew it."'

Being donor conceived had never occurred to her before; but Erin had always wondered if she was adopted. 'I was just trying to figure out how did I get here, because this whole mom-and-dad thing isn't adding up quite right,' says Erin. 'It just seemed like there was another variable. And when she told me, everything made sense. My personality made sense. My face. How I look. I found out my biological father is half Ashkenazi Jewish, and I definitely got a lot of those genes.'

When she was finally told the truth, her response was excitement. 'I thought it was so fascinating, and weird, and strange,' she says. 'And as someone who writes for a living, and reads books, I'm like, "Oh wow. This is the best story I've ever heard in my life. This is insane."'

Although I wasn't quick off the mark like Erin, it appears we went through a similar thought process: 'I really took [finding out the truth] as an opportunity to rethink my entire personality and identity. And it was great,' she says. 'I cut away the parts I didn't like. I forgave myself for not meeting the expectations of my parents … and I felt oh, there's a reason I am who I am. *And I was always meant to be this person.*'

It also helped to know that all along, she'd been right. 'I thought I was nuts for thinking there was something that wasn't being said in my family. So knowing I was right – it was very validating.'

But Erin wanted to know how her experience compared to others'. 'I wanted to know, are my feelings normal? Do other people feel this way?' The research she found didn't answer those questions. 'I felt like what was available was not really satisfactory. There are a lot of studies with young kids, and in some cases the parents were essentially answering on behalf of their own children.'

So Erin began what would become an annual project: the We Are Donor Conceived survey. First conducted in 2017, it is unique in that, as you might expect, it's run by donor-conceived people. It's also a website and a Facebook group for donor-conceived people only. The latest survey, conducted in 2020, comprises the views of more than 480 donor-conceived people from fifteen different countries. Respondents ranged between thirteen and seventy-four years old, but 87 per cent were aged between twenty and forty. The vast majority were conceived via donor sperm (95 per cent), probably a reflection of donor sperm having been in widespread use longer. Seventy-eight per cent were raised primarily by heterosexual parents. And 86 per cent of respondents were female. (In my experience, more donor-conceived women are open to talking about these issues than donor-conceived men.)[5]

Once again, it appears heterosexual parents chose not to tell the truth early – or in fact at all. 'Family arrangement is the single biggest predictor of openness. Three quarters (76%) of those raised by a single mother or same-sex parents learned they are donor conceived as a child or infant. By comparison, only 9% of respondents raised by heterosexual parents knew they were donor conceived as an infant or child,' the study found. At least 34 per cent of all study participants did not find out that they were donor conceived from their parents.

At the core of the findings is identity and family. Seventy-seven per cent of all respondents said they agreed with the statement: 'My donor is half of who I am.' A huge 91 per cent wanted some form of relationship with their donor and 96 per cent said it was important to have a complete family health history. Ninety-four per cent said all donor-conceived people should have the option to know their donor's identity, and 83 per cent wanted the option to know their donor siblings' identities. Seventy-four per cent said anonymous donor conception was unethical. And an upsetting line: 71 per cent agreed with the statement that 'the method of my conception sometimes causes me to feel distressed, angry, or sad.'

For Erin Jackson, what stands out – year on year – is the commonality of the experiences and attitudes of those who are donor conceived.

'I feel like our experiences, no matter where we're from, have a lot of similarities.' She says that goes for not just the survey, but the online We Are Donor Conceived discussion group – which currently numbers more than 2000 donor-conceived people from around the world. 'We all have a similar way of looking at being donor conceived and how we feel about that reality.' And that includes opinions on what we want, and what needs to change.

What's important about that, Erin Jackson says, is those attitudes straddle both groups: those who were told the truth young and those who found out much later.

'People who were told young, like so young they can't remember as a child, they are less likely to be distressed, angry or sad about being donor conceived,' she says. 'But they're no less likely to support ending anonymity, or you know, having limits on the amount of offspring per donor.'

Ninety-two per cent agreed that the fertility industry had a responsibility to act in the best interests of the people it helps create. That question followed on from a finding in the previous year's survey, where 86 per cent of respondents agreed that sperm banks/clinics 'do not adequately understand or respect the emotional needs of donor-conceived people'.

That's more than four out of five donor-conceived people surveyed, from around the world, saying this industry is not treating them well.

BACK IN 2011 when I first started searching, I couldn't find anyone like me. You may think you don't know any donor-conceived people. And you mostly haven't seen us shaking up the world the same way adoptees have. Our lower profile is because far too many of us don't *know* we are donor conceived. We are silent because we have no idea that our parents are not our biological parents. We are silent because other people have decided for us that we will never have all our fundamental human rights. We will die from preventable diseases, we will unwittingly have children with our siblings, we will live forever at the centre of a big and poisonous family secret that bleeds into our upbringing and our own selves, without understanding it. That's not living in happy ignorance. That's just dangerous.

Particularly for heterosexual couples, who don't have to tell the truth, who can 'pass' as a child's full biological parents, the impulse to lie appears to be strong. But being a parent – being a good parent – means being braver, and stronger, and more selfless, for your child. It means doing things that you don't really want to do, for the sake of your kids. It means putting them and their future first.

And it means telling them the truth about themselves, and all of their family, and valuing those connections. It means being honest about what you did to make them.

CHAPTER 9

SECRETS TAKE TIME, energy and luck to unravel, often exponentially more of all three than it took to actually create the secret in the first place.

Without my mother's permission to look at the files on my conception held by IVF Australia, I was allowed access to nothing. The woman being treated is a patient, but the result of that treatment is not. I'd had enough.

I managed to get hold of the medical director of IVF Australia, Associate Professor Peter Illingworth, by phone. I told Illingworth that destroying donor codes and telling me there were no answers was not good enough. After that call, he emailed me (and Mary) to set up a meeting.

On 29 September 2011, I walked into the Sydney headquarters of IVF Australia. It was a glassy, shining building on the highway of Sydney's Lower North Shore. It was just over the road from the Royal North Shore Hospital, where I had been made in Clinic 20 and where my mother still worked. A short distance up the road was the small townhouse where I spent the first six years of my life. I could have ridden my bike to these offices. Somewhere in this building, I thought, was the name of my biological father.

In a room, all white and glass, I met with Peter Illingworth. I took notes. And I took a support person, my boyfriend at the time.

'What I would like to do is to do as much as we possibly can to help you with this,' he began. 'That includes doing as much detective work as we can, to gather the information we can.

'We have to also be cognisant of everybody else's interests in this as well. Other people have entitlements to privacy. Arrangements were made a long time ago that were the arrangements at the time, accepted by legislation and medical practices and society as the right thing at the time.'

Well, not quite. As we have seen, there was no law at the time I was born.

'Now, we recognise that a lot of that was wrong,' Illingworth continued smoothly. 'These are not things that would ever be done again, but all we can do is just to help you try and piece as much of it together as possible.'

I took a breath. 'What Mary has told me', I began, 'is that for some reason, the donor code has been deleted from my file, the file which she cannot release to me because it's not mine, even though I am that file. So basically, I can't access the file and the donor code's not there anyway. What can you actually do to help me?'

'Well, what would be very helpful would be for your mother to write, to give us permission to show you that file,' Illingworth said.

'But what good does it do if the donor code's not there?' I said. I deal with non-answers for a living.

'Well, what we are doing is going through all the donor records, to try and identify which donor was involved,' he said. 'We will not be able to know for certain. But I could have a good guess, maybe. Let me put that in context as to what was happening at that time historically.

'The donation was given to your mother on the basis of anonymity,' Illingworth said. Hence donor codes, not names, being used in the files of women like my mother. But then, at some point, clinic staff went back and obliterated all mention of the donor code from each sheet of paper in women's files.

'It seems to be [for] about a year or so, including the time that your mother went through treatment,' Illingworth said calmly.

'How is that legal?'

'Well, at that time it wasn't *illegal*. There was nothing in the law at that time to stop you from doing it.'

Cutting holes in medical files was still trashing NSW Health Department minimum standards, set out in its circular on record-keeping in hospitals. And just because something's not illegal doesn't make it right.

Illingworth also told me that when I was conceived and born, donor sperm was either frozen and held in a bank, or a donor would come by, drop it off fresh, and it would be used that same day for treatment. Inside, I was screaming: what kind of screening is possible on sperm *dropped off fresh and used within hours or even minutes*? But Illingworth was still going.

'So those were the days just before the AIDS epidemic broke,' he continued, 'and in fact there were cases in Sydney at that time where women died from AIDS infections contracted through that practice.'

Dead women, from HIV-positive sperm. There was a roaring in my head.

'That was in western Sydney, at Westmead Hospital. So from that point forward, that was what made clinics stop deleting any donor records. From that point forward, the donations were all carefully recorded,' he finished. He paused.

'So there was no legislation, no general guideline, no ruling that codes should be deleted?' I prodded.

'Not at that time,' he said.

'Just someone at that clinic deciding to manage the records themselves?'

'Yup.'

'And who', I asked, 'would that have been?'

'That would have been the clinic themselves, the staff involved at the time, all of whom are long gone,' Illingworth said.

'Do you have any records as to who they were?'

'Uh, it's something we can look into, but they're all retired now; they're all long gone.'

'As long as they're not dead.'

'Uh —'

'That was a joke,' I said coolly. 'How many times would you use the sperm of one man?'

'Sometimes, quite a lot. Sometimes not very many. In those days, sometimes sperm was used to create up to twenty families.'

Twenty families? Not twenty children – twenty *families*?

'What kind of tests were they running? Obviously none picked up the AIDS virus?'

'No, that's not true. At that time, they had just started checking for that. But the problem was then, and is now, that an initial AIDS test does not pick up an infection that is brewing. And so nowadays when we're using donor sperm, we will only use sperm that has been frozen, quarantined and retested after a period of three to six months. But in those days that wasn't known to be an issue.'

'Were they running any tests?'

'They were running some tests for general health, making sure the man was generally healthy. Generally, men with serious medical histories, serious genetic problems, were not allowed to be used as sperm donors.'

'How would you know?'

'Because they saw a doctor, and the doctor would take a medical history.'

'Could they just lie?'

'They can, but people can lie to us, all the time, in any form of life, and there's nothing we can do about people who lie to us,' Illingworth said soothingly.

'If I had AIDS,' I said, 'I would presumably know by now?'

'You would know by now, yeah, be assured that you would have known it by now,' he said.

'Jesus Christ,' I said. There was a silence.

IF I HAD the virus, I would know by now, but I would also be dead by now. So would my mother. In 1982, when I was conceived (and for many subsequent years until the mid '90s), being HIV-positive was a death sentence. HIV would become full-blown AIDS. You would become shockingly, debilitatingly weak. You would become terribly vulnerable to both major and minor illnesses. And you would, within a short timeframe, die.

I couldn't believe that fertility clinics would consider sufficient a verbal assurance that a donor did not have any inheritable conditions. But somehow it had been enough. Consider, too, that a clinic would want that donor to donate, in order to allow the clinic to be able to offer (increasingly popular) donor conception. You're looking at a recipe for green-lighting essentially everyone.

ONE WEEKEND, I was invited around to Donor Conception Support Group co-founder Caroline Lorbach's house for lunch. She and her husband have three children who are donor conceived, now all adults. I drove to a comfortable family home in Sydney's west with a bright dining room and a table already set. Caroline offered something else over the course of lunch: since the DCSG was now defunct, she was getting rid of all the old files and notes. There were also newspaper clippings, papers, submissions to Parliament and letters. Did I want to look through them? Yes, I did.

On small, square pages seemingly from an exercise book, one man had written a long, rambling treatise to the DCSG. A lot of it made no sense. It was also extremely graphic. He ranted about 'spawn' and spoke about women and their body parts – to put it politely – in extremely disparaging terms. He also doodled all around the margins. The cartoons were nightmarish. They were of demon babies, and monsters, and vaginas with teeth, and various combinations of demons-monsters-toothy vaginas. This was clearly the feverish work of someone with a mental illness. And this man, apparently, was a sperm donor in Australia; that was why he had contacted the DCSG.

The DCSG had no way of verifying absolutely that this man had donated sperm, and that his donation resulted in live offspring, because, once again, the clinics hold that information and do not give it out. But I was horrified. If this was the kind of stuff that was in his head, how on earth had this man presented to the fertility clinic itself? Had the receptionist noticed something was going on with him? Had a nurse? Had the fertility specialist? Or had everyone turned a blind eye because they wanted to harvest his material?

Imagine finding out that this man was your father. I flinched. What kind of trust do you put in a fertility clinic, as a paying customer? You trust that the donor – whose genetic material will be placed inside your body and become part of your future child – doesn't have any transmittable disease. You also assume that he is not violent, not a sex offender, not any other kind of serious criminal, and not insane. But in Australia, for instance, there is no jurisdiction which requires a police check on sperm or egg donors prior to donation. What assurance do you have that your trust is not misplaced?

Another handwritten letter to the DCSG caught my eye. It was spidery old lady writing. It was from one Shirley Lock, Tasmania. I have tried to find her, without success. In her letter, she explains that she is enclosing a copy for the DCSG of a 'somewhat tardy' submission she had made to a New South Wales state review of artificial reproduction techniques. The year is 1998.

'My attention was drawn to this debate by the desire of people conceived in this way to discover their genetic background and <u>paternal</u> records,' she writes (emphasis her own).

'As a registered nurse, I worked in Canberra in 1982/3 and at times "relieved" the regular sister at a private practice (gynaecological). At this surgery I was required to give AI [artificial insemination] in which I was told the semen was a mix of donor and "husbands".'

Semen mixing? It's usually explained as something entirely cosmetic that treats the social anxieties of the commissioning parents and nothing else. If you mix semen, donor and husband, you can hang on to a slim hope when that child is born that it *may* be your husband's biological child. On a purely medical level, mixing the sperm of different men and then injecting the resulting multi-gamete mess into a woman really doesn't sound like something any registered doctor should be doing. And what if the sperm of more than one donor was mixed in? And whether it was one donor or several, how on earth could that clinic claim to know how many babies had been born from whom, whose family medical history relates to whom, and who is donor conceived, if it was shaking up these kinds of cocktails?

'It seems to me that the legitimate desire of people to research their genetic histories is therefore made difficult, socially and scientifically without meticulous records and genetic testing,' Shirley Lock writes in 1998. 'Is this practice (or former practice) of semen mixing fully recognised?'

I contacted Andrew Refshauge, NSW health minister at the time. He said he remembered Lock's startling letter and question, but not whether it was investigated.

Driving home from Caroline's, I added Shirley Lock to a short list in my head: the people who kept their eyes open and saw the storm coming.

CHAPTER 10

Although many, if not most, heterosexual commissioning parents fail to tell their donor-conceived children the truth about themselves, they do tell other people. Other adults, that is. My mother and father – my mother and social father – had told three people in their lives the truth about me. Obviously, I wasn't one of them. My paternal grandmother and grandfather were.

In terms of love though, it didn't, and it doesn't, matter. I am one of the lucky ones: instead of donor conception creating some kind of rift with my social-not-biological family, Oma and Opa in Adelaide (otherwise quite steeped in the mores of their generation) loved me unconditionally. I was their family. I loved them right back. I remember this vividly, even though Oma died when I was only a few years old. Opa died when I was a teenager, a scant half year after my father had flatlined in a hospital bed.

One of my maternal uncles also knew the truth about me, but I suppose that situation was a little different. After all, he *is* genetically related to me, through my mother. Perhaps all of this felt like a distant issue to him – a concern for the in-laws. In any case, he never mentioned it to me either.

I'm not angry at any of these people in my family who knew the truth that I was denied for so long. I'm not angry with my social dad, and I never have been. He might have eventually told me the truth, had he not died when I was fifteen. Or he might not have. Who knows? But this much is true: he loved me like his own. He loved me more than anything except my mother. And when my mum told me the truth, I was shocked and angry, yes. But I'm no longer angry at my poor mother, either, who bore the full brunt of the whole situation simply because she was the one who finally confessed.

For months after she told me the truth, I kept asking Mum for permission to access the records of my conception held by IVF Australia, but every time I raised it, it didn't go well. She, like commissioning parents all around the world, had been told – by the clinic – to go away and pretend it had never happened. Artificial insemination is an intrusive, confronting act on a woman's body. Patients are vulnerable. You can imagine the damage if even your own doctors are suggesting that this is something shameful: this is a secret, do not speak of it. Then imagine you followed their advice. How do you overcome almost three decades' deep shame? At that time, Mum didn't want me picking over the files: going through what had happened, stringing this out. For her, the moment of truth was more than enough pain.

What changed her mind was cancer. A lump had been found in her breast, for the second time. It was small, considered benign, and the prognosis good, but when it comes to breast cancer treatment, no-one messes around. Almost immediately she was looking at months of surgery, recovery, radiotherapy, rehab.

I said to her, 'What if someone on the donor's side has breast cancer? Or more than one person? Mum, I need to know this stuff. I need to know *risk*.'

She exhaled. 'Okay. Fine,' she said.

That was it. That was all I needed. I wrote an email to the clinic, and she signed it.

A COUPLE OF months later, I was back at IVF Australia. This was the day of days. This was the meeting in which they would finally hand over the pages, however mutilated, of how I had come to be.

And there was some hope. Mary had rung me, a month after the first meeting. She'd told me that they were trying to contact Douglas Saunders, the man who had run Clinic 20 and taken it private to form NSART. But Saunders wasn't in the country, Mary warned.

Mary said there was another (once again, highly conditional) way they might be able to work out who my donor was. Women were inseminated on a number of different occasions per cycle of treatment (each cycle corresponded to a woman's ovulation cycle). IVF Australia would check the dates of insemination in the cycle during which my mother fell pregnant with me. Then they would see which donor had had their sperm used on those insemination dates. A match, if there was one, could only be confirmed by genetic testing, with everyone's permission, etc. But it was something.

My mother had been treated five times in the cycle during which I was conceived. There were five dates, clues as to which donor might be my biological father.

'Now,' Peter Illingworth began. Mary was sitting in on this, too. 'This is the file. I'd just like to walk you through the issues and the dilemmas.' My heart sank.

First they showed me the relevant pages. Out of the whole fat file, only two sheets of paper related to my conception. These were the only two pages recording the treatment cycle in which I was conceived. Each A4 page had a table on it, with four columns: Date, Insemination by (with initials of staff members), Motility and – at the very end – Code. To record the donor code.

On those two precious pages, under 'Code', there is only a blank. The entire column has been cut out and another piece of paper stuck over the hole with sticky tape. Then the damaged pages have been photocopied, and the photocopies kept as the record, so that there is no answer to be found, ever.

'That's normally a real no-no in medical terms,' said Illingworth brightly. 'So it's not something you would normally come across, to be honest.' He'd seemingly forgotten his statement last meeting that this was something accepted by the law, society and medical practice.

'The covering must have happened in 1982,' he said. 'Because when we look at the other records, there's only a small number that have had this happen to them.'

'Going back how many years?' I asked.

'Oh, not very far.'

'So what period were they erasing the donors?'

'I think it was happening some time in '83 or '84, they looked back and said —' he checked himself and then continued: 'There must have been some threat to donors' privacy at that point. They must have said, look. At that time they were entitled to do it. At that time there was nothing illegal in what they did. It's just with the knowledge we now have about how important this all is, it's just a terrible thing that's happened.'

'So you're saying they stopped recording '82, '83, '84, and they started recording again in '85?' I asked. I meant, when did they decide to retain donor codes in files: they seemed to be writing them down okay, but then, later on, cutting them out.

'Mm-hm. Yeah.'

I found out later that 1985 was an important year, for reasons that Illingworth either didn't know or didn't tell me. In 1985, following a sharp, horrifying uptick in medically acquired AIDS, Australia began universal screening for HIV in both donated blood and semen. If codes were deleted up until that point, Clinic 20 was destroying any information which could uncover a link between an HIV-positive sperm donor and infected women and children.

By the time of this second meeting, Illingworth had managed to contact Professor Douglas Saunders, the former head of Clinic 20. Saunders is another pioneer of the baby business. He helped found the Fertility Society of Australia. He was head of obstetrics and gynaecology at the University of Sydney, and in 2001 he became a Member of the Order of Australia for his work in infertility.

'He [Saunders] doesn't *recall* the decision to do this,' said Illingworth. 'But he thinks there must have been some sort of threat to the privacy of the donors.'

'So he takes responsibility for that decision, he's the one who made it?' I asked.

'That was the decision made in that unit at that time.'

'By him?'

'I don't know, he doesn't recall that decision at all.'

'Was he leading that unit?'

'He was at that time, yeah.'

In our previous meeting, Illingworth had told me that when I was conceived, Clinic 20 used a mix of frozen and fresh sperm. Today, he told me that Saunders had remembered, 'quite categorically', that all sperm used in late 1982 was frozen and quarantined for six months. Last time, Illingworth had told me that the same donor could be used for up to twenty families; today, he said no more than ten siblings were created from any one donor.

'Was that a regulation?' I asked.

'It was certainly the rule in that clinic at that time,' Illingworth said.

'And they wouldn't have broken that rule?' I asked.

'No, no,' Illingworth said.

As it turns out, he was wrong in that too.

SIX YEARS BEFORE I met with Illingworth, in 2005, Professor Douglas Saunders had appeared in an investigation by ABC TV's *Four Corners*, 'Secrets of the Fathers'. It's an investigation which was well ahead of the curve.

'Professor Douglas Saunders,' ABC journalist Janine Cohen reports in that story, 'now chair of the fertility industry's licensing body … has himself attracted criticism.'

Saunders was so big in Australia's fertility industry that he was the chairman of the Reproductive Technology Accreditation Committee for five years. Earlier, I said that the fertility industry in Australia is self-policing. RTAC is part of the Fertility Society of Australia – the professional association of those in the baby business – and audits all clinics in the country for compliance with its Code of Practice.

Saunders was head of RTAC during the years when RTAC itself conducted all the audits of clinics. They later contracted it out.

When Douglas Saunders was chairman of RTAC, the Code of Practice said that no clinic was supposed to use a donor for more than ten families.

'*Four Corners* has obtained a copy of a letter written in 1997 where a family complains to Professor Saunders about his own clinic,' Janine Cohen declares in 'Secrets of the Fathers'. 'The patient said she'd discovered her donor contributed to at least eleven families, although she'd been promised the clinic's limit was ten.' If Saunders, the chairman of RTAC, was breaking the rules, what hope was there that any other clinic was keeping them?

'Why do your RTAC guidelines work if you say ten families?' Cohen asks. 'If you can't stick to the guidelines or to the rules why should anyone else be able, expected to be able to?'

'Well,' says Saunders. 'We can only try, we can only try.'

'Do you think, given instances like this, is RTAC the right body to be the watchdog over the industry?' Cohen asks.

'I believe it has worked well over the years, and I still say this: there has, there is no evidence that harm has been caused over the years,' Saunders says.

'How would we ever know?' Cohen asks. 'There's no records.' (Here, she's referring to a national register of donor-conceived people.) 'How would we ever know?'

'Yes,' replies Saunders. 'Yes.'

EVEN AFTER SAUNDERS retired, and RTAC contracted outsiders to audit fertility clinics, the audits themselves remained mysterious.

In 2010, Peter Illingworth appeared at the federal Senate inquiry into managing donor conception information. Illingworth was then the President of the Fertility Society of Australia. Under questioning by Labor Senator Trish Crossin, Illingworth said that RTAC's annual reports on clinic audits weren't publicly available – or even written down.[1]

'Can you provide us with the latest copy of their annual report?' Senator Crossin asked.

'I think it is a verbal report,' Illingworth replied. The role of RTAC, he said, was to set a code of practice. 'That Code of Practice is publicly available,' he said.

'All right,' Senator Crossin replied. 'But we are talking about a body here that has the power to regulate or not regulate fertility clinics, which then have the power to create or not create life in this country, and yet it does not provide a public annual report, it is not accountable to any Commonwealth agency or department and not subject to any federal legislation. We would not have the same situation with our pharmaceuticals in this country, would we? We would not allow the Therapeutic

Goods Administration to just report to a society and tell us that the drug they have tested is okay.'

More than a decade after that exchange, I check the RTAC website. At time of writing, only one annual report of RTAC is there: the 2018–19 report. It's not even the latest.[2]

BACK IN THE meeting room with Illingworth, I was impatient to run away with my precious papers, to read it through on my own, pore over it, see what they'd missed. Despite everything, I still thought there might be the key to an answer somewhere: maybe I could puzzle out how I had been made. But there were more unpleasant revelations to come.

Mary took over. She'd been checking the dates of the cycle in which my mother had been treated with donor sperm and fallen pregnant with me. And she'd also gone through the unsuccessful cycle before that. And, she said, their andrologist had looked through all their sperm donor files, to find corresponding dates of usage. And they'd each checked twice.

'We haven't been able to find that match of dates,' she said. 'I've looked for those dates and for inseminations around those dates —'

'There's no inseminations at all?' I asked, astonished.

'Yeah,' she said. 'For some reason, looking through, and unless we've missed it, and I've looked through twice, through all the files, and there are quite a number of files, as I've explained, where we've gone through, and there is no match for those dates.'

It was hard to take in.

'It seems odd that it would happen to all of them,' I said blankly. 'So, do you have records of *any* sperm being used on those dates?'

'No, we can't find records of any sperm being used on those dates,' Illingworth said.

My mother was treated with artificial insemination on five different days in the cycle in which she fell pregnant with me. In the preceding, unsuccessful cycle, she was treated on four different days. That's a total of nine days of clinical operation for which IVF Australia is telling me there is no record of any sperm being used at Clinic 20 at all.

And yet I exist.

How many other children were made in those same nine days for whom there is no record of any sperm donation being used whatsoever? And how many *other* days of Clinic 20's operations sailed by without anyone recording any donor sperm being used at all?

I felt dazed. But I'd come in with a grab-bag list of questions. I thought I might as well finish it. So, in an abrupt tangent, I asked Illingworth why men donated sperm back then. Why do it?

'Generally, they were often students,' he said. 'At the end of the lecture, the professor would say "We need some sperm donors, hands up fellas, I'll give you ten bucks or something, expenses, to be a sperm donor". And half the guys in the class would put their hands up.'

Since that meeting, I have heard this tale often, from fertility specialists around the world: the donors in the '70s and '80s were all medical students. In fact, the classroom callout for sperm isn't true for all of them, but it seems to be true for some. One of my friends once went through the yearbooks of Melbourne's Monash University, crosschecking every man who graduated from medicine over three or four years against one or two other details, in an attempt to find her biological father.

Illingworth's account filled me with dismay. Imagine: you're a young man enrolled in a very demanding university degree. Your professor (male, and probably quite eminent) asks you for a favour, at the end of the very same lecture in which he taught you. Maybe you're not a top student. Or maybe you are and want to stay that way. Something else that you sometimes hear, accompanying this tale, was that the inducement to these young students wasn't just money: it was a little 'extra credit'. Extra credit, in return for sperm.

'It happened to me at university,' Illingworth confided. 'I didn't donate, by the way, but I can remember the head of the IVF clinic saying "Anyone want to be a sperm donor?" and three or four of my friends put their hands up … And the professor then felt a duty to protect these young kids … from,' he paused, '*complex* decisions.'

'Why?' I asked. 'They were adults.'

'Well, it's a different thing now, Sarah,' said Illingworth. I was getting very, very tired of that response. I was also just plain tired.

I left, clutching my envelope of neutered papers.

CHAPTER 11

It was international Women's Day. The sun shone, the highway was clear, and a show called *Girls to the Front* was on the radio. As I drove, I wolfed a late lunch in the car.

I was on my way to meet a woman I'd thought about since my meetings with Peter Illingworth at IVF Australia. She was hard to find. She'd grown up, changed her name, moved, and her close family had passed away. Finally, I tracked her down. Her name is not Jessica, but that's what I'll call her.

I parked outside a house in a wide, quiet street. The letterbox was at the top of a rise, and a curving brick driveway next to it led down to the front door. I knocked and the door was opened almost before I'd finished. 'I saw you pull up,' she said.

Jessica is blonde, with hair pulled back in a high ponytail, and that day she was wearing loose, flowery green pants and a black top. We settled in the living room, on a giant L-shaped couch. Her husband, David (not his real name), was already there. On the glass-topped coffee table there was a black plastic folio, fat with newspaper clippings. Jessica and David looked at me expectantly.

Jessica had an open, straightforward manner. She occasionally toyed with a gold cross around her neck while she spoke but was otherwise calm. David was guarded. He had one hand protectively across the back of the sofa, behind Jessica's shoulders. Hanging on the wall above my head was a framed photo of Jessica as a toddler, with her mother and her father. In the photo, a young Jessica is also grabbing a necklace, which hangs on a chain around her mother's neck. Her mother is smiling, looking straight at the camera. She is beautiful.

In the 1980s, Noelene Cliff and her husband George were trying for a baby. Noelene was desperate to start a family: she was the child of a single mother, who'd given her up for adoption shortly after birth. Noelene grew up in a children's home. Family was particularly important to her. George and Noelene had been trying for almost a decade.

'All they wanted was a child, especially my mother,' Jessica said.

The problem, doctors explained, was on George's side. So they suggested a donor insemination program.

In photos, George Cliff looks like a bit of a rock 'n' roll dad: he has aviator-style frames, and a brown beard and moustache. He was self-employed, running a promotions business, which included gigs and clubs. He loved Noelene to distraction.

The Cliffs enrolled in what was then called the Artificial Insemination by Donor program at Westmead Hospital. The Westmead clinic was the second fertility clinic in the state, after Clinic 20.[1] Westmead is another large public hospital, servicing Sydney's west. Today, Westmead has a battery of specialists across a wide range of disciplines and is home to multiple research institutes plus a leading children's hospital. Westmead is no two-bit operation.

Noelene Cliff underwent three blocks of artificial insemination, treated over months with donor sperm from three different men. After an early miscarriage, she fell pregnant again around October 1983, with sperm from Donor Three.

In May 1984, a tiny Jessica was born, twelve weeks premature. There is a picture of Noelene, fixated on her newborn child, stroking Jessica's dark hair carefully with just the finger and thumb of one hand.[2] Jessica is intubated, her little body covered in monitor patches and medical paraphernalia, and fast asleep with her head to one side.

At first, Jessica lived in the neonatal ward, steadily gaining weight and progressing well. Noelene breastfed her. After Jessica had spent nine weeks in hospital, Noelene could finally take her child home.

'She was just a doting mother,' said Jessica. 'She slept in my room for the first year.' Noelene couldn't tear herself away from her baby, kept for so long in a grey hospital wing.

The adult Jessica sitting across from me today is a practising Christian. Her faith comes up frequently when we talk. What her family has been through is so extraordinary, with such seemingly unlikely twists and turns, that she believes God must have been with them.

'God has his time, and his purposes, and his ways. If she didn't sleep in my room for the first year, and then they got that call, things could have been very different,' Jessica said.

David added, 'They had one year of magic. That's how George described it.'

In March 1991, George Cliff gave evidence to a NSW parliamentary inquiry on medically acquired AIDS.

'The fertility clinic contacted us approximately one year after the child was born,' George Cliff told the inquiry. 'And jokingly said, "There has been a case of AIDS overseas." Something flippant. "We are testing all of our patients, would you and your husband and child come in?" We joked about it, we really thought it was a joke.

'At no time did they tell us that the actual donor at that stage – that Noelene's donor – had tested positive.'

In the early '80s, HIV was spreading with terrifying speed, largely through men having unprotected sex with men. At that point, women were less likely to contract the disease; the social stigma and fear surrounding it was huge, and myths about how it spread abounded. Rumours flew about how you could get it from shaking hands, from hugging, from sharing cups.

George Cliff told the inquiry that Noelene went into Westmead Hospital to be tested for HIV in June 1985. Two weeks later, the Cliffs had a phone call. The results were positive.

Jessica's biological father was Donor Three. But George Cliff said that Westmead staff revealed that Donor One – the donor used for months in several of Noelene's previous, unsuccessful treatment cycles – had come back to the program and told them he was bisexual. Donor One had donated sperm regularly, they said, in 1982 and 1984. Staff told the Cliff family that three other women at the Westmead clinic had also contracted HIV through donor semen. Decades later, the Westmead fertility specialist responsible would confirm this number: four HIV-positive female patients. For all of them, it was a death sentence.[3]

The Cliffs were never told the names of these women, fellow victims. I can't find their names either: the other infected women never came forward publicly. They carried their disease in private to its terrible conclusion. In 1988, an article in *AIDS and Obstetrics and Gynaecology* reported that none of these four women passed the disease on to their husbands, 'despite unprotected intercourse', and that three of them had a child by other donors but did not pass the disease on to their children.[4] All of the women were killed by AIDS. From the mid '90s onwards, antiretroviral therapy changed a diagnosis of HIV from a death sentence to a chronic, manageable condition. But in the early '80s, HIV was fatal. However, you wouldn't know it, George Cliff said, if you were going by the advice of Westmead Hospital.

'Initially, we were led to believe that there was a mortality rate in the vicinity of 10 per cent,' George Cliff told the inquiry. As if that weren't concerning enough, he said no-one warned the Cliffs that George might also be at risk. 'The risk of further infection was not adequately explained, and Noelene and I maintained a normal sexual relationship for an extended period. Fortunately … I [was] spared.'

It wasn't just George who escaped. A child born to an HIV-positive mother not on antiretroviral therapy runs the gauntlet: the disease can be transmitted from mother to child in pregnancy, during birth or through breastfeeding. Without intervention, the UN agency UNICEF says that about 35 per cent of HIV-positive pregnant women will pass HIV on to their children at some point during those three stages. The risk is greater the longer any HIV-positive mother not on antiretroviral therapy continues to breastfeed her baby.[5]

Although her mother bore her and, according to her father, breastfed Jessica for the first nine months of her life, Jessica escaped HIV.

But tiny Jessica was not the only baby at risk. Because she was premature, she lived at the hospital for more than two months. Noelene Cliff had excess breastmilk. 'They used a lot of Noelene's milk for all the other babies in the neonatal clinic ward,' George Cliff told the parliamentary inquiry. An unknown number of other premature or at-risk babies were also put in harm's way. It would not be discovered that HIV could be transmitted via breastmilk for another year.[6]

'There's other cases, are you aware?' Christian Democratic Party MP Reverend Fred Nile asked.

'They told me that everyone was cleared,' George Cliff responded. 'All the other babies. They tested them all.'

That exchange sinks into the transcript of the parliamentary inquiry like lead. After what happened to Noelene, believing that no babies were infected with HIV at Westmead is hard to take on trust.

George Cliff added that, after Noelene's diagnosis, their treatment by Westmead was less than ideal.

'After the initial approach from Westmead Hospital in 1985 until 1986 when the first symptoms became apparent, we had no contact from Westmead Hospital,' George Cliff told the inquiry. 'It was not until such time in mid-1986, after visiting the Albion Street AIDS Centre [a different facility] that Noelene first became fully aware of the implications of being HIV antibody positive. She was informed by medical staff that her life expectancy was short.'

George Cliff told the parliamentary inquiry that his wife went into first shock, then acute depression. To make matters worse, George himself had a bronchial condition from having whooping cough as a child. He had become seriously ill and was unable to work. Meanwhile, Noelene began to deteriorate. She lost a huge amount of weight. Like all AIDS sufferers, with her immune system compromised, this woman who had enjoyed the rudest of health now came down with everything: meningitis, a badly infected arm, chickenpox. The night sweats began. 'Every couple of hours she'd wake up, I'd have to change her, change her singlet, everything, the bed, strip it down, possibly four or five times a night,' George Cliff told Parliament. Noelene now spent her life in and out of Westmead Hospital with appointments or with complications. It was hard on both her and her husband, and it was no place for a child.

'We had to be treated with all other AIDS patients in a public hospital, which included prisoners from the jail, with two heavy prison guards sitting alongside of them with guns,' George Cliff said. 'We were expected to sit in this waiting room, with our child, who was possibly about two or three years old at the time. The prisoners would frequently use foul language when we were kept waiting and drug addicts as well were there. We would have to wait up to one hour and a half to three hours.' Unpredictable wait times continued, he said, regardless of Noelene's deterioration, almost until her death. 'One month before she died, we went back to that clinic, she had to wait one half hour ... Finally, she couldn't sit up any longer. She had to lay down when she finally got in to see the doctor.'

When Noelene Cliff was admitted for months on end as an inpatient to Westmead, attitudes at the hospital inflicted further pain. Some staff behaved as if they could catch HIV by coming near their own patient. 'She had to put up with staff bringing her trays, leaving them outside the door, not wanting to bring them into her room,' George Cliff would recall. It upset Noelene hugely. 'I was sitting in the room with the little child and I said to these people, "Do you think I would be sitting in this room if you could catch AIDS, with a little child, just by being in an air-conditioned room?"'

By 1990, the Cliffs had almost no money. They'd received no compensation from the public hospital which had given Noelene the disease, or indeed the government itself. And George was on sickness benefits for his bronchial condition. 'Whenever we got any extra money, we knew there wasn't any hope for her, we tried to do a few things like go and stay in a hotel,' George Cliff told the parliamentary inquiry. 'Then we wouldn't have any money left when we needed it some months later, but everything was done so that we lived every moment for the time.'

George Cliff told his story to the NSW Parliament in March and August 1991. Noelene Cliff had died in December 1990, at the age of forty-two. Westmead had treated her for some five years. George told Parliament he received condolence cards from all over the world, but not one word from Westmead Hospital.[7]

IN 1994, THE *Sun-Herald* announced that the NSW Government, under Liberal premier John Fahey, would reverse years of denial and grant compensation totalling $36 million to 230 people in New South Wales who had medically acquired AIDS.[8] New South Wales was the last Australian state to do so. 'Between 1980 and 1985 Australia had the highest rate of transfusion AIDS cases in the Western world. NSW, with more than 100 known cases, was responsible for the worst domestic rate,' the *Sun-Herald* reported. Jessica thinks that her father received around $200,000, which George told her was 'a very small amount [compared] to what many others had because [Noelene] had passed'.

The Cliffs contemplated suing Westmead, but the expense and the complexity of the case put them off. Jessica's father told her the records of Noelene Cliff's fertility treatment were completely destroyed by Westmead before the Cliffs could launch any legal action.

'He just said that because [Mum and Dad] tried to go them [Westmead], and because [Westmead] were aware that something was possibly going to happen, they destroyed the records,' Jessica told me. 'We couldn't get anything. We couldn't get any information.'

Westmead Hospital and the Western Sydney Local Health District declined my request for an interview.

George Cliff died in September 2015, succumbing to his long battle with lung disease.

IN THE FRAMED family photo on Jessica and David's living room wall, Noelene is young, with a mass of permed '80s hair and colour in her cheeks. At this stage, she has the disease and knows it. George is holding his wife and child. Both George and Noelene have full faces and are smiling.

Jessica lost her mother at the age of six. Afterwards, when it was clear that the young Jessica herself had escaped HIV transmission, Westmead staff grew interested in her. George Cliff would later confide in his future son-in-law, David, that Westmead wanted to know what secrets Jessica's little body could reveal.

'They believed she might have carried an antibody to AIDS – because she was able to survive – and they wanted to test her,' David said. Throughout our interview so far, David had betrayed little emotion; but now his voice had an edge of fury. 'And that never happened. No way in the world would George go back into that system that destroyed their lives. And the nerve to ask that question,' David said vehemently. 'After everything. I think it just shows the complete arrogance of the individuals who are involved.'

Malpractice in fertility treatment does not end with the birth of a child or the death of a commissioning parent. It echoes down the generations. It colours people's lives. George Cliff drank himself into insensibility for two years after Noelene's death. Even after he pulled himself out of that hole, his bronchial condition meant his health was never good. Jessica grew up looking after her father. For her, that was normal.

To this day, Jessica will not set foot in any part of the Westmead medical precinct. Jessica and David have two young children. Westmead is conveniently located for her family, but whenever her kids are sick, she will drive them miles away to a private hospital and pay through the nose for emergency attention.

Her biological father, Donor Three, may still be out there somewhere. Jessica doesn't have access to Noelene's treatment records, and has never tried to find him, nor has she had the emotional space to do so. There's been much bigger things going on. The man who infected Noelene, Donor One, is dead of AIDS.[9] Jessica has considered this. She genuinely bears no animosity towards him for passing the disease on to her mother and killing her.

'[Sperm donation] was one of these things that you just did for getting some money. They probably would not have thought for a second there was anything more to it,' Jessica said. 'They may not have even known they had the virus. I'm not angry at them, because I don't know that he knew [that he had HIV].'

The fertility industry, however, is another matter.

CHAPTER 12

DUE TO THE opacity and lack of regulation surrounding donor conception itself, the story of the HIV/AIDS epidemic in donor conception is largely unknown, and the death toll is far from clear.

In 1980 and 1981, AIDS was sweeping through gay communities across the US. At first, the new disease was actually called GRID – gay-related immunodeficiency disease – and some scientists and authorities publicly speculated that perceived aspects of being homosexual were the cause, in particular having a lot of different sexual partners.[1]

Noelene's Donor One first began donating sperm to Westmead Hospital in 1982. That year in the US, the Center for Disease Control reported on the disease also surfacing in heterosexuals, particularly those with additional risk factors: intravenous drug users, haemophiliacs, as well as Haitians. By September 1982, nearly 600 cases of AIDS had been reported to the CDC – and more than 40 per cent of those people were already dead.[2] At the end of 1982, the first AIDS case was formally diagnosed at St Vincent's Hospital in Sydney.

At the start of 1983, 'epidemiological evidence from CDC's investigations strongly suggested that blood and blood products transmitted AIDS and that the disease could be transmitted through intimate sexual contact.'[3]

In January 1983, America's National Haemophilia Foundation said high-risk donors, such as gay men, should be barred from donating blood, sparking outrage from gay rights activists, who were already fighting entrenched homophobia.[4]

In January and February 1983, the *Journal of the American Medical Association* and the *New England Journal of Medicine* canvassed the risk of AIDS transmissions to haemophiliacs and whether blood donors should be screened.[5] In March, the US Public Health Service adopted the position that members of groups at increased risk for AIDS – including gay men – should not donate blood. The American Red Cross and the American Association of Blood Banks complied.[6] This was a significant step. Some blood bankers were extremely worried about advocating a measure that would hit their supply of blood donations. The reaction from some groups was outrage, as Columbia University's Professor Ronald Bayer explains: 'Gay organizations just coming to grips with a new threat to the survival of their communities were concerned that an explicit ban on blood donations by gay men would add to stigmatization and homophobic attitudes.'[7]

Soon it would become evident that the truth of transmission wasn't as discriminatory as some feared. HIV was transmitted through unprotected sex, but it didn't have to be *gay* sex. Transmission didn't even require sex at all. In 1983, HIV was already in blood bank supplies in both the US and Australia[8] – and in Australia, because of Noelene Cliff, we know it was already in donor semen. (The first US case of HIV transmission via donor sperm appears to have occurred the following year, in 1984 in New York City.[9]) AIDS killed people of all genders and all sexualities. It killed young and old. Children who had never had sexual contact of any kind would die. It killed babies. The stakes were of the highest kind.

It strains credulity that Australian doctors and health authorities remained unaware of the cataclysmic changes sweeping the US. By May 1983, that became even less likely, after the head of the Sydney Blood Transfusion Service, Dr Gordon Archer, sensationally went on national television calling on homosexuals to stop donating blood.[10] Archer also stunned his BTS counterparts in other Australian states by proclaiming that it was 'a virtual certainty that AIDS was in the blood supply'. There was no test for HIV at this stage; prevention was the only course of action. Dr Archer's plea made the front page of newspapers the following morning. A media storm ensued. Archer was labelled a bigot, and gay rights activists protested outside the Sydney Blood Bank.[11]

The next month, on 21 June, a New South Wales state politician sent direct telegrams to state and federal Cabinet ministers requesting urgent action to restrict the spread of AIDS in Australia.[12] He suggested 'a total ban on homosexuals donating blood ... or semen to the Artificial Insemination Donor Service', reported the *Newcastle Herald* a few days later.[13] That politician was the Reverend Fred Nile, a hardline Christian and no new entrant to this space: Nile was (and continues to be) famous for his extremely strong anti-LGBTIQ+ views. Two and a half weeks later, the first officially documented Australian death from AIDS occurred in a Melbourne hospital.[14]

In October 1983, the heavyweight *New England Journal of Medicine* published an article directly addressing the risk of HIV transmission in donor conception. It specifically raised the possibility of HIV transmission through not blood, but another bodily fluid: semen.[15]

In November 1983, AIDS experts from around the world gathered at World Health Organization headquarters in Geneva, Switzerland, for the first international meeting on the AIDS epidemic, which had by now been reported in nations around the world.[16]

In October 1984, staff at the Melbourne Blood Transfusion Service quietly began to question its donors in private about their possible exposure to AIDS, including sexual history, and excluding those deemed at risk.[17] By November, blood donor declaration forms had been introduced by each state blood transfusion service – but there was no corresponding statewide (or nationwide) action at Australia's fertility clinics. Some, including Sydney clinics, continued to use fresh sperm.

That same month, November 1984, the Australian public was horrified when Queensland authorities announced that three babies had been infected with HIV/AIDS through blood donated by a gay blood donor. By the time they announced it, the babies were already dead. Twenty-four hours later, the Queensland Government passed a law imposing criminal sanctions on any blood donors who lied about their history of homosexuality or drug use when donating blood.[18]

There were zero such measures in any state for sperm donors.

In May 1985, Australia began universal testing of potential donors for both donated blood and semen.

IN THE HEART of my city sits the golden sandstone establishment the University of Sydney. It has produced seven Australian prime ministers, a few football teams' worth of other members of Parliament, many captains of industry and a veritable plague of lawyers, including silks, judges, and justices of the High Court of Australia. It counts Douglas Saunders, the man who ran Clinic 20, as an emeritus professor.

In Sydney University's SciTech Library, an angular space open to the public, I find a slim red volume. It's a self-published book by Saunders, titled *Fertility Society of Australia A History: Its "precipitate" birth & the story of IVF*. Saunders, it becomes clear, has an erratic approach to punctuation.[19]

My eye is caught by the word trapped between Saunders' quotation marks. The adjective 'precipitate' means 'something that is done sooner or faster than expected and without enough thought or preparation'.[20] Perhaps Saunders didn't understand the word that he was using, or – more worryingly – he did.

On the cover of Saunders' book is the Fertility Society of Australia logo, 'a stylised image of an ancient Umbrian fertility symbol'. It looks like a baby in a triple-layered cage.

The book consists of a series of interviews with fertility heavies, covering a period from the '70s to the '90s, about the 'challenges faced during this time'. Each chapter is a first-person account by a different fertility professional, based on recorded telephone interviews conducted by Saunders. Each chapter has a similar title: Conversations with Alan Trounson, Conversations with Geoff Driscoll, Conversations with Gab Kovacs. There are twenty-seven accounts, including Saunders' own contribution (which, rather strangely, is titled 'Conversations with Douglas Saunders': it appears he interviewed himself). Only one interviewee mentions the interests, or the welfare, of any of the children made by this industry. One of the few women interviewed, she covers this in two sentences. Conversely, wine features *a lot*.

I find a chapter breathlessly titled 'Conversation with John Tyler – Risks of Donor Sperm and AIDS (HIV)'. Along with Geoff Driscoll, John Tyler co-founded Westmead Hospital's fertility clinic. Tyler recounts his career, starting with 'hamster penetration tests' in the UK, followed by time working with mammals at Harvard. 'So my animal experience set me up for human IVF,' Tyler concludes. In three paragraphs, he discusses giving women the HIV-positive donor sperm that killed them.[21]

Tyler states that he unknowingly recruited a bisexual donor into the Westmead program. According to Tyler's account, at the time, HIV screening was unavailable, and the world was still ignorant about the potential for HIV transmission through sperm. When a clinic patient tested positive to HIV in 1984, the source of infection was traced back to the insemination. This news, Tyler baldly continues, meant it was too late for four patients in the Westmead program. All of them, plus the donor, died from AIDS. Tyler goes on to reflect on the impact this 'horrendous time' had on him and how patients in reproductive medicine leave the clinic better than when they entered. He then claims that, within twenty-four hours of the case coming to light, all Artificial Insemination by Donor programs were shut down by the government, and mass-testing among panicked patients ensued.

When I met with Peter Illingworth at IVF Australia, he didn't mention a full government shutdown. I haven't found official mention of it anywhere else in my searches. Wouldn't such a thing be up in lights?

I went to the NSW Government. 'According to former fertility specialist John Tyler, in the 1980s there was a full government shutdown of all fertility clinics due to concerns about HIV. Can you confirm whether this was the case?' Their response: 'This is not information held by the Ministry of Health, and we would recommend speaking directly to the scientist, John Tyler.'

It's not a definite no. It doesn't necessarily mean that there *wasn't* a full government shutdown of all fertility clinics because they were killing women with HIV/AIDS. Although it does seem like a strange thing to forget.

Then I asked the federal Health Department whether they ordered a national shutdown thirty-five years ago. They sought the advice of an independent health policy consultant, who had worked in the field for decades. He couldn't find any history of any such order, nor of any trigger.

Finally, I tracked down John Tyler himself. He'd left Westmead in 1987 and moved on to other clinics. By the time I found him, he'd been quietly retired for some time. We spoke on the phone. He was wary. But in the end, he answered my questions via email.

His answers were short. They differed from the Cliffs' account and from the state and federal government responses.

Instead of George Cliff's evidence regarding a 'flippant' phone call from Westmead to come in for an initial HIV test, Tyler said he discovered that HIV was in donor semen when 'Noelene had herself tested at Crown St clinic and told us'. Tyler said he couldn't remember how long the full shutdown of all fertility clinics lasted, but it applied to all fertility clinics in Australia, centrally co-ordinated by the government. He said the records of patients attending Westmead's fertility clinic, like Noelene, were never destroyed. However, records of donors 'pre HIV' were destroyed 'as per usual practice of the time', and that donors and recipients were all aware this would happen and consented to it. 'Post Noelene all new donors had their records retained,' Tyler wrote.

What measures did Westmead take after discovery of HIV transmission to prevent future transmission? I asked. 'Actually can't remember apart from stopping the clinic for a considerable time,' Tyler replied. Were any fertility clinic staff at Westmead disciplined or otherwise investigated following discovery of the transmission of HIV? 'Yes me alone.' What was the nature of that investigation or discipline? 'I cant [sic] actually remember, only that a legal team spent about a week with me in the lab looking at multiple things before deciding I could not be directly blamed,' he replied. I asked him whether he was aware, in 1983, of rising concerns about HIV in donor blood and semen in the US and Australia: 'No.' Or if he'd come across any articles in professional journals like *JAMA* or *NEJM* about HIV in donor semen: 'No.'

I asked him if Westmead staff told patients that HIV/AIDS only had a 10 per cent fatality rate. I asked what (if anything) they told infected patients about how the virus might be transmitted, and whether all the babies in the neonatal ward who had been fed Noelene's breastmilk had been tested for HIV. To each of these, he replied: 'No idea I was a scientist and did not see patients.'

At the end, he wrote: 'I was sued by George Cliff but it never went to court as the legal Teams deemed I could not be held responsible.'[22]

I TURN TO another volume from the archives: a bound report of the NSW Law Reform Commission, published in November 1984. The year before, the state's attorney-general had asked the Law Reform Commission to report on any need to make laws on human artificial insemination, among other aspects of the industry (IVF, surrogacy, other fertility treatments).

The LRC's Discussion Paper is a report into the practice of 'Artificial Conception and Human Artificial Insemination' in New South Wales. It was published at the end of a year in which John Tyler says it was discovered that the first New South Wales woman had been effectively handed a death sentence by her HIV-positive donor insemination, triggering a full government shutdown. But I found no mention of that in the LRC's report. John Tyler acted as a consultant to their work. 'Did you tell the LRC about HIV transmission through donor sperm at Westmead?' I asked him. 'I think that's why I was involved,' he replied, 'or it may have been because of the *Women's Weekly* Survey on DI [donor insemination] I carried out.'

Two-thirds of the consultants to the LRC report are fertility specialists (nine of thirteen). Douglas Saunders, whose clinic by then had presumably destroyed not only my donor code but many others', is another such consultant.

Perhaps, then, it's no surprise that the Law Reform Commission finds that 'the Australian community is justified in relying upon its medical profession to conduct the practice of artificial insemination by donor ethically and efficiently'. There's no need for the law to intervene in donor conception: 'the community should be reluctant to introduce detailed regulation of the practice of artificial insemination by donor'. The LRC concludes: 'We are not aware of any practices or activities in relation to artificial insemination on the part of hospitals or the medical profession that could be considered to be unacceptable to the community at large.'[23]

AUSTRALIAN FERTILITY DOCTORS weren't the only ones giving would-be mothers HIV/AIDS. Years later, another article in *JAMA* reported that at just five clinics across the US and Canada, hundreds of women had been treated with HIV-positive donor sperm prior to 1986. The clinics were in California, Arizona and Vancouver. Five HIV-positive donors had donated sperm to these clinics. (This is not necessarily the total number of HIV-positive donors to these clinics – or the total number of clinics with HIV in donor sperm – just the parameters of the article.) Two hundred and thirty women had been inseminated with sperm from these five HIV-positive donors alone, which is an average of each man inseminating forty-six women. Of the 230 women, 199 consented to HIV testing. In 1995, seven of those 199 were HIV-positive.[24] Of the thirty-one not tested, I find myself wondering if any were already dead, or subsequently died of the disease.

None of those seven HIV-positive women ever had a baby from the treatment.

The authors concluded that HIV transmission via donor sperm was 'a potentially serious threat to women'. They recommended that public health policies 'requiring retrospective identification of HIV-infected semen donors and patients receiving AI before 1986 ... should be considered routine'.

GOING THROUGH MY mother's treatment file from Clinic 20 at the Royal North Shore Hospital, I come across a page which is almost blank, but not quite. It's a note from a different institution: the Department of Immunology at St Vincent's, a Catholic hospital in Sydney. At the top, a small column lists my mother's name and the details of her specialist, Professor Douglas Saunders. The date is July 1985. My mother is tested for the 'AIDS Retro Virus'. She was tested for HIV a month after Noelene Cliff. My mother tested negative.

ON THE FIRST page of Douglas Saunders' book, there is a quotation. Saunders has chosen to open his history of the Fertility Society of Australia with a famous line by the Nobel Prize–winning author William Faulkner.

It reads: 'The past is never dead, it's not even past.'

CHAPTER 13

I AM THREE, IN a dark blue velvet dress with coloured smocking across my chest. My thick hair is pulled back from my face with a ribbon, which is a good thing, because I'm leaning forward to blow out candles on a birthday cake.

In that moment, I'm not looking at the camera. Like any child, I'm focused on the treats in front of me, and so are all my friends, fanned out around the table. Behind me are a few smiling adults, including my mother. And in the background is the nurse who destroyed my donor code.

Her name is Diana Craven, and she was a nurse at the Royal North Shore's Clinic 20 – in fact, she was the only nurse at that clinic until 1983, the year I was born.[1] She and my mother got on well – after all, they were both nurses working at the same hospital; it just so happened that my mother was also a patient at that hospital's fertility clinic. I see Di Craven in other photos from my party that day. She has a short, Princess Diana–style haircut. She wears a soft, creamy turtleneck top and grey corduroy overalls. The secrets in the shadows of cake and pass-the-parcel that day were worthy of a daytime TV soap.

As well as granting me access to the file of her fertility treatment, my mother had given me a potential lead: she'd mentioned Diana Craven. I vaguely remembered Di as a pleasant figure from my childhood, so I tracked down her phone number. I wanted to know if donor code destruction at Clinic 20 was total, if there were any back-channel ways of finding out more. I wanted to know if she remembered any clues. I hadn't spoken to her since I was a child, but I trusted that she would help me, as you'd trust any honorary aunty or close family friend who watched you grow up.

It took a while to steel myself. On the last day of 2011, eight months after my mother had told me the truth about my origins, I dialled Craven's number. She picked up.

She was warm. I explained, delicately, why I was calling. I hoped she could help me: the donor codes had been destroyed at Clinic 20. Did she remember anything? Was there any scrap of information she could pass on?

'I've often thought I was going to get these kinds of calls,' Di Craven said. 'There were a couple of other girls [she meant Clinic 20 patients] that I was friendly with, in the same situation.'

Diana Craven wasn't surprised by my call. She was ready for it. She knew about the code destruction and she knew it was wrong.

'At the time, the thinking was it was best not to have the information,' she said. I kept quiet. 'There was a group of people who didn't feel it was right,' Di Craven confided. Now, that was interesting. 'When your mother had treatment,' she continued, 'the donors were chosen by me.'

The woman leaning over the sandwiches at my birthday had made me. Not my parents. She had chosen the straw that would go on to create my particular mix of genes. She had chosen that mix, out of a whole range of possible versions of Sarah. I was stunned. Diana Craven didn't even realise the enormity of what she was telling me.

If I didn't have to worry about being mass produced, or dying of preventable disease, or sleeping with a half-sibling, or my own mental health – if I didn't have a massive stake in the truth – I would say that no-one should ever meet their disinterested, non-parental maker. Not like this. You should never meet the person who ensured that you exist and all other possibilities missed out, because their importance to you will never, ever match your importance to them.

Di Craven was still talking. 'We [chose donors] on the basis of the physical characteristics of the [social] father,' she said. 'The donors were all medical or university students. They were different to the donors we have now.' The same old story. I think it's supposed to be comforting. I'm not sure why – is it really better to think that your biological father was chosen from some select cohort for breeding?

'There's a couple of donors who might've been it,' Di Craven mused. 'One might be yours.' She didn't say the words. They never say the words. No-one in this industry is ever willing to use the terms 'biological father' or 'biological mother'. It's always 'donor', which is a straight-up lie. You're not a donor if you get paid.

'They were paid,' said Di Craven. '$20 – no, $60 – no, $10 a donation.' This was confusing. 'That was reasonable money then. It wasn't payment, but they were given money as "expenses". I think they still get expense money.'

They do.

ACCORDING TO THE inflation calculator of the Reserve Bank of Australia, even $10 back then wasn't small change. Ten Australian dollars in 1982 is equivalent to about AUD$36 in 2020. That's a few beers in a pub. That's an evening with your mates if you're an impoverished university type. And AUD$60 in 1982 is the equivalent of AUD$217 in 2020 terms. That's most, if not all, of your weekly rent in a low-budget (read: student) sharehouse. Just for a single male orgasm.

Today, the going rate depends on whether you have sperm or eggs to offer. It also depends on which clinic and which country. In Australia, for example, I've spoken to a man who donated sperm ten times in 2006, and was paid $100 each time. In 2015, it was reported that Australian fertility business City Fertility Centre was offering egg donors a flat $5000. That is a lot of money for a supposed 'donation', and there were concerns raised around 'inducements'.[2]

In the US, researchers have reported ads for egg 'donors' offering up to USD$100,000. Payments to egg donors are also taxed by the Internal Revenue Service.[3] But eggs, unlike sperm or blood, are not replenished by the body on a regular basis. A baby girl is born with all the eggs she will ever have in her life, and that number dwindles over the years. Through the IRS, the US Government takes a direct slice of women selling their own irreplaceable human tissue.

The problem is – speaking as a product of these things – *all* money is an inducement, high or low, and it certainly does not make donor-conceived people feel good to know there was a price tag on their DNA. Children are not supposed to be bought or sold. There's a word for that: trafficking. If you want to donate, as an informed and consenting adult, donate. But you shouldn't expect money in return. The clue is in the name: donor. In Australia, people are not paid to give blood, even though this literally saves lives. This is in line with World Health Organization policy, which says: 'the safest blood donors are voluntary, non-remunerated blood donors from low-risk populations'.[4] This is not a new recommendation. The WHO has called on all countries to obtain all their blood supplies through voluntary, unpaid donors since 1975.

In Australia, you do not get paid money for blood, because it's human tissue. You might get a couple of biscuits afterwards: fine. Anything more than two biscuits is problematic. If you do not get paid for blood, by the same logic, you definitely should not be paid for your DNA. If giving away your DNA or your child without financial compensation incurs too great a cost to your wallet or your health – don't do it. All of this is completely optional.

The national *Prohibition of Human Cloning for Reproduction Act 2002* prohibits the payment of 'valuable consideration' for a donated oocyte, sperm or embryo – but allows the payment of 'reasonable expenses' incurred by the donor.[5] 'Reasonable expenses' are not fully defined and have no monetary limit. Every state in Australia also has a *Human Tissue Act*. They are 'substantially similar', according to the Australian Law Reform Commission.[6] New South Wales' version also prohibits donors from selling their own human tissue, but says they can be reimbursed for 'expenses' which are 'related to the removal of that tissue'.[7] In the case of sperm donors, it is hard to see what expenses you incur watching some porn and masturbating.

But complying with these laws, insisting that paying expenses is not paying donors, becomes even more sketchy when we look at what Australia's National Health and Medical Research Council says you're allowed to offer in donor conception. Its ethical guidelines, once again, contain some alarming loopholes.

'The current situation in Australia is that gamete donation must be altruistic,' the ethical guidelines say, 'and that commercial trading in human gametes or the use of direct or indirect inducements is prohibited by legislation. This position reflects concerns about the potential exploitation of donors (particularly egg donors) and the potential risks to all parties.' Sounds good – but wait.

'While direct or indirect inducements are prohibited, it is reasonable to provide reimbursement of verifiable out-of-pocket expenses *directly* associated with the donation.'[8] These include medical and counselling costs, both before and after the donation. You might think: that's reasonable. But it also includes travel and accommodation costs within Australia. A donation holiday, perhaps? In 2010, the Australian Senate reported that one clinic, Reproductive Medicine Albury, had offered a package to Canadian men that included return airfares, accommodation for two weeks and an allowance of $150 each day in exchange for sperm donations.[9] 'It was estimated that the total package was valued at about $7000 at that time,' the Senate report said. Troublingly, the NHMRC itself 'was involved in overseeing the ethics of this offer'. And after a six-month 'investigation', *The Australian* reported, the NHMRC gave it the green light.[10]

Extraordinarily, the NHMRC Ethical Guidelines also say that gamete 'donors' (the term becomes increasingly ridiculous) can be reimbursed for loss of earnings where the donor takes unpaid leave from their job to donate. This, effectively, allows the fertility industry to pay your salary while you're doing treatments, check-ups, egg collection, sperm donating, counselling, whatever. Fertility can become your employer, sanctioned by the only national guidelines for this industry. To me, this appears to skate very close to the prohibition set out in laws state and federal.

I wondered if the Australian Government does what the US Government does – draws revenue from taxing the money paid to individuals for extracting human tissue – despite the fact that (unlike the US) it outlaws people selling such tissue? I also wondered if the Australian Taxation Office was monitoring any of this. So I asked them. The ATO media liaison officer was very nice and not a little surprised by my question. He asked around, and an intriguing answer came back.

'The reimbursement arrangements are between the recipient of the sperm or egg donation, and the donor,' a spokesperson for the ATO said.[11] Good lord, I thought, it's even more under the table – even less regulated – than if it were the clinics paying lost wages to donors. The money's going from private individual to private individual. Does anyone monitor that transfer at all, I wondered?

Then my conversation with the ATO turned to something much more up its alley: income reporting.

Unlike the salary you receive from your actual job, in the case of someone else reimbursing you for lost wages, no tax has been withheld by your employer. Therefore 'amounts received as reimbursement for lost salary and wages are taxable as ordinary income,' said the spokesperson for the ATO, 'and should be included in the donor's income tax return.'

I have never met an Australian donor, male or female, who told me they declared money from donating gametes on their tax return.

FORMER CLINIC 20 nurse Diana Craven – in that first phone conversation with me, at least – was full of answers.

'As soon as a baby was born and healthy, the donor code was destroyed,' Di Craven said matter-of-factly. 'We cut it out so that it couldn't be traced. Deep down, I knew it wasn't going to be the right thing – you shouldn't ever lose that information. [But] donors were told they wouldn't be contacted.'

And then she gave me a donor code. Dredged from her memory. Two codes, actually, either of which she thought might have been the one she cut out from my file.

'AFH,' she said. 'He was not unlike your dad in colouring. He was a science student, a young bloke in his early twenties. There was another one, ADZ, less likely. I know this other friend of mine, she definitely had ADZ. It's never left my brain. [But] AFH is the most likely. I can't remember his name.'

AFH. Was that him? Did the letters mean something? An Andrew? The surname Harris? I knew that the codes at Clinic 20 were random, not tied to names, but I couldn't help possibilities stampeding through my head. ADZ? Adam something? I wrote both codes down frantically. Briefly worried that the 'Z' wasn't clear enough, I went over it so many times it's a wonder the pen didn't punch through the notebook. Then I squashed everything I felt – again – and focused on my list of questions. Di was in a chatty mood. What else, what else could I ask her?

'Who gave the order for the codes to be destroyed?' I asked.

'Professor Saunders would've given the order for codes to be destroyed,' Di Craven said. 'But it was what everyone in Australia was doing at that time.' *What?*

'Professor Saunders is a lovely guy,' Di said. 'I could call Doug Saunders to ask him for codes – just so I could look at a list of donor codes … Maybe if I looked through the codes, I could match those with the right height and hair colouring [as your social father].'

'Would he be okay with that?' I asked, doubtful.

'I still talk to Doug,' said Di Craven comfortably. 'I have a good relationship with him. I can ask him and he'll give me an honest answer. Give me a few weeks or so, I'll get back to you as soon as I can.'

'Okay,' I said encouragingly. To me, it really didn't sound like a conversation Saunders would welcome, but I wasn't going to say so.

'We've come a long way with a lot of things,' said Di. 'It's not the same world now. It was a very naive world; [you'd] stick your fingers in your ears and hope the problem goes away.'

But of course, the problem didn't go away. I didn't go away.

DI CRAVEN HAD said that clinics across Australia were destroying donor codes. Why on earth hadn't this come out before? And the dearth of records more broadly? How could you have baby factories – many of which were public facilities – covering up which humans they were breeding, and how often? How had these people continued to practice and be venerated? Why wasn't this a national scandal?

But it wasn't just clinics across Australia. It was, and is, much worse.

Today, I am in touch with thousands of donor-conceived people from around the world, from places like the US, the UK, New Zealand, Canada, South Africa, the Netherlands, Belgium and Portugal. We are adults. This group doesn't yet include younger entrants born of the industry in the popular fertility destinations of choice in more recent years – poorer countries, as wealthy foreigners harvest the DNA and bodies of the less fortunate: Nepal, Ukraine, Mexico, India, Cambodia, Thailand, Greece.

And what I've found is a lot of similarities. Despite being made in different countries, we have received similar treatment from fertility clinics. We have been given the same excuses, ranging from the improbable to the implausible.

'Who here,' I began one day, in an online donor-conceived group, 'has had their records destroyed? And if so, do you know when they were destroyed or how? (Fire/floods/shredders etc. all count.)'

Dozens of responses rolled in.

There were those who'd been told everything had been destroyed a long time ago, or – even worse – that their fertility specialists never kept any records in the first place.

'There were no records to be destroyed because nothing was kept, intentionally … They sketched my social father and my parents told them their requirements and the doctors got to play God.' Missouri, USA.

'They lost almost all records of my donor and have no explanation for it. I got in touch with them 2 years ago to seek info and it took them over a year to admit they had no records … They did eventually find the handwritten original donor form he filled out but they had no record of my birth or any others as coming from him.' Auckland, New Zealand.

'I have been told that minimal records were kept, if any at all. If there were any they were long destroyed … Neither of my parents knew donor sperm was involved. They thought they were having THEIR baby.' Michigan, USA. (Deception of both social parents is not unknown.)

Another common, and international, explanation given for the lack of donor conception records is fire.

'There was a "fire" in the records room when the clinic was being investigated for fraud … I have copies of the fire report/investigation. The report claims it may have been started by an electrical issue, but they weren't really sure. It happened in 2003. I'm not sure what happened with the investigation either.' Los Angeles, USA.

'The wife of the fertility doctor destroyed the files after he retired, she burned them. The doctor had a private practice (his wife worked there as well) … I learned from former assistants that when he wasn't retired yet they got the instruction that if something would happen to them (for example an accident) they had to destroy the files immediately.' Antwerp, Belgium.

'When I confronted [my fertility specialist] years after his retirement he admitted to burning most of the files in his fireplace.' Rotterdam, the Netherlands.

Precious documents around the world, up in flames. But it seems the industry isn't just plagued by fire. There's also the opposite problem: water.

'Unfortunately [my fertility specialist] died before I got to know I was donor conceived. I did speak with his wife who informed me that the records got wet in their garage.' Melbourne, Australia.

'Told my records were destroyed by a flood, and placed in a tip … high court judge thought it sounded fishy. Was 52 Harley street London.' That's Jo Rose, a prominent donor-conceived advocate from the UK.

Then there's the trifecta:

'I was told fire AND flood AND "destroyed after 15 years because there was no need to keep them". That was three separate phone calls to the clinic over a few months in 1996. However, when I met with the doctor in 2013, he told me the records were out the back, that he never destroyed anything, and voila! My records were there (they wouldn't give them to me though).' Brisbane, Australia.

'Same,' said another woman, also in Brisbane.

'You were given conflicting answers by your clinic too?' I asked her. 'And the same answers – fire, flood … oh no, they're here?'

'Yep,' she said. 'And the good old, "you are not our patient so you get nothing".'

ALL THESE STORIES are geographically so far apart, and yet, for their similarities in approach to record destruction, they could be in the same city.

I've always been more inclined to suspect a cock-up over a conspiracy. But the avalanche of outlandish, yet common 'reasons' for fertility specialists not providing records about the babies they were making occasionally makes me waver. Did some of them learn from each other? Did they ever discuss with each other how to expedite breeding and minimise paperwork? And do some still do that today?

I WAITED FOR Diana Craven to have her chat with Douglas Saunders about the donor codes, and ring me back. And I waited. I didn't want to nag.

After several months of waiting, I finally cracked and rang her again. She didn't answer. Later, she left me a confused voicemail, saying she must have been mistaken: neither AFH nor ADZ were my codes, and I should trust that IVF Australia was doing the best it could for me.

They got to her, I thought. I'd expected nothing less.

But it left me in limbo. And I believed I deserved better than a voicemail. So, four-and-a-half months after our first call, I got her on the line for our second. To keep myself on track, I'd written down questions, like: What did Saunders say? You seemed so sure about the code, why did you change your mind? And, if the conversation went to hell in a handbasket: How would you feel if I were your daughter?

I started with why she was mistaken about the donor codes. 'Well, I thought, I had in my mind that's who it was,' she said. 'But when [IVF Australia] looked through their records, they found it couldn't be that particular donor.'

'Why is that?'

'I spoke to that girl, lady, I think you spoke to her.' (Di Craven meant Mary, the first person at IVF Australia I'd dealt with.) 'She looked at all the dates concerned. And the donor I thought it was wasn't used at that particular time.'

'Okay. Di, I'm going to tell you something,' I said firmly. 'What they told me was they had *no* donors used on the dates that I was conceived. They didn't record them.'

'Yes, that's what she, what she was doing,' stammered Di. 'Because when we used to use samples, it went on sheets, like a bank record of the stock, you know the stock that was being used.' Great choice of words. 'Some of the sheets she didn't have access to for one reason or another, whether they were misplaced in the move or whatever, but she was going to get back to me.'

That's not what Mary told me. She hadn't told me her search was incomplete. She'd told me that she, and the andrologist, had gone through all the paperwork, of all the dates, of two different treatment cycles, twice. 'And if [Mary] found anything from those dates,' Di Craven said, 'because there were no signatures, I said I would come and see her, look at the records she had, and see if any of those signatures [signing off on the sperm used] were mine.'

'How many suspects do you think that will leave you with then?' I asked. If more sheets existed, and Di Craven found her signature, would that be even remotely useful? 'Like three, four, five?'

'Yeah, maybe four or five,' Di said.

'Mm hm,' I said. 'And then what?'

'What we're trying to do is a process of elimination,' said Di. 'Then what happens is, they contact the donor, if they *can* —'

'Yeah, I know,' I interrupted. 'I know all the power rests with the donors. I know that.'

'Because at the time they donated,' said Di, 'they were told that they weren't —'

'Yeah,' I interrupted again. I didn't have time for another round of the opaque excuses that led nowhere. 'So, it rests on [Mary] being able to find something even though she's already said there's nothing to find.'

'Mm. That's right,' Di Craven said pleasantly. 'She *is* trying.'

'You said you were going to talk to Professor Saunders,' I said lightly. 'What did he say?'

'I did. He put me onto [Mary].'

'So he didn't actually say anything?'

'Well, he said, he said she's the person, the one looking after all the enquiries,' Di Craven said.

'Did Professor Douglas Saunders seem open to the idea of me finding my donor?' I asked.

'Yes,' said Di emphatically. 'Very open, but understanding that, you know, if these people [the donors] say no, they don't want to be contacted, there's nothing he can do. It was the arrangement they made at the time.' A huge loophole: how would I know if they ever actually asked any donor, let alone asked that donor in a *fair* way? How could I trust them to handle any of this?

'Did [Mary] give you a timeframe in which she'd get back to you?'

'No. She's doing the best she can. And when she – just hang on a sec, Sarah,' Di said. There was a pause. Then she came back to the call. 'Sorry, Sarah.'

'I'll let you go,' I said. 'I know you're busy.' There was nothing else to be gained from this conversation, clearly.

Di said as soon as she found out something, she'd let me know. I'd heard her say that before.

CHAPTER 14

No answers from IVF Australia. Di Craven shut down. What else could I do?

The NSW Government, I discovered, has something called a Central Register, and part of that is the 'voluntary register'.

The voluntary register is a register for donor-conceived people born before 1 January 2010 in New South Wales. (That is, most of us.) After 2010, all donor-conceived people born in New South Wales are supposed to have the identifying details of their sperm, egg or embryo donor(s) recorded on the Central Register and kept by government. The government relies on fertility clinics to submit this information. A lucky post-2010 donor-conceived person can then access identifying information about their donor on the Central Register once they turn eighteen. Which means, at time of writing, that the Central Register has been used precisely zero times.

For all of us born before 2010, there's only the voluntary register.

If you know you are donor conceived, born before 1 January 2010, you can fill out an application form to go on the voluntary register. Then the NSW Government will 'verify' what you say with your fertility clinic and ask them for the information about your donor. If the fertility clinic has a matching donor record, you're in luck. If they don't, your details alone go on the register. But your prospects of being linked with family – never high – are virtually nil.

Then what? If your donor becomes aware of the voluntary register and makes the effort to put themselves on it and is happy to have contact with their potential offspring, a government staffer might match you with your donor, and you may have some form of communication. It's the same deal with your donor-conceived siblings.

When I found out about the voluntary register, I knew all the caveats, but I still felt it was important. It was productive. It was official. It was something I could do. I filled out an application form with my details. Allergic to penicillin, mild asthma. I even noted down the 'AFH' donor code, adding 'code may be incorrect, due to shoddy record-keeping'. I received an official notice of receipt from the state government in December 2012. Then silence.

AROUND THIS TIME, I checked the IVF Australia website. A big fertility player, IVF Australia has an ethics committee. It 'provides advice to IVF Australia on ethical aspects of clinical infertility practice'. It ensures that 'the care of our patients and the research we carry out is guided by community views'.

Professor Douglas Saunders was listed as a member of the IVF Australia Ethics Committee.

So was Diana Craven.

TWO YEARS LATER, in 2014, I had a conversation with a friendly bureaucrat in the NSW Department of Health. I mentioned that I'd sent off my details to their voluntary register. I'd had a reply saying that the state government would provide that information to my fertility clinic, now IVF Australia, to see if they had a donor match for me, or other information.[1] After that, nothing. Did the government ever get an answer from IVF Australia about me?

She checked. And came back with an odd answer.

'The original request seeking donor details was returned unopened and unclaimed [from IVF Australia],' she said. Had they sent it to the address of that big shiny building on the Pacific Highway, I asked? Yes. IVF Australia was still there. They'd never moved. The Department of Health knew how to contact them. Why had this one letter failed to make it?[2]

'We at the Ministry of Health never followed that up, so we didn't send it out again,' she said. 'So we never got back to you confirming your registration on the register. Looks like the process stalled. I know that was two years ago, and it's not good. I'm sorry.'

After a while, dealing with this kind of Orwellian super-control over your identity, you start to suspect everyone. Can you blame me?

Two years had passed. A key part of the lone government process set up to help me find family had gone nowhere, and the government had only learnt this because I checked. So what now? I asked her. Could she put me on that register without verification from IVF Australia?

'We'll act like we've only just received your application, and send it to IVF Australia again,' she said. 'You're on the voluntary register, and your [self-provided] donor code is here with your disclaimer.'

IN 2015, I made an investigative radio documentary, *The Donor Detectives*, for the ABC's Background Briefing. It was about how donor-conceived people in Australia were turning to unorthodox methods to find their biological parents and siblings, because official systems and the medical profession were failing them. The resulting investigation was cited in the Oxford scientific journal *Human Reproduction*.[3] (Although the documentary was about others, not me, I disclosed my own background as a donor-conceived person in the story.)

As part of the documentary I interviewed Kay Dekker, a woman who had been conceived in Western Australia – one of only three Australian states in 2015 that even had a voluntary register.

Kay was on that voluntary register for a decade with no match. She had the name of her clinic and the fertility specialist, but that was about it. Her records had been destroyed. Then she went online and found an Australian forum for donor-conceived people, run by another West Australian, Adam Quinlivan.

'And then Adam sent me a message saying, you know, not many people are under Dr Colin Douglas Smith, what information do you have?' Kay told me. 'And I gave basic information and we sort of just chatted back and forth. Our information was similar and it was the only information we had, so Adam had said to me "Would you consider doing a DNA test?", because he had already done one.'

So she did. The DNA test confirmed that Adam and Kay were half-siblings. Both were utterly floored. They are just five months apart in age. But here's the thing: by the time they met, both Kay and Adam had been on that same voluntary register run by the Western Australian Government for fourteen years without being matched. Neither of them had any records from the fertility clinic which they could provide to the register. That meant, as far as the government was concerned, there was nothing to be done. Kay and Adam's details sat side by side in the database for more than a decade.

Both Kay and Adam questioned the point of being on the register if no proactive steps are ever taken by register administrators. Even after Kay and Adam found each other, Kay said, the situation didn't change: '[The state register] said they would never, even if someone else came on to the register, and they had similar information to Adam and mine, they still would not make that connection.'

'So you could have more siblings, and they won't match you with them if they know about them?'

'That's right,' Kay said.

If your records are incomplete or destroyed, tough.

I decided to revise my assumptions – specifically, my assumption that these voluntary registers worked at all. So I asked the NSW Government how many matches its voluntary register had made – the only central matching point for thousands or possibly tens of thousands of donor-conceived people born in my state before 2010.

The answer was: one. One match. In its history. Which I reported in the documentary.

In my own personal situation, I decided to forget about the voluntary register.

WRITING THIS BOOK years later, out of curiosity I decided to ask the NSW Ministry of Health about the voluntary register again.

How many donors who donated before 2010 were on the voluntary register? I asked. And how many pre-2010 donor-conceived people were on there?

Out of the thousands of donor-conceived people born before 2010 in New South Wales, as of 2019, there were precisely 100 on the state's voluntary register.

The only good thing about that paltry number was it was almost matched by the number of donors (eighty-five) who wanted to be known to their biological children.

The last question I asked the Ministry of Health about the voluntary register was how many successful matches they'd made between biological parent and child, or between two siblings. Five years on from *The Donor Detectives*, I thought, it was time for an update on 'one'.

Turns out, the government didn't know.

'The Ministry does not keep statistical records of matches made of donor offspring to their donors. Where a match is made, the relevant parties are notified and sharing of information facilitated in accordance with their consent,' was the reply.

I don't wish to turn the screws on individual public servants, but keeping track of how many matches are made from a register designed with the sole purpose of making matches does seem like a key performance indicator.

And why, then, had they told me in 2015 that only one match had ever been made?

I despaired. You could chase any one aspect of donor conception for the rest of your life, and you still wouldn't get a straight or satisfying answer.

WITHOUT A PROACTIVE register and matching service, without central government collation of records, without records, without any advocates or allies, all I could do was conduct my own random searches. So I went hunting for sperm donors. It sounds funny and a bit gross. In reality, it's emotionally gruelling.

I decided on this course of action, then couldn't do anything more for a few months, then found a name or two with numbers, then couldn't bear to ring them. There's a good reason why adoptees have independent support services, counselling and formal information points when they go searching. You need to be emotionally ready to find the name of a person who could be your biological parent. You need to be strong enough to even read the name on the damn page or screen. It was not like being a journalist investigating someone else's story. I couldn't even pretend that I was doing this on behalf of someone else. To verify this stuff, you have to share personal information with strangers – often very personal information. The kind of personal information that makes you vulnerable.

Once, I found one man in a random forum online who said he'd donated to Clinic 20 around the right time. His donor code – which he knew – was similar to what Di Craven had come up with. But her memory might have been slightly off – or his. I gathered strength. Then I rang him to find out more. Let's call him Paul.

Paul told me he donated in 1978 and 1979. 'Then they suspended my donations in the 80s, because of AIDS,' he said indignantly. 'It was a knee-jerk, horror reaction. They threw out every donation.'

Paul wasn't a medical student: he said he'd studied engineering, and later become a bus driver. 'The Royal North Shore Hospital used to trade sperm,' he told me.

I don't know what 'trade' means, but I do know if you send off one guy's sperm to another operation, in the absence of any central collation of records, there is no way of knowing when a family limit is reached. I have also been told that the Royal North Shore Hospital sent sperm to clinics interstate. The 'rules' on family limits, such as they are, differ by state. Even if you're adhering to the family limit rules in one state, you could be breaking them in another – to say nothing of the difficulty in tracing eventual groups of siblings.

'They made me really nervous,' he said. 'I was incredibly naive.'

Naive or not, Paul kept going. He told me that almost a decade ago he'd started donating again – on what I suppose you could call a freelance basis, outside the clinic system, to a lesbian couple. Then another. At the time I rang him, Paul said he had had thirteen children by lesbian couples – in addition to however many children he had created through fertility clinics. Paul estimates that the total number of children he has fathered will be somewhere between forty and 200, from the RNSH and his freelance activities. I felt sick. I finished the conversation and hung up.[4]

Given Paul's dates of sperm donation to the RNSH, and assuming that Clinic 20 was using only fresh sperm in those days, as Illingworth told me in our first meeting (but then denied in our second), it seemed – on balance – unlikely that Paul was my biological father. Paul had been forthcoming and believed any children of his had a right to know who he was. But I was still shaken. I suspended individual sperm donor searches for the time being.

CHAPTER 15

EVERYWHERE IN NEW South Wales there were brick walls. However, across the border, things were better for people like me.

In forward-thinking Victoria, donor-conceived people had had some major wins. In 1984, Victoria was the first jurisdiction anywhere in the world to create a central register for donor conception information.[1] The register applied to births from 1988 onwards. It did not abolish donor anonymity – identifying information could only be released with the parties' consent. But it was a huge step.

In 1995, Victoria banned anonymous donation of eggs or sperm – a full fifteen years before New South Wales did so.[2] The ban was for all donations from 1998 onwards. It was another major step.

After 1998 in Victoria, then, there existed three rules for the same group of people. Donor-conceived people born pre-1988 were entitled to nothing, and often got nothing. Those born between 1988 and 1998 could have access to non-identifying information about their biological parent(s). They could have access to identifying information – if their biological parent(s) consented. Those born after 1998 didn't need permission: they were entitled to access identifying information about their biological parents (although not their biological siblings).

Then Victoria entered a really interesting phase. It was argued that having three different rules for donor-conceived people and their families was discriminatory: that all donor-conceived people should have the same rights, regardless of when they were born. In 2010, a Victorian parliamentary inquiry began to examine whether or not all Victorian donor-conceived people should have the right to access identifying information about their biological parent(s), regardless of birthdate.

This would require a retrospective change to the law. It would mean that Victorian donors who had understood that, legally, they could stay anonymous if they wanted to would have that taken away.

Retrospective law can give lawyers, members of Parliament and policymakers alike a severe eye twitch. Retrospective laws are considered by some to be inherently unfair, no matter what the issue.[3] Retrospective criminal law is verboten in the US, although retrospective civil laws are allowed. It is possible to enact retrospective legislation in the UK, both civil and criminal, but very rare.[4] Australia follows the British path: we allow it.

But that doesn't mean we do it often.

The war of words was lively. Those opposed to retrospective changes included some sperm donors, as one might expect, but they 'did not appear to be in the majority', as professor of health law Sonia Allan wrote. In her book *Donor Conception and the Search for Information*, Allan says of the debate in Victoria at the time: 'Notably there are more than 120 sperm donors on the voluntary register in Victoria, and many donors supported information release.'[5] On the other hand, the inquiry heard from just three donors who were opposed.[6] One of the three made it clear that his main fear was not the release of identifying information – it was any contact that followed.

This is an important distinction. Knowing who your biological parent is, and actually talking to or meeting them, are two different things. In adoption, a compromise had already been found: contact vetoes. Contact vetoes have been made available around the world, as adoption records have been retrospectively opened by jurisdictions. In practice, contact vetoes are used sparingly. This is how they work.

In New South Wales, for example, an adoptee has the right to identifying information about their biological parents. But if the biological parents do not wish to be contacted, some (where the adoption order was made before October 1990) may lodge a contact veto. The adoptee, in return for the identifying information about their biological parents, has to sign an undertaking agreeing not to make contact with them.

And vice versa: an adoptee adopted out before October 1990 may lodge a contact veto against their biological parents. Contact vetoes are legally binding.

In Australia today, contact vetoes are very rarely lodged. In 2018–19, there were 2468 applications for identifying information in relation to an adoption. The total number of contact vetoes lodged during that year? Three. Of the three, two were lodged by adoptees against their biological parents, and one was lodged by a biological parent (a mother) against their offspring.[7]

If Victoria was going to retrospectively change the law and allow all donor-conceived Victorians identifying information about their donor(s), contact vetoes were one tried and tested way of going about it.

While only three donors fronted up to the Victorian inquiry and objected to ending anonymity, there were many more powerful organisations and fertility specialists who were strongly opposed. These included: the Fertility Society of Australia; the Victorian branch of the Australian Medical Association; Melbourne IVF; the Victorian Infertility Counsellors Group; and two of Victoria's fertility specialist 'heavies', Professor Gab Kovacs and Professor David de Kretser – the latter having recently stepped down as governor of the state of Victoria. This powerful list argued the case for donors remaining untroubled by the consequences of their actions, in the notable absence of a large group of donors voicing that themselves.

Both Victoria's branch of the Australian Medical Association and the Fertility Society of Australia said that donors should not be contacted these days, at all, even just to ask whether they would now consent to any request for information. They should not be given that option.

Why would these medical professionals resist change so vigorously? That is, indeed, the question.

On the other hand, there were a number of sperm donors who publicly supported ending donor anonymity. They recognised the child's right to family and also said that the child's preference, and welfare, should come first. Essentially, that's good parenting. It's an unselfish recognition that in this situation, the child's basic rights trump your own.

Ian Smith, a sperm donor whom I've met and had a number of chats with, knew he had seven donor-conceived children at the time of the inquiry. All were the result of pre-1988 sperm donations – meaning, they were entitled to absolutely no information about their biological father whatsoever. And Ian couldn't find out anything about his seven donor-conceived offspring, although he wanted to.

'I would dearly love to know something, to at least meet them once, but I may never do so. If I had the opportunity to do so, yes, I certainly would wish to,' Smith told the inquiry. But Smith stressed that he wouldn't push. 'You have got to protect them, is my view,' he said. 'If the legislation were to change and it would allow me to make contact with those people, I personally would be very reticent in initiating that, inasmuch as I do want to, I would love to meet those people, but it comes from my philosophy that they are at the core of this and it is their human rights that are paramount.'[8]

Other donors felt the same. Michael Linden is the biological father of one of my friends, Myfanwy Cummerford, a prominent advocate for donor-conceived people in Victoria. Myf's search for Michael, conducted years before my own, was just as fruitless – until she took the extraordinary step of talking to *The Australian*, which put a big photo of Myf on the front page, along with an article. Michael happened to pop into a 7-Eleven that day and bought the paper. Appearing in the only national newspaper (and making the front page) succeeded where all other avenues had failed. Today, Myf and Michael have a relationship and are in regular contact.

Michael is also the biological father of four other donor-conceived people, three of whom were unknown to him at the time of the inquiry. He told the inquiry: 'I feel there is no difference between my circumstance and that of the relinquishing parent in the context of adoption. My need to connect with them, and my curiosity about their whereabouts and how their lives have transpired, is of the same order I believe and likewise should not be summarily negated because I somehow gave them away.' But in terms of contact, he was respectful and succinct: 'It is their call; not mine.'[9]

I stumbled across this highly strung debate in Victoria as the parliamentary inquiry neared its end. My journalist brain fired up.

Donor conception strikes at the heart of what it is to be human. How is life made, and who gets to make those decisions? How much is nature, and how much is nurture? What should you, personally, be entitled to, in order to be human and to be sane?

This would make a good story, I thought, when the inquiry reports. Then I came across Rel.

NARELLE GRECH: BIG brown eyes, a massive smile, dreadlocks to the waist, and a fighter to the last. I would come to see that this whole inquiry, inasmuch as a parliamentary inquiry can ever be about one person, was about her. We were the same age. She found out she was donor conceived at fifteen. And she became an activist.

'There are not enough words in the world to begin to write about what it is like being a person who was conceived via anonymous donor sperm ... It has been an obvious blessing and it has often felt like a cruel curse,' an adult Rel would write in 2010.[10]

Teenage Rel was given mere scraps: her biological father was 5'7", brown-haired, blood type O+.

'When I inevitably became more curious and wanted to know more I was met with fierce denial and a lack of compassion from the very professor and the very institution that helped to conceive me,' she wrote. This was Professor Gab Kovacs, who would go on to oppose change at the Victorian inquiry. 'The "donor" was anonymous, and I was told that because my parents and the donor all agreed to this anonymity I would have to just accept this and get on with things.

'I cannot begin to describe how dehumanising and powerless I am to know that the name and details about my biological father and my entire paternal family sit somewhere in a filing cabinet in Melbourne, with no means to access it.'[11]

This search would dramatically shape Rel's life. 'When I began becoming active in the DC community I realised that one way I could make a difference is to channel all of this passion into a career. To help other people in my situation some day,' she said. She gained a social work degree and began work in foster care and child protection.[12]

Rel was tireless. She pressed and pressed. She somehow wangled out of someone that her donor was Maltese. This made Rel very happy: her biological mother and social father were also Maltese. She discovered that her donor code was T5. Then she and Myf worked out that at Rel's particular clinic, this meant something in itself: he must have been the fifth sperm donor to that clinic whose surname began with T. 'It delighted me to think that my actual initials were N.T.!' she wrote. Rel found out that she had eight donor-conceived half-siblings – five sisters and three brothers, all born within three years in Melbourne. At twenty-seven, the age I discovered my own truth, Rel had known hers for twelve years. Yet she wrote: 'I still do not know myself like I should … I have moved through so many phases; shock, curiosity, anger, loss, grief, disconnectedness, disempowerment and hopelessness.'[13]

Rel always stressed that she loved the parents who had raised her – a lot – and she respected them for telling her the truth. That wasn't the problem, she wrote.

'The real dilemma is that no one with authority stopped to properly consider what the thoughts, wishes and needs of the DC person might be … I did not sign anything stating that I would be happy for my father and paternal family to be kept secret from me. I was not a party to this agreement and I believe that this information should be shared with me.'

To me, Rel's words nailed the basic problem. When a donor-conceived child, by design, cannot know their biological family, the result is the deliberate stunting of the donor-conceived person's identity and humanity.

The year was 2010, and Rel's own life was about to change drastically.

UNTIL THIS POINT, Rel had enjoyed excellent health. 'I had never been ill in my life,' she wrote.[14] But that changed in 2011. Her large bowel ruptured. Rel had to have emergency surgery. She had a large tumour. It was bowel cancer: terminal. Rel was only twenty-eight years old.

Rel's surgeon told her that Stage 4 bowel cancer, at her age, was most likely due to genetic factors. There was no history of cancer on Rel's mother's side of the family. 'At this point I cried,' she wrote, 'not only for the fact that I was now terminally ill, but also as I most likely inherited this disease from my paternal family and my anonymous sperm donor T5.'[15]

By December 2011, Rel had undergone twelve rounds of chemotherapy.[16] 'I cannot work or enjoy the life that I once knew. I feel like my youth has been taken away from me,' she wrote. 'I cannot explain what it's like to have to face such questions about mortality at the age of 28.'

And there was an extra kick in the teeth: 'I am furious to think that this could have been prevented.'

If Rel had known of any genetic risk, she wrote, she could have been screened earlier for this type of cancer.

'The choice to be tested would have been mine, and this is the most frustrating thing in all of this,' she wrote. 'The system that has helped to create me has also left me powerless to know basic information regarding my identity, and more importantly my own health. If I had this knowledge upon finding out at 15 years of age, I would [have] been able to make the decision to be tested for this type of cancer ... I am not ready to die.'

Rel made submissions to parliamentary inquiries on donor conception, state and federal. She pleaded that she needed to find her biological father and her siblings. This preyed on her mind: her time was running out. And she needed to warn them.

'I am also concerned that my eight half siblings ... may be walking about and carrying this possible disease without knowing it,' Rel told the Victorian parliamentary inquiry. 'They may also be terminally ill. They may have passed this illness onto any children they have. This diagnosis does not only affect me, it possibly affects so many other people, and they should be made aware if this is the case.'[17]

The files remained shut.

I FIRST RANG Narelle Grech in 2012. I'd pitched a story on the Victorian inquiry to ABC TV's nightly national current affairs show *7.30*. I felt I had to disclose to my executive producer Sally Neighbour that I was donor conceived, which was really quite painful; I still wasn't used to explaining any of this, particularly in the workplace. To her credit, she told me to go ahead. The story would be subject to all the normal editorial processes. There was no issue.

Rel was the first person I lined up and my main talent. She was really energetic and bouncy on the phone, despite her health and what we were discussing. I got on a plane.

I didn't tell Rel I was donor conceived. Some journalists might think it would be an advantage. I thought to myself, sternly, that if I couldn't get talent across the line *without* telling them, I wasn't any good at my job. My boss had okayed the story and not told me that I had to disclose; the story was about Victoria, not about me. And telling my boss had been painful enough. I wasn't about to start telling others. Walking this kind of line was a whole new experience for me as a journalist. It definitely did not make my job any easier.

Rel lived in a suburban sharehouse. We drove up, the cameraman and I, and she let us in. She was wearing a skirt over baggy pants, a necklace on a leather thong, and her dreadlocks hung down her back.

Her housemates were out. Rel's room was a dark palace of cushions, fabric, candles and incense. She walked us through the tidy kitchen, where her medication sat on the counter; she showed us the backyard and the veggie patch. Then we settled down to do the interview.

She was strong. The only time she wavered was when I asked her about her diagnosis. 'The doctors asked almost instantly, "Is there a history of bowel cancer in your family?"' Rel said. 'There are tests if it's in the family that young people can have from about 15, so had I known that there was a potential risk of bowel cancer I could have caught this, before stage one even.' She stopped and blinked. We paused the tape to let her breathe.

People are often a little bit quiet after an interview like that: such upsetting stuff takes a while to come back from. I let Rel and the cameraman sort out a kitchen scene – it was time for Rel to eat something anyway – and felt the pressure in the room return to normal. She ate, we chatted more, we packed up and left. My mind was churning. She'd already given me the interview. She'd spoken to me about life, and death, generously. She was in a truly miserable situation. I made a decision.

'I have to go back in,' I said to the cameraman. 'I left my jumper.' I dashed back to the front porch.

I knocked and she let me in again, surprised. I shut the door. 'I don't have long,' I said in a rush. 'I just have to tell you something. I'm donor conceived too.'

Her eyes widened and she squeaked. Then she burst out, 'I *thought* you got it!' and we both roared with laughter. There were a few minutes of 'What? And when you said —' 'I know, and I was so —' 'I can't believe —' It was joyous. We made plans to speak soon. Then I ran back out.

The report came together well. Rel was happy with it, and we kept Skyping after, just talking about whatever. We were both in our late twenties, got on like a house on fire, and we became friends. She was so funny, and so fun, that (to my shame) I often forgot she was sick.

Once, when we were Skyping, she was bemoaning being single. C'mon, I said, there are some good guys out there. I asked about someone she'd met recently. She just looked at me.

'Do you know how hard it is to date with a colostomy bag?' she asked.

Rel needed a guy who was nice, smart and funny – and also okay with her sketchy health, a probable decline and a very finite end to any relationship. It's hard to date with a colostomy bag. It's hard to date when you're dying.

PROFESSOR GAB KOVACS, the fertility specialist who made Rel, was another Australian fertility 'pioneer'. He ran the donor insemination program at Melbourne's Prince Henry Hospital from 1978 for two decades until it closed. There, he treated Rel's mother and an estimated 1500 other couples.[18] From 1998 to 2007, Professor Kovacs practised with the private Monash IVF (motto: 'Let's be brave together'), treating another estimated 1500 couples. In 2015, Fairfax newspapers described him as the man who 'has overseen the insemination of more Victorian women with donor sperm than almost any other doctor'.[19]

I interviewed Gab Kovacs for the *7.30* story. Professor Kovacs, unlike some others in this industry, is not afraid of the media. He doesn't try to hide behind a company or a written statement.

'She's a very nice young person,' he said, 'and we feel terribly sad about her illness, but I just can't see what else we can do.'

To the end, Rel and the Grechs firmly believed that 'as her mother's doctor and the man who could access [the donor's] name, Kovacs had put up roadblocks'. Gab Kovacs, on the other hand, maintains that 'he did everything the procedures permitted' (Fairfax's *Good Weekend*, 2015).

I asked Rel about Gab Kovacs.[20]

'So when I was 18, I made an appointment to see Professor Kovacs. I wanted to know whether there'd be any more information he could tell me, and he said, "Unfortunately if I were to tell you your donor's name, I'd go to jail",' she replied. (I am not aware of any criminal provision stating that fertility specialists will go to jail for telling someone who their biological father is.)

'So he knows,' I said.

'He does know,' she confirmed.

I put that to Gab Kovacs in 2012. His answer was: he couldn't remember who the donor was, and, in any case, he no longer had access to Rel's records.

BUT THERE WAS a massive win on the horizon for Rel. The Victorian parliamentary inquiry had finished. It found *all* donor-conceived Victorians should know who their biological parents were, regardless of previous law or what promises were made.

However, the inquiry's recommendations were not law. And the rest of Parliament, which hadn't sat through the hearings and listened to all the arguments, was not yet convinced. Instead, it was decided there be an extension, to ask more donors their views. Only donors.

While Parliament filibustered, Rel's life was running out. She had been hospitalised. Myf told Clem Newton-Brown, the chair of the inquiry, who asked Victorian premier Ted Baillieu to authorise a search for Rel's donor. In what would prove to be one of his last acts in office, Baillieu intervened personally in Rel's case, ordering the state public records office to find T5.

This, finally, forced a breakthrough.

After a decade and a half of searching, it took nothing less than the personal order of the premier of Victoria to defeat the forces arrayed against her and deliver Rel what she needed.

In February 2013, Rel received a letter from Victoria's attorney-general. It said that her donor had been found. His name was Ray Tonna. He lived in regional Victoria. It was that simple.[21]

When she got his name, Rel called Myf, who straightaway found a picture of Ray on Google. The resemblance was striking. 'I remember saying to Rel, "It's him Rel, we've found your gypsy father",' Myf told me, 'because she always thought he must be where she got her free-spirited nature.'

Ray Tonna wasn't in the least bothered about contact. In fact, he told authorities to give his newly discovered daughter his email and phone number. Their first call went for three hours.

I remember Rel telling me how she drove to his place with her best friend Danielle, a while out of Melbourne, nearly jumping out of her skin with excitement. When she met Ray, she was delighted and amazed. In personality, they were extremely similar: Ray is arty, empathic and an old-school hippie. Rel said she spent hours at his house, happily going through old photos. She met his wife and son ('My brother!' she told me, laughing. 'I have a brother, Sarah!'). Ray was elated she'd turned up on his doorstep. He would have been happy to meet her fifteen years ago. He would have been happy to have known her from the start.

'The moment we actually met was like an amazing dream come true – nothing prepares you for something like this,' Ray Tonna told me, years later. 'I almost felt as overwhelmed as when our [social and biological] son was born. It was like the birth of this person I didn't know. I thought it was a wonderful thing from the word go.' There is a beautiful photo of them both, hugging.

About six weeks later, Rel was dead.

Her hospitalisation had become permanent and she was in a lot of pain. Ray visited her in Melbourne two or three times a week – they had about a month and a half of knowing each other, biological father and child. They should have had years. It was what they both wanted. It shouldn't have been in anyone else's power to prevent that.

Rel died on 26 March 2013. She was just thirty. I'd recently started seeing Sam, who's now my partner. Sam and I were going to the movies that evening. I turned up outside the cinema a complete mess: we bought whiskey and went to a park instead. Night fell, and I sat outside in the dark with him, crying.

NEARLY THREE YEARS after Rel's death, Victoria finally passed its world-first legislation, granting all donor-conceived people the right to identifying information about their donor. The law also provided for contact vetoes. Rel's family was in the gallery to see its passage through the upper house.

Victoria's *Assisted Reproductive Treatment Amendment Act 2016* is known as Narelle's Law.

TODAY RAY TONNA is free of the disease that killed Rel, and so is his family. He has been told that he may carry a genetic predisposition for bowel cancer, which, if combined with another's similar predisposition, could result in the disease.

Since meeting Rel, Ray has been able to find four of his other donor-conceived children. He has been able to tell each of them to get tested for bowel cancer.

CHAPTER 16

AFTER THE VICTORIAN parliamentary recommendations which would become Narelle's Law, in New South Wales I fronted up to my own state parliament.

I was there with an old friend, Lesley. Lesley has watched me grow up: she was my teacher in Year 3. I went to a tiny primary school with a close-knit community. Back then, Lesley had no idea that I was donor conceived. But she knew my dad, and she knows my mother, and she has always supported me unconditionally.

I was at Parliament to address a bunch of politicians about the most personal, sensitive part of my life – about which, at that stage, I still hadn't told many people in my life, including family. I was going to dredge all this up in a setting where I also work as a journalist. Later on, I was probably going to have to interview these MPs on some other topic and hold them to account. I can think of more fun ways to torpedo my career.

We signed in, rode the lifts with a staffer, and entered a featureless meeting space. Seated around a boardroom table were six men in suits, ranging from their mid-thirties to their late sixties. Only men. I was there to voice my outrage about the protections built around elusive biological fathers, and every politician – every person there with power – was male.[1]

IN EARLY 2012, NSW Parliament began hearings for an inquiry into a single aspect of donor conception. Very different to Victoria's, their focus was the donor conception equivalent of a first-world problem.

A year previously, in 2011, a NSW District Court judge had made the decision to remove a man from a child's register of birth. The child's social parents – the primary carers of the child – were two women in a same-sex relationship. The biological father was a sperm donor. The same-sex couple and the sperm donor had found each other through placing ads in magazines.

A WORD ABOUT this sort of 'freelance' networking to create a child: my focus is the fertility sector, dominated by the big clinics, and the need for regulation in this sector. Some peer-to-peer arrangements, you might argue, will always fly under the radar, so why go after the industry? Well, just because some people may seek out a random on Facebook to have a baby doesn't mean the multi-billion-dollar global baby business – sanctioned, subsidised and taxed by governments – gets to escape scrutiny. But I would also like to make clear that I think sourcing your own unknown donor online is a terrible idea, for both would-be parents and the child. The list of dangers is long and includes STDs, inheritable genetic disease, late-onset inheritable conditions which the donor might not even know about and which you will not discover until it's too late, masses of siblings, potential for exploitation, potential for lawsuits, potential for personal attacks. To say nothing of the fact that your child will probably, once again, not know their biological parent(s) and all their siblings.

THE MAN AT the centre of the 2011 New South Wales court case had agreed to donate sperm to the two women. He made it known from the start that he wanted to be involved in the child's life. One of the women fell pregnant and in 2001 had a child, a baby girl. The birth certificate only allowed for the naming of a male and female parent. Only the biological mother was on the birth certificate.[2]

The biological father was known to the child, maintained a close relationship with his daughter, and provided financial support during the pregnancy and every week after she was born for some years. By 2011, District Court Judge Walmsley SC found that not only had the sperm donor 'had a close and loving relationship' with the child all of her life, but 'so have [the donor's] mother and his sister'.

But it wasn't all rosy. Within months of the child's birth, the relationship between the two mothers and the sperm donor had deteriorated – not unknown in private donor arrangements. So he applied to the Family Court for contact orders, with success. He was granted access every second weekend and, with the agreement of the two women, in 2002 the biological father was listed on the baby's birth certificate.

When the girl was about four and a half, her mothers' relationship broke down, and they split. There were new court orders, which also increased the amount of time the biological father had with his daughter. It was a triple-parenting situation.

When the girl was nine, her non-biological mother wrote to the biological father, asking him to agree to be taken off the girl's birth certificate, because she wanted to go on there instead. There had recently been a legal change allowing two people of the same sex to appear on a birth certificate as parents. However, the number of names could still only be two. The non-biological mother wrote to the biological father: 'You always will be her biological donor, and you will still maintain your relationship and spend time with her … this is not a reflection in any way on your relationship with [her], but is merely putting in place what should have been written when she was born.'

The man replied that 'as a sign of good faith', if it was possible to have three names on the birth certificate, he would agree to this. 'But I will never agree to have my name removed. [She] is my daughter just as much as she is yours and [your ex's].'

However, three names on a birth certificate wasn't, and isn't, possible.[3] Cue legal action. The man lost. In August 2011, Judge Walmsley said although he had 'considerable sympathy' for the biological father, he had to find in favour of the biological mother. This was because of a New South Wales law, the *Status of Children Act 1996*.[4] This Act says if a child is born of a fertilisation procedure, and all the adults involved (heterosexual couples, same-sex couples, single women, donors) agreed to that procedure, then the donor, if male, 'is presumed not to be the father of any child born as a result of the pregnancy'. The donor, if female, 'is presumed not to be the mother of any child born as a result of the pregnancy'. The commissioning woman who carries the child is deemed the mother, whether she uses donated sperm, a donated egg or a donated embryo. Any partner she has at the time, of whatever gender, who agreed to the procedure is the other parent.

The upshot of this 2011 case was that NSW Parliament decided to hold a full parliamentary inquiry into inclusion of donor details on the Register of Births, because one man – one parent – who still had a legal right to see his child felt aggrieved that he was no longer on a piece of paper. And I can understand why that hurt him. But all of this was a niche issue, a tiny fleck on the dark iceberg of donor conception.

This case was, once again, all about the parents and not the child. This case did not represent what the majority of us donor-conceived people struggle with. This man knew, loved and had contact with his daughter. She knew that he was her biological father. She could ask him anything she wanted about whether she had any other siblings (she didn't: he had donated sperm only once and had no other children). She could ask him anything she wanted about family medical history. There were no secrets. The legal fight, essentially, was a fight *for* her, by three parties who all knew and loved her. Given the full spectrum of problems with donor conception, this seems like a good problem to have.

But, predictably, the court case got a lot of media coverage. Lesbians! Sperm donors! An ugly private spat in public! So New South Wales decided to hold a parliamentary inquiry into this aspect of donor conception – and nothing else.

It didn't matter. At this point, to me, any opportunity was a good one. I wrote a long, confidential submission to Parliament. I told them the issue which had sparked their inquiry was a red herring. I told them everything that had happened to me and everything I'd found out: deliberate record destruction in public hospitals, lies, AIDS, dozens if not hundreds of batches of siblings, and so on. I added, grudgingly, that if they were intent on pursuing only this birth certificate thing, then they should not enshrine lies on what is a cardinal document – a document from which all other important legal documents are derived.

In Australia, a birth certificate is used to obtain a passport, a driver's licence, a Medicare card. It trumps all. Kept by the state-based registries of Births, Deaths and Marriages, it is each state's record of its citizens. It should contain biological truth. Have three parents on there, have five. But there should always be, named, the biological father and the biological mother. This is not about the parents. This is to protect and uphold the rights of the child. If you've been lied to all your life about the very fact of being donor conceived, or who your biological family is, the only thing in your life that would ever tell you what you really are is just such a birth certificate. In our current, permissive, self-regulating fertility industry, a birth certificate is, I wrote to NSW Parliament, the only opportunity for a government to tell its own people the truth.

So that's how I ended up in a room with six male strangers, about to spill my secrets.

THEY STARED AT me. I gripped the back of a chair. I did not sit.

'Thank you for coming to tell your story,' the chair, Nationals MP John Barilaro said. 'We appreciate you being here to speak in confidence.'

'My name's Sarah,' I began. 'And I'm donor conceiv —' Suddenly, shamefully, my voice rose to a squeak. I shut up immediately. My throat nearly closed over, with the painful tightness you get when you're about to cry. My eyes stung. Oh god, no. I hadn't even said anything yet.

I struggled for control for what seemed too long, and then tried again, my voice still high and strained.

I know I got through everything I wanted to say. I told them everything, all the holes in the system. All the twists and turns and self-serving caveats that kept me from my own family.

I'd also taken along a copy of my mother's treatment records and handed them the two pages with the donor code cut out. There was a silence as they passed the documents from one man to the next.

At the end, the oldest MP in the room – the one who'd been the least responsive throughout my hearing – suddenly spoke. 'Well, I think she should know who he is,' he said.

I was astonished. Around the table, there were small, sympathetic signs: some nods, a smile. Then he spoke again. 'What if,' he said, 'there was another page attached to the back of a birth certificate? Or a note saying there was some more information?'

I nearly groaned out loud. 'Well,' I said carefully, 'you still wouldn't be telling people what they need to know. What if they never looked up that extra information, because it didn't seem important? What if their commissioning parents ripped off the extra page?'

This didn't seem to convince him, or some of the others, and there was a round of murmurs and polite disagreement. But it was okay. I'd spent an hour with them, an intense hour, but it was still a very short crash course in all these issues.

Lesley and I debriefed at a cafe. We rolled our eyes about the suggestion for an extra page on the birth certificate. 'That was ridiculous,' Lesley said. 'I felt like yelling, "Who are you trying to protect?"'

We finished our cake, had a last hug, and I went home to wait for their report.

THE REPORT DROPPED a few months later, and I really don't think I could have asked for much more.[5]

The terms of reference for the New South Wales inquiry – that is, what the committee were supposed to focus on – were brief and narrow: 'whether there should be provision for the inclusion of donor details on the register of births maintained by the Registrar of Births, Deaths and Marriages.' That was it. But the committee went above and beyond, I thought, to demonstrate that they knew there were much bigger issues in play.

I went through the foreword to the report by the chair, John Barilaro, with growing elation. 'Throughout the inquiry it became evident that this issue was complex and that it required significant examination,' Barilaro wrote. 'The Committee struggled with a position due to either conflicting information, or the lack of information. At times the Committee also struggled with the intensely emotional and personal reflections we heard from inquiry participants …

'The Committee considers that donor-conceived people have the prevailing right to know the identity of the person who contributed to their biological makeup.' I punched the air. 'Members of the Committee favoured the principle that the rights of donor-conceived people were of a greater value and paramount to that person's wellbeing in the future.' Another air punch. They'd listened. They hadn't seen me as crazy. I breathed out and read on: 'The Committee considered that mandatory naming of donors on birth documents would not be an appropriate way to encourage parents to tell their donor conceived child the truth about their conception ... The Committee has instead recommended that an addendum indicating that further information is available be attached to birth certificates that are issued to donor conceived adults.' Oh, for god's sake. But there was a lot more. 'Retrospective access to donor information, in relation to births occurring before 2010, was a key issue for those affected by donor conception ... These issues will be examined in detail by the Committee as part of an upcoming inquiry.'

Another inquiry! Into a retrospective change to the law in my state!

At the end of the committee's report was an appendix listing all those who had given public evidence in person over two days of hearings. They were lawyers, bureaucrats, commissioning parents, academics. A few were great advocates for donor-conceived people, like Caroline Lorbach. The rest were not. There was not a single donor-conceived person who spoke publicly.

But there was a final note: 'The Committee also met privately with a donor conceived individual.' Just one. That was me.

The lesson is terribly cheesy. One person can make a difference.

THE SECOND NSW parliamentary inquiry was held hot on the heels of the first. Five of the six (still all-male) committee remained the same, including the chair, John Barilaro, so the knowledge accumulated from the previous inquiry was retained. It was all about whether or not to allow retrospectivity. Or, as the terms of reference stated:[6] 'whether people conceived by donor conception prior to January 2010 should have access to donor conception information, including information that identifies their donor and donor conceived siblings'. The rest of the terms of reference were about how to do that, if that were to happen – who would manage the information, should there be counselling or other supports, and 'any other relevant matter'. A damn good start.

I participated, of course. They'd already heard my story, but I wrote another confidential submission. So did other donor-conceived people, including at least two from New South Wales – word was getting out, despite a lack of self-knowledge, a lack of advertising and very little media attention.

Unfortunately, New South Wales was not going to go as far as Victoria. The report of the second inquiry stopped short of calling for access to identifying information for all donor-conceived people, set out in law. Frustratingly enough, there was the same stumbling block: donors who were opposed. And not actual donors. But the possibility of donors who were opposed. In the end, just one donor had made a submission to the second inquiry. He said that donor-conceived people 'have an inalienable right to know the details of their conception, their donors, their ancestors and siblings'. That is, the only donor who bothered to give evidence supported us.

The committee, however, said: 'In light of the lack of direct evidence received from donors, the Committee is unwilling to recommend substantive change in relation to access to donor conception information.'

Donors were allowed to override best efforts to secure the basic human rights of donor-conceived people, simply by doing nothing (apart from that one guy). By doing nothing, they were able to outweigh our own emotional journeys, time, written submissions and personal appearances. Don't ever tell me that the system favours children.

I also found this a bit jarring. Why was it okay not to hear from us, but important to hear from donors? And if the committee really wanted to find donors: well, why not put the hard word on the fertility clinics? There was no doubt this committee was definitely hearing from the baby business.

The Fertility Society of Australia had made a submission, making clear that it was also speaking for its powerful sub-groups:[7] the IVF Medical Directors Group, Scientists in Reproductive Technology, the

Australian and New Zealand Infertility Counsellors Association, and the Fertility Nurses Association. Unsurprisingly, they were all 'strongly opposed to compulsory retrospective registries'. One big fertility clinic, Fertility East, also made its own submission. Fertility East said that allowing all donor-conceived people the right to know who their own biological family was 'would have a devastating prospective effect on every aspect of medicine ... this concept could be extrapolated to every branch of human endevour [sic] with untold consequences'.[8] Adoptees being granted access to their original birth records hadn't led to the downfall of society, but apparently we might.

One fertility specialist from the public Concord Hospital, Professor David Handelsman, wrote: 'Becoming a sperm donor was explicitly envisaged as a social generosity, with the understanding that there would be no further contact, disclosure of identity and other recriminations.' It is telling that he viewed 'disclosure of identity' as a 'recrimination'.

'The claim that a genetic history from the sperm donor is essential for the medical care of offspring is incorrect and misguided,' Handelsman wrote firmly – a few pages after he admitted that his own practice had twice had to contact a former sperm donor regarding 'a genetic disorder newly diagnosed long after donation in either a donor offspring or in the donor himself'. He continued: 'There is no remote basis for such an oppressive legal approach as retroactive suppression of their legal and privacy rights of innocent sperm donors on the basis of genealogical curiosity by offspring.'[9]

So there were no retrospective changes recommended. It wasn't all bad, however. The committee did recommend that 'as a matter of urgency', the Ministry of Health should 'engage specialists to liaise with donors, donor-conceived people and recipient parents, to facilitate access to identifying information with the consent of all parties'. They also recommended the creation of a whole new agency to collect and manage donor conception information. And there was one more recommendation in there that electrified me.

'The Committee heard alarming evidence that information held by independent organisations may, at times, have been tampered with or destroyed, either deliberately or through a lack of correct process,' the report said.

'The Committee recommends that, as a matter of urgency, the Attorney-General amend the *Assisted Reproductive Technology Act 2007* to make it an offence to destroy, tamper [with], or falsify any donor conception records.'[10]

It was a win. It was, for obvious reasons, very close to my heart. If this recommendation were followed, no future donor-conceived person would have to go through what I did. Accountability and transparency would be one step closer. And finally, I would feel I had formal acknowledgement that what was done to me was wrong.

BUT A REPORT is not law. Two reports are still not law. The NSW Government responded to both the committee reports in April 2014.[11]

'The Government recognises how important it is for donor-conceived people to be able to access information and learn about their biological origins. International law enshrines the rights of the child, including the right of a child to know his or her parents and preserve his or her identity,' the government said. So far, so good. But, having acknowledged that, the government proceeded to deny that right.

There would be no right to identifying information for all donor-conceived people. There would be no new agency set up to manage donor conception information. And donor conception records would be left with the clinics. Years later, the government would finally make it illegal to falsify or destroy records: but you had to bring any proceedings within just two years of that destruction – and if the records were all with the clinics, how would you know?[12]

A *Sydney Morning Herald* article summed up the recent focus of my life in two sentences:

'The NSW government had agreed to transfer the donor files from clinics, which had been caught destroying records, to a central electronic database after a recommendation by a 2013 NSW parliamentary inquiry. But lobbying by the IVF industry, which claimed it would be too expensive, has resulted in a significantly watered down bill being introduced to NSW Parliament this week by Health Minister Jillian Skinner.'[13]

CHAPTER 17

WHY COULDN'T WE break through? Why were fertility specialists, clinics and even the broader medical organisations so ranged against us?

There's three sorts of answers to that question, some more likely than others.

Firstly, full transparency would uncover just how many rules were broken, how often, and by which medical professionals. How many giant sibling groups exist; the prevalence of inherited disease, both venereal (like HIV/AIDS) and genetic; how many donors were allowed to donate when they should not have been. How many clinics deliberately destroyed records. How donors, and commissioning parents, were misled. How both sperm and eggs were traded.

A woman called Kate Dobby gave scorching evidence on this to the Victorian parliamentary inquiry in 2010. Dobby was the registers officer for four years at Victoria's state Infertility Treatment Authority, administering all of Victoria's centrally held donor conception records and the register of donors and donor-conceived people.

'There was egg swapping that occurred at a specific clinic,' Dobby revealed. 'Egg swapping is a practice whereby you have multiple female patients in and you retrieve some eggs and say you have got one person there and you produce four eggs and then you might give one to the other woman there ... That stuff happened, and I know that the clinic that practised that has very poor records on that.' Dobby said the women having eggs extracted, as part of their own fertility treatment, were at that point 'encouraged' to give some – their excess – to someone else. She pointed out to me the potential for exploitation was high: 'I always got the impression that these weren't planned decisions & therefore that the donations that took place were ad hoc & that patients weren't adequately counselled about the implications of their decisions ... I'm not quite sure how a woman could offer informed consent to this process ... Asking them to donate their eggs in this context is arguably exploitative.'

Dobby's account makes me furious. Human eggs are not common property for doctors to farm out at will. Human sperm, of course, is also not common property. But there is an extra dimension to human eggs. Extracting them exacts a significant physical toll on the body of the female patient, which sperm donation does not. Women inject cocktails of hormones to stimulate their ovaries to super-produce. It is also a mentally vulnerable, and taxing, time. Human eggs are extracted with risk and pain.

'There was an instance where we were contacted by a woman who was told that a child had resulted for another patient,' said Dobby. 'Another patient had got pregnant with her egg, while she had failed to get pregnant with her egg. So there was another woman who had had her biological child but she had not had one herself. She ended up having one a few years later via egg donation herself.' Such colossal, wilful, unnecessary damage – which should be criminal. One can only imagine that putting all that down in writing would create a certain liability. Dobby also said that there were 150 or 160 babies conceived in Victoria using sperm from another state, South Australia, which came with no identifying information whatsoever. And that at the same time, Victoria was sending sperm to South Australia. That is, sperm trading, through 'personal relationships between doctors and clinicians'.

That wasn't all. Dobby was lifting the lid on Victoria – supposedly the most highly regulated, forward-thinking state in Australia, which in turn is supposed to be one of the leading countries in the world of fertility – and it was not pretty. 'A lot of donors reported to me that their identities were not verified correctly or that they were actually encouraged to donate under pseudonyms,' Dobby said. Doctors suggesting donors use fake names? How is that, in any universe, good professional practice? 'I know that there are donors who, when they would apply to the voluntary register at this time, they would say, "I may have also donated under this name, this name, this name and this name," saying that the clinics sometimes encouraged that to occur,' Dobby confirmed.[1]

Through her job, Kate Dobby spoke to a lot of donors. 'Donors were offered benefits in exchange for donating, which I guess we know,' Dobby said. 'I can remember there was one donor in the Prince Henry's [program] who, under "Reasons for donating", wrote "beer money".' Prince Henry's was the clinic presided over by Professor Gab Kovacs. It was the clinic that made Rel.

I have heard this 'beer money' story before, as have many donor-conceived people. Recently, an Australian donor-conceived woman received a text from her biological father and shared it with our group. She'd asked him why he donated sperm all those years ago. 'It might sound callous but back then it was just to get 10 bucks to go drinking on a Friday night … nothing more! I didn't even give the consequence much thought,' he'd replied. She appreciated the frankness but was taken aback.

Hearing that you were made in exchange for a few pints is not the origin story a human deserves. Personally, I used to fear meeting my biological father and finding out that I was just another round of alcohol. What I mean is: I used to fear meeting someone I would despise, who would make me, in turn, despise myself. Then I simply decided that if my own creation was so trivial, so insulting, it was no fault of mine. That realisation was a gift. It was one of those rare moments in life where, suddenly, years of worry slide off and you're light as a feather. Certainly, no-one from any fertility clinic helped me reach that place.

It wasn't just beer for sperm, however. In a supposedly altruistic donation system, donors were enticed by everything from alcohol to surgery on the house. 'I know that other donors were offered free vasectomies and things like that,' said Dobby. (The logic is twisted: if you want to stop having children, make a bunch of them for us first.) 'The other thing is donors who were patients. Maybe you had a couple who were in treatment and the male partner was encouraged to donate.'

Anyone who has been through fertility treatment knows it strains relationships – sometimes even ends them – and can undo mental health. How is it ethical for a doctor to put the hard word on a man, or a woman, in that situation? How can they give proper, fully informed, considered consent?

Kate Dobby also attested that family limits were being broken. Under Victorian law, donation was permitted to no more than ten families from a single donor. Dobby said one case alone broke this legal limit three times over. 'I know that there were other instances where there were up to thirty separate families, or in excess of forty children, over a very short time period from one specific donor,' Dobby said. 'This happened after legislation. Donors were re-coded, sometimes within the same clinic. They had a donor on the books and they used them again, giving them a separate code.'[2]

PERHAPS EXPOSING THE unsavoury truth is the main reason why the fertility industry (and wider medical organisations) strongly oppose granting all donor-conceived people the right to know their biological family. But what are the others?

The second sort of answer to this question is all about defending the silent, besieged donor. This is definitely the sort of answer which gets a public airing.

Professor Gab Kovacs made a submission to the Victorian parliamentary inquiry in 2010, championing privacy – while also protecting the honour of the medical professionals involved. 'Retrospectively removing the anonymity makes liars of the clinicians who recruited these donors, including such eminent clinicians as Professor Carl Wood, David de Kretser … and myself,' he wrote.[3]

'Pre-1988 donors [in Victoria],' wrote the Australian Medical Association of that state, 'agreed, in good faith, to assist other families to conceive and did so on the proviso that their privacy would be maintained.' It wasn't just an agreement, according to the AMA.

There's a myth that all donors across Australia who were promised anonymity signed watertight legal agreements after appropriate counselling. 'Contractual assurances were given to those who donated prior to 1 July 1988 that their identities would not be revealed to donor recipients nor to donor-conceived people and that they would be able to remain anonymous,' wrote the AMA (Vic).[4] Well, that sounds definitive, doesn't it? A contract?

Let's compare that with the evidence of Kate Dobby. Instead of a sweeping statement that all donors signed contracts, this woman got down and dirty in the paperwork for records across her state.

Dobby wrote: 'Granting access to this information creates issues regarding past donor consent to being anonymous. However, sometimes *evidence of this consent cannot be found or did not accurately represent the needs or wishes of the donor at the time*.'[5] (Emphasis added.) So, not a stack of legally binding contracts, then.

What seems more plausible: that all fertility clinics everywhere had comprehensive counselling for donors, accompanied by perfectly drafted contracts, kept in meticulous order? Or, given what happened to my mother's treatment records and many others, that fertility clinics' paperwork and professional practice has been often pretty terrible across the board, including for donors? Dobby had already warned the Victorian Government of the state of donor conception records in 2010: 'There has been a history of this information being destroyed or haphazardly collected by practitioners and clinics.'

In any case, Dobby believes, consideration has to be given to comparative standards of consent. 'The historical context needs to be taken into account,' Dobby wrote. 'What most people would consider to be informed consent now, is very different from the situation 20 or 30 years ago. Community attitudes towards assisted reproduction have changed, and people are now more likely to be open about their involvement in it.'

Even if Parliament had found a massive filing cabinet of bulletproof donor consent agreements, I would still challenge them. I would still say that when it comes to us and our right to know who our biological parents and siblings are, all those documents are invalid. Not only because of the UN Convention on the Rights of the Child, and all the domestic law that flows from that Convention. But also because *we* never agreed to give up that right. We never signed anything. And we are the vulnerable parties in all this, the children. Our rights should be paramount, despite concerted efforts to destroy them.

THE THIRD SORT of answer to the question of why the fertility industry opposes donor-conceived people finding family is the kind of answer that hides in plain sight. It's always there, mentioned casually every now and then. But because no-one wants to ascribe gross mercenary motives to an industry that cloaks itself in babies, it never becomes the headline.

The fertility industry says that removing donor anonymity – being open about their baby-making practices – threatens their business model for donor conception. 'The Society is concerned that retroactive laws in the context of gamete donation may jeopardize the whole practice by destroying the trust of candidate donors and recipients,' wrote the Fertility Society of Australia to the NSW Parliamentary Committee.[6] How would removing anonymity do that? What did they mean?

David Handelsman, andrologist at Concord Hospital, spelled it out. 'The universal experience of sperm donor programs is clear that the introduction of the mandatory disclosure requirement produced a dramatic, near total, reduction in willingness to become sperm donors,' he wrote. 'This was our experience in screening over 600 men who provided over 200 sperm donors, 90 per cent of which were pre-1997. Whereas recruitment had previously been easy and abundant, under a mandatory disclosure regimen, recruitment slowed to a trickle.'[7]

Allegedly, removing anonymity damages the business model. It attacks supply.

There are several things to unpack in Handelsman's submission. Firstly: you'd want to know more about the screening process and conduct detailed opinion surveys before you could draw any definitive conclusions.

Secondly, the question of 'abundance'. And its nemesis – shortage. We hear very little about abundance. We hear a lot about shortage. A quick online search turns up the following: 'How a sperm donor shortage led Carrie to look outside the box in her quest to be a mum' (SBS's *Insight*), 'Calls for public egg and sperm bank to curb state's donor shortage' (*The Age*), 'Australia turns to American [sic] for sperm donors after massive shortage of Aussie blokes' (*Daily Mail*).

There's also the persistent image of a 'drought'. In Australia, we understand drought. Drought equals bad. Quite a few subeditors have had the same brilliant idea: 'The Sperm Drought' (*The Monthly*), 'IVF diary of a single woman: the sperm drought down under' (kidspot.com.au), 'Men told to get a wriggle on and end the sperm drought' (*The Sydney Morning Herald*).

If journalists looked beyond what they were told by the fertility industry, touting for more supply, they would see something quite different.

To understand if removing donor anonymity reduces the ranks of donors, you need the actual numbers, before and after. You need trends, and you need a control group. Like so many aspects of the fertility industry, these numbers are largely not public, nor are they centrally held. However, in 2016, three Australian academics – Damian Adams, Shahid Ullah and Sheryl de Lacey – published a peer-reviewed article in the international *Journal of Law and Medicine*. The title was: 'Does the removal of anonymity reduce sperm donors in Australia?'[8]

The answer: no. In fact, after a ruling that Australian donors needed to be identified, overall donor numbers increased.

The authors examined more than a decade of data, from the year 2000 to 2012. Around halfway through, in 2005, the National Health and Medical Research Council Ethical Guidelines changed. From 2005 on, the ethical guidelines told clinics not to accept donations unless the donor agreed to release identifying information about themselves to their resulting children. Before 2005, no jurisdiction in Australia required clinics to do this, apart from Victoria, which had set this out in law since 1998; after 2005, all of them were supposed to do it. Victoria, therefore, was the control group – changes to the guidelines altered nothing there.

To obtain the information on donor numbers, the authors used data reported to authorities (mandatory and public in just three states) and they also wrote to the clinics themselves. They wrote to all the fertility clinics in the country listed as accredited by the Fertility Society of Australia. There were eighty. All up, thirty-eight clinics provided data, including twenty of the major providers.[9]

Whether you look at the numbers for the state of Victoria, for the rest of Australia, or for the country as a whole, the trend is one way: up. 'The first year of NHMRC Guideline implementation (2005) saw an increase in total donor numbers in all groups,' wrote the authors. In fact, the upwards trend was most noticeable in the jurisdictions where previously anonymity was the norm. And there was also 'a relatively consistent increase in donor numbers per year over the entire study period'.

A similar phenomenon had already been documented in the UK. 'In 2005, the United Kingdom underwent a transition from a system using anonymous donations to one using only donors who agreed to identity release. Published data showed that overall numbers of donors increased following the removal of anonymity,' the authors wrote.

'This study has shown that the impact of removing donor anonymity in Australia is positively correlated with donor numbers ... [this] contradicts claims that the removal of donor anonymity would compromise donor insemination (DI) procedures through a reduction in donor numbers.'

So what were those screaming headlines about? And what on earth was the Fertility Society of Australia talking about when it said that removing anonymity would jeopardise the practice?[10]

I can't answer for the Fertility Society of Australia, of course. But I can highlight one key distinction, which a slew of lazy media coverage has failed to identify, but which any economist could tell you in their sleep: there is a difference between supply and demand.

Supply is your concrete numbers of donors and donations. But demand is the number of people who want donated human tissue, and that's subject to a whole range of different factors. Demand is driven by the changing composition of families, including single mother by choice families and LGBTIQ+ families; the occasionally quite arbitrary definition of 'infertile'; and increased numbers of women, and men, leaving it till later to have children, who perceive donor gametes to be a safety net. Add to that list: celebrities announcing donor-conceived babies; advertising; and fear.

Driving the market is a consumer culture, in which the payment of money means you get something in return. Even a baby. But, although some in our society will tell you otherwise, having a child is not a right. Having a child is a privilege.

If everyone who wants a donor-conceived baby is automatically supposed to get one, then you will have a shortage of donors. You will always have a shortage. It doesn't matter how many women's ovaries you harvest, or how many men are assigned to a room with porn, or how many couples you pressure to hand over their 'spare' embryos. There will never be enough to satisfy human want. You will never be able to fulfil everyone's desire (and since when was that the role of medicine?) unless – and this is a terrible look into the abyss – you agree to lower all standards and safeguards. You say that it doesn't matter how we came by this egg, this sperm, this embryo. It doesn't matter how many children a man fathers, or a woman mothers. It doesn't matter if this baby was made on the other side of the world in a medical setting that you yourself would never deign to use. It doesn't matter if you bought your child, if you bought a Ukrainian egg and South African sperm, implanted them in a woman in Greece, took the baby from her when it was a few hours old, and left the country without once looking back. It doesn't matter if you lie to your child about all of this. It doesn't matter if they are never made aware of a truth which would sicken them and rock them to the core. Nothing matters, except you, and what you want, and the good money you paid, and the baby that the machine delivers in return.

Why do we find it so hard to say 'no' to some people who want to use the bodies of others to have a baby? Those people who are outraged when they face any obstacle, any restriction whatsoever? Because, perhaps, mainstream society does not perceive those wants as immediately damaging. Babies are often seen as a good thing to want – and moreover they are a want which sanctifies the wanter.

But unregulated, unchecked, uncontrolled, those wants hurt us all. They certainly hurt children; they will hurt children who are not yet born. Lots of people will not like me saying this, but in the oft-quoted words of a former Australian of the Year: the standard you walk past is the standard you accept. I cannot accept a baby business that does not uphold the rights of the child. And all adults should know that just because you want something, doesn't mean you always get it. Particularly if what you want is another human being.

A FINAL WORD on demand: currently, the Victorian Government is considering possible changes to its entire framework of fertility laws.

In 2018, the state government commissioned a review of the state's regulation of fertility treatment, to 'strengthen current laws to provide more safeguards and support to women accessing these services'. The terms were quite broad, but key issues included whether the existing regulatory framework was 'appropriate' for 'an evolving market for assisted reproductive treatment'.[11]

The author of the report, Michael Gorton, is a principal lawyer at law firm Russell Kennedy, on whose website he is described as 'an experienced commercial lawyer with a focus on the health sector'. The Gorton Report (delivered in May 2019) and its recommendations are mostly about the adults who use fertility treatment, not the products of the baby business. A formal government response to the whole thing is yet to come.

But Victoria has already acted on one of Gorton's recommendations. In 2020, it got rid of a requirement for couples and individuals to undergo police and child protection order checks before accessing fertility treatment. This requirement offended many customers of fertility clinics. Patients, *The Age* reported, 'felt the checks were "unfair, humiliating and a cause of distress"'.[12] The Victorian Department of Health and Human Services tells me that removing these checks gives would-be parents 'easier and fairer access' to fertility treatment. A spokesperson confirms the checks are also gone for anyone wanting donor conception.

Consider, again, the case of adoption. Would you happily adopt out a child to anyone who had not undergone, and passed, police and child protection order checks? If the answer is no – then why would you object to those checks for people who wish to commission a child from third-party material? Another child which they could not obtain within their own social relationships, but one they could buy? I weigh potentially causing offence against potential for harm and the best interests of the child. And 'offence' loses. Every time.

The abuse of donor-conceived children is not an abstract notion. There are at least two Australian instances where concerns around such harms have arisen. One case involves Australian child sex offender David John Farnell, who had twenty-two such convictions to his name and served time in jail for his offences. Farnell's past sexual offending included three female victims who were aged seven, ten and eleven.[13] Yet in 2014, Farnell and his wife commissioned and took home a donor-conceived baby girl from Thailand, gestated by a Thai surrogate, to raise in their own home. 'Legal experts believe Mr Farnell would not have been allowed to enter into a surrogacy arrangement in Australia because of his criminal past,' the *West Australian* newspaper reported in 2014. But at that point in Thailand, Farnell wasn't flagged. (After bringing the baby home, Mr Farnell told Australian media he'd received counselling in prison, and his sexual urges towards children had '100 per cent stopped'.)

The second instance involves another heterosexual Australian couple, who commissioned donor-conceived twins – also in Thailand.[14] In 2014, the husband was charged with sexually abusing both twins when they were under the age of ten. In the ensuing legal action, court documents revealed that he was also charged with possession of child abuse material. Childline Thailand, a child welfare organisation which runs safe houses, was asked to help with this case. I contacted them. Due to privacy conditions around court cases involving children, and because Childline Thailand was not involved in the criminal prosecution itself, even their organisation, they told me, was not notified of the outcome. They were unable to disclose any details regarding the children's care.

In both these cases, the children came from donor eggs and were carried by a commercial surrogate. In Thailand, there were no police checks on commissioning couples' backgrounds. Both these cases hit the headlines in 2014. In 2015, Thailand outlawed commercial surrogacy.

I DON'T USE this phrase often, because it's a terrifying statement, but in the very particular context of donor conception and police and child welfare checks: if you have nothing to hide, you should have nothing to fear.

CHAPTER 18

AT HOME, I took stock of my situation, sitting at the kitchen table and staring out at the street. The parliamentary inquiries in New South Wales had taken years and resulted in zero change. I tried to think clearly. Surely what happened in my case was wrong? Surely doctors and nurses couldn't just cut holes in medical records whenever they felt like it? Let alone do it to cover up the truth about the babies they had made?

I rang a high-profile legal firm. And I rang Legal Aid. (May as well cover off both ends of the spectrum, I thought.) If there was no possibility of answers for me, then maybe there could be justice. Could I sue for the deliberate destruction of my donor code? For destroying not just my link to my biological father, my brothers and sisters, my full identity, but also robbing me of potentially crucial family medical history?

I had long chats. Both said no. It was too long ago.

But I hadn't even realised that I was donor conceived until I was twenty-seven, I argued, so how could I possibly have sought redress sooner? It didn't make a difference, they said.

All right. Maybe there was no case I could fight through the courts. (Probably that was a good thing: no-one's ever launched legal action, let alone a test case, because it was both fun and easy.) But these people had surely committed professional misconduct. How could you use taxpayer money to run a baby factory where you deliberately covered up what you were doing? How was tampering with those medical records okay?

In my state, the independent government body which investigates and prosecutes medical complaints is called the Health Care Complaints Commission. I filed a formal complaint with the HCCC about the head of Clinic 20, Douglas Saunders, and the nurse from Clinic 20, Diana Craven. I felt somewhat bad about the complaint against Craven, the woman from my childhood birthday parties. It's hard to puzzle out. I still liked her. The problem is, no-one should deliberately destroy donor codes, and therefore those who do should be held to public account. I don't believe in exceptions to the rule when the act is so egregious.

Seven weeks after I filed the complaints, I hadn't heard anything from the HCCC apart from an automated receipt, so I gave them a call. I spoke to an assessments officer I'll call Michelle, who had been assigned to my complaint. She told me that the Medical Council of NSW 'consulted' with Douglas Saunders about the matter, and after that the Council, as well as the Commissioner of the HCCC, had decided to 'discontinue' my complaint because of the 'lapse of time'. Michelle said the HCCC was still waiting on the Nurse and Midwifery Council to 'consult' with Diana Craven, after which they would make a decision in her case. It was unlikely that would amount to anything either.

But, I said, Saunders and Craven were both still active in their fields – in fact, Saunders was teaching at a university in the US. And when the codes were destroyed, I said, I couldn't do anything. I couldn't bring a complaint. I was a baby.

'The way the Commissioner and the Medical Council look at it is risk to public safety, and whether it's within practitioner guidelines,' Michelle said. 'The Director of Assessments advised me it was approved by the ethics committee.'

No-one had ever mentioned code destruction being approved by an ethics committee before. Where did this body suddenly come from? I asked her which ethics committee that was. She said she would ask the director and get back to me.

'We have the discretion not to deal with things more than five years ago,' Michelle added.

'But', I said slowly, 'that means you will never investigate anything that's done to a child.' Without their parents' support, I meant. Unless, of course, a miraculously composed genius of a four-year-old decided not to go to the playground one afternoon and wrote a formal complaint to the HCCC instead.

'Oh,' she said quickly, 'we *always* investigate child sexual abuse.'[1]

A WEEK LATER, I received a formal letter from the HCCC's manager of assessments. It mentioned my phone call with Michelle: 'I understand how dissatisfied you must be feeling,' said the manager.

'The Commission investigates individual health practitioners only when there is a reasonable likelihood that disciplinary action would follow ... I also wish to note that the concerns raised about destroyed donor information during the 1980s is not new to the Commission, the Commission has in fact received a few complaints of this nature.' *Oh, really*, I thought. Nevertheless: 'The Commission in consultation with the Medical Council of NSW has decided to take no further action with your complaint,' he said.

There followed a bunch of reasons, all of which only raised further questions. 'Dr Saunders' conduct at the time would have been an accepted practice,' the manager said. 'The Commission is not basing its decision on whether Dr Saunders did or did not destroy the records, as noted, the decision is based on the fact that it was accepted practice at the time; if this practice occurred today, it certainly would not be condoned and it would not be accepted conduct,' the manager continued. So they weren't challenging whether Saunders did it. And others had also complained about record destruction too. But it was fine because it was all, somehow, 'accepted'. It was fine because the human products were not worthy of the same consideration as the humans who made them. We were throwaways. 'In the 1980s,' the manager wrote, 'assisted reproduction was considered experimental.'

Formal confirmation from the state of what I am, I thought, via a few blank-faced lines. Dr Frankenstein's creature came to mind.

'The Commission is advised that with regards to the destruction of donor codes, this would have been approved by Northern Sydney Local Health District equivalent's Ethics Committee,' the manager finished.[2]

No-one – not Diana Craven, who told me she cut out my code, not a single fertility specialist or clinic, not the NSW Voluntary Register, and no-one who fronted up or made a submission to any parliamentary inquiry in any state – had ever mentioned any 'Ethics Committee', for a public or private clinic, which authorised the destruction of donor codes. In fact, I hadn't come across mention of an ethics committee at any New South Wales fertility clinic in the '80s or '90s full stop. If an ethics committee had existed at my publicly funded hospital, they should have at least been able to tell me its name. You can't just capitalise 'Ethics Committee' and say that it must have been real. Show me a single piece of paper with its letterhead? Who was on this committee? What powers did it have? When did it meet? What did it do? And finally, where's the paragraph of ethics committee policy that authorised medical professionals to cut holes in treatment files?

A month after that letter, I received a second, from the same manager of assessments. There would be no action taken against Diana Craven. It was too long ago.

'The destruction of these records is noted that to [sic] have had a significant impact on you,' the manager wrote, 'however it does not represent a significant ongoing risk to public health or safety.'

MY FRIEND AT NSW Health urged me to request a review of the HCCC decision. Inside, I felt that I'd given up on the parliamentary process, and the legal process, and now I'd given up on the healthcare regulator. But my friend was right: you should jump through all their hoops. It leaves them with no shred of excuse.

'The HCCC believes code destruction was "accepted practice at the time". By whom?' I wrote. 'If it was, it should have been outlined in government policy documents, medical law, clinical policy, donor confidentiality statements, public hospital codes of practice, etc. What documentation can the HCCC provide to prove that it was an "accepted practice"? Who are you getting that from?

'The HCCC believes code destruction "would have" (that seems lazy) been approved by the "Northern Sydney Local Health District's equivalent Ethics Committee". No-one else has ever claimed this – including Saunders himself … Once again, where is the documentation to support the HCCC's assertion? … Most disturbingly, the HCCC says that in the 1980s "assisted reproduction was considered experimental". Therefore, I am the product of a human experiment,' I wrote. 'Putting to one side the highly irresponsible, hurtful, and damaging way in which the HCCC has communicated to me that I am a human experiment: this is research involving humans, creating live babies. As the HCCC should well know, there are a whole raft of legal and ethical rules which come into play once anyone determines to conduct research involving humans. I am willing to bet the RNSH research most definitely did not comply. If the HCCC chooses not to investigate the human experiments it says were being conducted at the public hospital the Royal North Shore throughout the 1980s, creating hundreds, if not thousands, of live babies, I demand to know the reasons why not … Once again, I ask the HCCC: who are you really acting for?'[3]

The HCCC did not uphold my request for review.

IT'S A TRUTH universally acknowledged that when the government, the law and the system in general fail you, you talk to the media. This is true even for journalists themselves. Pretty much my only avenue left to seek redress, and also maximise chances of finding family, was to go public with the whole thing.

It scared the living hell out of me.

I'd kept most of my personal story inside for years. The thought of broadcasting it was about as appealing as slowly drilling a hole in my own foot. But if you're going to go public, you may as well be as public as possible. I needed to have two awkward workplace conversations: one with my immediate boss in radio current affairs, where I was working at that point, and then with the head of ABC Editorial Policy, Alan Sunderland. Both gave me the go-ahead. I was going to be part of an *Australian Story*.

AUSTRALIAN STORY IS a national half-hour 'award-winning documentary series with no narrator and no agendas – just authentic stories told entirely in people's own words', its website states, a program which puts 'the "real" back into reality television'. The show is a powerhouse. *Australian Story* has massive national reach. People adore it. And it's the perfect vehicle for a personal story, although it's definitely not an unfiltered you talking to an audience. Despite its claims of the 'real', *Australian Story* is highly produced. Any half-hour documentary show which doesn't use a reporter's voiceover is going to have to direct its talent very closely to keep the story moving.

MY PARTICULAR PROGRAM had been years in the making. In 2012, I'd started talking to an *Australian Story* producer, Belinda Hawkins, about what happened to me. She lived in Melbourne, and through a neighbourhood connection had heard about one of my friends, Lauren Burns, who is donor conceived and had just managed to track down her father after four years of searching. Lauren had previously looked up swathes of medical students, to work out if any were her father, without any luck. It was prior to Narelle's Law in Victoria, so Lauren had managed the near-impossible only through the intervention of the doctor who had made her. Fertility specialist Dr David de Kretser had decided he would assist and contacted Lauren's biological father, Ben Clark, on Lauren's behalf.[4]

'I wrote to Ben, indicating that there had been some interest arising out of the research project that he had participated in many years ago,' de Kretser would tell *Australian Story*. There's a troubling term: research project. Like other donors, Ben Clark was open to communication. He and Lauren wrote to each other. Then they spoke on the phone. Then Ben invited her to come visit.

By 2012, Lauren and Ben had met, had a few chats, and their relationship was a friendly one. No hostility is the best you can hope for when you're donor conceived. Of course, there are many of us who hope for much more. And, on some occasions, you get it. But from what I've observed, 'friendly' is a great outcome: it can be much, much worse. People are cruel. Donors can refuse all contact and all answers.

Another recurring experience – which is more hurtful to my mind – is that there will be initial, positive contact with a donor, followed by extreme hostility from his immediate family circle and the end of all contact. From my observations, if he's a male donor and heterosexual, this is almost always led by his wife. Sometimes, the wives of sperm donors feel threatened by us, even though we weren't conceived out of a previous love – or even lust – for a female rival. These wives feel that their worlds are threatened by our petitions for basic answers. In response, they can deploy a scorched-earth policy. They do this even if they know that their husband has donated sperm in the past: these women appear to have buried that knowledge in some dark place, and when we turn up, they react with fury. I've been told of one situation where the wife not only knew her husband was a sperm donor but was in a relationship with him at the time and encouraged him to donate. Yet when his child, an actual human being, tried to contact her husband – as a result of the activities both she and he had explicitly condoned – the response was nuclear.

EVENTUALLY, THE *AUSTRALIAN STORY* program took shape. Lauren decided to go for it. Ben, astonishingly, agreed as well. It turned out Ben was the son of famous Australian historian Manning Clark – who was in turn Lauren's grandfather. This celebrity connection could have been tailor-made for an *Australian Story* audience. Belinda would film with Lauren in Victoria and me in New South Wales.

THE *AUSTRALIAN STORY* became a two-parter, rare for that program, an hour split over two weeks. We'd waited for a long time – I was half convinced it wasn't going to happen at all – and now it was suddenly a double-header. It was the story of Lauren (Mystery! Celebrity! Happy result!) and the late Rel, pieced together from all the file footage shot of her over the years, and me (No answers! Scary questions! Cautionary tale!). It's a bit annoying to be reduced to someone's tragic case study, but it was, probably, good for me. Every journalist should cede control of their own story to someone else once in their life. It gives you a bit of insight into what you ask members of the public to do every single day: how much you expect them to trust you. Except, of course,

I'm a journalist myself, so I wasn't going to surrender totally. The weekend in between the two broadcasts, I wrote a long, first-person feature for Fairfax newspapers' *Good Weekend* magazine. It was called 'Misconception', and it had all that I wanted to say which *Australian Story* hadn't covered.

'Let me be clear: I don't need another parent,' I wrote in that article. 'I couldn't have asked for a better father than the man who brought me up. But I could do with some answers about why I am the way I am, who my family is, and what genetic time bombs I should watch out for. I would like to know who my biological father is, and to have an amicable relationship with him. You'd think that the former, at least, would be a legal right.

'The reality is that I'll live my entire life as an only child who probably has more brothers and sisters than most people I know ... What happened to me in the 1980s could be happening right now. There is no national law keeping this industry's practices in check or protecting the rights of the child. Without the right to the truth about our genetic origins, donor-conceived people will remain products of industry, not human beings.'[5]

THE POWER OF television is in pictures and emotion, not details. The problem that Belinda encountered in my case was there was no-one to speak for me – except me. *Australian Story* relies on families, and sweet, counterpoint interviews with pathos. You don't get that if there's no family. Except my mother, and she was a whole other kettle of fish.

What happened with my mother, in a way, illustrates much of what is wrong with donor conception and the damage it does. There had been no support for my mother, or father, to deal with their own very personal involvement in a government-sanctioned human experiment. There was no follow-up. No encouragement to tell the truth, or parenting tips. In fact, there was the opposite – there was shame, and active encouragement to lie. She had only told me the truth after twenty-seven years, and it hadn't been easy since.

My mother had initially agreed to be part of the *Australian Story*. I'd said I didn't want to be involved in any of those negotiations: it was her choice. Belinda had a long chat to her over the phone. Apparently it was a positive one. I was dubious. You don't wind back all of that history of hurt and secrecy in one conversation. Belinda set up a shoot, flew herself to Sydney and turned up at my mother's flat. My mother said she didn't want to do it. That was it.

Hearing about it afterwards, I felt guilty. Was I being unreasonable to be part of a TV story in the first place? Did my mother feel like she'd been forced into something? But – on the other hand – wasn't that the whole heart of this problem? People not being told the truth? People not being asked or having a say?

As it turned out, my mother had decided she didn't want any of this made public at all. A lot of donor-conceived people who want to be more open about their lives face this pressure from family at least once, if not all the time. There's the incredibly common, 'I'd like to try to contact my biological parent, because it's important to me, but it would upset my social mother/father/mothers/fathers/everyone', or the 'I really support changes in the law, but I can't speak about it because it would hurt <insert family member here>'. If you've already had half (or more) of your family ripped away from you, you're understandably quite reluctant to risk any more.

This is, in a word, shit. It puts the donor-conceived person always in the position of trying to make everything okay, not for themselves but for everyone else, scrambling to make things right for the very people who created the problem you are in. Even though you love them and they love you. That's never going to end well. (I would add: it's impossible to control anyone's happiness except your own.)

I don't expect anyone, least of all my mother, to speak to a journalist if they really don't want to. You always have a right to say no. I was actually a bit relieved she didn't do the interview; I didn't think she was ready – a suspicion borne out. But, conversely, there is always a right to say yes, and choose to speak to a journalist. You can't stop other people from doing something just because you don't want to do it yourself.

It's a terrible question. Where does the individual end and the family begin? Who owns the truth of your collective unit?

Every culture, and every family, has a different answer. But the answer I came up with for me, which I still hold, is that I have the right to the truth about my own life, and I have the right to tell it if I choose. This was my truth: believed a lie till twenty-seven, fought for access to files, found those files had been deliberately tampered with, zero redress, zero justice, zero change, zero apology from the medical sector, the law, or government. I watched my friend careen towards death without answers, the same answers I was fighting for myself.

The difference between my mother and I was perspective. I was attempting (with only limited success) to understand what on earth had happened in the baby business: the whole damn thing. My mother was trying not to think about any of it. That goes back to what the fertility clinic told her to do at the very start. Go home, and pretend it never happened.

I'm glad I told my story publicly, because being restrained from doing so when I was already so snookered by all other parts of the system would have been maddening. But there was a price. After the resulting *Australian Story* 'Searching for C11' aired in 2014, my relationship with my mother took a nosedive for quite some time.

Everything usually ends happily on *Australian Story*, but here's the thing that bothered me about 'Searching for C11': donor conception is not a happy tale. There are some donor-conceived people who are very happy about how their lives began and are, and I love that. Their stories are often beautiful, and their views are important. What these people have in common is total openness with their parents, right from the start. Their families give them the truth and understand their need to know, if not connect with, biological relatives. These families show how it can be.

But of the 2000 donor-conceived people I'm in touch with, it seems to me like the 100 per cent happy ones are definitely the minority. The majority have had, or more often still have, significant concerns – which largely go ignored. Donor conception is not miracle babies from good-looking, clever, famous strangers. It can be deeply fraught for all parties, but most of all the child.

CHAPTER 19

I DON'T WANT TO sound ungrateful about *Australian Story*. There was a huge response to 'Searching for C11'. The power of that program, and its reach, is undeniable. For many viewers, I think, 'Searching for C11' humanised donor-conceived people. Until then, we were eternal infants in people's minds. Before that *Australian Story*, to the mainstream, it was largely the parents who mattered: either the tragic couple who couldn't have babies, or the blissfully 'modern' family with a cuckoo child of their very own. After the *Australian Story*, audiences began to realise that babies grow up – and it's not okay to lie to them.

Lauren had gone travelling by the time Part 1 finally aired. She'd decided to take some time out, so the media requests came to me. I was doing live Q&As (which, as a journalist, was fine) about my personal life (which was excruciating). 'What does your mother think about you doing all this?' was one predictable question.

Fortunately, the act of writing for *Good Weekend* not only made me feel like I'd actually said what I needed to say, but it had also forced me to puzzle out how to say it. Explaining everything in my own words then allowed me to repeat those words without pain. Well, mostly.

One interview wrapped and another started. After the broadcast of Part 2, I took the next few days off work and hid. Social media, of course, was worse; at least all of the journalists I spoke to kept it civil. There were a lot of men online making a lot of remarks about sperm. Classic Neanderthal stuff. I blocked the lot.

I WOULD MAKE the same choice again. Going public with my own story unwound something in me. I didn't feel like I had something dark and huge to hide, at work, with friends, with family. It was already out there. I didn't have to feel frustrated that certain things would be difficult for me to discuss and it would hurt me to explain why. If someone had missed the show, or not read my article, or any of the other articles or stories or interviews I'd done on donor conception since, well, it wasn't my fault. I was being ridiculously upfront.

One reason why I'd done this was a last attempt at finding my biological father. I'd exhausted all other avenues, including my own research (translation: I was sick of talking to misfits from the internet). From the million-plus audience each episode of *Australian Story* draws, I thought some men might come forward. But life doesn't work like that.

Out of all those viewers, just one man got in touch with me. Turns out he was a selfish, self-absorbed crank. All he wanted to do, I realised with growing scorn, was whine to me about some legal dispute he was in regarding his own biological son whom he'd fathered through a social relationship and then abandoned. He was outraged the boy wanted to be recognised as his child. It had nothing to do with me or donor conception whatsoever. What a prince. I hung up.

But the good far, far outweighed the bad. What I hadn't anticipated was how many donor-conceived people would contact me after *Australian Story* and *Good Weekend*, both to say thank you for sharing some of the less puppies-and-rainbows stuff, and more importantly just to say hi and tell me a bit about themselves. Mostly, they'd never spoken to another donor-conceived person before. Given how many of us there are, I cannot stress how weird this is. It's like an adoptee growing up, becoming an adult, starting their own family, all the while being the only adoptee on earth. Never seeing another adoptee's story, never even reading about one. Keeping it all inside, to save other people face, at your own private cost. Something that big should not be something you have to hide or bear all on your own. Particularly when there are lots just like you.

Damian, Myf and my other donor-conceived friends had run an online forum for years, but we needed something more immediate.

Facebook, I suggested. We created a Facebook group just for donor-conceived people. No would-be parents (who packed out most other spaces online, with their incessant pleas for sperm, eggs or embryos); no parents of donor-conceived people speaking instead of their own children. No agencies. No 'experts'. No-one but us. It was only for Australians. Each time someone got in touch with me, I asked them if they wanted to be part of the group. They usually did. Donor conceived issues gained traction in the media and more of us started doing interviews. Every time that happened, more people would join. Then the group expanded to include New Zealanders. We're trans-Tasman cousins, after all.

There were a few soul-searching moments: once, I remember, we had a request to join from the mother of a twelve-year-old donor-conceived child, so that her kid could ask us questions. She felt her kid was too young to have a Facebook account themselves, so she wanted in on her child's behalf. We considered it. Many of us grew up not knowing other donor-conceived people and suffering in some way because of it. Not knowing others in your complex situation is not good. And it's a big deal to suddenly be potentially lumbered with a twelve-year-old's mental health. But ultimately, we said no. The rules were the rules. We had a safe space for us, only us, and there would be no parents. We didn't know why this mother wanted in: there are crazies out there, believe me. A lot of commissioning parents online simply want us to legitimise their choices. They want us to say that everything is fine, or if we won't, they want to be able to dismiss us as dysfunctional. Quite a few of us have been attacked, or removed, or even doxxed, for trying to talk about the rights of the child. There was at least one group literally for happy people in donor conception, with many parents of donor-conceived people and donors as members. If you're in that group and not happy about your own donor conception, you get kicked out. They don't want to hear it; it's a massive red flag.[1]

Our donor-conceived-people-only Facebook group grew and grew. Currently, we have more than 450 members, one of the biggest such groups of donor-conceived nationals anywhere in the world.

One of the donor-conceived people who contacted me after *Australian Story* was a woman called Rebecca. She was also made at the

Royal North Shore. *Well*, I said, and there followed a long discussion about Clinic 20.

Bec had known since she was eleven that she was donor conceived. This, in theory, is a good thing: the earlier you know the truth, the easier it will be to deal with. But, like so many of us, Bec had found out the truth in a horrible way. Her parents hadn't told her. But they'd told some adult friends. The friends had casually mentioned it to their daughter, who was the same age as Bec. Then Bec's parents split up and her father remarried.

'It was the night after my dad got married for the second time and I was staying with [that girl],' Bec told me. It was a sleepover. 'I was feeling a bit down because I guess my new stepmother wasn't a fan of the fact that I existed, to put it bluntly … and this little friend … just looked at me and said, "Well, I don't know why you're so upset. He's not your real dad anyway."'

Eleven-year-old Bec had no idea what to make of this astonishing, upsetting statement, so she parked it. Some time later, she asked her mother about it. Her mother was chopping up vegetables for dinner.

'And Mum just froze,' said Bec. 'She stopped chopping, and she just kind of stared ahead for a minute. And that was the first time I realised, oh my god. It's true. I didn't really take it seriously until that point.'

Bec's mother explained it as best she could: she said that because Bec's father didn't have a very high sperm count, they used someone else's sperm to 'boost the numbers', in Bec's words. Bec says her mother was told by the clinic that her father's sperm would be 'mixed in' with the donor's sperm, so there would be a 'chance' that her father might still be her biological father.

'But then Mum said [Clinic 20] never took a sperm sample from my dad,' Bec said. 'So I'm no geneticist, but I'm pretty sure that means it's a slim to none chance.'

Bec didn't have a file from RNSH/IVF Australia, so I told her to ask her mother to apply for it. Eventually, it appeared. And Bec's donor code had also been cut out. She was the first other RNSH kid I'd met, and they'd done to her exactly what they'd done to me.

WE MET UP in a cafe in the city, both with files, and compared them. This piece of paper the same, that form for your mum, can't find that for my mum, and so on. It was exciting. And fun. We became good friends. Bec is lovely. She's tall, with curly brown hair, green eyes and Mediterranean olive skin: her mother is Italian. We're just two months apart in age. Bec has worked as an occupational therapist in a public hospital; she understands the vagaries of the state health system in a way I don't. She's warm and generous. And she's super sharp – after she got that file, she was coming up with some damn good questions in zero time.

'You know,' she said one day to me on the phone, 'there's that law in New South Wales, the one that says we're not legally the children of our sperm donor.'

'Yeah?' I said. She meant the *Artificial Conception Act 1984*, intended to prevent donor-conceived individuals from making financial demands of their donors. That law had been raised before, usually by those in power, to rebuff people like us.

But Bec had thought of something else, and it was brilliant.

'Well,' she said, 'that law was passed in 1984. But we were born in 1983. Does that mean we *are* the legal children of our sperm donors?'

I blinked. Then laughed out loud. 'You should've been a lawyer,' I said. Her reply was unprintable.

THE *ARTIFICIAL CONCEPTION ACT 1984* remained in force in New South Wales until it was replaced by the *Status of Children Act 1996* (which contained similar provisions). If you're surprised that such a law existed in New South Wales in the early '80s, so am I. Neither foresight nor legislation are the hallmarks of fertility treatment. However, a reading of this (short) Act makes it clear that this is situation normal. This law protects men, ignores women, and incidentally condones the troubling practice of sperm mixing.

The *Artificial Conception Act 1984* is that startling piece of legislation which says when a woman becomes pregnant using donor sperm, the donor shall be presumed not to have caused the pregnancy.

As previously discussed, the world's first pregnancy using a donor egg was reported in Melbourne in 1983, and the world's first live birth following an egg donation was reported by an American team in 1984. Yet the *Artificial Conception Act 1984* doesn't make any mention of egg donors – all donors are 'semen donors' – which raises the fascinating question as to whether women who donated in New South Wales from 1984 until 1996 were still the legal mothers of the children produced (and, presumably, could have been hit up for money). The Act says it applies even if the sperm used on the woman 'was a mixture of semen, part of which was produced by a man other than her husband and part of which was produced by her husband'. Yes, sperm mixing is acknowledged in law.

Bec's idea – that because she and I were born prior to the *Artificial Conception Act 1984*, we were the sperm donor's legal children – was a hilariously clever one. But when I read through the Act, it became clear that we'd missed something. 'The provisions of this Act apply … whether the pregnancy occurred before or after the commencement of this Act … [and] whether or not the child was born before or after the commencement of this Act.'

The *Artificial Conception Act 1984* applied to all time.

Funny how the fertility clinics didn't howl and carry on about the unfairness of that particular retrospective law.

AFTER THE *AUSTRALIAN STORY* program went to air, I formed a support group for donor-conceived people in New South Wales. I'd had a few chats with Amnesty International, who were sympathetic towards our right to know family, and they agreed to let us use their office. It was centrally located in the heart of the CBD and there was always at least one Amnesty person working there late, keeping it open.

So I put the word out on Facebook. It started one evening after work. I brought gin. Bec, more sensibly, brought crackers and dips. And we waited. Soon people started to turn up; in the end, there were eight of us. Eight. Whereas just a few years ago I didn't know a single one. Where the NSW Government couldn't find anyone else in the state apart from me. And, even more remarkably – there were not one but two guys.

From going to donor-conceived meet-ups in Melbourne, I knew that donor-conceived men were almost like unicorns. Donor-conceived men seemed less likely than donor-conceived women to talk about this stuff, be open about it or seek answers. It's more common for the men to bury it. Even if they grow up knowing the truth, many of them pack it away in their minds, either because they can't deal with it, or because they don't want to, or both. I know heaps of donor-conceived men now, of course, who are the exact opposite: but the more you know others like you, the more likely it is that you'll feel okay talking about all of this.

The Melbourne meetings were run under the auspices of VARTA – the Victorian Assisted Reproductive Treatment Agency. VARTA, formerly known as the Infertility Treatment Authority, acts for all parties in assisted reproduction: commissioning parents, donors, clinics and us, the products. A VARTA counsellor usually attended the Melbourne meet-ups for donor-conceived people. That didn't sit right with me. New South Wales doesn't have a VARTA equivalent, but even if we did, I wouldn't include them. I'd founded this support group because everything else about the system had failed us. I was tired of gatekeepers and mediators. I certainly wasn't doing this so an outside 'expert' could sit there and psychoanalyse. We were all adults and yet no-one treated us as such. This group was just for donor-conceived people, to vent, to say anything they wanted without the exhausting self-censorship that weighs us down in every other forum: talking in public, talking to doctors and government, talking to family.

I can't tell you exactly what was said in those meetings, of course – you don't found a support group to publish its secrets. The numbers changed every week, but we had a great mix of occasional attendees, walk-ins and regulars. I can tell you that G&Ts were drunk, absolutely terrible jokes were made, and we shared – a lot. Donor conception isn't something you can, shall we say, set and forget. It's baked into your family. It's always there, acknowledged or no. And as such it can affect the entire family unit, in a myriad of ways, for life.

If there's a complex problem in the family – for example, long-term illness, any form of abuse, messy divorce or separation, substance addiction, tragedy – donor conception can almost always be relied upon to make everything worse. No-one in our group had the same story, but every story had similarities. No-one had had it easy. And no-one in that group had so far been able to find their donor or their siblings.

THE FALLOUT FROM telling my story on national television continued. I received an email through my work account, from a woman I'll call Lucy.

'I worked at Royal Prince Alfred Hospital in the '80s,' Lucy wrote. The Royal Prince Alfred is another major public hospital in Sydney, which backs onto the sandstone of Sydney University. Lucy said that she'd been a medical forensic photographer at RPAH, and her unit also worked with Sydney University. She and her colleagues 'became close friends with the many scientists/doctors in various areas and you would be shocked to hear some of the stories they told over lunch.'

'It was hot talk among staff re: the scientists/doctors being the primary donors for IVF due to their own knowledge of biological, health and physical attributes often sort [sic] by parents,' I read. 'There was much excitement and interaction between the Royal Prince Alfred Hospital and the Royal North Shore Hospital [Clinic 20] with exchanging ideas and celebrating successes. It was well accepted that sperm donors were keep [sic] to a minimum based on successful inseminations/health of the sperm and availability of donors inhouse.' Ugh. In-house donors: why ever step outside the hospital doors.

'At RPAH only a handful of interns or staff were used regularly as the norm,' Lucy confided. 'Who knows how many children these individuals fathered.'

I was so grateful to this woman for getting in touch. But, as always, the more I found out, the more repulsed I became. Was doctors getting their mates to donate worse than getting their students to donate? Or was the worst of all the doctors themselves inseminating their own female patients? Maybe. Probably. It's all bad.

'Your story I feel is not an isolated incident,' Lucy wrote. 'Perhaps look closer at the original technicians and doctors on the IVF program when you were conceived.'

Oh god. A pit opened in my stomach.

Lucy had been moved to write to me, she said, because I'd exposed donor code destruction at the Royal North Shore Hospital. 'Your story rang alarm bells as RPAH records were often found to be tampered with when a doctor or technician moved on or a department restructured,' she wrote. More destruction of information? In another public hospital? How many were we even up to now? I jotted down a quick list of Australian fertility clinics where, one by one, donor-conceived people had told me their records had been destroyed. Six in New South Wales. The biggest fertility business in Queensland. The private practices of at least two fertility specialists in Victoria. Another major public hospital in South Australia, Queen Elizabeth's Hospital. That's at least ten baby factories in four different states deliberately getting rid of the evidence.

This is beyond any state parliamentary inquiry, I thought. This is national. This is Royal Commission stuff. I had no authority to make these hospitals, clinics and individuals divulge their secrets. I was just someone they'd trampled along the way.

At the bottom of her email, Lucy explained further why she was writing. She was an adoptee, absorbed into a new family at the start of the 1960s.

'I also would like to find my biological father,' she said. 'His name wasn't recorded, however I know my natural family know who he is but it's hidden by "generational secrecy" – they say "there's no need to visit the past". I have lived a whole life not knowing who I am biologically. It's cruel.

'Babies are not commodities,' she told me, 'they are people. Laws need to be rewritten. We are entitled to an identity and knowledge of our genetic makeup just like everyone else.' I'm with you, Lucy.

'It's a small world out there, and from my own experience of meeting my biological brother (then unknown to me) and being attracted to him, heaven help the outcome if we had become lovers,' Lucy confessed. 'The medical profession seems to create all these anomalies without much concern for the future fatalities, emotion [sic] and physical.'[2]

Being attracted to your own family: horrifically disturbing. And yet another aspect of donor conception that the industry doesn't want to talk about.

CHAPTER 20

ACCIDENTAL INCEST. The polite term, coined in the '80s by American writer Barbara Gonyo, herself biological mother of an adoptee, is genetic sexual attraction or GSA.[1] Four decades later, the risk of GSA, in the context of adoption at least, is gaining recognition. I came across an adoption support document on GSA from Cumbria County Council, in north-west England:

'What some adopted people and their natural relatives lack is a shared experience of childhood to provide a common frame of reference for their feelings,' it says. 'Bringing up a child from birth to adulthood, or being reared with other siblings by one parent allows us to safely label our emotions within the context of the family. The danger occurs when blood relatives meet as adults without that shared experience, and then try to reconstitute the family relationship without being able to put a familiar label on their emotions.'[2]

Now imagine that up to 90 per cent of the people you're talking about have not only been brought up in isolation from their biological family, but don't know that they have some, or dozens, or even hundreds of other half-siblings out there. 'Genetic sexual attraction … occurs between two consenting adults who may know nothing of their familial ties prior to meeting and, in some cases, have no idea they are even related when they meet. This phenomenon is believed to be caused by several factors, mainly the fact that there is a basic human attraction towards those who have similar physical attributes to us,' says the adoption support information from Cumbria County Council.

I wanted to scrub my brain. I ran through all my exes. I'm probably okay, I thought frantically. Here's a tip: it helps to date mostly foreigners. That's my gift to you, dear reader. After all, your parents could be lying to you, too. Unfortunately, as a rough rule of thumb, dating foreigners is only a protective factor for those born in the twentieth century. Thanks to this century's rising global trade in gametes, for younger donor-conceived people that's no longer any guarantee of safety.

The council website lists no less than four different UK support groups and hotlines which can help those in adoption address any concerns they may have about genetic sexual attraction, in addition, of course, to 'your adoption support Social Worker'.

What do donor-conceived people like me have? Nothing between us and the horror.

ONE OF MY donor-conceived friends in Australia once spoke to me about her concerns that she'd briefly dated a half-sibling. She hadn't found her donor, or his biological family, but at least she knew the truth about herself. When she realised early on that her date was donor conceived too, it was 100 per cent over. Being able to protect herself like that, however, didn't make it any less disturbing.

The full range of consequences of genetic sexual attraction are serious. GSA doesn't just harm your mental health: the risk of genetic abnormalities is high.

The risks for children born of incest – or 'consanguineous [same blood] relationships', as it's also known – start with cousins. The authors of an article 'Inbreeding and Genetic Disorder' in the 2011 book *Advances in the Study of Genetic Disorders* say that consanguineous marriage 'is usually defined as a union between individuals who are related as second cousin or closer'. 'In general,' the authors say, 'the rarer the disease, the higher the proportion of consanguineous marriage among the parents of affected individuals. Similarly, the closer the inbreeding, the higher the effect.' Much of the article discusses the outcomes for children born of the unions of first cousins. Relationships closer than that are taboo around the world, the authors note: 'Regarding incestuous unions between biological first degree relatives (father-daughter, mother-son, brother-sister), a universal taboo for nuclear family mating exists in all societies.'[3]

It's taboo and illegal, yes. Including in my own country. The *Federal Marriage Act 1961* (Cth)[4] specifies that a marriage is void where it is between a person and their whole- or half-blood brother or sister. But no-one gives donor-conceived people the information they need not to break the law – or fully protect themselves from such a devastating act.

A FEW YEARS back, I reported for the ABC that I had obtained the personal sperm donation records of one donor in Sydney. This man, it seems, was the careful, diarising type. I called him John.

'Set out on two pieces of pink notepaper are the personal records of how many times a single man donated sperm around Sydney. For the record: 318 times,' I reported.

John had donated his sperm to six different fertility clinics. Six. They included the fertility clinics of five of the biggest public hospitals in Sydney.

'John's serial sperm donations occurred not in the distant past, but as late as the '90s,' I wrote. 'John made his sperm donations under the condition of anonymity. What that means is his own biological children would never know who he was, or (far worse in this particular situation) they wouldn't know who all their half-siblings were.'

John's sperm donating zeal was not documented by any Australian national register, because there isn't one. It also wasn't picked up by any state-based register, because there wasn't one of those either in New South Wales until 2010.

How many children John has fathered as a result of his activities is unknown. It all rests on how fertile John was. You can make multiple straws of semen from a single donation. (One ejaculate, a leading fertility specialist tells me, can be used for seven or eight inseminations. Other fertility clinics say anywhere from five to twenty.) Each straw is a treatment. Each straw can, potentially, become a child. It also seems unlikely that these five public hospitals would have been keen for John to donate sperm hundreds of times if his sperm was, to be blunt, completely useless. It is reasonable to assume that John was able to father children.

How many children, then, could John have? John may have fathered as few (!) as dozens of children. But, if he was particularly fertile, he might have fathered thousands – all in the same city. My city. Does the risk of accidental incest seem more real now? And John is just one serial sperm donor. There were, and are, many others.

WRITING FOR THE UK's *The Spectator* magazine, on the fortieth anniversary of the first IVF baby, journalist Ross Clark said there were plenty of children unknowingly born of affairs in the UK, 'but that is a risk which is hard for government to guard against. The increasing number of children who are conceived with donor eggs or donor sperm — an activity that is regulated by the state — is quite another matter ... it recently emerged that there are seventeen men who have each fathered at least thirty children via donating their sperm and a further 104 with between twenty and twenty-nine children.'[5] Or, as *The Telegraph* put it, 'Seventeen British sperm donors have fathered more than 500 children between them, new figures show.'[6]

In the UK, only donor-conceived people born after April 2005 have the right to access identifying information about their donor, once they turn eighteen.[7] (Unless anonymous gametes donated pre-April 2005 were used, in which case: tough.) Britain, like most states of Australia except New South Wales and Western Australia, also has a donation limit of ten families. In Australia, we know this limit is broken even when set out in law, as the former VARTA worker Kate Dobby told the Victorian Parliament in 2010.

Let's assume, though, that Britain is better. Let's assume the rules are followed. Even if all clinics obey a ten-family limit, having seventeen men who each father at least thirty children doesn't seem surprising; it is, instead, foreseeable. None of these children have a right to know all their donor-conceived siblings.

In the UK, once a donor-conceived person turns sixteen, they can know how many donor-conceived siblings they have, their ages and genders. That's it. Once they turn eighteen, they may register for Donor Sibling Link, which will facilitate contact between them and any of their siblings who have also registered. If no other sibling has registered, again: tough.

But the UK also has another surprising, horrifying, resource for some donor-conceived people. Those who are sixteen or older, and worried that they're having sex with a half-sibling, can apply to a government regulator to find out if they're related to their new crush. 'If you're over sixteen and are thinking about starting a physical relationship with someone, you can make a joint application to us to find out if you're genetically related,' the website of the UK's Human Fertilisation and Embryology Authority says cheerily.[8]

I find it hard to take in the fact that that process even exists. Who on earth thought this would solve the problem? Think of all the sixteen-year-olds you know. What poor kid, grappling with all the crap that being late-teens brings, and finding someone they like, and having sex for perhaps the first time in their lives or even just considering it – what poor kid is going to say to their new boyfriend or girlfriend, hey, let's make a formal application to a government authority to find out if we're siblings?

While I find it particularly unconscionable that teenagers are left in this situation, alone, without the basic information they need to protect themselves, the UK measures are good, relatively speaking. Because at least there exists a national government regulator of the fertility sector, with a website, which has a mechanism to allow some people to check if they're committing accidental incest.

No such service exists in Australia. Nor in the US. To say nothing of other countries all around the world.

IN 2010, AN Australian politician sounded the alarm in Federal Parliament. Joanna Gash was the longstanding Member for Gilmore, an electorate on New South Wales' beautiful south coast. On 25 October 2010, Jo Gash rose to speak – but not about tourism, fisheries or agriculture. Instead, it was something completely out of left field. Something which had surfaced in her electorate, which worried her.[9]

'Several months ago I was having a regular catch-up with the CEO of the local division of GPs when we stumbled upon an interesting topic: unintended marriages between siblings and the potential side effects for their children. Some say that the occurrence of this kind of extraordinary situation is on the rise, with the increasing uptake of IVF technologies as well as changing attitudes within our society about children and marriage,' Ms Gash told Federal Parliament. She called for those affected to contact her office.

As Gash told Gilmore newspaper the *Illawarra Mercury*, her concerns were not abstract. 'Mrs Gash said she knew of one case in her electorate in which a half-brother and half-sister married without knowing they were related. It is understood no children have yet been conceived,' the *Mercury* reported.[10]

'You wonder how many people there are [in that situation] ... you don't find out unless you have a blood test,' Mrs Gash said. 'I thought it was time to bring it up. Maybe it will start people thinking about where they come from, because some people don't know enough, and the repercussions can be quite severe.'

This is the first and only instance I can find of anyone publicly warning that accidental incest between donor-conceived siblings in Australia is not only a real risk – but has already occurred. A decade on, I rang Jo Gash to find out more. Had that poor couple split up? What happened? She told me the case had come through a senior medical professional. I contacted the medical professional, who was unable to disclose further details. At the best of times, doctor–patient confidentiality and privacy are big things to negotiate – let alone on something as upsetting as this.

In 2010, Jemma Tribe was a key staffer to Jo Gash. She says the prospect of raising accidental incest in Federal Parliament caused major concerns in the office.[11]

'Jo was hoping to start a conversation about it,' Jemma Tribe told me. 'Most MPs will rave about a service in their electorate which will get them a write-up in the local paper. Bringing up a topic like that isn't what everyone wants to hear, necessarily.' (Understatement of the year.) 'We were hearing from someone in the industry that two donor-conceived people had married and wanted to start their own family.

What would that mean if we don't have any mechanism in place to prevent that?'

But accidental incest is an awful topic for any conversation, let alone politics. After the *Mercury* article came out, Jemma Tribe said, '... it didn't really go any further ... I think a lot of people were very uncomfortable about it at the time'.

At least Jo Gash said something. At least she tried.

WHAT IS THE risk of accidental incest among donor-conceived siblings? The answer depends on the donor, the clinic and the country. Even in the (better) regulated places, it's probably higher than you might think.

Ross Clark had a stab at estimating it in his *Spectator* piece, 'The Incest Trap'. 'Take [one] man who has fathered thirty children [in the UK]. The risk of at least one of his children entering into an incestuous relationship rises to one in 18,000,' wrote Clark. Clark was making some key assumptions, it's true: for simplicity's sake, he was assuming half the children were male, half were female, all would be heterosexual and all marry someone, from Britain, within five years of their own age. Within those parameters, then, Clark estimated: 'The risk that at least one of those seventeen sperm donors will father children who go on to have an incestuous relationship rises to one in 1060.'

However, there's a few other things to take into account. 'This [rate of 1 in 1060] assumes that use of donor sperm is widely dispersed about the country and that relationships are random. Neither of these is the case,' wrote Ross Clark. That, certainly, is correct. We've already covered genetic sexual attraction. And equidistant dispersion of donor sperm is neither the case in the UK, nor in Australia, the US, nor anywhere. You can't assume that all commissioning parents will naturally self-distance their new donor-conceived families across a nation, spacing themselves evenly. And yet this is a myth which prevails.

In 2019, two Brisbane parents were shocked to find out that their own donor-conceived children had not one but three half-siblings living in the same neighbourhood. Same-sex couple Shannon Ashton and Lisa Quinn had used a 'blue-eyed surfer' as a sperm donor to make their kids. Turns out, so did a lot of others. Ashton and Quinn have five kids in their family unit. Those five children have another forty-three donor-conceived siblings, three living locally. One was in the same daycare group as one of Ashton and Quinn's own daughters. Suddenly, the chance of meeting a half-sibling was a dead cert.[12]

Ashton and Quinn had IVF, using this donor, at the biggest fertility operation in Queensland, the private Queensland Fertility Group. When they discovered just how close to home their kids' siblings were, QFG's Dr David Molloy had to downplay this revelation: 'It is usually planned that the mothers would live thousands of miles away from each other,' he told the media. (How can he possibly plan that? Are doctors forcing pregnant women to live in houses spaced out across the Simpson Desert?) 'It is also a very rare situation that there would be five children from the same sperm donor in one family,' he said. What? QFG helped them to do so in the first place.

Apart from the ridiculousness of assuming that commissioning parents who are utterly unknown to other commissioning parents will, somehow, self-distance from each other, there's also the confounding factor of physical matching to consider – a phenomenon which is practised by both commissioning parents and the clinics themselves. In my case, it was done wholly by Clinic 20 staff. They noted my dad's height, eye colour, hair colour, and so on, and then found a sperm donor to 'match'. This would, in turn, facilitate the lie that I was my dad's child. In *The Spectator*, UK-based Ross Clark wrote: 'Donors tend to be matched physically with the people to whom they are donating – with the result that [the donated material] is more likely to be used in the same community and same part of the country where it is donated.'

Clark argues that the British government should impose far stricter limits on donor conception in order to prevent incest, a problem which, he says, the government has been reluctant to even consider. 'No government has been brave enough to interfere with a process that allows single women and same-sex couples to bear children (one of whom, in the latter case, is the natural parent),' he wrote. 'Why not limit sperm and egg donors to donating to a single family – and preferably draw them from people who do not have their own children?' I can only imagine the howls of protest from the fertility sector if each donor were only allowed to donate to a single family. Unlike removing anonymity, this probably would destroy their supply chain.[13]

But in terms of government reluctance to move against same-sex couples or single women who desire to be parents: that's not the full picture. There is a tendency to assume that donor conception is mostly or only practised by same-sex couples and single women. This is not the case. The majority of donor-conceived people I am in touch with are the children of heterosexual commissioning couples. In fact, in years gone by – and in some jurisdictions to this day – singles and same-sex couples were, and are, specifically excluded from accessing donor conception.[14]

The damage in donor conception, for decades, was done solely for and by heterosexual commissioning parents. To ignore that is to ignore most of us.

No government is brave enough to protect all the donor-conceived children of heterosexual couples from harm, either. And, as we have seen, heterosexuals, unlike same-sex couples, can lie about using fertility treatment in the first place.

I WOULD LIKE to be able to run the same rough calculations as Clark and come up with an idea of the risk of accidental incest among Australian donor-conceived people. But I can't. I don't have any numbers to begin with. Because as bad as seventeen British men fathering more than 510 children around the country may be, at least Britain knows about it.

In Australia, we don't keep that data, and we never have.

CHAPTER 21

As more Australians joined our group online, I'd become aware of other big networks of donor-conceived people, too: lots of us from around the world. It was the strangest, most delightful relief. Suddenly, I could ask anything about donor conception that popped into my head, and a dozen people from multiple nations would reply, most of whom were probably wondering the same. In these fora, no aspect of being DC is taboo. Including how donor-conceived people themselves feel about the risk of accidental incest.

I threw the question out to one of the international groups on Facebook: 'Have you ever worried that you actually *have* dated a half-sibling (i.e., had reason to think they were a half-sibling) – or ever had a near-miss sibling dating experience?'[1]

Nearly thirty people responded, some in-depth: it seemed to be a common fear. Mostly 'no' responses came back to the second part of the question, along with some interesting self-protection measures (always dating foreigners or people obviously of another race were risk mitigation strategies, conscious or otherwise). But a few people from the US had troubling stories. 'I messed around with a boy in high school then years later we found out we were both DC. There is only one sperm bank in Montana and only a handful of donors when we were conceived. He hasn't done a DNA test or anything,' said one. 'I did get a really strong deja vu feeling when I met my bio-dad in person,' wrote another. 'He reminded me SO MUCH of this one guy I dated in high school it was uncanny.' 'Yes, a fear I had,' replied a third. 'Turns out it was well founded as my half brother was in the same year at school and only one town over in our rural area. My social, donor-conceived, brother and I both married immigrants and I don't think that's a coincidence.'

A fourth person pointed me to a 'Dear Prudence' advice segment, hosted on washingtonpost.com and *Slate*. The advice of this particular 'Dear Prudence' was given by Emily Yoffe, contributing editor of *The Atlantic*, to a male reader who wrote:

'When my wife and I met in college, the attraction was immediate, and we quickly became inseparable,' said the man. 'We had a number of things in common, we came from the same large metropolitan area, and we both wanted to return there after school, so everything was very natural between us. We married soon after graduation, moved back closer to our families, and had three children by the time we were thirty.' Both the man and his wife were donor conceived. He'd never bothered to trace his sperm donor, although his wife had found out who hers was, and thought her husband should too. You can guess what's coming.

'Our anniversary is coming up and I decided to go ahead and, as a present to my wife, see if my biological father was interested in contact as well.' (Oh no.) 'He was, and even though our parents had used different sperm banks, it appears so did our father, as he is the same person.'

The same donor, donating sperm at different places: something that can only be prevented by a compulsory, policed, broad-based donor register.

'I can't help but think "This is my sister" every time I look at [my wife] now,' the man continued. 'I haven't said anything to her yet, and I don't know if I should or not. Where do I go from here? I am tempted to burn everything I got from the sperm bank and just try to forget it all, but I'm not sure if I can.'

Emily Yoffe replied: 'I understand your desire to burn everything. But if you are now looking at your wife and thinking, "Hey, sis," I don't see how you can keep this information to yourself.'

Yoffe recommends 'seeking out a counsellor who deals with reproductive technology' and finally, jarringly, adds: 'I don't see why your healthy children should ever be informed of this ... I think there's way too much emphasis put on DNA. Yes, you two will have had a shock, but when it wears off you will be the same people you were before you found out ... I think you two should be able to file away your genetic origins and go on.'[12]

I definitely don't agree with lying to the next generation, the children of these two donor-conceived people, about the truth of their origins and the key to their own physical health. And I have no idea what Yoffe is suggesting by filing this information away and going on. Just keep having sex with your half-sister, because you've already had kids anyway?

I'm finding this hard to write. I'm sorry. I know it isn't pleasant to read either.

THE BEST WAY to prevent genetic sexual attraction, and accidental incest, is to know who is in your biological family. This includes *all* biological siblings. For a commissioning parent, it is not good enough to say, well, I won't lie to my own donor-conceived child about their origins – if they ask – and think they will be safe. They will never be safe if they have 200 unknown siblings out there, to say nothing of the donor(s) themselves. You are leaving them to deal with that on their own.

That Cumbria County Council information for adoptees is interesting. The phenomenon of genetic sexual attraction, it says, is 'overridden within families due to the Westermarck effect which turns off the sexual attraction part of a person's brain to relatives when they are raised together as a family and label their affections differently. When separation occurs early within families this effect does not occur.'

Therefore, to fully ensure your donor-conceived child is safe from genetic sexual attraction, they need to know the identities of all their donor-conceived siblings and have some form of contact with them while growing up. No-one expects you to have a house big enough to accommodate them all. But your donor-conceived child needs to see them, see photos of them, communicate with them, hear you talk about them and acknowledge their existence. Hear you explain the connection as family. Not just with some of their siblings, but with all.

This can and does happen in 'known donor' parenting situations. For instance, some people in same-sex relationships ask a third friend to be the donor. As long as that friendship survives, and the donor is present in their kids' lives, there is a much greater likelihood that it will be known if that donor has other children, and how many. It will also be known if the donor suddenly develops some late-onset inheritable disease. Their kids can ask the donor all the questions they may have, and connect with that person, and any other siblings.

Have you ever come across a parenting situation like that, using a donor put forward by a fertility clinic? One where all the offspring are assured of knowing, and growing up with some knowledge of, all their siblings?

I haven't.

AS PROBLEMATIC AS the system in Britain or Australia may be, there's always someone else who has it worse. In the world of Western donor conception, that's often someone from the US, where pretty much anything you can imagine has already happened somewhere, including at one point a so-called Nobel Prize sperm bank set up to produce a new (white) super-race of geniuses.

The Donor Sibling Registry, a private organisation which helps people trace their siblings, has members from around the world but is primarily US-based. By 2011, the DSR had already registered one group of 150 siblings, all fathered by the same sperm donor. This, it would seem, is far from the upper limit.[3]

In 2015, I first interviewed American Matt Doran, who's donor conceived. Matt was born in the '80s but didn't find out the truth until he was an adult.

Matt says he'd always had a sense that something wasn't quite as it seemed. Then, in June 2012, he was looking rapt at a screen which was displaying the sonogram of his twenty-week-old baby.

'The first time we saw my child in the womb it kind of changed my life, that, "Wow. I'm going to be a father,"' Matt told me. 'I saw the heartbeat, and it awakened sort of a repressed question that I'd had since I was probably at least maybe twelve.' So he rang the man who'd raised him. He asked his dad: 'Is there something you're not telling me about my conception?' His father came clean.

'It felt like an out-of-body experience,' Matt recalls. 'Everything in my life, all of a sudden, made sense. And then I also felt all this urgency to find out who my biological father was. That was my first question: 'Do you know who he is?' And [my dad] said no, he was anonymous.'

Matt was told his records were burned. However, through his own investigations, Matt eventually traced his biological father, a 'donor' who sold his sperm at the University of Kansas Medical Center, in Kansas City. 'I don't call him a donor because in my mind that's a made-up word by an industry to make it sound like it's a good thing,' Matt told me in that first interview. 'It's really just mostly a money-making scheme and that's what he did, my father I call him. He paid his way through medical school with his sperm.'

The man Matt calls his father is a man called Kip Wendler, but he's also been labelled 'Dr Papa'. In 1992, national current affairs program *Hard Copy* ran an investigation on Kip Wendler. 'Tonight on *Hard Copy*,' the presenter boomed, 'Dr Wendler may have fathered up to 500 children.' 'Can that possibly be?' a woman shrieked in response.

Matt watched this program many years later, in the living room of a male cousin, who'd recorded it on VHS. He watched as Wendler estimated the number of children he'd produced through donating sperm: 'probably over nine years probably a couple of hundred, conservatively'. A minimum of 200 half-siblings, or a maximum of 500? In 2015, Matt told me a mere 200 was unlikely, given that Wendler had been active for a decade. Wendler has since rejected the moniker 'Dr Papa' – he says that was a nickname for a different donor – and says only thirty deposits were made for $5 each. Matt, to this day, is unsure where the truth lies.

But the idea that he might have had 500 half-siblings took its toll on Matt. 'It was honestly like life-shattering for me and I completely, basically, hit rock bottom,' he said frankly. 'I used alcohol to cope with my depression.' The risks to health, the risk of genetic sexual attraction, these are concrete, physical dangers. But donor conception – particularly donor conception en masse – can come with a less tangible curse: the feeling of utter exploitation.

SURPRISINGLY, TODAY, MATT says he and Wendler have a good relationship. It's taken years. Matt says, looking back, he had 'a lot of fear' when he first approached Wendler: 'I had a background report on him that he had been in prison and lost his medical licence and then divorced twice, and just, it looked bad on paper. So I approached him in that mindset, and it kind of put him on the defence.' That first approach didn't end well.

After that, Matt says that every year, he would message Wendler on Father's Day: 'Sometimes "Happy Father's Day", or sometimes a little spiteful, "Happy Anonymous Father's Day".' For years, Wendler didn't respond. 'And then in 2017, I think I texted something and he responded with this huge text and it was like, whoa, OK, this is different,' says Matt.

Wendler told Matt that his mother, Matt's grandmother, was dying. 'I said, well, why don't we give us a second chance,' Matt recalls. Wendler asked if they could talk in six months: his terminally ill mother was living with him in his house, and he needed to get through the situation at hand first. 'So eventually we finally had a phone conversation. I think it was after my grandmother had passed,' says Matt. 'And that was really hard because I could have met her, and I'd actually been to his house, standing on the street just looking at his house. I didn't have the courage to go knock when I was there.'

The phone call went well. 'We talked for like an hour. We had so much in common … we talk every day now,' says Matt.

What, now, does Matt think of Wendler's donating history? 'My dad told me that he [only] did it thirty or forty times,' says Matt. But Matt says Wendler was a student, and then a resident doctor, for about a decade. 'I don't know how many years out of that he was active with [University of Kansas Medical Center] and the sperm bank.'

Matt hasn't yet come across hundreds of siblings. 'There's a lot of me that wants to really try to give [Wendler] the benefit of the doubt. And there's also the side of me that says maybe he's just a complete fraud and, you know, he's lying, and he did donate hundreds of times. And it's true. I don't really know. I'll never know. So I just try to focus on giving him the benefit of the doubt, and not harbouring anger or resentment.'

BEING DONOR CONCEIVED isn't a club you choose to join. It's something you are, quite literally, born into. Consequently, among donor-conceived people there are a wide range of views on everything, including on donor conception itself. In that first 2015 interview, Matt came up with the words that no commissioning parent wants to hear: the words that some people like us carry inside. An inconvenient truth.

'I'm against the entire industry,' Matt said simply. 'I think this whole practice [of donor conception] should be banned.'

This statement had nothing to do with Matt's situation in life when we spoke: by that time, he'd long since pulled himself out of the alcohol-fuelled crash. He had a wife and a child whom he loved. He was happy. But you can be happy with your present and yet still recognise the wrongness you feel.

'The world and the industry wants to sell this idea of family as if it's like something out of a magazine, or like we're pets, like dogs or something,' Matt said, with brutal directness. 'We're not like a commodity that's traded, that should be regulated. That's still treating me as an object. I guarantee you, whoever chooses to put those regulations in place is not going to do it, be *able* to do it in such a way that people have full human rights.'

That's it right there. That's the truth that even I handle with care: sometimes, no matter how much money parents pay, no matter what assurances clinics give, no matter what kind of life ensues, sometimes even we feel so exploited that we believe we should not exist. Why would you do that to a child?

I ASK MATT, five years later, if he still feels the same way. Today, Matt knows his biological father. He's also found a half-brother whom he loves: he sends me photos of them together, at his half-brother's wedding. They look strikingly similar.

But Matt's views on donor conception itself, he says, haven't changed.

'I am saying I shouldn't exist,' he says baldly. 'But that doesn't mean that I should *cease* to exist, now that I'm here. I can have a purpose in my life and make it meaningful.

'But the things that I've had to go through in my life because of my donor conception have been extraordinarily difficult. I would say traumatic, in different ways, at different times. And I don't wish that upon anybody. And I think it's wrong for many reasons.'

Matt was raised by a heterosexual couple, but it didn't matter that he had a social father, he says: he still needed to know his biological father. 'I think fathers are very important. I don't think fathers are disposable. And I think it causes a lack of development in areas for the human to not be connected with both his biological parents in a healthy, loving way. I mean, that's my views on it. I couldn't imagine having children and not being in their lives every day. My kids are so important to me.

'I don't even get it. How do people do that?'[4]

CHAPTER 22

THE SYDNEY OPERA HOUSE auditorium was packed, and I was nervous. There were seven women on stage with me, including the French author Muriel Barbery, Emmy-winning artist Lynette Wallworth, poet and critic Fiona Wright and singer-songwriter Sampa the Great. It was the Women of Letters session at the All About Women Festival.[1] We were there to each read 'A Letter to My Unfinished Business'. Of the locals, Sampa was fierce, Lynette was hilarious, and Fiona was both hilarious and biting.

Literary maven Marieke Hardy set the rules: no recordings, no videos, no podcasts. Although there was a big audience, the idea was that each letter could live and die in that moment; it would never be replicated anywhere again by anyone if its author chose not to publish it themselves. I chose the moment. I stuck to that for years, until I came to write this book.

'To whom it may concern,' I began. 'I realise it's a bit of an impersonal opening. My name is Sarah. You should know that despite the complete ambiguity of my greeting, I care about you deeply. That's why I'm writing. You are already in my heart.

'I have no idea what you look like. I don't know what music you listen to. I don't know what your favourite drink is, or even if you drink, but it doesn't matter. You are my unfinished business.' The house was quiet.

'I'm still alive, and if you're still reading this you're still alive, so the sample wasn't HIV positive, because if it was we'd be dead by now. It's one of the comforting things that doctors have since told me.

'That's also one of the few things that I know for sure …'

I STARED INTO the dark of the Opera House. My letter was nearly over. Here I go, I thought.

'This letter is for all of you' – I read – 'my dear brothers and sisters.

'You might not even know you're donor conceived. I'm sorry to cause you pain; I'm sorry to blow your world apart.

'But you need to ask your parents if you really are their child.'

That was it, that line: that was why I was, once again, doing something excruciating in public. All else was bait for the hook. If our parents lie to us, if society obliterates us, we need to ask for the truth, because the truth will never come to us. I wanted to make each and every person listening to me doubt. I wanted to make them doubt their own selves.

'There's quite a few people in this room who could be you,' I said, gazing at the audience. 'Similar age. They're watching me and they don't think this letter relates to their lives. Or relates to anything they know. They are also being deceived. It's been estimated in years gone by that there are more than 60,000 donor-conceived people in Australia … so you might not even realise that your parents are not your parents. Or you might know, but you might not realise that you and I share a lot of DNA. You might be exactly the same age as me. The way they used sperm, they created litters of children. *Big* litters.

'Donor-conceived people are all different, and some of them are sweeter and nicer than I am,' I said frankly. That got some smiles. 'But if you're my siblings, maybe you understand me. I'm angry at the fundamental lack of respect for human beings. Made in a lab. Farmed out. Raised in ignorance. I'm not saying don't do it at all. I'm saying, treat humans better than you treat dogs. My dog has more paperwork than I do.

'So I'll leave you with that, guys. Don't feel you have to get in touch. But I wouldn't have written this for you if I didn't care. I've tried to set out what is known. Any more than that, and I'll need your help.

'One thing's for sure.' I grinned savagely at the audience. 'Our dad is a wanker.'

Laughter. Applause.

AFTER I'D GONE public, on *Australian Story* and in the *Good Weekend*, the gloves were off. There would be no favours, no counting on goodwill from anyone in the fertility game for any family information. I'd revealed destruction of medical files. I'd accused them of 'cowboy medicine'.

I didn't get any blowback for asserting that fertility doctors, using HIV-positive sperm, had killed women. But what the nurse Diana Craven had told me about those two donor codes – the codes she thought might be mine, AFH and ADZ – seemed to hit a nerve. Peter Illingworth, the medical director of IVF Australia, left a voicemail on my phone, saying there was something we should discuss. I emailed him back asking him what it was.

'It was during the lead-up to the *Australian Story* programme,' he replied. 'We did turn up one or two minor details … I'd be happy to have a talk with you about it on the phone.'

Right. What did that mean? What 'minor details'? I was done with calls, chats and back-channels; whatever this was, it was going to be set out in writing.

'Phone conversations aren't the best for me unfortunately, because I'm working rather long hours right now and as you can appreciate, I prefer not to receive these calls at work,' I replied. 'Could you put the one or two minor points in an email? Thanks.'

The response was silence. For weeks. Fortunately, I'd already set my expectations to zero: now I was just curious to see how this would play out.

After a while, I gave him a nudge.

'It's been more than three weeks since my last email, and I haven't heard from you about what these "minor details" might be,' I wrote. 'Belinda Hawkins provided you with the two donor codes I was told by Di Craven could be my donor code. The most likely was AFH. I understand IVF Australia was going to investigate that information by looking up the donor files corresponding to that code, among other avenues. Have you found anything?'

Silence – for another ten weeks.

Then, finally, a reply.

'Hi Sarah, Apologies for the delays,' Illingworth wrote briskly. 'What I am sending you is the last page of the donor records for AFH and ADZ.'

What?

I couldn't have access to the medical file about my own conception without my mother's written permission, but I could have other people's?

What doctor just hands out pages of individuals' medical files at will? Let alone the medical director of a flagship fertility business owned by an international corporation which in turn is listed on the Australian Stock Exchange?

'You will see on these that all of the samples in store for these two donors were used on the dates shown in April and May 1982 and that underneath this in each case is the word "FINISHED",' Illingworth wrote. 'This seems to have been the notation that was used at that time to indicate that there are no more samples of this donor in store. We certainly have no further records of either of these donors after this time.'

I was baffled. I looked at the two pages. Both were headed 'Royal North Shore Hospital Cryostorage Sperm Motility Study'. Was this … a study? Or a record of actual use? One page was for donor AFH, the other for donor ADZ. Each page had a table – although actually filling in the columns appeared to be optional. The column titled 'Straw no.' appeared to have no data. 'Donation no.' was similar, with the exception of a single note reading '2 outside' for AFH, and '4 outside, 2 centre' for ADZ. What did that mean? I hazarded a guess. Did these men mostly masturbate at home ('outside'), then bring in a jar? Or did it refer to something else entirely? The column 'Pre-freeze motility %' seemed to host the data which should have fallen under 'Straw no.' – for instance, in ADZ's table, 'Pre-freeze motility %' was just the numbers from one to ten. Pre-freeze motility itself, or the percentage of all moving sperm in a sample before freezing – a common indicator of sperm quality – was apparently not recorded at all.

There was also a column for 'Date received' and another for 'Date withdrawn'. The latter, perhaps, was when the sperm was used to inseminate a woman. Or maybe the sperm was merely withdrawn for 'study', as per the heading. How did all of this prove anything? And, on AFH's page, almost all of the 'Date received' was five or six months after 'Date withdrawn' – that is, this document seemed to suggest sperm was somehow being withdrawn from storage before the donor had even made the donation in the first place.

It was a bit of a mess.

'We think this is a transcription error,' Illingworth wrote, referring to the 'withdrawn' vs 'received' date snafu, 'entering the year wrongly, by the technician who was thawing the sample.' If that were the case, the technician wrote down the wrong year six times.

On both documents, below the column data, it did indeed say FINISHED. But these, according to Illingworth, were just a single page from each man's donor file. What if there were other pages with more insemination dates? In fact, the photocopy of AFH's page showed another page peeking out from underneath. It contained data right to the bottom row – potentially another thirty-six instances of donor insemination. I wouldn't know, of course. Illingworth had only sent me what he deemed the highlights.

'It remains theoretically possible that there are still other records in existence at Royal North Shore to indicate collection of further samples by these donors after that but we have found no evidence of this,' Illingworth wrote.

'All of this makes it seem to us very unlikely that either AFH or ADZ were the donor that was used in your case.'

That was what all this was driving at. Forget the codes you have.

'Nonetheless we did explore the two donors further and tried to contact them,' Illingworth added. 'We were, however, unable to make contact with either of them.'

I put the pieces together. Illingworth was not only sending the private medical documentation of two men he didn't think were connected to me – he was doing so, by his own admission, without having asked either for their permission. I was astounded. Even in releasing non-identifiable information, what had happened to all those stern industry pronouncements about donors and their absolute, inviolable right to privacy?

'Given that we don't actually think that either of these men are the donor from whose donation you were derived, we decided to leave it at that point,' Illingworth finished. 'I am sorry to again be giving you disappointing news.'

If he thought that would end it, he was mistaken. I replied that afternoon.

'Hi Peter,' I wrote. 'That's a lot to take in, particularly from a single page of a file which obviously contains more detail, including potentially more detail about sperm usage (because I can't see the whole file, I don't know).' I listed a further seven questions about the columns and data.

He replied an hour and a half later. It was brief. 'Hi Sarah, I agree. It's a lot to take in, particularly when the subject is so important for you. I'd much rather sit down with you to go through it together, rather than sending emails back and forward. Could we please do that?'

I sent a response within twenty minutes. 'Hi Peter,' I said. 'You chose to send this rather confused donor information without much explanation by email, so it seems odd to do that first and then ask for a meeting. In any case I'm going overseas on holiday shortly, so I would appreciate email answers. Would you be able to send any other pages from those two files of ADZ and AFH?'

Silence for a week and a half.

Three days before Christmas, I received a few lines: 'I think it would be much better that we meet to discuss this further. Let me know when you're back … I don't see any useful purpose in further email discussion.'[2]

JUST BEFORE THE *Australian Story* program went to air, producer Belinda Hawkins emailed me. She said that on the day of his on-camera interview, Illingworth had told her he'd just discovered that IVF Australia had copies of my mother's treatment files – but not the originals. The originals might still exist, Belinda thought, with the Royal North Shore Hospital. I was stunned.

'Did [IVF Australia] tell you they only had copies of the records, not the originals?' Belinda asked me. It was three days before the broadcast of Part 1.

'Neither Illingworth nor anyone from IVF Australia nor the RNSH nor any doctors at all have contacted me there is a possibility the RNSH has intact records of my conception. The only person who's told me that is you,' I replied.[3]

I put in an urgent request with the Royal North Shore Hospital for the original file. The RNSH responded: once again, they needed my mother's permission. That old chestnut. My mother was in Japan, without her mobile phone, staying with an uncle of mine who didn't know about any of this. The timing was classic. So the RNSH manager of Health Information Services was going to call my uncle in Tokyo, who didn't know I was donor-conceived, to get through to my mother, who hated talking about me being donor-conceived, to once again try to get her permission for something which (if denied) could affect the documentary going to air within hours, the piece I'd written for *Good Weekend* which was going to the printers, and, far more importantly, my relationship with my mother and the rest of my life.

Just once, it would have been nice to have the power to make decisions about finding my family myself, without being utterly dependent on good luck and other people.

I wouldn't have put money on a positive outcome – but I would have lost. From Japan, my mother did a wonderful U-turn – and gave the go-ahead.

After a stressful back-and-forth over signed consent forms, the day after Part 1 of the *Australian Story* program was broadcast, the Royal North Shore Hospital finally delivered. I was cc'd on an email from the hospital to my mother, containing a scanned PDF of the original medical records held by the RNSH.[4]

There were no surprises. There was no intact original file. The code was cut out.

The main difference between what RNSH gave me and what IVF Australia had given me was colour. The RNSH file was in full colour, not black-and-white: something which was irrelevant 99 per cent of the time – except for those two crucial pages where the donor code had been removed. You could see, on those pages, the pale yellow ghosts of sticky tape, where blank paper had been stuck over the holes cut in the file. It proved the code destruction was complete.

The manager of Health Information Services wrote a note to my mother – not me – to accompany the file: 'Royal North Shore Hospital Health Information Services is deeply concerned with this discovery and as a result will launch a full internal audit of all of the hospital's former Assisted Reproduction Treatment clinic records … I apologise for any distress this may cause you.'

An internal audit. *Good*, I thought, *about damn time*. The story went to air and to print. My own small world was exploded.

A FEW DAYS after broadcast, I'd recovered from the initial rawness of being so exposed and started to think again. An internal audit sounds pretty good, except there was no detail on what that actually meant. They certainly didn't tell me, the whistleblower/victim. Why didn't I know anything about this? Shouldn't I, at the very least, have an understanding of what they were doing and a timeframe?

I wrote back to the RNSH manager of Health Information Services, Nicole Stanzer. 'Thank you for sending on the records,' I said. 'I assume you meant to include me in your expression of concern, as this destroys my chances of finding my biological father and half siblings, not my mother's.' I asked to be kept up to date on the audit's progress, and I added a list of questions about it.

A week went by, with zero response. So I sent another email, voicing my concerns about her silence: '… I have very little trust in any of the professionals or institutions involved in the process of my conception and its associated record keeping. Destruction of medical records, particularly such fundamental records as these, is severe medical malpractice.'

Three days later, I received a reply – not from her – but from the Northern Sydney Local Health District's media team. The fact that the reply came from the media team was the first of many indications that they were dealing with me as a journalist – not a victim.

Senior communications officer Melissa Chain wrote: 'I can advise that a full and independent audit of the medical records of the former Assisted Reproduction Treatment clinic, including IVF records at Royal North Shore Hospital, is currently being conducted in accordance with statutory obligations.

'The audit will review the IVF records for any physical signs of tampering, editing or missing information. It is expected to be completed by the end of September, 2014.' An end date. At least that was one concrete piece of information. But she clearly had no idea what she was talking about. I wasn't an IVF baby, and nor were most babies from my time. I was conceived through an entirely different medical procedure: donor insemination.

'We will provide your mother with the outcome of the audit,' wrote Chain.

After all I'd done and been through for the last three and a half years – after blowing the whistle about my life on national television – they were going to conduct some in-house inquiry and not even tell me the outcome? Only my mother?

I emailed again, angry about their non-recognition of my rights, even though my mother had already given permission for me to be kept informed. I repeated my list of questions about what, exactly, this audit involved. 'I expect to hear from you soon.'

Silence. A week went by.

I wrote again. I repeated my questions. Then, at the end, I added something which had occurred to me about privacy. If they were so worried about privacy, why weren't they worried about mine?

Why was my case passed on to the media team? I asked. 'Nor do I know who, or how many people in the Northern Sydney Local Health District are now handling personal information about my case. As with my questions regarding the RNSH internal audit, I expect and would appreciate an explanation.'

Silence, for another three days. Then an official response, on NSLHD letterhead: the first time that had happened. Melissa noted the removal of donor codes and said she was 'sorry for the distress this has caused you and your mother'. 'I would like to assure you that every effort is being made to thoroughly investigate this matter ... Once finalised, a report will be provided to Nicole Stanzer, NSLHD Manager of Health Information Services for consideration.'

So we'd come full absurd circle. The report of the investigation would go to the woman who'd flicked me on to the media team in the first place – but still not to me. 'In relation to your concerns about your matter being referred to the NSLHD Communications Team,' Melissa Chain wrote, 'the people handling this matter are properly authorised and are aware of their privacy and confidentiality obligations.'[5]

Layers and layers. No matter what I did, no matter the blatant wrong I'd wrested from the archives, no change. So many managers, bureaucrats, authorisations, procedures. No clear answers. I took a couple of weeks' break from the frustration and the fight. It was turning into a full-time job. And I already had a job. Quite a challenging one, in fact.

ON 29 SEPTEMBER I checked the IVF Australia website.

I noticed that IVF Australia had changed their ethics committee details on the website. Professor Douglas Saunders and Di Craven had been wiped from IVF Australia's Ethics Committee list, along with everyone else.

They stopped naming any members of their ethics committee. There was now no transparency as to who was on IVF Australia's Ethics Committee at all.[6]

That same day, I came back to the fight and sent another email to Melissa Chain.

'[YOUR] LETTER PROVIDES absolutely no information on the RNSH internal audit. It also fails, once again, to say that I will be advised of the audit's findings,' I wrote to Chain. 'You do not even tell me who the independent auditor is.

'This is a cover up. I demand access to the full report of the internal audit. Originally you said this would be completed by the end of September. So, is it finished? … It would be nice if you answered all of my questions, but you haven't actually answered any. I will paste them below, again.'

Silence for another week. I emailed her again. 'Dear Melissa, It's been another week since my last email. All my questions still stand.'[7]

Silence for another month.

I'D KEPT NATIONALS MP John Barilaro and also Labor MP Guy Zangari in the loop about all of this – the two most interested politicians from the committee conducting the donor conception inquiries in New South Wales. ('Me and Guy, us Italians,' Barilaro said to me once, 'we understand the importance of family.') Now I decided to add a third. Greens MP Jamie Parker hadn't been a part of the inquiries, but he was at that point my local member. I emailed Parker and told him what was happening (or failing to happen). 'I cannot find out anything about a process which is apparently supposed to be investigating the extreme malpractice against myself which the hospital admits took place ... It is very easy for me to believe that they are lying and that nothing is being done,' I wrote. I told him it wasn't just me either: I knew of others, like Bec, who were made by Clinic 20 and had also had their donor codes destroyed.[8]

As it turned out, Parker was a good choice. Within just two days of that email, Jamie Parker had raised my case on the floor of NSW Parliament. 'Many members would know about a constituent of mine whose story appeared on the ABC's *Australian Story*, on *AM* and in Fairfax's *Good Weekend* ... We do not know who is conducting the audit and when it will report. We do not know whether other people conceived like my constituent will be contacted to advise them of any process or risk ... [The NSLHD] said she is not entitled to details because she is not a patient and it will only deal with the donor recipients, such as the mother. This is a major problem because in addition to her conception there, my constituent was born at Royal North Shore Hospital, and basically no-one could be considered more a patient than this young woman.'[9]

A fortnight after Parker's speech, I finally heard back from the manager of Health Information Services. Instead of a progress report or answering my questions about the audit – she just told me that it was all already over.

'Dear Sarah, Thank you for your ongoing correspondence,' she wrote. 'As you are aware RNSH … launched an independent audit …'

Then I stopped scanning and instead read every word slowly. 'This audit was undertaken by NSW State Records and covered all medical records between 1979 and 2005.' (What? But the practice was sold in the 1990s?) 'This audit did not resolve why the donor code was removed, when it occurred nor who may be responsible.

'Clearly a full investigation is required, which the RNSH is committed to following through. As such we are currently in the process of appointing an independent external investigator to conduct the work.' Another investigation? 'I understand this does not provide closure for your personal circumstance and I am sorry for any ongoing distress caused by this situation, however RNSH is still unable to answer many of your questions.'[10]

MY RESPONSE WAS predictable. I sent Nicole Stanzer a barrage of questions about this second investigation. A brief reply came back, expressing regret that no further information could be given and thanking me for my patience.

A couple of weeks later, she got in touch, unprompted, with an update – the first time anyone had done so.

'As of today we have appointed an external investigator for the RNSH ART Clinic investigation. The external auditor is IAB and the investigation will commence immediately,' she said.

IAB. I'd never heard of them. I looked them up – the Internal Audit Bureau, owned by the state government.

I looked up the name of the investigator I was given. The bulk of his expertise appeared to be in workplace bullying.

I didn't have a good feeling about this.

CHAPTER 23

I TOOK A SUPPORT person to the meeting with IAB: my friend Steve, who is also a lawyer, with significant experience in dealing with the state government. I took a copy of my mother's treatment file. I took along copies of the notes of all my conversations with Di Craven, Peter Illingworth, you name it.[1]

Steve and I sat down in a tiny office with the investigator, a middle-aged man. I went through everything. I gave him all my paperwork. The investigator kept reassuring me that I shouldn't worry, he would find the proper records, he would find them, he would get to the bottom of this. This had the opposite effect. Wasn't he listening at all? I kept trying to explain that in fact, there was nothing to find, the information had been destroyed and it was a major scandal.

I really don't think the investigator knew how to deal with a situation like this. We were, after all, talking about malpractice, human life, and what was essentially long-term trauma beginning at conception for an unknown number of people. It was quite clear that IAB dealt only with workplace issues relating to adult public servants.

I was glad Steve was there. Not only for support, but to compare notes afterwards.

'He didn't … really seem on top of it, did he?' I asked Steve.

Steve grimaced.

A COUPLE OF months later, all leads had dried up. There had been no word from IAB. So I tried another tack. Donor-conceived people are often warned that no-one can break the agreement with the donor. Well, for that to be a legitimate argument – there had to be an actual agreement to point to.

By this stage, you may have guessed that I'm a glutton for punishment. I emailed Peter Illingworth. 'I am writing to formally request a copy of the contract or agreement with sperm donors in the public hospital system during the years 1982 and 1983,' I wrote. 'The records of that unit were subsequently taken over, along with the clinic itself, by IVF Australia. I would like a copy of whatever agreement was given to sperm donors in those years at the Royal North Shore Hospital and signed by them. This does not breach privacy laws.'

Five days later, I hadn't heard back. It was mid-February 2015. By now, I'd digested the strangeness of those two pages Illingworth had sent me from the files of donors ADZ and AFH. He'd wanted a meeting to discuss them. Why the hell not?

I emailed him again, suggesting a meeting to chat about the pages. He replied two days later. It was a thoughtful message.

'I do understand how angry you are about all of this. On the other hand, I also understand that how [sic] traumatic it is for you to visit the clinic and go through these very painful and sensitive issues with us,' Illingworth wrote.

'Personally, I would be absolutely delighted if, at the end of it all, we were able to get you all the answers you need and put you in touch with your donor. However, I'm just not optimistic that that's possible, given what's happened.

'I will bring copies of all the documentation that we have related to the questions you are asking. With the passage of time, I can't categorically say what consents were always in use at RNSH at that time for the donors but I will bring some samples of consent forms from that time so you can see what some of the donors at that time were signing.'

Great, I thought. He suggested some times. I looked at my shifts and tried to work out when I'd be awake and emotionally ready. I left it alone for a little while, to calm down and to prepare.

Two and a half weeks later, before we could meet, Illingworth dropped another bombshell.

'Since we last spoke, there has been a major development,' he emailed. 'We have been contacted by Royal North Shore Hospital. They have reminded us that all of these records relate to treatment provided at Royal North Shore Hospital and that they are therefore their property, not ours … They have now come across and reclaimed all of the donor records.

'We now do not have the records for any patient or donor where treatment took place before 31st December 1995. Accordingly, we are not in a position to provide any more information and can only refer you back to Royal North Hospital [sic] for any further information.'[2]

By that point all I could do was throw my hands up in disgust.

IT SEEMED A little strange, though. The massive IVF Australia had effectively been raided by the Health Department? I emailed my department contact: 'Is it true that the RNSH has taken back all donor records from IVF Australia? And left IVF Australia with no copies?'[3] And I emailed Belinda, the producer from *Australian Story*: 'I can't keep up. These people are shifty as f**k.'

I also replied to Illingworth. 'Did they leave you with any copies of patient or donor records pre 31st December 1995?' I asked.

'They've taken everything away,' he replied promptly. 'I do hope this doesn't in any way impede your search for the information you are seeking.'

Thanks, I thought. Apparently Illingworth, too, found the whole situation rather curious: 'The RNSH arrangement was fairly unique. It's the only public hospital programme that morphed into a private programme … I'm still not clear why the public hospital records were allowed to leave RNSH at all when the clinic moved out into the private clinic in January 1996,' he wrote.[4]

I updated Belinda on this latest round.

'Plot thickens. Like a thriller,' she replied.

MY DEPARTMENT OF HEALTH contact got back to me about the apparent records raid on IVF Australia. She knew nothing about it.

'IVF Australia has not informed NSW Health of this development … NSW Health will write to IVF Australia to seek confirmation of the fact that they no longer hold RNSH records. I suggest you contact RNSH for confirmation.' What was going on?[5]

Sometimes, in public bureaucracy, the left hand has absolutely no idea what the right is doing. I emailed Nicole Stanzer at the Royal North Shore Hospital. One month down the track, she came back with some very concrete details about what the hell had happened.

The day after Illingworth's thoughtful email to me, suggesting some dates and times to meet, he'd had a visit from the IAB investigator. This was to negotiate 'for the release of clinical records for sperm donors held by IVF Australia, dating back to July 1977, previously held by the [RNSH] ART clinic.' These records were 'physically transferred together with a copy of the donor database to RNSH on Monday 9th March 2015 for examination and secure retention'.[6]

So in the two and a half weeks I was steeling myself to name a date with Illingworth, he was negotiating, collating and farewelling the files that I was coming to see. Not once did he mention that. Until they were gone.

NICOLE STANZER SAID that if I wanted to see a copy of any sperm donor contracts for Clinic 20 donors, it would have to go through to the state government's Privacy Officer, who handled formal freedom of information requests (known as GIPA requests in New South Wales). GIPA requests take a long time, and, if there are records which can be released, money. Finally, what you get may simply be pages of redactions. As an additional middle finger to media applications, sometimes government agencies release the documents publicly at the same time as they give them to the purchasing journalist – so everything that you've waited and paid for is suddenly your rival's for free.

I shelved the idea of GIPA for now. I had too many other rabbits to chase down first. Like, for instance, what the hell was happening with the IAB investigator. It had been four and a half months since Steve and I had gone to see him, and I still didn't know when he was supposed to finish his investigation, if ever.

'Do you have a timeframe for the completion of the IAB report?' I asked Nicole Stanzer. And: 'Now that IVF Australia does not apparently hold the sperm donor records, I would like RNSH to investigate whether AFH or ADZ are my father, and if not, provide full documentation proving why not.'[7]

There was no response.

NINE DAYS LATER, I was in a cafe in Melbourne's north. I'd flown to Victoria for work. It had been a nonstop day of early flight, travel and interviews, and it was coming up to late afternoon. I hadn't eaten all day and I was starving.

I was at that light-headed stage of hunger, swallowing the first few bites of a sandwich ravenously without really chewing, when my phone rang. It was Nicole Stanzer, from the RNSH. The IAB report was finished. They would be releasing the findings at a press conference the next morning in Sydney. A press conference?

'But I'm in Melbourne,' I said in disbelief. 'I can't be there.'

Well, was the response, maybe some other journalist can go.

Some other journalist? Had she actually forgotten who I was? I was the victim who had sparked this whole thing.

'Do I get a copy of the report?'

No.

'But you're giving it out at a press conference?'

They weren't giving it out, she explained. They would merely be discussing some of the findings. No-one would get the report. There would be a press release, of course.

'Well,' I said furiously. 'Will I get a copy of the press release?'

Yes, she said, I would get a copy of the press release. I would get a copy of a press release about my life.

I hung up. Thank god I'd finished all my interviews for the day. I was a mess. I couldn't even fly straight home. I had more interviews to collect the next day in Melbourne and I couldn't just cancel work travel and do things later. Maybe I should have done so anyway, and sorted it out myself afterwards, but I was in no fit state to make any decisions.

It was a strange night, alone in Melbourne.

AS IT TURNED out, I waited. And I waited. And nothing arrived. The media conference was scheduled for 9:30 am the next day. There was no press release in my inbox. At 9:34 am, I sent Nicole Stanzer a furious email.

'I've had virtually no information about what the findings of this investigation are and no written information of any kind, let alone a copy of the report,' I wrote.

'I asked if you would at least be kind enough to first send me a copy of the press release about this announcement by email, as the affected party whose situation started this investigation and the previous investigation into what is clearly serious malpractice at the RNSH.

'I have received absolutely nothing from you, not even a press release, and I understand the press conference is about to start.

'Your treatment of me is reprehensible. I am a human being. You're not even treating me with the same consideration you would another journalist. I have no press release. Instead, as the victim of all this, and the person who has lost the most, I am treated as neither victim nor journalist. I'm just ignored.

'I expect a full copy of the report.'[8]

THE ABC SENT a journalist or two to that press conference, of course. After all, this was the big news break from *Australian Story*, an ABC show. My colleague Lindy Kerin went for ABC radio current affairs.

Lindy managed to tell me what had emerged at the press conference. IAB had found that Clinic 20 had destroyed donor codes in eighty-eight out of 3160 files.[9] Eighty-eight. Why? Why? IAB had also found that there were 'no formal documented policies or chief legislation' regarding sperm donors. Apparently, in the absence of any such documented policies, clinic staff – public servants – destroyed codes, and this was all okay. The removal was 'permanent'. No-one was named. No-one was responsible. There was no evidence of 'malicious management'. The Northern Sydney Local Health District 'deeply regretted any distress' these findings caused former patients, 'as well as their donor-conceived children.'

That was it.

Lindy was covering the story for *The World Today*; she wanted to interview me.

'Well, it's clearly a whitewash,' I said coldly. 'I mean they say they've uncovered eighty-eight records where the donor codes have been removed and they say that apparently nobody is responsible? I find that very hard to believe. I have given names to the public hospital inquiry, to the Royal North Shore, of people who did this. I have made complaints about these individuals to the Health Care Complaints Commission. They have declined to investigate any of these people.'

Andrew Montague, the executive director of operations with the NSLHD, had spoken at the press conference, trotting out the same hackneyed excuses. If I'd been there I would have flayed him alive. But you get the journalists you get on the day, and none of them specialised in this area quite like I did.

'At the time between 1977 and 1984, assisted reproductive technology was in its early stages and it's like a lot of new technologies, there's not legislation in place and it very much is the practice at the particular time. Certainly from the investigation, what we have seen is that it was a standard practice and really the key thing at that point was that all donors were given unconditional guarantee that they would be anonymous,' Montague said.

An undocumented policy of record destruction: clearly, all above-board, nothing to see here. If the guarantee of anonymity given to sperm donors was so important – why wasn't that written down either? Why would decades of doctors, governments, bureaucrats and now investigators bend over backwards to defend what was both reprehensible and entirely invisible?

I didn't even believe that number of eighty-eight affected files, out of thousands of files. After all, I had no reason to trust anything else they'd said. Why would I suddenly start now?

The Royal North Shore Hospital 'urges those concerned about their medical records to get in touch', *The World Today* reported.

They weren't even going to tell those eighty-seven other women they claimed had had their treatment files deliberately damaged what had happened, let alone their children. Andrew Montague and the RNSH were going to leave it up to those eighty-seven (or however many) other women to first of all hear about code destruction, then understand what it meant, then overcome fear and shame – and finally, one by one, struggle with the bureaucracy of the Royal North Shore.

All that would mean, of course, was that there was a good chance no-one else would ever be publicly identified as being affected or make any sort of fuss. It would dampen the whole thing down. Widespread, deliberate donor code destruction, reduced to just me making noise.

THAT EVENING NICOLE Stanzer emailed me a reply.

'I advised you our Corporate Communications unit was handling the media statement,' she said. 'They were unable to provide any information before the press conference. All media requests were provided the same response last night and all media news desks – no individuals except two who made requests directly to the Corporate Communications unit – were provided the media alert early this morning.' Well, why wasn't I one of those two, then? At the very least?

'You were provided the information that was in the media statement by myself in our phone conversation.' I had no idea if that was true, because I still hadn't been given the damn statement. 'The press release statement has been issued this morning and placed on our website,' she said.

'I can confirm that you will be receiving a formal letter as an affected party of the investigation. You may also apply for a copy of the report under GIPPA [sic].'

At the bottom of the email, finally, she'd attached the press release.[10]

THAT WAS THE end of April 2015. I had to stop. I knew I had to stop. I'd pushed so hard in so many directions. Now I swallowed my anger and tried to forget about it. All of it. I'd tried to right a wrong in the system, a massive wrong done to babies. I'd fought this in multiple arenas: Parliament, health regulation, the law, the media. In the end, I could count the total number of people in power who really gave a shit on the fingers of one hand, and still I'd have fingers left. All systems had failed, through arrogance and bureaucratic violations. I would never get answers about who my family were. I would never get change, redress, an explanation or an apology. None of us would. And I needed to look after myself. I was done.

IT WAS ALMOST Christmas. I was in Melbourne again for journalism's Walkley Awards. I'd thrown myself into something completely different that year, and made a two-part documentary on radicalisation, de-radicalisation and the rise of Islamic State. It was nominated in two categories, which felt good. At least I had a career left. At least I was still functioning.

I was staying at my brother-in-law's place, asleep, when my phone rang. I rolled over to the edge of the bed. 'Hello?' I mumbled.

It was Harriet Alexander, health reporter with the *Sydney Morning Herald*. I'd never spoken to Harriet before in my life, but I knew her byline. She explained that she'd put in a request to government for the full copy of the IAB investigation under freedom of information laws. It had taken months, like all such requests do, but she now had the partially redacted IAB report. Could she interview me about it? I slid off the bed onto the floor in a tangle of sheets.

'I've never read it,' I said. 'They never gave me a copy. They refused to let me anywhere near it. What does it say? Oh my god. Can you send it to me? I'll do an interview. I just need to read it.'

A few minutes later, it was on the screen in front of me, and once again I fell down the rabbit hole.

CHAPTER 24

THE FIRST PAGE was headed: 'Strictly confidential. Security classification: Protected. Investigation report into possible tampering of clinical records for Assisted Reproduction Technology.'[1]

The IAB report revealed that the first audit – the one which I was told nothing about except that it was suddenly over – had 'identified eighty-four clinical records where it appeared that sperm donor codes had been removed, or possible tampering had occurred'. These records spanned the period 1979 to 2005, including the period from April 1994, when Clinic 20 was privatised. Those new owners took with them clinical records of public hospital patients over the previous seventeen years, staff, and 'materials'.

How were they allowed to do that? Why not name these individuals? What did these new owners pay for the files and the sperm? Why was Clinic 20 privatised? Did it go out to tender? The report answered none of those questions. It didn't even ask them.

The public Clinic 20, the IAB report said, had had two types of records, with 'clear separation' between the two. There were the 'clinical records' of donation recipients and the 'clinical records' of sperm donors. Both groups, therefore, were classed as patients. No egg donors or donations were mentioned, or embryos. I was unsure whether this meant Clinic 20 dealt only in sperm donations, or if the IAB report simply left them out.

Clinic 20's system assigned each sperm donor a three-letter code in order of arrival. The system started at AAA: the next was AAB. Once AAZ had turned up, the second of three cogs would start spinning: ABA, ABB, ABC.

Interestingly enough, the IAB report noted 'the generally consistent presence of sperm donor agreement and consent documentation' although 'the practices around sperm donor records at the ART Clinic at its inception in 1977 were, compared with current record keeping standards, minimal'. So Clinic 20 was good at indemnifying itself, but not at actual medical paperwork? IAB had located 'extensive confidential sperm donor records which were held by IVF Australia'. These were more than 700 public Clinic 20 sperm donor records in IVF Australia's possession, 'physically transferred' back into the Royal North Shore Hospital's possession, as Nicole Stanzer had informed me.

IAB had examined 3160 recipient files and more than 700 sperm donor files: 'approximately 4000' in total. They spanned a period of more than twenty years, from 1977 until 1996/7 – several years *after* Clinic 20 had been privatised.

'There was a need to ensure that a coded identity of the donor continued to be maintained in order to limit the number of potential successful pregnancies for which each sperm donor was responsible,' the report said. 'Records examined suggest that the ART Clinic policy at the time was to limit the maximum number of pregnancies achieved by any one donor to ten pregnancies. There was also a requirement to maintain the identity of the sperm donor in the event that clinical staff needed to contact the donor if, for instance, a contra-indication to use of the donor sperm was identified.'

Donor semen, said IAB, could be cryogenically stored at Clinic 20 'in some cases beyond ten years' – and some donors made 'multiple donations … with references to multiple (in some cases, hundreds) of retained straws in storage for individual donors'. *Hundreds.* Each straw could potentially result in a child.

Clinic 20's three-month quarantine period for sperm donations, said IAB, was doubled to six months 'at approximately the time HIV testing appeared to have been encompassed in medical screening', around January 1985. Puzzlingly, the report quoted a letter sent to a potential sperm donor in February 1985. The potential donor had concerns 'about A.I.D.S. and a doctors' dispute with Medicare'. Clinic 20 responded: 'The AIDS epidemic has not affected the In-Vitro Fertilisation Program, neither has the doctors' dispute as we are in a Private Hospital.' The Royal North Shore Hospital was public and always had been. I added that one to the mental list I called 'Baffling errors of fact'.

'From the late 1970s until the early 1980s,' the IAB report said, 'identified records and correspondence indicated that it was the policy (not identified as documented at that time) of the ART Clinic with regard to anonymous donations of sperm that if a pregnancy resulted, the sperm recipient's clinical record identifying the sperm donor's code was physically removed and destroyed'.

There it was – code destruction. Apparently undocumented, but somehow still accepted as a 'policy'. The fact that such destruction was entirely counter to other stated policies was not investigated by IAB.

'Following the ART Clinic's privatisation in 1994,' IAB continued, 'sperm donor recipient records previously maintained by the ART Clinic were closed off, and new records created for ongoing sperm donor recipients who continued as patients of NSART.' Surely this break in the chain exacerbated the likelihood of the ten-pregnancy limit being exceeded. 'Both the sperm donor recipient clinical records and sperm donor records remain strictly confidential New South Wales Department of Health records.' Illingworth definitely should not have been emailing me pages from sperm donor files, then.

Interestingly, there was a brief, tantalising mention of an ethics committee. 'We further noted references in multiple clinical notes to referrals to an Ethics Committee in relation to various aspects of approvals for donor sperm to be made available by a donor recipient.' No mention of who was on that ethics committee, of course, nor whether it had functioned for all of Clinic 20's years of operation. The only example of a committee decision was this nosey policing of an unmarried couple: 'non-approval of release of donor sperm to unmarried recipients (and subsequent release on proof of marriage).'

Searching for further details on the ethics committee, I noticed something else. At the bottom of one page, out of nowhere, IAB included a single offhand sentence: 'We further examined these sperm donor files and noted that their sperm donations were still available and viable from donations they had made since 1977 and subsequently.'

What? Sperm donated in 1977 was still being held for use? IAB's report was delivered in 2015. That's thirty-eight-year-old sperm. It's nearly zombie sperm. There's a reasonable chance the biological father might already be in the ground if that sperm was thawed and used in 2015, or even earlier. There are medical and ethical concerns to be answered about the degree of deterioration for sperm that old, plus a raft of other considerations that leap out at me. And did any of those sperm donors sign a consent form agreeing that their sperm could be held and used in perpetuity? I doubt it.

It is a good example of just how loose the fertility industry is. There is no law or guideline outright banning the use of these undead gametes. Currently New South Wales law says donated gametes can be stored for a maximum of fifteen years, but you may obtain authorisation from the Secretary for the Department of Health to keep them for 'longer', with no uppermost limit specified.[2] (IAB did not mention whether any authorisation was sought.)

Australia's national *Ethical Guidelines for Assisted Reproductive Technology*, issued by the National Health and Medical Research Council, also fail to impose any meaningful limits on storage and use. The ethical guidelines say that fertility clinics should not use donated gametes collected before 2005 'without the consent of the gamete donor to the release of identifying information for any future treatments'.[3] But there are two massive exceptions. If you're using the mature gametes to create a sibling for a donor-conceived child who already exists – or if embryos have been made, and stored, but 'the donor cannot be contacted' – then go for it.

That's a staggering loophole. Who polices that? How hard does a clinic have to try? Do they half-heartedly ring a landline that someone provided in 1977? And what if we're talking about a clinic that destroyed donor codes and records, which we most certainly are. What if the clinic was unable to contact a donor as a result of the clinic's own deliberate attack on medical files?

Clinic 20 destroyed donor codes. And yet sperm donated to that public clinic was still there, decades later, in private hands, ready to be thawed and used to impregnate some unsuspecting woman.

It's Jurassic Park. In your uterus.

IAB had been able to find a consent form used for Clinic 20's sperm donors. Only two paragraphs of it were included in the report. One had the sperm donor agreeing never to know the recipient of their donation or be known to them. The other said: 'I agree never to seek the identity of any child or children born following upon the artificial insemination of any recipient of my semen nor seek to make any claim in respect of any such child or children in any circumstances whatsoever.'

So recipients would never know donors, and donors would never know recipients, and donors weren't supposed to seek out their children either. A stunted arrangement, imposed by doctors. But there was nothing there about me, about offspring. It appeared I could do as I pleased. Which, I supposed, was fortunate, considering the action I'd taken to date.

Despite finding that donor code destruction was a 'considered', albeit 'undocumented' practice at Clinic 20, IAB had apparently been unable to work out who'd done it. 'The party or parties who removed donor codes where a pregnancy resulted from a sperm donation have not been identified,' said the report. It also found: 'any staff member who undertook such action as removal of donor codes was acting on the instruction of management'.

IAB just left it at that.

I should not have been surprised at the shallowness of the investigation. I told you Diana Craven admitted to it, I thought. I gave you my notes. I told you how to contact her. In addition, if they'd looked a little bit harder, they would have found Douglas Saunders' self-published book, as I did.

In that book, Diana Craven admitted to removing donor codes, along with other staff at Clinic 20. Craven's account was edited by Saunders himself. Yet in 2014, the year after it was printed, Professor Douglas Saunders told *Australian Story* in a statement that 'he had "no personal knowledge of the code being removed and, if it was, when, by whom and in what circumstances"'. In 2015, IAB published its report, naming no-one, exculpating everyone.

THE WAY THE report picked its way carefully around key issues was interesting in itself. The IAB audit confirmed record destruction took place not just at Clinic 20 but at other clinics and dubbed all of this 'enduring anonymity' – a term which makes the practice sound thoughtful, as opposed to illegal. The issue, for IAB, was whether records had been '*intentionally* tampered with' (emphasis added):

'We have been particularly mindful of the pejorative nature of the term "tampered with" as suggesting that there was an intention of deception ... We found no evidence of such intention, noting the consistency of removal of donor codes in all cases where a successful pregnancy resulted until 1984.'

Therefore, destruction of donor codes was not 'tampering' because it was done to every baby. Because they maximised the damage, IAB reasoned, Clinic 20 was somehow off the hook.

'The likely time frame for removal of the donor codes in virtually all cases preceded the enacting of the *Artificial Conception Act 1984* (assented to on 5 March 1984). The practice of removing donor codes then ceased within a period of three months following the enacting of that legislation,' wrote IAB.

How could they possibly know that? And later, seemingly untroubled by the contradiction, IAB described more donor code removal years after the introduction of the *Artificial Conception Act 1984*. In a recipient's file dated 1989, there was a donor code that 'appeared to be obscured by "whiting out"'. Apparently the code in that file 'was obscured even from the reverse side of the document'. This, decided IAB, was 'likely to have been a clerical error', because another code had been written over the top.

IAB reasoned that destruction of donor codes ceased to become necessary with the introduction of the *Artificial Conception Act 1984*, which asserted that we were not the children of our biological parents. According to IAB, 'the last of the donor codes that were removed were cut from clinical records in June 1984'. Well, except for that 1989 situation. And except for a Clinic 20 letter that IAB had found, to a donor, saying that because of code destruction they couldn't work out if he'd fathered any children, a policy which was 'substantially reviewed around 1986'. But let's go with what IAB says for a second. Let's assume the last donor codes removed were for clinical records dated June 1984. What else was happening at that time?

A wave of medically transmitted HIV.

It's possible, even probable, that because of AIDS, staff at Clinic 20 were mostly scared into preserving donor codes after June 1984 – which, prior to that date, they'd destroyed. Taking a darker view of things, it's also possible that staff at Clinic 20 destroyed donor codes for files up until June 1984 to obscure who had been treated with what. If any of those women or live babies contracted HIV through contaminated sperm like at the Westmead program, well, there would be no way of proving that it was the fault of Clinic 20. When the act of destruction for any code took place, we'll never know. At best, we can only tell the period for which records are missing.

An incident at the Westmead clinic did score a mention in IAB's report. It wasn't HIV-related – but it did underline just how ruthless 'enduring anonymity' could be.

The IAB investigator had found some internal Royal North Shore Hospital correspondence about a particular sperm donor at Westmead. It was dated 1991, and it was not good news:

'... Subsequent to this, Westmead removed him from their Programme, however, did not inform him that an abnormal foetus had been the result of one of his donations. Miss XXXXXX informed me that it had been their policy at the time to maintain absolute anonymity in their programme.'

This Westmead donor had fathered an 'abnormal' foetus, and no-one had told him. However, the 'abnormality' was sufficient to make Westmead drop him.

Unaware, that man might have gone on to father more 'abnormal' foetuses in his own social relationships or donated sperm elsewhere to other recipient families. What anonymity would have been broken by telling him of the abnormal foetus at Westmead? None.

Did Westmead recognise any responsibility for any later 'abnormal' babies born, dead or alive, by that man? For any colossal pain or lifelong heartbreak which might have ensued for that man or recipient parents?

The IAB report didn't canvass those questions. After all, abnormal foetuses at Westmead weren't in their terms of reference.

IT SEEMED EVEN the professional investigator appointed by the state government wasn't going to ask the questions I thought were important.

There was one course of action left: to ask Professor Saunders himself. I sent him an email to his private email address, telling him who I was (in case the name didn't ring any bells by this point) and asking him for an interview. The email didn't bounce. But there was no reply.[4]

Nearly four weeks later, an unknown number rang my phone. The caller had the clipped, gravelly tones of an elderly woman. It was Douglas Saunders' wife, Margaret.[5]

Douglas Saunders, she explained, couldn't be of any help because he was too unwell. She could try to answer my questions instead.

I don't know if Margaret Saunders knew I was the one who had blown the whistle on donor code destruction at Clinic 20, because she seemed, in fact, not to know anything about the destruction itself. Nor the media coverage. Nor the two government-prompted investigations that followed.

'Even as an obstetrician, Doug had to keep the records of his patients for twenty-five years,' she said.

'Was that ... as intact records?' I asked. 'Or could he get rid of some of the pages?'

'Oh, heavens no,' she replied. 'No ethical person would.'

I explained that I was asking because there was a report done for the Department of Health which found that the records at the RNSH fertility clinic were systematically damaged.

'Well, certainly I can tell you right now, not by Doug. He's probably one of the most ethical people I know and have ever known, and not because I am his wife,' she replied. 'But,' she conceded, 'if that's the case, nothing was ever mentioned to us at all.' What? 'So that must have been sometime later, I suspect.'

Utterly baffling. Douglas Saunders had been asked, and had answered, questions about donor code destruction at Clinic 20 put to him by the ABC. On top of that, Peter Illingworth of IVF Australia, Di Craven of Clinic 20, and the Health Care Complaints Commission told me that they had all put questions to him about the destroyed donor codes on my behalf. A government investigation found that Clinic 20 had destroyed donor codes. Douglas Saunders had been at Clinic 20 for its entire existence. What on earth did she mean by 'later'?

I said that Douglas Saunders had published his book in 2013, and one of his interviewees, Di Craven, had mentioned code destruction at Clinic 20.

'I don't think that's the case,' Margaret Saunders said.

But it was, I said. 'She told him that for the book. And he published it.'

'Okay. Well then, uh … follow the book, is all I can say, for what he said on that,' she replied.

She did, at least, agree that donors were promised anonymity, and for good reason. I asked why. 'If that [code] was allowed to be kept in the records of who they were, they could then come back twenty years later,' she replied. 'If you were a child that had been born and had some disabilities or problems, you could come back and go to the father and say, you owe me,' she said.

'So it was to protect sperm donors from children who might have had a claim from having some disabilities?'

'Yeah,' she replied.

After a diversion on the lower quality eggs provided by overseas donors ('most of them are so poor and hungry'), Margaret Saunders said if I had any more questions I could put them in writing and send them to her. She would also ask Douglas Saunders for his input, although she couldn't guarantee he would be able to say much. She gave me their private mailing address.

I wrote down all the questions I could think of, including a chunk about Saunders' years in private practice and teaching, and sent them off.

ABOUT A MONTH later, I received a reply.

It was not from either Douglas or Margaret Saunders. It was a message, on NSW Government letterhead, from the director of Medical Services at the Royal North Shore Hospital.

'Dear Ms Dingle,' it said. 'Mrs Saunders has forwarded to me your set of questions.'

The RNSH director of Medical Services was suddenly gatecrashing my correspondence with the Saunders.

Seemingly unaware of years of exposure and investigation, he suggested I direct my questions to the head of the Northern Sydney Local Health District. Again.

'Further contact to [Professor Saunders] and Mrs Saunders would be inappropriate,' the director warned, 'as he is, for health reasons, unable to assist.'[6]

Even when I wanted to ask about Saunders' private practice, it seemed, the public health system was still running defence.

At the bottom, the director noted that the letter was cc'd to Mrs Margaret Saunders.

CHAPTER 25

THE IAB REPORT had failed to deliver any answers about my own personal situation. I didn't know who my donor was, how he came to donate, nor how many times he did it.

I also didn't know how much he knew about the whole process. Did he know the clinic would destroy donor codes, so that he would never be found? Did he realise that there was no law against them keeping, and using, his sperm indefinitely? Was he okay with all of this, or had he been deceived too?

I'M CHATTING TO a man whom I'll call Bob. These days, he's an associate professor at an Australian university. He's asked for me not to use his real name.

Bob is a sperm donor, although it's only recently that he's realised it.

'This is a really strange story. You probably won't believe it,' he says. Try me, I think.

In the early '80s, Bob was a student at the University of Sydney.

The University of Sydney has had strong ties, right from the start, to the fertility sector. Douglas Saunders, the head of Clinic 20, founded Sydney University's Department of Obstetrics and Gynaecology in 1972. He remained on staff with that department – on top of running Clinic 20 – for the next thirty-one years. Westmead Hospital's fertility clinic – the outfit which saw HIV transmissions in the '80s – is today wholly owned by the university.

One day in 1981, Bob was on campus, and something unusual happened.

'A large set of caravans and trucks turned up at the University of Sydney,' he said. 'And this was associated with some major hospital, and they said that they had this problem: they couldn't get decent people for sperm donors, they only had drunks and druggies.' Charming. 'And they were going to have this competition between faculties to see which could come up with the most donors... So somebody was keeping a check to see how many arts people versus science people versus engineering, sort of thing.'

It sounded like some sort of O-week activity.

'They sort of built up this competition atmosphere between the faculties,' said Bob, 'and in those days, there were very big ideas about, you know, "arts students are stupid" and all the rest of it. And, you know, the engineering students used to come in and bash up the arts students, and all these sorts of things that used to happen. So there was something that they could build on. There was this enmity between the students.'

'Wow,' I said. I had no idea what to say. This sounded utterly ridiculous. Very macho, very bro-culture. And completely plausible.

'This [competition] happened on the university grounds, all official-like,' said Bob. 'And at that stage in my life, I thought, I'm not going to get married. I might as well do it.'

So Bob went into a caravan. 'It all happened, all the rest of it,' he said delicately. 'And they only did a very minor look at anybody's health. As long as you could walk, I think,' (he laughed) 'they'd take you. And I then forgot about this event.'

Bob remembers the caravans were from a major public hospital, but he can't remember which one.

I couldn't let go of the idea of a competition. 'So how was this competition supposed to play out?' I asked. 'Was it purely *numbers* of donors? Or were they going to take that sperm away, and test it, and then tell you how impressive it was?' (Sometimes I can't help myself.) But Bob was thinking about more serious matters.

'No, I don't think they tested anybody. For anything,' he said firmly.

There were just two rules. 'It was only research students,' Bob said. 'Research students who weren't in any sort of arrangement, like a marriage or something.' The whole act was sold, he says, as 'you were doing a good thing for women. And of course, you were doing a good thing because you're *smart*. I think, you know, there was something to do with, you know. They were trying to have better children, of course.' He finally got it out: 'You know, I think it was some experimental, *eugenic experiment* is my guess.'

Bob chuckled awkwardly. Fair enough: eugenics is very far from palatable. And what he was describing was eugenics practised by public hospital medical staff, without any legal oversight. There were no laws around artificial insemination by donor in New South Wales in 1981.

'It happened sort of in a couple of days,' says Bob. 'And then the whole thing disappeared and was never heard of again. And apparently, there were lots of problems, with people who had diseases and things and what-have-you occurring.'

Afterwards, Bob didn't think about this much ever again: mostly, he forgot it had ever occurred – which might sound strange, but consider the circumstances of this so-called medical process, and the atmosphere. For Bob, this whole incident only resurfaced in his mind a few years ago.

'This was an incredibly unethical process,' said Bob, 'but it really did happen … it's very hard to think about, actually.

'The more you think about it, the more insane it becomes.'

AROUND 2017, BOB got an email. It was from a woman called Lauran Wassell. Lauran is donor conceived, the same age as me. She was born through the fertility clinic at the public Royal Hospital for Women in Sydney's east.

'Lauran said, "I think you might be my father",' said Bob.

That was a shock, to say the least.

Lauran knew she was donor conceived from a young age – around five years old – and had done plenty of detective work of her own over the years. She'd also enlisted the help of other donor-conceived people, including Geraldine Hewitt, who was made at the same fertility clinic. Both women say the records of their donor conception were destroyed. The Royal Hospital for Women comes under the South Eastern Sydney Local Health District. The SESLHD declined to answer any of my questions, including whether records were destroyed.[1]

Together, through sleuthing, Lauran and Geraldine worked out Lauran's donor might be Bob. So Lauran found Bob's contact details online, and sent Bob a message, with her contact number.

'He bloody rang,' Lauran told me, sounding amused. 'He rang within like 15 minutes of the email. It was insane. And he said "I don't think I could possibly be your father. I'd actually forgotten I donated sperm. That was a long time ago."'

Bob hung up. Had a think. Then he called Lauran back.

'And he goes, "I do remember donating",' Lauran said. 'He said, "But I didn't donate for like, for *children*."' Bob again described to her the caravans and the faculty competition. '[He said] it was all about testing,' Lauran recalled, 'to see who was the smartest, and how they could manipulate it, and how they could make these super babies.'

'And thinking to myself,' Lauran said, 'I was like, try not to be too offended here, Lauran, because I don't think he's put two and two together here that *babies were made*.'

LAURAN AND BOB did a DNA test together. Lauran and Bob are very closely related. But Bob is not Lauran's father. Another relative is.

Bob is not the only person in his family who donated sperm.

ALTHOUGH DONOR CONCEPTION has existed for more than a century, and become particularly common over the last four decades – we still do not realise just how big it has grown. How deeply it has sunk into the layers of our society. How close to home it really is. We allow it, engage in it, keep it quiet, and do nothing to accommodate its intergenerational consequences.

You may be reading this book because you find it interesting – I certainly hope you do – but you may also think that its contents relate only to others. In fact, given how long society has allowed donor conception to proliferate, there are no guarantees that your parents are your parents, outside of a DNA test. Which I recommend, if you have any doubts.

Donor conception hides in families, whether you are a commissioning parent who has used it and lied, a donor, a donor like Bob for whom – it turns out – donating sperm is something of a family quirk, or a donor-conceived person who has never been told the truth.

Sometimes, you might be more than one of these things.

IN 2005, AN Australian man in his mid-twenties I'll call Rob decided to become a sperm donor. Rob was in a committed relationship at the time. His partner already had kids, and Rob didn't think he would ever want to father any children through his own social relationship.

A fertility clinic happened to advertise for sperm donors at the gym of Rob's university. Rob was already a blood donor. 'Why not donate sperm to help people have a family?' he thought at the time. 'The process was simple. You call up and say you're interested, you meet with a member of their team for a family history health check, then the next appointment is with a counsellor who asks you what will your family think if they found out, and what might I think about it in the future.'

Back then, Rob was untroubled by any of this. 'I figured if the children wanted to find me, they'd have to get the written records, and at the time I couldn't comprehend why they would bother,' he said.

'And even if they did track me down, it wouldn't be until they are an adult twenty years into the future. I didn't think my family would ever need to know. I believed that if someone went to the trouble of going to a legitimate fertility clinic, then they must be really motivated to have the child and would look after them well. So hopefully the children would be happy enough with their lives that they wouldn't want to seek me out.'

Rob was then 'a poor student with three part-time jobs and full-time study'. As a donor, he received a cool AUD$100 per sperm donation. There was a six-month quarantine period: you received AUD$20 for each donation upfront, then after six months, if your second blood test checked out, you received the remaining AUD$80 per donation. Rob donated ten times. That was about AUD$1400 in 2020 terms.

Life went on. Rob's relationship ended. He graduated. His father and mother were both originally from the US and had moved to Australia. Rob performed that move in reverse: he went back to the US, to his roots, found a job, met a girl, got married and ended up having children through that marriage.

'I was always interested in family history, I think in part because I didn't have the best relationship with my parents,' Rob said. 'Knowing more of my family history made me feel more connected to a wider network of people.' So in 2016, he took a direct-to-consumer DNA test through a large genealogy company.

A few years later, Rob got a message from someone else who had done a test with the same company. The person shared a certain percentage of DNA with Rob: they were half-siblings.

Rob didn't believe it.

'I thought it was a Russian hack, because I had been using the face-ageing app,' said Rob. 'Then they sent me more photos. So I called my mum, who confirmed it.' She told Rob the truth for the first time: he was donor conceived. Rob was thirty-six.

ROB'S EXPERIENCE – FINDING out that he was donor conceived through a DNA test – is a common one around the world. These DNA tests are finally revealing the truth. The truth is certainly what we all deserve.

In the 2020 We Are Donor Conceived survey of 481 donor-conceived people from around the world, aged thirteen to seventy-four, fully one-third (34 per cent) said they found out they were donor conceived from a DNA test.[2]

Their parents did not tell them the truth as a child, a teen, or an adult, and no-one else did either.

The science doesn't lie. But it is not in a person's best interests to find this out from a website.

Society has an obligation to donor-conceived people not to leave them to find out the truth in this way.

WHEN I FIRST spoke to Rob about his discovery, he had lived with the knowledge that he was donor conceived for less than two months. He was still very much coming to terms with it. The first month, he said, was pure shock.

'Now I oscillate between sadness and loss, but other times it's anger. I partly set up my life in the US because I thought I was descended from a line of American men,' Rob explained. 'Turns out that's a lie, but I'm now married with a family over here, and can't easily get back to Australia.' Some days, Rob said, he feels angry – he feels duped.

'Don't get me wrong, my life is great, but I thought it was one of my choosing,' he said. 'I now know that some of my choices were built on a lie.'

The discovery has changed his relationship with his parents: 'My respect for my parents has reduced. I see the choice not to tell me as a reflection of their weaknesses, insecurities and small-mindedness … Not telling me was not for my benefit, but for theirs … I see my dad as my social dad, not my biological dad. He's no less important to me and will always be "my dad", but there is a different context to it now.' The truth also explains a lot: '[It] exposes years of secrets from my developmental years that I could sense, but never comprehend, until it all came out.'

Today, when Rob considers those ten occasions when he himself donated sperm in his twenties, he feels very differently. It never occurred to him that he *himself* was the product of such an act. Back then, he said, 'I couldn't relate to what it might be like to not know your biological parents. I took my understanding of my family for granted.'

He's now thinking about sperm donation from completely the opposite perspective – what it means to the resulting child.

'I wouldn't have done it if I knew at the time,' he said.

'I would have known the grief and difficulties of going through it all, and I think that would have led me not to want to impose that on others. The world has enough people, so I now think that if you can't have children, then find purpose and meaning elsewhere. I have asked the clinic that if any of my samples are left could they please destroy them.'

Rob says the clinic agreed but warned that if any embryos had already been made, none of them could be destroyed. (This is standard practice in Australia.) It also told him that his donations had already resulted in seven children. Rob says if any of those kids come to him for information, he will provide it. That, at least, makes him feel good.

Rob was just twenty-four when he donated sperm. 'I don't think you can make those longer-term decisions as a young man … It is impossible to think about those things earlier in your life. So I do think services target poor young men who aren't really in a place to fully understand the ramifications of their choices.'

The other thing is, Rob says, if he'd known he was donor conceived, he probably would have been ineligible to donate sperm anyway. 'I couldn't have given accurate medical history to the clinic, because I didn't know it myself at the time.'

DONORS CAN BE a generous lot, sometimes to their own detriment. Donors are also vulnerable to exploitation. When that happens, the question must be asked: who is failing their duty of care to these people?

Australia lays claim to the woman known as the most generous egg donor in the world: Faith Haugh. 'World's Best Baby Egg Donor', screamed the *Herald-Sun*. 'Melbourne Supermum', cried the Adelaide *Advertiser*.[3]

Victorian woman Faith Haugh donated eggs for seventeen years, beginning when she was just twenty-three.[4] This is notable for a few reasons. First of all: it's an incredibly long period of time. Secondly, the Victorian Assisted Reproductive Treatment Authority, or VARTA, says that 'preferably' donors of either sperm or eggs are aged between twenty-five and forty, and have already completed their own family.[5] That is, donors should already have had all the children in their own social relationships that they ever want to have – before they donate. But these safeguards are not mandatory. VARTA notes that fertility clinics 'may have their own policies'. And Victoria is one of the most, if not the most, well-regulated jurisdictions in Australia when it comes to donor conception.

Faith Haugh failed both these donor criteria: she started donating when she was younger than twenty-five – and she never completed the family that she wanted.

Faith Haugh began donating in 1993. In total, she would undergo forty-two cycles of hormone stimulation and egg extraction. All but one were conducted in Australian fertility clinics. Forty-two is an astonishing number for any woman. Nearly every single time, it was for other people.

Extracting eggs is hard on the female body: it's an arduous process. A woman will inject hormones daily for days or weeks to stimulate her ovaries, so that instead of releasing usually a single egg per menstrual cycle, she releases many more. Those eggs can then be extracted by a fertility specialist in a batch lot through a procedure sometimes known as 'egg pick-up'. The cocktail of hormones you inject, and the degree to which your ovaries are stimulated, depends on what your fertility specialist prescribes. For instance, one brand of injectable hormone is known as Gonal-f. It is produced in the ovarian cells of Chinese hamsters.[6] Once a woman is injecting Gonal-f, the number of eggs she will release in that stimulated cycle depends on the amount of stimulation and on the ovary itself. Gonal-f's manufacturer mentions a 'target oocyte yield' of eight to fourteen oocytes on its website.[7]

Women injecting such hormones run the risk of side effects – everything from headaches and nausea to ovarian hyperstimulation syndrome.[8] This is when the ovaries swell and become painful as a result of excess hormones. Symptoms of OHSS can range from mild to severe: from abdominal pain and vomiting, to blood clots, enlarged abdomen and rapid weight gain. Severe OHSS may result in hospitalisation.

Faith Haugh took Gonal-f. It is a commonly prescribed medication in fertility. She also took a number of other drugs as prescribed by the fertility clinics she was attending, the dose and type of which varied per cycle, as directed by her fertility specialists.

Faith Haugh first began donating eggs, Fairfax newspapers reported, 'when she saw an ad in *The Age* newspaper placed by an infertile couple. Through an IVF clinic at a public hospital, she anonymously donated her eggs to them, which led to the birth of twin girls.'[9]

At that stage, Faith had not yet met the man who would become her life partner, Glenn Watson. She had one daughter of her own, born when she was just eighteen. Glenn tells me that Faith's first egg donation at age twenty-three 'was pretty positive [for her]. At the time she wasn't feeling 100 per cent. I guess her self-esteem was pretty low. She felt like she was actually helping someone. So it boosted her worth, I guess.'

VARTA says that 'preferably', donors should 'keep both physically and mentally healthy' and should be 'responsible and settled. It is advisable that a donor's life is stable and they have a good support network.' Once again, however, none of this is 'essential'.

Faith kept donating eggs. She kept donating after she met Glenn. 'It was just constant, constant,' Glenn Watson says. And Faith didn't always tell Glenn how much donating she was doing. He loved her generosity, but he didn't want her to go overboard. 'If you've got ten kids out there, why do you wanna go for, say, thirteen? … You've given a certain amount of people a gift. And it's an invasive procedure.' So Faith sometimes kept the full details to herself.

Glenn himself has donated sperm in the past, at Faith's suggestion. He knows he has four donor-conceived children. 'That's enough for me … But when you've got someone ringing you saying, "Oh, we've got this person, you know, they need this and that", it kind of gets the ball rolling.'

Which, says Glenn, is what happened to Faith. He says the doctors 'took advantage of Faith's good nature'. And she produced so many eggs, 'it was like a gravy train'. Glenn Watson said one fertility specialist in particular, from Monash IVF, would ring Faith, personally, to solicit yet another round of egg donation. And again. And again. 'He'd just ring her. Out of the blue.'

'Do you think that's appropriate?' I asked.

'No,' Glenn said immediately. 'And I think Faith was, you know, she was the golden ticket for a lot of people. Because they knew that she produced a lot of eggs, and they were good eggs. And she was only a phone call away.'

Faith was not a person who would say no. In photos, she has straight blonde hair and fine features: she is a comfortable, maternal shape.

Her face is youthful and kind. 'I'm pretty sure,' said Glenn, 'she had thirty-two or thirty-three hormone treatments.'

I pause. I've gone through official documentation on Faith's medical background, which Glenn has kindly shown me. He keeps it, but it's not something he reads regularly, or wants to. 'It says,' I say cautiously, 'she went through forty-two cycles.'

'*Forty-two*?' Glenn repeated.

'Yeah,' I say awkwardly.

In Faith's medical file from Melbourne IVF, you can see part of the process unfold. Six eggs extracted from her one cycle. Seven eggs the next. Nine eggs extracted, in one of her last cycles in an Australian facility, aged thirty-eight: old in terms of the fertility game.

Not all Faith's egg donations were conducted at the same clinic. She donated to Melbourne IVF and Monash IVF, two of the biggest fertility entities in Victoria, and also said that her first donation was to a public hospital clinic. But all Victorian clinics are supposed to report donors and their donations centrally to VARTA, the state authority.

GIVEN HOW ARDUOUS egg donation is, it's a little challenging to understand why Faith did it as many times as she did. Glenn states firmly that Faith never got paid for any eggs donated in Australia (she also did a single round of egg donation in India, where she did receive payment in return). Altruism is one thing, but forty-two cycles of hormone treatments, keeping the details of many a secret from her own partner – and others – makes you start to wonder.

In 2003, after a full decade of egg donation, Faith was referred to an endocrinologist. She was worried about weight gain and pelvic pain. An ultrasound showed she had polycystic ovaries (a condition which, long term, can carry a heightened risk of diabetes, cardiovascular disease, and endometrial cancer).[10] But the report of the endocrinologist who assessed her made no mention of her current hormonal stimulation for egg donation. The endocrinologist, in fact, seemed unaware Faith was donating eggs. Instead, he puzzled over her deranged hormonal levels. He wrote that he was unable to explain them.[11]

There is no doubt Faith Haugh was a generous woman. But looking closer, Glenn's account of how Faith derived self-worth from her first egg donation makes a terrible kind of sense. As she continued to donate eggs with some secrecy, the picture starts to look more like an addiction. Something you hide from the ones who love and worry about you, something which gives you a small hit of feeling good, and that hit sustains you until you need another.

But unlike a smoking habit, or a gambling addiction, every time Faith donated eggs she was engaging in a fertility system where people were supposed to keep track of what she was doing, for both her sake and the sake of any future children: the fertility clinics she donated to, and the state authority, VARTA.

GLENN WAS STILL processing the fact that Faith underwent forty-two rounds of hormone treatments.

'Yeah, that's … that's insane,' Glenn said slowly. 'That's negligence, really. You wouldn't do that to a puppy, would you.' He pauses. 'At the end of the day, and they will always say this' (he means Faith's doctors), 'it was her choice.

'But there's got to be some sort of duty of care somewhere. Someone has to take the responsibility of saying, No. You've done enough.'

IN 2011, FAITH Haugh told the *Sunday Mail* she was the biological mother of nineteen donor-conceived children, and just one of her own. The latter fact was not as she would have liked it.[12]

Several years earlier, after so long helping others to have their families, Faith had decided she wanted to have a second child, with Glenn. But then she discovered something that made her shelve those plans abruptly. In 2007, she'd gone to her general practitioner, complaining of persistent abdominal pain and lethargy. Initial scans and tests pointed to 'small areas of focal nodular hyperplasia and a large hepatic adenoma' on her liver, according to one official report.

These are two different conditions. FNH is usually asymptomatic, without long-term consequences. Hepatic adenoma, on the other hand, according to Melbourne liver specialist Professor Christopher Christophi, 'has the potential for complications such as bleeding, rupture and malignant transformation to Hepatocellular Carcinoma' – a malignant liver tumour. Hepatic adenomas are strongly associated with the use of oral contraceptive pills (also prescribed to Faith as part of her egg donation process) and other estrogens.[13] One liver specialist quoted in Faith Haugh's records says that 'multiple cycles of IVF, combined with the use of oral contraceptives, could be genotoxic [that is a genetic driver of the development of hepatic adenoma]'.

However, a number of later tests diagnosed the large mass on Faith's liver as being FNH. At least two Australian surgeons, including Professor Christophi, told Faith that removing it was not safe – and it was also unnecessary. Although FNH is benign, the mass is repeatedly referred to in Faith Haugh's medical documents as a 'tumour', which may help explain what Faith did next. She wanted it gone. She was convinced it was cancerous.

'Once I get through this cancer the first thing I'm going to do is try to get pregnant,' she told *The Age*, in 2008. 'But I'm going to freeze an embryo, just in case.'

Faith would never raise another child of her own.

Faith, Glenn said, was experiencing a lot of pain. The mass on her liver kept growing. She wanted an embolisation to shrink it. She was convinced that she needed it. She was convinced, says Glenn Watson, that the tumour was life-threatening.

In 2009, Faith travelled to Thailand to find a doctor who would conduct the procedure. It was apparently successful in shrinking some of the tumour and she returned for two further procedures in 2010 and 2011. Her health was not good. In 2011, a specialist noted that she had a lot of significant health issues, including obesity and persistently abnormal liver function tests as well as the liver mass.

In 2012, against the advice of Australian surgeons once again, Faith managed to find a Thai surgeon who was prepared to remove part of the tumour at Bangkok Hospital. She was discharged five days later. A week and a half after discharge, Faith and Glenn flew back to Melbourne, arriving in the evening. The next day, Faith began vomiting. Two and a half weeks after the surgery, she was admitted to Royal Melbourne

Hospital with multi-organ dysfunction, including liver failure. She was critically ill. She stayed in intensive care for a number of weeks, went through several bouts of surgery, but ultimately died on 1 December 2012, aged forty-two.

Australian fertility clinics had nothing to do with each of Faith's decisions to undergo procedures in Thailand, including that last, lethal surgery. Those decisions look like the acts of a desperate woman, as indeed they were. But you could also say that Faith's decision to shop around, effectively, and find medical procedures on tap, followed a pattern set over *seventeen years* of egg donation, in which time I cannot find any documentation showing that any fertility specialist ever refused her donations – or told her no.

In donor conception, there is personal choice. And there is medical duty of care. And also present, unacknowledged but powerful, there are the forces of guilt, obligation, vulnerability and positive reinforcement.

IN AUGUST 2007, the Infertility Treatment Authority sent Melbourne IVF a warning letter about Faith Haugh and donor limits.

According to Victoria's Central Donor Register, by 2007 Faith's eggs had already created nine families (there were no details of how many children had been produced in each family). 'Licensed centres must not knowingly allow the donated gametes of one person to be used to produce offspring in more than ten families,' the ITA's Chief Executive Officer, Louise Johnson, warned. She also said that it would be important to check whether Faith had donated eggs interstate.

The nine families Johnson referred to did not include Faith's own daughter, raised by her. Faith's eggs had already created ten families, if you include her own.

The ITA did not tell Melbourne IVF to stop using Faith as a donor. Instead, it left that up to the clinic.

'It is up to Melbourne IVF to make a clinical decision in relation [to] whether to use Faith Haugh as an egg donor taking into account the guiding principles of the *Infertility Treatment Act 1995*, and the health and welfare of the parties concerned,' Louise Johnson wrote.

That same day, Melbourne IVF sent a letter to Faith Haugh, asking her to complete a statutory declaration. In it, Faith declared that apart from the existing nine families – seven with Monash IVF and two with Melbourne IVF – she did not have any other donor-conceived offspring from any other Australian fertility clinic, or any remaining embryos in storage either in Australia or overseas.

However, this declaration does not appear to include Faith's very first donation at a public hospital, reported by *The Age*, which resulted in twin girls. If you count that, Faith had already hit ten donor families.

Years later, I contacted the ITA, now VARTA, to clarify how many donor-conceived children Faith Haugh's donations had finally created, to how many families, and whether that public hospital donation was included in the count. They replied they were unable to provide that personal information to me, or even seek it out. However, VARTA said, no egg donor had ever breached the ten-family limit.

Five days after making her statutory declaration, Faith Haugh signed a Melbourne IVF consent form to donate eggs yet again.

Documents show Melbourne IVF would go on to extract another twenty-two eggs from the ovaries of Faith Haugh.

I PUT A number of questions regarding Faith Haugh to Melbourne IVF. To all of them, it responded: 'Unfortunately due to confidentiality reasons, we cannot comment on individual patients.'

MIVF is part of the giant Virtus Health. Virtus CEO Kate Munnings said: 'We take our responsibility for the care and outcomes of our patients and our donor programs very seriously and with great pride … We strive to lead a modern, socio-culturally responsible donor program.'

I also put a number of questions to Monash IVF about Faith Haugh, including whether one of their fertility specialists personally rang Faith to solicit donations. Monash IVF also replied that 'for privacy reasons we are unable to comment on any individual case'. It added: 'the safety and wellbeing of our patients and any child born as a result of assisted reproductive technology (ART) is paramount in everything we do. This is in keeping with the strict legislative and regulatory guidelines that we operate under.'

CHAPTER 26

TODAY THERE ARE countless sperm, egg and embryo donors around the world, in countries both rich and poor. Donors are described as givers of gifts in ads and in the media. If they're female, they're usually also 'angels' (albeit angels with working reproductive systems).

But if it's still rare to hear from a donor-conceived adult in the media (a donor-conceived person of age, interviewed without a parent in the background), think about how little you hear from all those many, many donors. Despite their numbers, have you ever heard any of them say they regret it, or that they're not 100 per cent comfortable with the bargain they struck?

And if not: do you honestly believe that every single one of them is fine?

IN 2014, A Sydney woman called Natalie Parker happened to watch the two-part *Australian Story* program featuring Lauren, Rel and me. She'd been mulling a big decision for some time, and, she tells me now, seeing us clinched it for her.

I can only describe this as a completely unforeseen consequence of my actions. I was horrified to hear her say so.

Natalie Parker and her husband had been through IVF to have their own biological children – two boys – and at the end of the process, they had three leftover embryos. They didn't want to have any more kids.

Natalie found herself in an ethical quandary familiar to many couples around the world.

'We created them with the purpose of being one of our children,' she told me over the phone. 'So do we then destroy them, or do we still give them the chance of life?'[1]

AROUND THE SAME time as Natalie was weighing this up, my own cousin asked me the same question. She's not really my cousin, if you define family by blood; I know this now. She is my (social) dad's niece. I rang her before the *Australian Story* went to air, to give her some warning of what was coming, and above all to tell her the truth myself first. When I was growing up, out of all my cousins, I absolutely idolised her and her sister. Little girls always look up to big ones. Funnily enough, as it turns out, they were the only cousins who weren't really mine.

She said exactly what I needed to hear. 'Of course you're my cousin,' she exclaimed. 'You'll always be my cousin.' We were both teary. She told me that it didn't matter. Then, out of nowhere, came something that I didn't expect. Quite often when I tell people the truth about the darkness I see in the fertility industry, they will respond in kind with their own. It happens with disturbing frequency.

My cousin and her husband had also been through IVF to have their own biological children. At the end of their treatment, they too had unused embryos in storage. And they were not in any way prepared for the emotional storm that ensued. Their choices were like Natalie's: donate them or destroy them. For years, my cousin and her husband had settled on a third, excruciating option: pay the fertility clinic in question a significant amount of money every year, to continue storing the embryos, so that they didn't have to make a decision. And yet, at the end of every year, they knew the decision itself hadn't gone away.

My cousin's particular clinic had a ten-year storage limit. After ten years, her clinic would automatically destroy the embryos itself, according to its own policy. My cousin and her husband were leaning towards that outcome of destruction by default. It would cost them a lot of money. But it would take the decision out of their hands. They would continue to pay the fertility clinic for a decade, simply to be spared the unexpected pain of choice. But, my cousin asked: did I think they should donate them instead?

'Well,' I said helplessly. (This was unexpected.) 'From everything I've found out about myself, I can only tell you what I feel: don't give away your genetic material.' I meant: don't give away your children.

'That's what I feel too,' she whispered.

NATALIE PARKER'S HUSBAND was all for donating their excess embryos.

'My husband isn't as emotionally invested as I am, and not very emotionally intelligent full stop,' she told me frankly. 'He was very much for donating, to give someone else a chance for a family.' That was how he saw the choice: between helping someone, and not helping them. Natalie wasn't sure it was quite that simple.

But she was aware of the demand for embryos. She'd read an article in the *Sydney Morning Herald* about the numbers of unused embryos in storage in Australia.[2] It stated that in any given year, around 120,000 embryos were in storage. It quoted an academic, who estimated up to 30 per cent of those embryos would ultimately not be used. (At the end of the piece, that 30 per cent figure was contradicted by the head of the Fertility Society of Australia, who said over time only 5 per cent of embryos would end up unused by the couples who made them.)

Astonishing as 120,000 embryos in storage is, with an (alleged) up to 30 per cent discard rate, that wasn't the hook of the story. The opening paragraph instead was all about a radical solution, proposed by that same academic: 'Prospective parents could receive discounted fertility treatment if they promise to donate some of the embryos created to other people, under one proposal for the thousands of unwanted embryos sitting in clinic freezers.'

Jesus Christ, I thought, reading that article which Natalie had sent me. It was a classic example of how assisted reproductive technology crashes through all social norms without forethought or discussion and then – to 'rectify' the situation – its cheer squad immediately rockets onwards towards compounding the damage.

Let's put aside the dubious ethics of giving people fertility discounts if they agree to bargain away their babies – like some modern-day

Rumpelstiltskin – and the legal questions which arise, including the concept of trading in human tissue, banned by Australia's Human Tissue Acts, and anti-trafficking laws. The sober response is *why*? Why are there so many unused embryos?

Are we over-treating some patients in the fertility sector – people who, in the case of heterosexual couples, may not even need expensive IVF in the first place? Should we divert some to lower-intervention options?

Yes, say doctors like fertility industry veteran Rob Norman. In 2013, more than 33,000 Australian women had a fertility treatment cycle. When I interviewed him in 2016, Professor Norman told me a large chunk of those women could have fallen pregnant without IVF, by using simpler, cheaper and less invasive methods: 'I think some people are getting IVF who shouldn't be getting it,' he said. 'My estimate is probably 40–50 per cent of people will get pregnant without IVF, and that is by understanding their fertility window, by tracking their cycle properly, by losing weight and [doing] exercise or having ovulation induction.'

After age, he said, weight was the number one factor affecting fertility for both men and women in Australia.

For those who do end up doing IVF – are we creating too many embryos? The head of the Evidence-based Women's Health Care Research Group in the Department of Obstetrics and Gynaecology at Monash University, Ben Mol, says the next questions to ask are: if you are going to do IVF, then how many embryos should you actually create – and how hard should doctors really be stimulating a woman's ovaries?

After that act, even more questions follow. Are we warning or preparing patients for the risk of creating too many embryos – that, having had all the children they want, they may find themselves facing possibly the toughest moral dilemma of their life?

And finally, are fertility clinics profiting, year in, year out, from the emotional anguish of couples, which results in mass storage of embryos that will never be used? Unquestionably. The problem is systemic. The solution is not a trading post where embryos are exchanged for fertility discount coupons.

Natalie had read this embryo storage article in the *Sydney Morning Herald*. She'd absorbed, not the offer of cheaper fertility treatment, because after all she was past needing any, but the number of unused embryos, the message about what a waste it was, and how sad it was for couples desperate to receive a donation. Then she saw me and my friends on *Australian Story*.

'After that *Australian Story*, I thought, as long as we have an open relationship and [any relinquished donor-conceived] children will know where they come from, then on paper, as long as you tick all those boxes, then that will be good, because you're giving that potential life the chance of a life, you know what I mean?' she said to me on the phone. I was appalled and astonished. That really wasn't what I thought the takeaway message was going to be from the show.

'We decided that it would be good to have a semi-open relationship [with the child] so it's something they grow up with knowing, it wouldn't come as a shock later on,' Natalie explained. She's right about that. But I didn't go public about what was done to me to encourage more donor conception. Stop, I told myself, put it aside. It doesn't matter. That was then. More importantly, Natalie has been through a hell of a lot since. She's now living a strange and painful reality, something no-one should have to endure. Once you create something – embryo or story – they can take on a life of their own.

In August 2014, just two days after Part 1 of the *Australian Story* documentary went to air, Natalie Parker hopped online and scrolled through a website called Embryo Donation Network. EDN is a small registered charity (tax deductible status: no) based in Sydney.[3] Its website is designed with soothing pastel hues of blue, green and purple, and inexplicably features a lot of photos of flowers and forest paths. EDN solicits financial contributions in return for its services: information resources (which seem to consist of links to other sites), an email address for any questions you might have, access to closed Facebook groups where you can 'connect with others in a similar situation', and – crucially – a classifieds page. For embryos. Essentially, a baby swap meet.

There was one ad which caught Natalie Parker's eye. Anna (not her real name) and her husband were looking for a donation of embryos.

Anna's ad sounded 'positive and upbeat and genuine', says Natalie. 'I'm pretty sure she mentioned that her and her husband would be open to future contact ... She described her husband as a "Saint Bernard walking through the snow with a keg around his neck" and herself as a "chihuahua" – maybe it was because I have a soft spot for dogs.'

What makes you connect with one stranger on a particular day and not another? Your mood, a single word, the fact that they mention dogs. Maybe everyone on that site was a dog person, but not everyone said so.

'It's a bit like the response to a dating ad,' Natalie says.

I SCROLL THROUGH the classifieds on Embryo Donation Network. 'We suggest that you seek independant [sic] fertility counselling, legal and medical advice about embryo donation before using the classifieds,' EDN says. There follows some brief instructions and a 'Donate' button – not for donating embryos, but for donating cash to EDN: bank transfer, Paypal, VISA and MasterCard all accepted.

As a product of the baby business myself, going through websites like this makes my flesh crawl. It's all, predictably, about the parents, both would-be and biological: almost nothing is about the child produced. As in the rest of the fertility sector, the actual human being created is elided from the discussion. The donors with embryos may think they're 'doing the right thing'. The problem is, they're doing the right thing for other adults, and rank strangers at that. Not their own children. In order to do the right thing by any children which may result, above all, you have to put *their* welfare and best interests first. At which point, you'd hopefully question why you were advertising your own child online.

Some of EDN's classifieds read like ads for puppies or kittens. 'Wife and I have 5 frozen embryos for donation to a good home. We are caucasian in appearance, both fit and healthy with no health issues. Both children born from this frozen batch are 8 and 4 and in good health, smart and good looking!' Good-looking white kids to a good home: prepare for inbox overload. Other ads are brief and raise questions: 'Embryos located in South Africa. We are looking to donate to a family close by. Embryos will be shipped to another country for the family to undergo IVF.' Why? Are Australian medical standards too high? Some ads highlight interesting 'selling' points: 'The child will be mixed race!' Another: 'We are well travelled globally … We would contact you back if we think you meet our requirements.' Only three classifieds out of a total of seventeen, on the day I visit the site, ask for the child to be known to their biological parents.

Further arrangements happen by way of contacting the parties privately, but it's easy to imagine that in some cases, money changes hands – including for the human tissue itself. Halfway down its FAQ page, EDN says 'in Australia it is not legal to exchange money for body parts including organs, sperm, eggs and embryos. However, all expenses incurred through the donation process are usually paid for by the recipients.' Who knows what 'expenses' means. Who knows how that's itemised. Certainly, such one-to-one transactions aren't being policed.

AFTER READING ANNA'S ad in the EDN classifieds, Natalie Parker decided to get in touch. She sent Anna an email: 'I found your contact details and ad on the Embryo Donation Network classifieds. I guess before I tell you my whole story, I should ask if you are still looking for an embryo? … I would love to hear a bit about you and your husband.'

Anna responded that same day. She sent Natalie a copy of her 'Profile' – an IVF Australia questionnaire form that she'd filled out, to be put on their list for donations. Marital status: happily married, 'hetrosexual' [sic]. No children, 'but not giving up …'. Sports played: 'Gymnastics (20 years), obstacle racing, sporty all rounder … volunteer my time at various charities … Favourite foods: salmon and home cooking. Chocolate [smiley face]'. Traces of unobjectionable personality. 'Main strengths: never giving up.' Anna said she'd tried unsuccessfully to conceive for eight years, using her and (presumably) her husband's genetic material as well as one round of donor sperm. Under the question 'Would you be willing to have contact or exchange of information with the donor or any of the children of the donor of any gametes or embryos?', Anna had checked both 'Yes, directly' and 'Yes, via clinic'.

At the end, under 'Personal messages', Anna had written: 'Your embryo will always feel wanted and loved. I would climb a mountain and cross a river to ensure they are happy every day of their lives. Thank you [smiley face].'

Two days after first contact, Natalie sent Anna another email: 'We are happy to come up Sydney for the Dr & counselling appointments … It looks like the ball has started rolling on everything, so that's exciting and a bit nerve wracking at the same time!' Once again Anna responded straightaway: 'Wow I just can't believe it. I'm sooooo excited. Anything that needs to be done on my end just let me know. I'm just packing at the moment for Bali … I will work around what ever times work for you. What ever you need me to do just say the word. Natalie I'm just in awe of what you are doing. Thank you again. You have made us sooooo happy. Feeling a little blessed right now.'

'It was hard not to get swept up in the excitement,' Natalie tells me now. She calls Anna's language 'charming': 'She was very flattering.' They conducted the process through IVF Australia, including a joint counselling session where the two couples met for the first time. 'They seemed really nice and genuine,' Natalie says. 'In the joint counselling she was saying all the right things, just the right things, to get what she wanted.' Natalie and her husband had to undergo blood tests at a cost of $140, a bill which they passed on to the recipient: 'That was a bit awkward,' she says. There were no other costs. 'I have no idea what [Anna and her husband] paid [to IVF Australia], but I guess it was part of their "donation package".'

At the same time as going through the steps for a potential embryo donation, Natalie and her husband were dealing with another big life change – they'd moved themselves and their two boys interstate. Anna's emails were constant throughout, and the language stayed 'charming', but also a bit relentless. Natalie had begun to have some doubts about the whole idea.

'When [Anna] was being quite pushy, repeatedly contacting me if I didn't respond straightaway, I spoke to a counsellor about that and how I was a little bit unsure, because it's a huge decision,' says Natalie. 'The counsellor said, "You know you can pull out at any time until it's the actual transfer". I said to my husband, "Should we go ahead?", and he said, "We can't pull out now, we've got their hopes up."'

Flattery, then guilt: again, two powerful emotions in donor conception, which go ignored by doctors and unrecognised by regulations. But in Natalie's situation, and who knows how many others', these two forces kept the whole process on the rails.

During the joint counselling session, Natalie says she was told that in the worst-case scenario she would be notified when a child (the biological child of her and her husband) was born. That was the bare minimum contact Natalie expected. The donation of two embryos went ahead, transferred to Anna and her husband in late 2014.

Emails from Anna went from constant to zero.

After the donation was finalised, 'we never heard from her again', says Natalie. That seemed strange, but fertility treatment can be a deeply affecting process for its patients. Natalie did, carefully, try: 'I asked her how she was going, and she didn't respond,' says Natalie. 'Life got in the way, and I didn't think about it.' Until twelve months later, when she got a phone call from the clinic. It was extremely businesslike.

'They said she'd transferred two embryos, but it didn't work. And that [we had] a third embryo left, and what did I want to do with it,' says Natalie. Apparently Anna had told the clinic she didn't want to try again with the last embryo. 'I thought, that's really strange, because she was so desperate to have a baby. I wondered why she just gave up.'

So Natalie found Anna's profile on Facebook. And, to her horror, she also found photos of someone else.

CHAPTER 27

NATALIE STARED AT Anna's Facebook page. Someone very familiar stared back.

'There was a child, who would have been conceived around the time of my donation,' says Natalie. 'He looked a lot like my younger son Hugo.' She immediately rang IVF Australia. 'I said, what happened, did she come back for a blood test? And they said no, she had bleeding, so she didn't come back.'

To Natalie, that was obviously a lie. The transfer had not failed. One of her embryos had successfully been transferred to Anna. And Anna had simply dropped out of all contact with IVF Australia, entering the health system as just another pregnant woman. Commissioning parents could just drop off the radar of fertility clinics at any time, and clinics didn't follow them up. It's one of the reasons why no-one has exact numbers on how many donor-conceived people there are in this country, let alone any idea who we all are.

'It didn't seem right, that the process wasn't followed through,' says Natalie now. 'When I rang up IVF Australia and told them what had happened, they got Peter Illingworth to call me. He said "It looks like she's done herself a grave injustice by not revealing this to anyone", and then I said to him, "I'm really concerned this has happened to other people", and he said "To the best of my knowledge this has not happened before".' Natalie was not comforted by that answer. 'I said I only found out through Facebook, and he was so patronising to me, I felt like he was patting me on the head.'

I asked IVF Australia's parent company Virtus Health whether this was an accurate reflection of that conversation between Natalie Parker and Peter Illingworth, whether this has happened before at their clinic, and if they had any comment to make on Natalie Parker's case at all.

In a statement, they replied that doctors were bound by patient confidentiality. 'As we have a duty of care to everyone involved, we are not in a position to make any public comment.'

THE BABY THAT Anna was now passing off as her own was biologically 100 per cent the child of Natalie and her husband.

'Do you think she stole your child?' I ask. Natalie feels the question is a bit bald, and the answer is more complex, but in essence, yes: 'It's kind of like saying when you go into a shop, you have to pay for whatever you buy – not that I'm saying it should be like a shop,' she replies. 'There was the condition that she was to follow through with the requirements. So it is like stealing something, if you really break it down.'

At a bare minimum, according to New South Wales law, the baby should have been recorded on the state's Central Register. And Natalie and her husband should have been listed as the donors. Those requirements would have cost Anna and her partner nothing and given the child a great deal: access to a second, biological set of relatives, with all the important protections that that knowledge brings.

But none of that happened. Was it too onerous for the recipient parents? Simply easier to lie? It is a terrible deception. The resulting damage isn't limited to the baby alone. 'It's hard,' Natalie says. She can still see that baby – now a child – grow up on Facebook. She knows where Anna lives. 'My husband said, oh well, we know his name, we can knock on his door when he's eighteen. And I was like no! That's not what you do! He needs to know while he's growing up.' Natalie is also worried about her two sons, who understand that they have a brother, but they can't contact or see him. 'I'm not really sure how to support them in it as they grow up,' she admits. I can understand her concern. As parenting dilemmas go, this is a terribly painful one.

Natalie has impressive resources of energy and determination. 'When it first happened, I felt quite violated,' she says. 'And I decided I wanted something good to come out of all this.'

After she realised her child existed, Natalie kicked into gear. She wrote to government, and she spoke to the media. Natalie told the *Sydney Morning Herald* that Anna had 'baby lust', a term that hovers around the fertility industry. It's an intriguing phrase which sounds like a topic for a thousand PhDs. But 'baby lust', once again, is a euphemism which reduces everything to the desires of the parent. 'Embryo heist' would be a more accurate description. Soft, petal-pink terms like 'baby lust' provide an excuse. What happened is not excusable. It is the theft of a child.

Natalie couldn't understand how legally Anna could get away with not disclosing her pregnancy. 'I just wanted to close that loophole in New South Wales, so there would be less likelihood of it happening in the future,' she says. She means the particular lack of regulation which allowed commissioning parents to walk away from fertility clinics after treatment, didn't force clinics to follow up, and left who knows how many donor children unrecorded, even after supposed legal protections were brought in. When New South Wales finally introduced legislation in 2010, post-2010 donors could no longer be anonymous. Their identities were supposed to go on the Central Register, information which could be accessed by their children once they turned eighteen. However, the whole system still depends on the commissioning parents telling their children the truth in the first place. And as I've discussed, for many, that is rare.

So Natalie wrote to the then NSW health minister, Jillian Skinner. The state government was then in the process of considering amendments to the *Assisted Reproductive Technology Act 2007*, following the two parliamentary inquiries it had held into donor conception – the ones where I'd spoken to the committee and told my story.

'Thank you for sharing your experience relating to the donation of your embryos with IVF Australia,' Health Minister Skinner wrote back to Natalie. 'The Ministry will also consider options to address the issues you have raised in relation to possible loopholes in the current system.'[1]

Natalie Parker also notified the Central Register of what had happened, telling them that her third biological child should be on their books as a donor-conceived child – and that she and her husband should be recorded as his donors, as per the law. The Regulation and Compliance Unit of the Department of Health's Legal and Regulatory Services branch began an investigation.

Towards the end of 2018, the NSW Government introduced a bill amending the ART Act 2007. They'd heard Natalie and they responded. From then on, as a result of Natalie's situation, fertility clinics and practitioners were required to collect information about the outcome of donor conception treatment. It also became an offence for a person to provide false information to a request for information by an ART provider: that is, it would be an offence to pretend that the fertility treatment didn't work.

Natalie reveals to me there has finally been an official ruling in her case. The state has found Natalie's terrible suspicion was correct: after disappearing, Anna did give birth to the biological child of Natalie and her husband. In March 2020, the director of the Regulation and Compliance Unit wrote to Natalie: 'I am satisfied that a male child was born on [birthdate] as a result of ART treatment provided to a woman using an embryo donated by you and your husband … I propose to record the particulars of the child's birth in the ART Central Register.'

Such a decision, the director said, will mean the boy's full name and date of birth are entered into the register – along with the details of the birth mother Anna and her husband, Natalie Parker and her husband listed as donors, and the sex and year of birth of Natalie's two boys. 'The purpose … is to ensure a donor conceived child, when they turn eighteen, can find out details about their biological heritage.'

Natalie rang the Regulation and Compliance Unit to follow up. She says she received verbal confirmation that the boy – her biological son – would finally be added to the Central Register of donor-conceived children in the next few days.

'There's no way of knowing if [Anna] will ever tell [the boy] that he is on the Central Register, but at least that information is there if he ever wants to access it,' Natalie says.

COMPARE THE PAIR. As a donor-conceived person, I had spent years meeting with New South Wales politicians and bureaucrats, telling my story, and uncovering systemic problems within a public hospital affecting dozens if not more of children and families, forcing official investigations. The systemic problem was not disputed. But no-one was held to account, and there was no redress.

As a parent and donor, Natalie told her story, revealing a serious problem which nevertheless had only been proven to affect one child. One month later she'd received a letter from the health minister herself, promising to consider options for closing 'loopholes in the system'. She achieved a result in her personal situation and managed to change state law.

Those 2018 amendments were the ones that supposedly followed on from the two parliamentary inquiries I'd participated in. They addressed Natalie's situation, but they completely ignored mine, as well as recommendations from the Parliamentary Committee about the plight of donor-conceived people. Nothing in those amendments prevented the actions of Clinic 20 from happening again.

Why did the state government listen to a parent, but not a product of this industry?

I come back to the profit motive. The fertility industry lobbies government. And the state government also has its own fertility clinics. Donors are key to donor conception, obviously, and in some ways they're also key to the rest of the industry, in clinics both public and private. Without donors, there is no donor conception, and therefore no final fertility safety net at the end of all the other treatments which the clinics can sell: without happy donors, there is no ultimate solution they can market.

Publicly unhappy donors threaten everything. They make the whole fertility industry look bad, plus the government which claims to oversee it. You can dismiss donor-conceived kids as 'children', you can dismiss donor-conceived adults as 'angry' or 'damaged'. And they do. But donors must be kept happy.

Donor-conceived people, on the other hand, do not represent any sort of profitable activity. Instead, we represent both financial cost and reputational risk. Maintaining our records imposes a financial cost. Dealing with us and our annoying queries, whether you're from the fertility industry or the health department, imposes a cost of time and therefore money.

And for both the private and public sectors, upholding donor-conceived people's human right to family imposes real risk, because it involves the truth. There's strong evidence to suggest that a lot of what was, and still is, being done to make us is pretty unsavoury. What if just one of those revelations upsets the real people involved? Public relations nightmare.

Donor-conceived people, therefore, are best ignored.

THAT DOESN'T MEAN that everyone listens to donors, though. The government may have acted when Natalie complained, but she says others in the embryo donation world stuck their fingers in their ears. Even those who'd played a role in Natalie's predicament.

'I had contact with the Embryo Donation Network,' she tells me. 'I wasn't very positive towards them.' Natalie had already posted about what had been happening in the embryo donation online support groups, so 'of course they knew about it', she says. 'However, when I formally sent them an email telling them what had happened, they sympathised and said that they also advocated for stronger support for donors and donor conceived individuals.' Natalie challenged them on what exactly that advocacy meant. 'I pointed out to them very clearly that having a "classified" service is treating these potential lives as commodities ... [and] they shouldn't be promoting embryo donation in States and Territories with no legislation. I can't remember what their answer was to that – but they're still doing it.'

I emailed the Embryo Donation Network with some questions about Natalie Parker. I asked EDN whether they accepted any responsibility for what happened to Natalie's embryos, given that the match occurred through EDN's classifieds system.

Embryo Donation Network replied: 'We are appreciative that Natalie has been able to document her story for the EDN website, as this has been beneficial in helping potential donors to be well informed as they make choices regarding their embryos. We look forward to continued collaboration with Natalie into the future, to work towards better protections for the embryo donation process and ultimately for the donor-conceived children who are born from these donations.'[2]

NATALIE'S VIEWS ON the Embryo Donation Network have, naturally, changed: when she looks through its classifieds section now, she sees something quite different – the commodification of potential lives.

'I really don't like it,' she says. 'People go there, they don't have any proper counselling beforehand. They can post whatever they want, make it look all glossy, but there's no substance behind it.'

These days, Natalie has the same kind of response to pro-donor conception stories that many donor-conceived people have. Which is to say: triggered. 'There was another story on TV recently,' she adds. 'It was another *Australian Story*. About someone who had donated an embryo to someone else and now they're one big happy family. And when I watch things like that now, I just cringe.'

Since covering the stories of Lauren, Rel and me, *Australian Story* has gone on to do a number of other 'fertility industry' episodes, all positive, and mostly niche. (*Australian Story* is by no means unique. No media outlet, seemingly, can resist a happy parent story.) There was the one about a single woman who used an anonymous sperm donor to have a baby. Afterwards, she tracked the donor down, there was a sexual attraction, they clicked, and began a real-life relationship. 'It's a bit of a fairy story, really,' said the woman's mother.[3] My thoughts on that were mostly unprintable, but I did wonder if the sperm donor cared about any of his other donor-conceived children whose mothers he wasn't having sex with.

Then there was the episode about a single woman who flew to the US, used donor eggs and donor sperm to create a huge batch of twenty-six embryos ('The reason I went with San Diego was that they gave a money-back guarantee.'), had one daughter, then decided to give all the other embryos away. Despite the fact that the embryos had no biological connection to her whatsoever, they were hers to dispose of – because she'd paid for them.[4]

Australian Story detailed this woman's grand plan to give these embryos only to people who agreed that her daughter could grow up with them as siblings, the idea being to create a 'village' for her own daughter. A new form of spoiling an only child, perhaps.

And there was the episode that Natalie was talking about on the phone. It was about an infertile couple and a couple with 'spare' embryos who negotiated an embryo transfer. This episode was called, creepily, 'Perfect Strangers'.[5]

'Henry is the face of successful embryo donation,' the *Australian Story* heading booms, over a massive close-up of newborn Henry. The success, and what matters, is that all the adults at time of filming 'Perfect Strangers' get on well with each other and are happy.

'I'm so excited and absolutely in a love bubble to have little Henry here in our life,' says the recipient mother, when Henry is born.

'It's almost a gift to them [the other couple] as you've gone through so much. You deserve this. And we're able to give this to you at no cost to us,' says the donating mother to the embryo recipients.

In 'Perfect Strangers', there's a moment when the donating parents visit the recipient parents in hospital, soon after Henry arrives. The donating parents bring their own children, Henry's full siblings.

'To hold him, it was amazing and the kids, they were really infatuated with him,' says Henry's biological father.

Henry's biological mother is firm: 'Not for one moment do I think that's my baby. We didn't make the decision of donation lightly. And when we made it we made it. And it was final.'

Natalie, watching 'Perfect Strangers' at home on TV, was horrified. 'Someone who watches that might think it was really good,' she says now. 'At the end of the day it's just words.' She knows first-hand how quickly these situations can change, how promises between adults can mean nothing.

I am horrified, too, but for different reasons. If you're a donor, you don't get to decide that 'that's not your baby'. If it's your biological child, it's always your baby. And how much, or how little, that matters is not up to you. You don't get to neatly arrange their lives, their humanity and their feelings. You made them. You are always on the hook as their biological parent. Biology is permanent. It cannot be erased.

And if you don't understand that, you should never have donated in the first place.

What I'm saying is that the decision about who Henry's parents are is Henry's decision alone. (I'm assuming that Henry's parents will continue to be honest with him about how he was conceived and born, although this is by no means guaranteed.) Whether Henry decides he has two parents, or four, or wants to be shot of the lot of them, that's his choice. He'll make it in time. And he's allowed to change his mind about that decision, however many times he wants, over the course of his life.

It also seems massively premature to be celebrating a successful transplant of parentage when Henry can't even sit up.

THERE IS NO happy ending for Natalie Parker: real life isn't like that. There are legal amendments now passed, and there is hope. She hopes what happened to her family won't happen to others.

But there's one more painful decision for Natalie.

Natalie still has one remaining embryo in storage, and she is still faced with the same quandary.

'I definitely didn't want to donate it until there was more provisions in place that the potential child would be on the Central Register,' she says. But even though she's achieved that change, and the amendments are now law, she hasn't made a move.

'I don't know. I still haven't decided.'

Trust, once utterly violated, is hard to restore.

CHAPTER 28

When I was small, I was always keen for siblings. There were several attempts to claim my best friends as my sisters, or the kid next door as my brother. After all, we were so alike: we had secrets, treasures, cubby houses, a whole intricate world of make-believe. Each time I'd think, hopefully, that perhaps saying it often enough would make it true.

Once, Bec and I had gone to see John Barilaro, the Nationals MP, about the Royal North Shore Hospital. Bec had discovered that her donor code had been destroyed too. I was glad she'd joined me in talking to him. It's one thing for the Royal North Shore to concede that code destruction had taken place, but quite another for politicians to meet multiple living and breathing victims.

Afterwards, Bec and I walked in the sunshine towards the train station. We joked about the meeting we'd just had: decompressing. Halfway down Martin Place, at exactly the same moment, we each reached into the navy handbag we each had slung over a shoulder, pulled out a lip balm, and applied it. Then we looked at each other, unnerved. It was even the same brand and type of lip balm.

It was pretty funny, but it was just a coincidence. In a 'normal' friendship setting, I probably wouldn't have noticed.

What's worse: having holes deliberately cut out in the records of your origins? Or having no records at all?

Apart from Bec, my closest friend from the New South Wales donor-conceived support group I'd started was a woman called Zoë. Zoë's also the same age as me. The man who made Zoë, fertility specialist Dr David Macourt, peddled his wares for several decades. He was the sole director of a private fertility business in Hurstville, a southern suburb of Sydney. It was a well-known clinic.

In the 1980s, Zoë's parents went to see Dr Macourt, hoping he could help them conceive a child. 'My mum and dad weren't married,' Zoë said, 'so they weren't eligible for the hospital [public] donor conception programs.'

David Macourt, on the other hand, didn't place any such restrictions on recipients. It was an attitude, Zoë said, which pervaded many areas of his practice. 'He was a bit looser with his criteria. It was more like, "You want to have a baby, okay, we can help you",' Zoë said. 'I think [my parents] probably knew he was a bit more of a cowboy even than the rest.'

Zoë has come across an intriguing early piece of paperwork from her parents' time at Macourt's clinic: a form signed by her parents before Zoë was conceived. It didn't have any details about how, exactly, Macourt was going to make Zoë, but it did have one standout clause.

'They weren't to hold him responsible if the baby came out a different race,' Zoë said matter-of-factly. She was startled when she came across this, to say the least. 'It was just weird to read it. To see something set out like that. To see it as a transaction.'

It's a strange thing to have to process.

'To me,' said Zoë, 'it makes me think he knew his record-keeping was not that great.'

THAT INDEMNITY-AGAINST-nonwhite-babies agreement is pretty much all the paperwork Zoë has found around her conception. And not for a lack of trying.

Zoë's parents told her she was donor conceived when she was a young adult. It was the summer holidays after her first year at university. After dinner one night, her parents indicated that they had something to tell her. 'My heart sank because it sounded a bit ominous.' She can't remember the exact words they used.

'But I do remember just feeling like the rug had been ripped out from underneath me, because it was such a surreal thing,' she recalled. For Zoë, the truth was completely unexpected, and it hurt. 'I always had a really good relationship with my parents. I always thought that they were very open and honest with me. I didn't think they hid anything. And so this seemed such a huge secret to keep, a fundamental part of who I am. I just couldn't believe it that they'd hidden it. I do remember just bursting into tears.'

Zoë's parents explained that there had never been a 'good time' to tell her, an argument which Zoë says she understands. But it is possible to understand someone else's position, without agreeing with them. In the weeks that followed, 'I did a DNA test with my dad,' Zoë said, 'just in case.' Just in case it was all a horrible, horrible mistake; just in case Macourt's treatment hadn't worked and her parents had conceived naturally after all.

'What was that like, doing a DNA test with your own dad?' I asked her.

'Sad,' she replied slowly. 'Getting the results … was sad.' The truth turned her identity on its head. At that point, Zoë didn't know any other donor-conceived people; she kept the sorrow, and the confusion, to herself. 'I didn't know what to do. I didn't know how to deal with it. And I didn't tell. I didn't start telling friends until I moved overseas, three or four years later, because they didn't know me from before.

'I couldn't talk about it without crying, for ten years.'

WHEN SHE WAS twenty-nine, Zoë began to search for answers. She rang David Macourt. She discovered that he'd sold his practice to another operation, Fertility First. She rang them too. There were no records of how Zoë had been conceived at all. And it seemed, Zoë said, that she wasn't the only one.

'I'm assuming that there aren't any records. I know that some were left with Fertility First when they bought his practice,' she told me.

'Just not yours?' I asked.

'They said they located some but, yeah, it was literally a box, according to them.'

Zoë was infuriated. 'The whole process felt like a series of brick walls, or doors slammed in your face ... it's like no-one's on your side.'

DR DAVID MACOURT made Zoë in 1983. The bad old days, you might say. Unfortunately, in assisted reproductive technology, the bad old days keep going.

Dr Macourt is known beyond the fertility sector for a legal stoush reaching all the way to the highest court in the land. This fight concerned his clinical practice, St George Fertility Centre. It revealed disturbing details about what went on in Macourt's treating rooms. But this was a fight between doctors about money – not people. The questions about people, exposed by each stage of legal judgement, are huge.

In 2002, Macourt had decided to get out of the game and sell up to another fertility specialist, Dr Anne Clark. Dr Clark already had her own practice, Fertility First, and purchased St George Fertility Centre from Dr Macourt. The deed of sale covered the assets of the St George clinic. Assets, as defined in the deed, included 'Records, Embryos (to the extent title in them can at law pass to the Purchaser) and Sperm ... Records mean all of the records of the Business, including all original and copy records of donor and patient screening records ... [and] lists of Sperm donors and patients, all patient records, consent forms and the vendor's Patient List'. All that paperwork was supposed to be in order. St George Fertility Centre warranted that 'the consents, screening tests ... and identification (including identification, contact details and physical characteristics) of donors of Sperm ... have been conducted in compliance with the [Fertility Society of Australia] guidelines.'[1]

It is an uncomfortable reality that Macourt sold off, and Clark bought, sperm and embryos like backroom supplies. This happens whenever a fertility clinic changes hands. However, what was to follow was even more disturbing: the legal process laid bare Macourt's approach to paperwork. Nearly two decades after he made Zoë without any surviving records, by time of sale in 2002, not much had changed.

Soon after purchasing Macourt's practice, Dr Anne Clark found that not all was to her liking. Macourt's practice had come with 3513 frozen straws of donor sperm, every one of which, theoretically, could make a child. Unfortunately, 3009 of these sperm straws, or 86 per cent, were unusable. Not because they wouldn't work: that was never the complaint. They were unusable because Dr Clark had no idea who they were from, whether they carried any disease, how many kids had already been made from them, and whether they'd been properly obtained in the first place.

In 2010, Associate Justice Macready of the NSW Supreme Court would lay out a vast range of problems with these thousands of straws of donor sperm.[2] Macourt's clinic had failed to identify sperm donors in compliance with industry code of practice. Macourt's clinic did not give Dr Clark records for all the straws of donor sperm. It did not give details of the sperm donors. It did not give details of sperm donor consent forms. It did not give details of the results of sperm donor screening tests. And it did not give Dr Clark a copy of the patient list.

What, then, had Macourt been doing in his clinic? The mind boggles.

There was a penalty for Macourt still to come: but it had nothing to do with the human rights of babies. It was all about business.

AS THE NEW owner of Macourt's clinic, Dr Anne Clark ordered a stocktake of its assets, including the sperm. The count began in January 2004. Dr Clark was left with just 504 usable straws of sperm, the remainder was destroyed.[3] The usable straws were all finished by December 2005.

So she went shopping. In the past, Dr Clark had purchased sperm from a number of Australian clinics, in a fascinating marketplace. Although no Australian donors are supposed to sell or profit from their own sperm, eggs or embryos, Dr Clark was able to buy sperm from Westmead Fertility Centre, Queensland Fertility Group (like IVF Australia, owned by the Virtus Health global behemoth) and Danish sperm bank Cryos. Among donor-conceived people around the world, Cryos has something of a reputation. It's a massive global retailer whose 'collection' has weathered various public scandals, including sperm from donors with inheritable genetic disease and sperm from a donor who was a murderer, convicted of killing his own two baby daughters.[4]

It is hard to see how this obvious market for the sale of sperm squares with legal prohibitions on trading in human tissue.

LET'S GO BACK a step. Why is it important to ban the sale of human tissue, including gametes, organs, blood and other body parts, and keep the trade – ostensibly – altruistic? Some might say: if the seller is willing, who cares? Unfortunately, that kind of unthinking statement is a wealthy first-world luxury, while in the developing world, kidneys are harvested from teens in slums.[5] Here, in rather more formal language, is the current Guideline on Ethical and Legal Issues in Relation to the Use of Human Tissue in Australia and New Zealand, by the Royal College of Pathologists of Australasia:

'Trade in human tissue for monetary payment is argued as commodification of the body. This is viewed as unethical because this, arguably, diminishes respect for the human body; opens vulnerable individuals up to exploitation; contravenes the "spirit" of the altruistic gift of help to another that tissue donation embodies; and may diminish the willingness of others to donate. These might collectively undermine the social capital derived from therapeutics and research reliant on human tissue donation.'[6]

When Dr Clark was shopping for sperm, the relevant state law – the *Human Tissue Act 1983* (NSW), still in force today, prohibited trading 'for valuable consideration ... the sale or supply of tissue from any such person's body or from the body of any other person.'[7] I've covered, already, how donors may be reimbursed for undefined 'expenses', a process which is not regulated. But there is another important exception to the ban on trading in human tissue. This prohibition doesn't apply 'if the tissue has been subjected to processing or treatment and the sale or supply is made for the purpose of enabling the tissue to be used for therapeutic purposes, medical purposes or scientific purposes'.

This means that clinics and doctors, in theory, aren't supposed to pay donors: but clinics and doctors can pay each other for human tissue once it has been 'treated'. So we claim that human tissue is not for sale – but really, it is. Writing in the *Medical Journal of Australia*, Nicholas Tonti-Filippini and Nikolajs Zeps noted: 'A practical legal and ethical distinction may have arisen that has not been articulated in any legislation or guideline. There appears to be an assumption that once human tissue becomes a tissue product … it may be offered for sale, that a price may be paid, and that profits may accrue to those who manufacture and sell the products.' This is a problem, because 'donors of human tissue typically presume that the tissue will be used for the benefit of the community through transplantation and research, rather than for profit to individuals'.[8]

DR CLARK WANTED to replace the unusable morass of frozen donor sperm she'd bought from Dr Macourt. However, she couldn't go back to her old suppliers. The 2005 NHMRC Ethical Guidelines had been introduced, and if she wanted to follow them – which she did – from now on Dr Clark needed to buy sperm where the donor had consented to provide identifying information to any offspring. Dr Clark turned to a US supplier: Xytex.

Xytex is no stranger to controversy itself. Following the global financial crisis, it offered a USD$200 'discount' to would-be families for 'select' sperm donors, in what was reported as 'a sort of clearance sale'.[9] The 'select' donors included donors who had donated many, many times. More recently, it was revealed that a donor that Xytex claimed had good health, a college degree and an IQ of 160 in fact had no college degree, a history of bipolar disorder and an arrest for burglary. Xytex had already sold this man's sperm to create thirty-six children around the world. Some of those families are already reporting significant mental health issues in their children.[10]

However, Xytex sperm did come with photographs of donors and recordings of them speaking. 'Patients could browse Xytex's website … and they could purchase even more information and additional photographs if they wished,' said Justice Gzell, who presided over the court action between Clark and Macourt. In any other universe, this would be called a 'marketplace'.

One can imagine that Dr Clark felt some frustration upon buying a business and then having to replace almost all of its stock. However, the first of three key court battles was brought not by her against

Dr Macourt, but vice versa – for failing to fully pay what she owed for the business.[11] Dr Clark then made a cross-claim against the company and Dr Macourt: she accused them of breach of warranty.

For the next few years, Dr Macourt's old clinic was hauled over the coals not for medical malpractice, nor for his terrible record-keeping, but for breach of warranty. Some of the best legal minds in the country were properly exercised as to what constituted 'damages' – not to any children born – but to Dr Clark, for having to make an order from Xytex.

In the third and final round of this battle, the High Court found that Macourt should pay Clark damages.[12] Macourt ended up with a bill of more than a million dollars. Dr Clark is still practising. The Xytex straws have, presumably, been doled out. There are no answers for the children Macourt made.

CHAPTER 29

THIS FIGHT THROUGH several courts from 2010 to 2013 was not the first time Macourt's clinical practice had been accused. There had been a previous case before the then NSW Medical Tribunal (which became the Health Care Complaints Commission tribunal). The decision appears to have vanished from the public domain. It's nowhere. Yet two people have told me it related directly to the health and safety of women and children, in a way the legal battle did not.

In the late '90s, a woman I'll call Jane was worried about her kids. Jane has two sons. Both are donor conceived.

In the 1980s, Jane and her husband went to their local GP after trying, unsuccessfully, to conceive. 'They tested my husband – and that was the problem,' says Jane. 'Look no further, basically.' The couple were told that it was either adoption or donor conception. They chose the latter. 'The GP that I saw tried a number of fertility clinics, and they all had waiting lists,' says Jane. All except one. 'Dr Macourt had no waiting list. That's how I got into Dr Macourt's clinic. I should have researched it a bit more, I didn't know much about donor conception.'

Jane was twenty-eight at the time, and not entirely comfortable with the path they were taking. 'I was very frightened, I wasn't at all sure this was what I wanted. I think some counselling probably would have helped me, but there was nothing. I had a couple of appointments with Dr Macourt, but he's not a counsellor. He just outlined the procedures available … he was very clinical, not that caring really. "We'll get you pregnant, do as I say."'

Jane did fall pregnant and had a boy I'll call Tom. A couple of years later, she and her husband wanted to have a second child and went back to Macourt. Their second son was born in 1990. I'll call him Ben.

Jane says Dr Macourt, like many other fertility specialists, told Jane and her husband to lie to their kids about their origins. 'He said, you don't tell the child,' says Jane. 'That just did not seem right to me.'

Unusually, Jane decided to do the exact opposite. 'I told the boys from when they could first understand, as young as two years old,' she says. Without any counselling, three decades ago, she did what parents today still utterly fail to do. I am heartily impressed.

'If they know the truth, then there's nothing to hide, and they will accept it,' she says.

However, Jane couldn't tell them what she herself didn't know.

When Tom, the eldest, was about ten years old, 'he started carrying on about was he going to lose his hair and go bald early,' Jane says. 'He definitely wanted to know more about his donor.' So, after a period of pestering, Jane says she went back to Macourt's clinic.

There was, according to Jane, a rule at Macourt's clinic where they were supposed to hold the records for ten years. Tom, unfortunately, was just outside the ten-year limit. 'He just wanted to know, was he going to go bald? And other non-identifying characteristics, like is the donor clever, and so on,' says Jane. But Jane says there were no answers to be had at all: there was no file for Tom. Jane thought that was bad enough. But Tom's younger brother Ben was a different story: Ben was only eight. Jane says there should have been a file for Ben.

'My youngest son was within the ten years, and there were no records,' says Jane. 'I heard talk [through the former Donor Conception Support Group] that Macourt didn't keep records at all, and he was quite pleased with himself.' The point of this, according to Jane, was that if there were no records, there would never be anything to find: 'He did not want us to contact the donors, they were promised anonymity, they weren't going to have their lives disrupted by people like me.'

Jane wasn't going to accept that there were no records for either Tom or Ben. Jane says in 1998 she joined a joint complaint made about Macourt, by a few former fertility patients of his, to the NSW Medical Tribunal.

According to Leonie Hewitt, the co-founder of the Donor Conception Support Group, that tribunal process 'took forever'. Hewitt and the DCSG were part of the process to support the families. Jane says there was a tribunal hearing at Ryde Hospital: 'There was a panel of three people, I think they were doctors, they questioned me about different aspects. Macourt sat opposite me with his lawyer.'

'[The tribunal] were loath to do anything about it,' says Leonie Hewitt.[1]

According to both Jane and Leonie Hewitt, there was another family party to that complaint: a mother with four kids. They say that mother had a compelling reason to seek out her children's records of donor conception. At least one of the children, Leonie says, had thalassaemia, a genetically inherited blood disorder which, in its severest form, can require regular blood transfusions and cause bone abnormalities. The only cure for the severest form of thalassaemia is a bone marrow transplant, but even if a donor can be found, the procedure itself could be fatal.[2] Today, it's suggested that all couples thought to be possible carriers of the thalassaemia trait get tested before having children.

For that family, according to Jane, finding records 'was a life and death matter ... And Dr Macourt still would not help them'.

She says Dr Macourt did not provide medical records of the babies he was creating in his clinic. Instead, it emerged at that tribunal that there were none to provide, according to Jane.

I can't tell you the outcome of that complaint because the NSW Medical Tribunal itself – these days known as the HCCC – can't find it. An HCCC spokesman told me they 'did prosecute a complaint against Dr Macourt which was before the then NSW Medical Tribunal'. Such decisions, they said, were public at the time. But 'due to the age of the matter', they had been unable to find a copy of the decision either within their records, or publicly.

One would have thought, if it had serious and ongoing implications for public health, such a decision should have remained publicly available.

ONE DAY, AFTER some rebuffed attempts at contact, to my utter astonishment I call a number and end up speaking to David Macourt himself. Not only that, he agrees to answer my questions, then and there.

David Macourt says he began offering donor conception at his fertility clinic from sometime in the '70s, and that the donors were medical students – his students.

'So did you let them know in your classes that they could donate or something?' I asked.

'Oh, yes, I asked them,' he replied instantly. He said he paid them perhaps AUD$10, or something like that, but he couldn't remember. 'I certainly mentioned it in tutorials.' He said he was teaching at King George V Memorial Hospital for Mothers and Babies – a public institution which today is part of the Royal Prince Alfred Hospital, the place where Lucy used to work. Lucy: who wrote to me to warn of medical staff known to be donors, who suggested I look for my biological father among the staff at my own Clinic 20.

'What was your record-keeping system when you were running your clinic?' I asked. There was a pause.

'Oh, I took notes,' he said eventually. 'Like any other doctor. I took notes. And probably names of donors at the time. But they were destroyed early on. Because they didn't continue. As soon as they stopped I basically destroyed their names. Er. Is that all you want?'

I asked him to clarify.

'Once they were a donor, I kept a note of them,' he said. 'Once they stopped being a donor, I destroyed their file.'

'Why was that?'

'For their anonymity.'

'Right,' I said, 'but how could you tell if, for instance, if one donor had any health issues, how could you tell, if you had destroyed files?'

'Oh, well, these were healthy medical students,' he said. 'In their twenties. It was unlikely they'd have a major health issue. I mean I questioned them early on ... Unless it's congenital. Or familial.'

'Yeah, well, exactly,' I said, 'if there was a congenital problem, how could you then —'

'Well, they wouldn't be accepted,' he interrupted. 'Wouldn't be accepted.'

'But how would you know?'

'I would ask,' he said. 'They were medical students, they weren't idiots.'

Okay.

I asked him about the court case with Dr Anne Clark, which revealed thousands of straws of unlabelled or inadequately labelled sperm at Macourt's former clinic.

'How could you know that, whether you were breaking any family limits, if you didn't label straws of sperm?' I asked.

'You're talking about after my practice was sold. I immediately destroyed everything.'

'You destroyed everything when you sold your practice?' I said, astonished.

'Yeah,' he said. 'Oh, well, anything about my donors.'

It is hard, hearing these things when you're donor conceived. It is even harder when you're also good friends with one of the people this man made. Zoë deserves better than this. And so does Tom, and Ben, and all the others Macourt made.

'And given that you had destroyed information, how could you know, or how could anyone know, whether you were breaking family limits?' I asked.

'Firstly, what *is* "family limits"?' he said.

I felt sick.

'Secondly,' he added, 'I mean, the number of donors I had was very large, so it was highly unlikely that I was breaking family limits, just because I was turning them over.'

'Did you have any sort of set family limits policy at your clinic?'

'Oh, uh, I think we did, yeah,' he said, 'but I can't remember it … I think they were accepted limits by the profession, rather than something I set up.'

I looked at my notes.

'Was there, in 1998, a Health Care Complaints Commission Tribunal about the state of your records?'

'I can't remember. Maybe there was.'

I said that the former Donor Conception Support Group had told me that two women who were former patients of his, recipients of donor sperm, had made a complaint that their children didn't have any files, and that in the case of one of the women there was thalassaemia in the family.

'Does that ring any bells at all?'

'No,' he replied. 'I've got no idea what you're talking about. I mean you're talking about something that's twenty-odd years ago, there's been a lot of water under the bridge,' he said. 'But I find it difficult to say I wouldn't remember that. But I don't remember that. But that doesn't mean anything. Because it's twenty years ago. Or more than twenty years.'

Okay.

WERE YOU GIVEN any formal documentation about the tribunal, I asked Jane. 'I think I was sent a letter thanking me for attending,' Jane says. 'That was about it.'

Jane was left with the strong impression that the health system protected its own. Tom and Ben have had to deal with an information vacuum about their biological families for decades. To this day, neither Jane nor Leonie Hewitt knows what happened to the family with thalassaemia.

CHAPTER 30

IN 2005, HELEN Edel and her twin sister Anne appeared on national television. The program was *Four Corners*' investigation 'Secrets of the Fathers', the same show where Professor Douglas Saunders was grilled about breaching family limits at Clinic 20.

Helen and Anne were in their mid-forties at the time, and they'd recently discovered that they were donor conceived. They'd also worked out who their biological father was. He was their mother's fertility doctor.

I tracked Helen down fifteen years after that show aired. She lives in regional Australia. Anne has passed away. Their childhood, says Helen, was not a happy one: 'Dad wasn't much of a father to us. We always got jibed at. We were belted when we were naughty. The domestic violence, it was shocking. Mum went out to work and we got controlled by a leather strap.'

By the time the girls were twenty-one, their parents had separated. Their mother married again. Their new stepfather 'was an awful man, he was a real creep,' says Helen. The twins were floored when, in the heat of an argument, their stepfather told them their dad was not their father. It turns out the twins' parents had been to see a Dr John Doherty, at Sydney's Balmain Hospital, and her mother had been artificially inseminated.

'Mum wrote a book about her life,' Helen tells me. To my astonishment, she manages to find it, scrabbling round at the other end of the phone line, and reads me extracts. 'Here was a chance to have a pregnancy,' Helen reads. 'Donor semen was to be used, and my husband agreed … The right time finally came and the little procedure was performed.' (The oddness of postwar language to describe fertility treatment is striking. It sounds like a 1950s homemaker magazine.) 'It remained a secret for almost twenty years.'

But then the truth came out. 'I was so shellshocked,' Helen tells me. The man who'd beaten her and her sister, and kept them at arm's length, wasn't even their biological father. 'It made me feel very angry. I never saw my father, I never even went to his funeral. I hated him that much.'

For the next two decades, from their twenties until their forties, the twins 'were always searching'. The effect of childhood domestic violence, Helen says, was 'big men issues', and the years after disclosure were a particularly bad time. 'There was a history of sexual violence towards my sister and me in our twenties,' Helen says. 'Rape, abuse, violence, we went through some awful things … Australia back in the '70s was a very racist and sexist country. It was hard being a female.' Helen doesn't know how much of it had to do with the childhood beatings, the low self-esteem or the donor insemination: maybe all three. 'Can you blame the artificial insemination for the domestic violence?' Helen wonders down the phone line. 'I don't know.'

Three years after discovering the truth, Anne wrote to Dr Doherty, delicately asking for information about their biological father. To her amazement, in February 1983 he replied. Helen sends me a copy of the stained, typewritten letter: 'The donor was a very bright young doctor who has since become a successful specialist in experimental medicine so the I.Q. part is quite O.K.,' it reads. 'Good family history except for hay fever. He was single when I knew him, but is now married with children.'

So far, so (sort of) normal. Then the letter becomes a little bit daytime soap: 'Physically, he was considered to be a ruggedly good looking young man with a squarish face and good teeth when he laughed. He was quite athletic.' And finally, a patronising admonishment to Anne: 'Real fathers are people who nurture you, love you, and want you from the time you are concieved [sic]. A Biological parent provides you half your genes to help you get started.'

As soon as Anne received that letter, Helen says, she rang Dr Doherty. 'He was really rude to us,' Helen says. Anne asked Dr Doherty who the donor was. In response, he screamed at her. 'He said to Anne, "How dare you ask who your real father was?"' Helen says. Anne cried and cried – and dropped the search.

In their forties, the twins contacted Leonie Hewitt and the Donor Conception Support Group. They showed Leonie the letter from Dr Doherty. Leonie thought the letter was weird. She told *Four Corners*: 'I very, very carefully said to [the twins] in a very gentle way, "Have you ever thought that the doctor could be the donor?"'

That devastating suggestion galvanised the two women. The twins traced Dr Doherty to a small country town, only to discover he'd died ten years before. They approached Doherty's son and asked if he would do a DNA test. And the son consented. Helen sends me the results. As the twins told *Four Corners*, the test proved the dead Dr John Doherty was their biological father. He had inseminated their unwitting mother with his own sperm. She thought it was an anonymous donor. 'He wanked in the other room to donate his sperm. It was fresh in those days,' says Helen frankly. By this time, their mother had died – she would never learn how her own doctor had deceived her.

'After the *Four Corners*, I got two phone calls from people who were my half siblings,' Helen Edel tells me. 'One woman was a lawyer in Sydney. She couldn't believe how much she looked like me. Her mother went to Dr Doherty. Their family was sitting on the couch watching the show, so she knew.'

The half-brother who'd consented to the DNA test was furious with the twins after they went on *Four Corners*. 'He never spoke to me again,' says Helen, fifteen years later. She's unbothered. 'I've probably had such a crazy life that something like that didn't affect me too much. Plus I was busy having my own family … I've got three beautiful kids and four grandchildren. I'm the head of a tribe. Fuck those Dohertys. I couldn't give a fuck about them.'

THE PRACTICE OF fertility doctors inseminating patients with their own sperm has occurred around the world. It is a next-level transgression. So many ethical and professional boundaries are trashed. Lies abound. Suddenly, dark and disgusting elements entwine the process. Was there any sexual gratification? A sense of power? And what recourse would any Australian woman have, if she wished to bring a case before the courts about her fertility doctor inseminating her with his own sperm? The answer is unclear.

Is it rape?

Other jurisdictions overseas have already had to consider this question. The answer, according to an American academic is: maybe. It's complicated. In the US, fertility doctors being unmasked as sperm donors is no far-off scandal, perceived or otherwise. It's all too real.

In the US in 1987, some physicians admitted to using their own sperm to treat their patients in donor conception – to none other than US Congress's Office of Technology Assessments. And they said they were using fresh, not frozen, semen.

The Office of Technology Assessments' report surveyed hundreds of fertility doctors. It found 22 per cent used fresh semen exclusively: still more used a mix. Doctors' 'sources of fresh semen' included: medical students, hospital personnel, other physicians – and 'few practitioners reported having used their own semen (2 per cent)'. Each practitioner who reported using their own semen as donor sperm said they did so for multiple patients – specifically, between four and fifty women.

That was 1987. Since then, a growing number of US fertility practitioners have been accused of fathering biological children through their own fertility clinics. The list winds its way across the country: Dr Donald Cline in Indiana, Dr Gerald Mortimer in Idaho, Dr Ben Ramaley in Connecticut, Dr Cecil B. Jacobson in Virginia, Dr John Boyd Coates in Vermont, Dr Kim McMorries in Texas.[1]

Troublingly, legal action has been brought against at least two fertility specialists, Cline and Jacobson, in two different US states – but at the time of prosecution there was no specific law against what they had done. In 2019, *Vice* headlined: 'Doctors Can Legally Inseminate Patients with Their Own Sperm in Most States'.[2]

Now, slowly, US legislators are moving to address that problem.

Canadian journalist Alison Motluk has been writing about reproductive technology for fifteen years. She runs her own online publication, *HeyReprotech*, which provides the kind of consistently thought-provoking coverage of this industry that almost all mainstream media organisations lack.[3] (Another notable exception is *Slate*.)

In February 2020, Motluk tackled the doctors-as-donors. 'One of the huge frustrations for families is that it is proving very hard to hold doctors to account. There are no laws explicitly prohibiting a physician from inseminating a patient with his own sperm.' Again, that old stumbling block of what the law has actually foreseen as a potential problem.

Motluk interviews Jody Madeira, a law professor at Indiana University who studies this dilemma. Not bringing these doctors to justice, Madeira says, is not an option. Letting them off 'creates the impression that such conduct is not legally punishable and runs counter to legal frameworks such as informed consent'.

Madeira has developed the devastatingly named theory of the 'three penetrations'. The first penetration is when the physician injects his own sperm specimen into the patient's uterine cavity. 'Patients have consented to this procedure, but not to its performance with the physician's sperm,' says Madeira. The second penetration is 'when the physician's biological material joins with the patient's, implants into her uterine lining, and forms a placenta, breaching her physiological barriers in the most intimate way possible'. It's uncomfortable reading. But it's important. 'The third penetration … follows from the child's birth. The resulting child is welcomed into the patient's family and held out as their own, obtaining legal rights and privileges to their emotional, social, and financial support,' says Madeira. The third penetration, then, is raising a cuckoo child, biologically the doctor's own.

None of this in any way denies the love a mother may have for the donor-conceived child she has carried and delivered. As with donor conception itself, understanding this requires us to have more than a good–bad, yes–no approach to a complex situation.

You can love your child to the ends of the earth. And the child is, clearly, innocent. But that does not make what was done to you okay. The end does not justify the means. The mother did not consent to the means. She has every right to feel violated, and she will be reminded of that violation on a constant basis.

'Is it rape? That's not clear … It is hard to find acts that are analogous,' says Jody Madeira … 'She wonders, however, if the closest transgression is physician-patient sex,' Alison Motluk writes, in *HeyReprotech*. 'Physicians are discouraged from having sex with their patients because it's generally agreed there is a power imbalance. That makes it hard for a patient to give meaningful consent.'

You might say that in this matter, it's not sex – it's a clinical procedure. 'But is a medical procedure like insemination still clinical when the physician performing the procedure masturbates to ejaculation in a nearby room, catches his sample, walks to the examination room where his patient is waiting and inserts his sample into her vagina via a syringe and catheter?' asks Madeira. Clinical touching that is performed solely to help a patient conceive, she argues, 'could easily cross the line to become sexual touching — performed at least in part for the physician's own gratification.'

Motluk agrees. 'There is something sexual — even rapelike — about this act. In many ways, though, it seems much worse than doctor-patient sex. The patient is vulnerable, both emotionally and physically … The patient is the victim of a deceit … The patient continues her life under an illusion … The patient loves the child but hates the act that brought the child into the world. The patient can never leave this behind, because the very act is embedded in her own beloved child. It smells like a crime to me.'

LAWMAKERS IN A number of US states have arrived at the same conclusion. Such an act is becoming formally known as 'fertility fraud' or 'reproductive battery', and it is a crime.

In 1996, California enacted a law following a scandal at the University of California, Irvine fertility clinic where reproductive endocrinologists used patients' reproductive material without their consent. California made it illegal for anyone to knowingly use or implant reproductive material for any purpose apart from that to which the provider of the material had consented. It carried a penalty of either three to five years in prison, a fine of up to USD$50,000, or both.[4]

In 2019, lawmakers in both Indiana and Texas became the second and third states respectively to enact fertility fraud laws. In both states, the changes were a result of a public campaign by donor-conceived offspring of doctors, and their mothers, who realised what the fertility doctor had done after DNA testing.[5]

In Texas, fertility fraud legislation was introduced in June 2019 largely due to the courageous advocacy of Eve Wiley, a donor-conceived woman in her thirties, and her mother, Margo Williams. Wiley told her story to investigative program *20/20*. Her mother thought she'd used an anonymous sperm donor to conceive. But when Wiley did a commercial DNA test, the result pointed to her mother's treating doctor, Kim McMorries.

McMorries admitted to Eve Wiley what he'd done – but insisted that he'd partly cleared it with her mother. McMorries told Eve: 'I spoke with one of my mentors ... and he said they were having better success by mixing samples.'[6] So McMorries said he mixed in his own sperm with the donor sperm that Wiley's mother had selected. He said he had discussed this with Wiley's mother, who had agreed to McMorries mixing in the sperm of an anonymous local donor. McMorries, of course, used his own. He admitted he did not tell Wiley's mother that the local donor would be hyperlocal: himself.

Margo Williams flatly denies any such consent. Instead, she says she told McMorries she didn't want to use local donors, because she was worried about the prospect of accidental incest for any resulting children. She selected a donor who was not local (and not McMorries).[7] Texan legislators agreed with Wiley and Williams: this kind of deception is now a crime.

Today, a Texan victim may bring legal action over any such act of fertility fraud for up to two years after the offence is discovered – thereby avoiding the chorus of 'it all happened too long ago'.[8] If found guilty, a doctor faces between six months to two years in prison and a fine of up to USD$10,000.[9]

Celebrating the passage of the law, Wiley said: 'I had a duty to inform other potential victims.' In a space where donor conception is usually presented, unquestioningly, as a boon for women's access to reproduction, Wiley invoked the language of feminism to celebrate her achievement.

'I have not made this about [the doctor], I have made it about protecting women's reproductive rights and the importance of consent.'[10]

At the time of writing, five states across the US now have fertility fraud or reproductive battery laws: California, Indiana, Texas, Colorado and Florida.[11]

BACK IN SYDNEY, I'm talking to a woman I'll call Catherine. She has two adult children, a son and a daughter, whom she loves, who know they are donor conceived but have no right to know their donors. Recently, another layer has been added to her son's identity.

In the late '80s, Catherine says she and her husband were five months into donor conception fertility treatment at a popular Sydney clinic without any result. She has her suspicions about what happened next. 'In the sixth month, I think [the doctor] must've just thought, let's try with fresh [sperm]. And he did it. I've come across one other patient of his where he used fresh.'

I can't check this against any paperwork, because Catherine is yet another person who has no records of any of her treatment with this doctor, who I'll call Dr Aarons. This was 1987, two years after the introduction of HIV testing of sperm across all Australian fertility clinics. Only frozen sperm can be quarantined to prevent HIV: not fresh.[12]

In the sixth month, Catherine fell pregnant and had her son, whom I'll call Josh.

A few years later, she and her husband decided they wanted another child. So they went back to the clinic.

'I asked to use the same donor again,' says Catherine. 'Aarons said absolutely not, that donor is not available anymore, he's gone overseas, I don't know where he is and I can't get in touch with him. A load of rubbish.' Catherine and her husband thought about it, and 'naively' decided to go ahead anyway. They had another child, a girl: Ava.

Ava and Josh have different biological fathers. Josh, in particular, grew up searching for answers about his biological family. In 2019, Josh texted Catherine a question. And her world shattered.

CATHERINE WAS IN a theatre, sitting in the audience in the dark. Her phone pinged. It was a message from Josh. 'Mum, does the name Aarons mean anything to you?' he asked. 'Because that's the donor.'

'*Shit*,' Catherine blurted out. People were staring. 'I had to go outside, and I cried. I was so upset. I thought, you've got to be kidding me.'

Josh had done a DNA test with one of the big commercial companies that help those interested in genealogy build family trees. Once you do a test, you're automatically linked with any family members you have who have already sent off their DNA to those websites. Josh had come up with some very close matches.

From those matches it appears, says Catherine, that Dr Aarons is Josh's father. Which, if correct, would mean that Dr Aarons inseminated Catherine with his own sperm.

Catherine says she feels violated.

'Abhorrent. Abhorrent,' she says vehemently. 'To find out it was a doctor, it's just unethical.'

A year on, Catherine is still in a bad place: she loves her son, absolutely no doubt about that, but she's utterly repelled by the thought that Aarons inseminated her with his own sperm. 'I feel ripped off. Cheated. I don't feel right about it at all. I feel mistreated. It's a bit in the area of Frankenstein,' she says, 'it just shouldn't have happened this way.' She sees Aarons in Josh. 'When I look at my son, I can see the shape of his head is similar [to Aarons], and the way he stands. It's quite noticeable to me … I remember Dr Aarons saying to [Josh's social dad] "We both have the same colouring" as we walked into his office. Little did I know that that was going to ring true.' There are many aspects of her treatment at Aarons' clinic that she now sees with different eyes. 'I remember Aarons saying to me, it was four months down the track [of treatment],' Catherine recalls. 'He said to me, "You're young", and he patted me on the wrist. "We'll get you pregnant."' There is revulsion in her voice. 'My husband was in the room with me every time I had the straw [of semen],' she says. Catherine and her husband separated a number of years ago. Josh has since told Catherine's ex-husband that he believes Aarons is the donor. 'I don't know what [my ex] thought. I think he was just more worried.'

A man clinically inseminating multiple women with his own sperm, in the presence of their husbands, sounds like behaviour which belongs in a cult. Catherine says when Josh texted her Aarons' name, she had a terrible sense of truth. She says this wasn't the first time she'd heard this about Aarons.

'I know I'm not the only family,' she says now. When her kids were still young, Catherine had volunteered to give a talk at a hospital: it was about how parents should tell donor-conceived kids the truth.

'One of the women came up to me and said "I'm a single mum, my child was born in 1990, and Aarons used fresh semen. Aarons is the father,"' Catherine says.

'How on earth did she know that?' I asked.

'Because he told her,' Catherine says simply. 'She said, "I had to accept fresh semen because I just couldn't fall pregnant".' (The myth that fresh sperm works better than frozen persists, despite evidence to the contrary.[13])

'She just had full knowledge that Dr Aarons had used his own fresh semen [on her]. I had to keep it very quiet. I mean, she's just confided this to me. I was gobsmacked. She's one. How many others are there out there?'

DR AARONS IS still alive, though no longer practising. Catherine has not confronted him, has not asked him for answers, and neither has Josh.

I requested an interview about donor conception in his clinic, and Aarons agreed. He told me that he destroyed records of donor conception. Which was in keeping with Catherine's account of having no treatment records at all.

'How many donor-conceived babies did you make over the years?' I asked Dr Aarons.

'I can't remember, I've got no idea. I don't think I've ever had an idea,' he replied.

I took notes.

'And did you ever inseminate any of your patients with your own sperm?' I asked him.

'No,' he replied calmly.

'Either fresh or frozen?'

'No.'

'Because I've come across a former patient of yours who says that DNA tests show that her son is biologically your child —'

'Well, how would she know what my biological makeup was?' he interrupted. It was a fair question. I spent a little while explaining the explosion of DNA databases and genealogical techniques.

'So this woman, her son says that you are his biological father. Is it possible at any point that you used your own semen?'

'Well, not that I remember,' he said.

This was startling in itself.

'And this woman also says that she met another woman,' I continued, 'another patient of yours, who was a single mother, who you inseminated with your own sperm, with her knowledge —'

'Well, that's not true.'

'Does that ring any bells?'

'No, that's not true.'

Seemingly, an impasse. But the allegations were serious, the act definitely not unknown in this game, and Dr Aarons had admitted to me that he destroyed his donor conception records. A thought occurred to me: if he *wasn't* Josh's father – which doubtless would bring Catherine a great deal of relief, in any case – then would he prove it?

'Would you be happy to do a DNA test to settle it?' I asked him.

He gave a short laugh. 'No. I wouldn't be happy to run around doing DNA tests for people. That's ridiculous.'

'Oh, okay.'

'Would *you*?' he asked.

'Well, if it was one-to-one, I don't see why not. If there was nothing to hide,' I said.

'Well, I don't like having blood tests to begin with,' he said. 'Let alone having them done because of someone else's request.'

'I think they can do them with saliva these days,' I said. (They can.)

'I certainly wouldn't be happy with people doing testing on me,' he said. 'I'd just find it an interference with my lifestyle.'

I paused. 'Right. Because it would be inconvenient?'

'Because it would be interfering with my lifestyle.'

'Oh.'

THE ONLY GOOD thing to come out of this is that Josh, finally, feels he's found answers about his biological origins. And he feels a sense of peace.

The idea that now haunts Catherine has ended Josh's decades of uncertainty and frustration.

'Honestly, Sarah, he's just so chuffed,' says Catherine. 'He's happy because he has answers. He's okay about it all. He's just glad he knows the truth.

'I'm sure Aarons thinks we're after money. All [Josh] wants is information. He wants to talk to Aarons. It's never gonna happen.'

THIS IS THE first time Catherine has told this story to a journalist, and she is nervous: understandably so. What she tells me is a gigantic step. This is the first time anyone has accused Dr Aarons of inseminating Australian women with his own sperm.

He is only the second Australian doctor ever to be accused publicly of such an act. But, unlike the first case of Dr Doherty and the twins, Dr Aarons is still alive. With Aarons there are answers to be had, either way, and, if necessary, a chance of justice – if any authority dares.

AROUND THE WORLD, more cases keep emerging.

Britain, 2012: filmmaker Barry Stevens and barrister David Gollancz reveal that at London's Barton clinic, founder Berthold Wiesner himself may have fathered between 300 and 600 of the clinic's children. 'A conservative estimate is that [Wiesner] would have been making twenty donations a year,' Gollancz said in 2012.[14] Wiesner died in the '70s. In 2007, DNA tests on eighteen people who had been conceived at the Barton clinic between 1943 and 1962 showed that twelve of the group were Wiesner's children.

Canada, 2015: the previously highly regarded Dr Norman Barwin, former president of the Canadian Fertility Society and a recipient of the Order of Canada (which he returned after admitting to professional misconduct) is found through DNA to have used his own sperm to inseminate patients at his clinic, where he practised for three decades until 2014.[15]

South Africa, 2018: the *Sunday Times* reports that a woman called Fiona Darroch and her two siblings – all from Australia – have found they are the biological children of their mother's South African fertility specialist, Dr Norman 'Tony' Walker.[16] Fiona Darroch says she confirmed the paternity through DNA testing with a nephew of Walker's. She says she's also discovered two other Walker half-siblings in the US. The *Sunday Times* reports that a Walker family representative refutes the claims, saying 'no genetic testing had been done on any of Walker's acknowledged children or grandchildren'. Walker himself committed suicide in 1977.

THE ACTIONS OF doctors-who-are-donors are revealed in retrospect, by donor-conceived people themselves, who grow to adulthood and go hunting for the truth. And yet none of the countries where such revelations have emerged have passed laws guaranteeing all their donor-conceived people the right to know biological origins.[17] The right to know – if it exists in law at all – is still piecemeal, depending on the year you were born or the part of the country in which you were made.

Instead, laws and systems still shore up guarantees of donor anonymity, past and present. So how do you know that fertility fraud is no longer a problem? You don't. If history is any guide, we will leave it up to the babies being born now to grow up and spend years searching for answers. We will leave it to them to deal with this mess.

CHAPTER 31

I'M OUT WALKING the dog, on the phone to my friend Bec. As we chat, I wander aimlessly through the streets, under trees, past bungalows and factory warehouses. No authority is willing to hold Clinic 20 and its staff to account, or help us find answers. We've come to a dead end – unless one of the many external parties who knows more about our origins than we do has a Damascene conversion.

'You and I should do a DNA test,' Bec says, not for the first time.

I stop to cross a road. 'Yeah,' I say doubtfully. 'I guess.'

SHE'S RIGHT, LIKE she is about most things. But it takes me a while to see it.

In the past, DNA testing was an expensive exercise usually ordered by a court. In those days, it was strictly one-to-one: two people went to a lab, paid hundreds and hundreds of dollars, and any genetic relationship to each other was officially revealed. If you're donor-conceived, this kind of procedure is in theory useful for finding your biological family, but in practice it has huge limitations. Primarily, you have to know who to test – that is, you almost have to have the answer before you begin – and they have to agree to do said test with you.

But recently, there's been something of a revolution. Direct-to-consumer DNA testing kits have been taking the bored retiree market (and others) by storm. These kits are for everyone interested in building their own extended family tree. They're easy to use: you get a package in the mail, provide a sample in the comfort of your own home and post it back. They're also relatively affordable – at or around the USD$100 mark.

The best thing about direct-to-consumer DNA testing, though, is that it has single-handedly ended anonymity. This craze has quietly delivered us the right to identity: which is Article 8 in the UN Convention on the Rights of the Child. For a price, that is.

This is the price: you surrender your DNA to a privately owned, commercial entity. There are a few big ones – Ancestry DNA, FTDNA, 23andMe. You want to go with the biggest, or several, or all. This means more than one of these entities might have access to your unique genetic code: the thing that makes you, you. I really don't feel good about that.

Once you hand it over, what do these companies do with it? They want to make money from it, of course. Take, for example, one of the biggest companies, Ancestry. Ancestry uses your results to study 'aggregated Genetic Information to better understand population and ethnicity-related health, wellness, ageing, or physical conditions'. It may share it with research organisations (either non-profit or commercial), and they may have a financial interest in that research arrangement.[1] It's possible that in the future, law enforcement agencies may gain access to your genetic information to investigate crimes, although so far Ancestry has refused.[2] And the company's own rules about either of these things, or anything else, could change. Did you even read that massive privacy statement the first time around before you clicked 'agree'? Will you sit down and go through the latest version, checking for updates? What if the company is sold or taken over? Ancestry claims all its privacy conditions would continue, but who really knows what will happen to your DNA?

It's not just DNA either. If we check the dataset that Ancestry acquires for each of its customers, it's significant. Ancestry compiles: your name, email address, password, payment information like your credit card number, billing and shipping address(es), sex, year of birth, any user provided content like mobile phone number or photos or self-disclosed family, your device's IP address, the websites you visited before and after Ancestry's site, geolocation information from your mobile phone if you allow it, the name of your internet service provider or mobile carrier, all your search requests and communications with other users and activity within the Ancestry site of course, plus some other things. It's quite a package.

What you buy with that DNA fragment of self, though, could make it all worthwhile.

This is what happens when you do a DNA test: you send off your saliva sample. You wait a number of weeks. Then the company delivers you your results and – crucially – adds you to its database. Suddenly you're on there, with an account, plus a whole bunch of suggested connections – mostly total strangers with whom you share a certain amount of DNA.

The databases for companies like Ancestry, or 23andMe, or FTDNA are now so very big that if you come from a Western nation, where these companies draw most of their users, you will definitely be matched with relatives straightaway. They may be very distant, like an eighth cousin; so distant, in fact, that the defined relationship is hard to imagine. You will probably have lots of these very distant kinds of relatives. When I say lots, I mean hundreds. Don't worry if you've never heard of them before.

The dream scenario for donor-conceived people is this: You get your results and boom! A half-sibling has already done a test and you're matched straightaway. Or your biological parent(s). Instant answers upon testing do appear for some donor-conceived people, probably more often than you'd think.

However, for the rest of us, there's a bit of work ahead. You have a list of distant relatives. You select the closest. You message them, asking nicely if you may see the family trees that they have built on the company's website. That's what everyone is there to do: people are mad for genealogy. Genealogy is often said to be the next most popular online hobby after porn, which may not be accurate, but it certainly paints a picture. Often, the people you contact on these sites will kindly grant you access. After all, if you're a relative of theirs, you should somehow be built into their family tree too.

Now you have a bunch of different family trees, which all join up to you somehow. You build them backwards in time to find common ancestor(s) with your distant relatives. Once you've found that common starting point, the one that makes all your connections fit, you build a family tree of that particular ancestor forwards in time, using not just the DNA of others on the site but also clues in historical records like births and deaths notices, marriage banns, newspaper articles, shipping notices, moves interstate and overseas, whatever. Until you come to, well, you.

What this means is: you can find your own biological parent, even if they have never done a DNA test.

You can find your own biological parent using only your own DNA.

It's a lot of work. It's a lot of time and painstaking research. As more people send off DNA kits, and join the databases, it becomes easier, but it can be a full-time job. One donor-conceived person I've interviewed worked on her own case for hours every night for a year. You may hit dead ends: you may be stuck, waiting for more crucial links to be uploaded to the database when some distant relative somewhere does a DNA test. But, sooner rather than later, you will have a breakthrough. And in the meantime, you can always try a second company's database. Maybe there will be other relatives there who hold the key. Or you could try a 'search angel': someone who's already gone through this process for themselves, or for other people, and is much more experienced. Because genetic genealogy – which is what this whole method is called – is such an obsession, there are plenty of armchair experts out there. And I mean that in the best possible way. Friendly advice abounds, whether you need a little assistance or want to outsource the whole thing.

There are several other major advantages in direct-to-consumer DNA tests. Firstly, these DNA results are ongoing. You're on those databases for as long as you want to be. The algorithm ticks away in the background, without you having to dragoon more individuals into going to a lab with you and paying hefty fees. You might have a sibling straightaway, and then in a couple of years' time be surprised by a second and a third, who do their tests and find you. Secondly, genetic genealogy is a process that you yourself can start, continue and leave. It is, finally, something donor-conceived people choose, and over which they have a certain amount of control. For the first time, in order to take the big step towards answers, you don't need to utterly depend upon the permission of others, or their goodwill, or their ability to perform their job with basic professionalism and competence. All you need is your own DNA.

Among donor-conceived people, interest levels in DNA are high. In 2018, I conducted a (completely unscientific) poll in one of my Facebook groups for Australian and New Zealander donor-conceived people. Around sixty people responded. Not everyone responded to every question: it's Facebook, after all, not an exam. However, what came out of that was pretty interesting. Fifty-seven out of sixty-one people, or 93 per cent, said they had already done a DNA test to find their biological family. The rest said they might one day. No-one said they would never do a DNA test.

Of those who had done a DNA test, two-thirds had found their biological father or siblings. From a base of almost no-one knowing any biological family, and being denied answers, this is an extraordinary success rate. And the third who hadn't found biological family through DNA, at that point in 2018, may have done so since.

DNA cuts through all the lies and deception. There is no more anonymity in donor conception. To any anxiously 'anonymous' donors reading this, let me say: you are so screwed.

But it doesn't have to be scary. Consider the other major trend from my poll. Of the thirty-eight people who said they had found their donor and/or siblings through DNA testing, thirty-two – or 84 per cent – said it had been a positive experience. Of the remaining six, no-one said instead that it had been a negative experience: perhaps they chose not to answer, missed the question, or considered the experience neither negative nor positive. I also asked if anyone had done a DNA test and regretted it. Zero people ticked that box.

It is hard to manage your own expectations at the best of times, let alone when you've been as kicked around as most donor-conceived people have. At a base level, I think, what most adult donor-conceived people want from their newly discovered biological family is openness, answers and civil communication.

Until now, those answers did not come easily – or ever. For most donor-conceived people, your own DNA is a high price, but it is the price you choose to pay.

Five years after learning that my father was not my father, after coming up against many, many brick walls, I bought an Ancestry DNA test kit. I spat into the little clear tube. And I sent it off.

JUST SEVEN WEEKS later, my initial DNA results dropped into my inbox. I speed-read my way through them. A close-ish match in the third to fourth cousin range, which meant I shared a great-great-grandparent with that person, or possibly a great-great-great-grandparent. Then a whole heap of more distant cousins. The nerdy nature of the genetic genealogy community meant that they mostly had full human names, too – no online aliases of 'cupcaaake99' or some such. This was important. Even the full name of a distant descendant was a clue.

But no biological father, no biological siblings. Bec and I had done an Ancestry test at the same time. She wasn't there in my matches. I knew it was a long shot, I thought. Since when does your friend turn out to be your family?

I'd already joked with both Bec and Zoë about the possibility of being related, of course. (When you're among donor-conceived friends, it doesn't take long for this to happen.) Zoë is slightly taller than me, with pale skin, blue eyes and long, light blonde, somewhat curly hair. She looks Nordic. Bec is a fair bit taller, with green eyes, tightly curled brown hair and the olive skin of her mother's Mediterranean roots. I look so Japanese that locals address me in that language when I'm in Japan. Together we look like some cheesy stock shot, keyword 'diversity'. But it's true, donor-conceived friendships are always tinged with the prospect of hard reality. What if we're siblings? We get on well because we're alike – is there a reason? After a while getting to know each other, you might even swap the ultimate compliment: 'I wish you were my sister.'

I sent a polite email to a few of my closest Ancestry matches, those distant cousins, asking to see their family trees. I said that I was searching for answers about my father's side of the family, but I didn't say why. Not in the first email, I thought. Who knows what prejudices lurk. But my particular genetic mix also provided my search with a great first clue. My undisputed biological mother is Malaysian Chinese. Just about everyone on Ancestry, seemingly, and certainly all of my matches were white. Therefore, 100 per cent of my Ancestry matches were from my biological father's side of the family. So, writing to these newfound distant cousins, I explained that we must be related through my paternal line. I hit send several times. Then I paused my search.

I couldn't sink too deep into my results. There was no luxuriating in the moment. No lingering over the racial breakdown that Ancestry provides (a rich font of self-satisfied procrastination if ever I saw one). No mulling over being 26 per cent Scottish and googling images of hard-bitten sheep crofters in the Outer Hebrides. The Ancestry email had arrived just as I was reporting for ABC's *Four Corners* for the first time.

I was trying to make a forty-minute television documentary in a couple of months for an extremely demanding show and not mess it up. I was more than busy: most non-work things in my life – like laundry and food – had already fallen by the wayside. So the night I received my Ancestry results, over-caffeinated and driving back from some shoot with the crew, I didn't have time for much more than a few quick emails to my top matches. And from the back seat, I dialled the Ancestry helpline, just to check if there was any more information to come.

The woman who answered had clearly dealt with this query before. 'There could be more,' she said patiently. 'These are your DNA test results, but it'll take between one to two weeks for the algorithm to calculate all your matches.' Apparently they had a new method of calculation. I hung up.

The next day, I rang Bec to check in. She'd had her Ancestry DNA results, and I wasn't in her list either. I shrugged. It was what I'd believed all along. We talked through her top matches. They were in a similar range of distance to mine. There were some more intriguing names, possible leads.

And then something happened. We realised that Bec's top match – a third to fourth cousin – was my top match – *my* third to fourth cousin. The same man. The same degree of relationship.

What did that mean? We were, somehow, (distantly) related. No expert, I tried to sort through other ways that could happen. It might not be through the paternal line. We might both be related to the same man through the maternal line.

But I, at least, could rule that out. All my European matches had to be from my paternal line. These days, Ancestry will mark your matches as 'Father's side' or 'Mother's side', but at that point it did no such thing. So my matches were key.

That didn't eliminate Bec's mother, of course. She's Italian, but there may have been some shared European ancestry between her and my paternal line. So therefore, either Bec and I were related because her mother and my biological father were related – or because both our biological fathers were related – or because we had the same biological father.

And then I parked it. I couldn't do anything without waiting for the full two weeks and final confirmation of results; speculation would get me nowhere. Work took over my brain.

IT WAS WHILE I was on another shoot in Melbourne that Bec rang me.

'Hiya,' I said distractedly. I walked away from the crew, into the grid of the city centre.

'Sistersss!' she crowed.

'WHAT?'

'Check the app,' she said. 'Check your matches!'

I didn't believe her. I checked. At the very top of my matches, something had changed. Bec was there. A lovely profile shot of her on her wedding day, and the predicted relationship: First Cousin.

'What?' I said. I was excited, but cautious. I'm not a believer by nature and this in any case didn't make sense. 'Cousins?'

'Nah, I think that's wrong,' she said – Bec had done a crash course in DNA analysis by this point – 'because if you look at the amount of centiMorgans that we share, we share too many to be just cousins.'

A centiMorgan is a unit of measurement in genetics. In the genetic genealogy context, according to the International Society of Genetic Genealogists, it's 'used to measure genetic distance. It is often used to imply distance along a chromosome'.[3]

I checked. Bec was right. Despite being absolutely nothing alike in height, colouring, features or any other physical characteristics, we shared nearly 1800 centiMorgans, which indicated one of the closest possible genetic relationships. Despite the suggested explanation, we were much too closely related to be first cousins. (My theory is that Ancestry's still-evolving algorithm had marked us as possible cousins because it was confused by our birthdates. Bec and I were born two months apart – something highly unlikely for full siblings, or even half-siblings born outside of donor conception – but completely normal for cousins.)

However, if you looked at the centiMorgan count, the answer was clear. According to the amount of DNA we shared, we were either half-sisters, aunt and niece, or one of us was the other's grandparent. We were both cracking up, talking it through.

There was no way the grandparent thing worked. Even with a terrifyingly long cryopreservation regime for donated gametes in New South Wales, I was clearly not the child of either of Bec's children, who were at that point, respectively, a toddler and an infant. There was no way Bec could be descended from me, because I had no children at all.

The aunt and niece thing also didn't work. For that to happen, she would have to be the child of one of my full siblings, of which I have precisely zero. Or I would have to be the child of one of Bec's full siblings. She only has one brother. He's much younger than both of us. Thanks to living in a temporal universe, I could, at least, rule out my own father being younger than myself.

That left just one option: half-sisters.

'I told you so,' she teased.

'You were right,' I laughed. 'You were so right.'

I have a sister.

WHAT DOES IT mean to have a sister? Where do they fall in your life?

Studies, theories and greeting cards abound for sister relationships – although I suspect the true answer is that there are as many kinds of sister connections as there are sisters themselves. Some contain good news. At least one American study has concluded that in childhood, all children report greater intimacy and companionship with sisters, rather than brothers.[4] In a UK study of sibling pairs aged between four and eight, out of all possible combinations (older brother–younger sister, two brothers, older sister–younger brother, two sisters) the older children who reported the most warmth in their relationship with their younger sibling were girls with little sisters. But rivalry is also seemingly ever-present with sisters: plenty of researchers and writers, both fiction and non-fiction, focus on the particular oscillation between love and hate that a sister bond creates. And yet a 2010 study found that having a sister boosted adolescents' mental health, whether that sister was older or younger: she would become a protective factor against ten- to fourteen-year-olds of any gender feeling lonely, unloved, guilty or self-conscious.[5]

All of this is fascinating, some of it heartwarming, and yet none of it applies to Rebecca and me. We didn't grow up together. We have no shared childhood experiences (unless you count, as strangers, having our donor codes destroyed by the public health system). And by the time we met, we were both adults, with established careers, partners, places in life. The need for rivalry is nil. We are friends. What more does sister status add?

When it comes to donor-conceived sisters finding each other as adults, the studies, theories and greeting cards all dry up. If there are few checks and balances regarding how we can be made, there are even less rules or norms for who we become. How alike are Bec and I? Outwardly, not at all – but the big question is: how alike are we on the inside? The full extent of that, I think, is still unknown. It might take the rest of our lives to answer.

I have to admit I also felt a certain amount of pressure. We were friends and then suddenly sisters, except I had no idea what a sister was. Bec, at least, grew up with a younger brother. What was I supposed to do? How was I supposed to behave from now on? If you judge me by extrovert standards, I suspect I'm not even a great friend. For me, constantly keeping in touch with people is exhausting, and I like to retreat, appear at random, then retreat again. I love my friends. But I also really appreciate it when they let me just pick up where we left off, no matter how long it's been. I'm genuinely terrible at regular friend maintenance.

What you need to know about Bec and me is that I think she's the better sister. She's extremely thoughtful, kind and generous. Both her EQ and her IQ are high. In a world where literally anyone could be my sibling, I won. And if there are no rules, no social expectations for how this relationship is supposed to play out, then I guess I can't be a failure. One hopes.

WHAT WE ARE as siblings is one thing: what I am, having found a sister, is another. In purely selfish terms, finding out that Bec was my sister was the best thing that had happened to me since all this began five years before. It was, if not an antidote, then most of the key ingredients for one. Having a known sister unlocked something in my mind. I had won back a part of my own humanness. I had snatched an answer from the endless churn of the baby factory. I was, all of a sudden, much happier. I was whole. I was a person, with two sides to my family, and I mattered.

I had proven that I was real.

CHAPTER 32

WHILE I WAS still trying to get my head around sisterhood, another Ancestry email dropped in my inbox. It was from a fifth to eighth cousin. Her name was Heather. Heather was a kind woman in her sixties, living an industrious life in the suburbs, finishing off a Master's degree, doing sudoku, and volunteering at her local hospital.

All of that is true, and yet it belies what she really is. Heather is nothing less than a force of nature. She would change both our lives forever.

'HI SARAH,' HEATHER wrote. 'Lovely to hear from you. I have several ancestry trees and have some people with the surname Dingle in at least one tree. Is this the surname you are researching?' (Absolutely not.) 'If you can give me a few clues as to some surnames on your father's side I may be able to send you a link to one of my trees … I have probably over 18,000 people in my trees and anything else you can provide may be a start.' (Good lord.) 'I may be able to help you if you can provide more details. We must share a common ancestor somewhere not too far back.'

Well, that sounded very nice, I thought. Then I realised that she'd sent another three emails that same day before I'd even responded to the first. Her brain was clearly pinging off in all directions. 'Hi again Sarah, I finally found your tree under DNA matches linked to a cousin of mine, John, who is in my tree and whose DNA test I am administering …

it seems you are more closely related to him and this may give us a clue …' 'Hi again Sarah, you can access the tree with John's father by clicking on view tree to the right of his match to you …' 'One more time for tonight Sarah, sorry John's father was born under this name. I think that other name may have been his grandfather.'

I had absolutely no idea what she was talking about. I hadn't even really checked out the full depths of the Ancestry site. Heather, clearly, was the business.

'Heather – this is amazing! Thank you so much! Dingle is my surname but not my biological father's surname – I genuinely have no idea who he is, or where in Australia/elsewhere he may have lived, unfortunately. All I know is that all the European in me comes from him. I am hoping to somehow triangulate family trees from various cousin relationships and work it out,' I wrote back. She responded immediately, with not one but two emails.

'Hi Sarah, I hope to be seeing John's wife in about three or four weeks so will see if she can help. Will ask her whether I can pass her name onto you …' Great, I thought. The next email was more intriguing: 'By the way Sarah, I managed to find my father's parents. He did not know who they were. I have also found DNA evidence to support my findings … so you may be lucky after all.'

I shot her a quick reply expressing my thanks. Hm, I thought. That part about her father was interesting. She might get it: she might be an ally. Maybe I should tell her what's really going on here.

As well as being the last (and only) hope for many donor-conceived people, DNA testing is also a beacon for adoptees, including those from older generations where adoption practices were, shall we say, somewhat loose, if not outright baby-snatching. I guessed that Heather's father might have been an adoptee. Which was good news in terms of my situation. I've never had to explain my desire to find family, or my rage at being denied it, to an adoptee. There was a very good chance that Heather already understood where I was coming from.

MUCH LATER, I found out I wasn't far off. Heather's father had been placed in foster care aged three, and he died aged fifty-eight. 'He went through his life not knowing who his parents were or why he was given up,' Heather told me.

Years after he'd died, in 1980, Heather went searching for those answers. It was before DNA companies like Ancestry. Heather did it the old-fashioned way: publicly available information and human intelligence. She found her father's birth certificate, with his mother's name, but not his father's. She researched his mother's life. Then she rang the Department of Community Services to inquire about her father's foster care placement. Surprisingly, they told her the name of her biological grandfather. ('They probably weren't supposed to, but they did,' she told me candidly.) And the contact information they had for him: the trade union's Worker Office.

Unfortunately, Heather's paternal grandfather had both a common first name and a common surname. When Heather searched for her grandfather's name through archives like the Electoral Roll, 'there were a million,' she told me. So Heather tried to work out, from her grandmother's life, address, and other scraps of information, which one her grandmother was most likely to have met and had a child with. She found a man who lived just one street away from where her father was born in inner Sydney. Heather cross-referenced this with records from the Births, Deaths and Marriages Office, confirmation that this man worked for the Worker Office, extreme physical resemblances from photos, and, many years later, Ancestry DNA test matches. She'd found both her father's biological parents.

Heather contacted their descendants, including her father's half-sister, Heather's own aunt. She had found answers for her father, 'a very sensitive, kind and gentle man who had a very hard life and a very sad past,' Heather told me. 'He had to fight the shame and rejection of illegitimacy for many years through no fault of his own.'

I asked Heather how it made her feel, to finally win the truth her father was denied all his life. 'Ecstatic,' she said immediately. 'It's like there was a big hole there, and then it was filled – Dad didn't just drop from outer space … It just felt really, really good.'

And Heather wasn't just pleased for her father's sake. 'It was a jigsaw, and this was the final piece that fitted in,' she explained to me.

'And it made a difference to me. I think it filled in these gaps in my identity.'

IT WAS DAY Two of being in touch with Heather. I checked my inbox. There was a bewildering array of information in not one but five new emails from her. I was astounded. She was clearly tireless.

'Good news! We can narrow the field even further! I have found a DNA link with you also (on page twenty-one out of seventy pages!)' Seventy pages of DNA results? By this point, quite frankly, I was just pretending to understand what was going on.

'So that rules out [Family A]'s distant ancestry and leaves the common links that John and I SHARE … namely, [Family B].' There followed a cascade of names and historical tidbits. Someone's ancestor had come from Donegal, Ireland. I was a descendant of the Donegal connection and his first wife, while Heather was a descendant of Donegal Man and his second wife.

I could barely take it in. But one thing was very clear: Heather was marching inexorably forwards in time, closer and closer to the 1980s, to the Royal North Shore Hospital in Sydney, to the day when I began. She was ripping answers from the void with furious speed. Before the second day ended, there was another message. She'd brought in the wife of her cousin John to help the search:

'It would be great if we could have your mother's name or at least surname and the area where she lived. Also, if you can tell us anything about her history this would be useful. If you were adopted then the Dept of Community Services would have records. If you were not adopted, then if you can get access to your mother's birth certificate it would be a great help.'

What they were after was social clues: how my two parents might have met in order to make a child. A perfectly reasonable question for any kind of baby – except a donor-conceived one.

It was time to come clean. Heather had also sent me her phone number, and I gave her a call.

I said I'd send Heather the article I'd written for *Good Weekend*, which would explain it. That article had proved invaluable: it was exhausting to go through everything all over again, both my personal story and the general mess caused by donor conception, and have to explain how the 'system' was no system at all. I sent that article to people who contacted me out of the blue, saying they were donor conceived and they wanted to know how to start searching for their donor. Should they contact the government? The clinic? Unless they were from the state of Victoria, I usually replied that neither would amount to anything, attached the article as proof, and told them to join our support group, either by coming to the meetings or online.

This time, though, I sent the article to Heather. And crossed my fingers. What if she was close to someone who was a sperm donor and saw everything through his lens? What if she decided I was altogether too messed up to have access to her family tree?

I needn't have worried. From searching for answers for her father – from searching for her own grandparents – Heather knew exactly how I felt. 'I wasn't judging you,' she'd tell me, years later, when I asked her. 'I was more thinking about you being denied the knowledge of your parent, and I thought that was terrible.' And her natural curiosity rose to the fore: 'I was excited by the challenge, and thought "Okay, I might be able to do some good here",' she recalled.

After I emailed Heather the *Good Weekend* piece, she didn't leave me on tenterhooks. There was a reply in less than half an hour. 'A great article! I will send a copy to John's wife and we will get to work to see what we can come up with. I can already see some similarities to [Family B] in you.'

Twenty-six hours later – this woman is a bloodhound, I thought – Heather sent me another email. 'Hi again Sarah, I am attaching a document as I have found some exciting news on two strong possibilities for you that would fit in nicely.' That was all. Two strong possibilities: could she mean …? I opened the attachment. There were the names of two men that Heather thought could be my father.

I'll call them the Timothys. For each Timothy, there were LinkedIn profiles, work addresses, Twitter and Facebook accounts, details of where they went to school, what their parents did, and even a write-up from one Timothy's win at a recent seniors' tennis tournament. One was a high school English teacher. The other was working at the state government's Roads and Maritime Services.

I was dumbfounded. I looked at the Timothys. My dilemma was: how much do I believe? How attached do I get to either possibility? Or do I tell myself that neither is him?

Heather's research was extensive. But she'd made a note that none of this was absolute, that there were more leads yet to hunt down. So in my mind – with a slight wrench – I dismissed both. Neither were my father: this was just the first step in what could be a very long process. As for the process itself, I felt a bit useless. Research is a core part of my job. But Heather was the master of a whole bunch of shared ancestral family trees covering thousands of key individuals. She was taking the lead on the search, for which – out of the two of us – she was eminently best equipped. After I got over the shock of the Timothys, however, I realised there was something I could do. 'I'm going to ask a contact of mine (a sperm donor from the '80s, nice guy, open to his kids contacting him) about how to approach men, what's a good way to go about it, etc.,' I wrote to Heather. By 'men', I meant sperm donors, of course. 'Yes, a good idea I think … and a very sensitive subject,' she replied. 'It may be a good reason to wait a bit, until everyone else has been eliminated … Will keep sending you stuff in the meantime, as options to think about.'

I should say that, while Heather was undoubtedly a genetic genealogist of terrifying speed and skill, she only ever used publicly available information. Everything that she was trawling through – old electoral rolls, wedding notices, social media – was open access. She'd built many a branch of her own family tree and had accumulated a lot of knowledge about convict-era Australia. She was, in short, exactly the person Bec and I needed; and after so many years – the first person with such access to information who was genuinely interested in helping us. Thank god for Heather.

We'd arranged to meet up the following month, to go through Heather's notes, and I'd explained that Bec was my sister. Bec, of course, had also popped up in Heather's matches as a distant cousin. The meeting expanded to four: Heather, me, Bec and Bec's baby Emily – my niece, extraordinarily enough. I had a niece! And a nephew! What did that mean? Another loop of confusion and self-doubt followed.

By now it was clear I was in the middle of a crazy ride, where if it wasn't for emails and the written word I wouldn't have had a clear sense of what was happening at all. A few months back, some producers from Screentime Australia had contacted me about donor conception, with an eye to making a series similar to one screened in the Netherlands. The Netherlands series followed a group of donor-conceived people who did DNA testing to find siblings, and it was lovely, genuinely compelling and sweet. I told the Screentime team about Heather and Bec, and our meeting, and the utterly wild journey of the last fortnight. The producers asked if they could come along and film us. Both Heather and Bec, to their credit, were okay with this. By this point, I think we were all outside the bounds of our normal lives anyway.

We decided to meet at Sydney University's Fisher Library. The Screentime producers managed to book a suitably atmospheric part of the Fisher, so we'd have some privacy. Which, as it turned out, was a very good thing. A few days beforehand, Heather had sent through another one of her bombshell emails.

'Just confirming Saturday,' she wrote. 'BTW, this time, I believe I really may have found your father! I have triangulated information from your DNA matches of seven different people on Ancestry, including myself ... I have put together charts to explain my deductions and included other information as well,' she finished.

What? I shook myself. It was probably just another good guess; it didn't mean anything. Long ago in Heather terms – which meant about a week – she'd discounted both the Timothys as she furiously winnowed through history. At the time, I was relieved I hadn't invested emotionally in either Timothy. I should adopt a similarly cautious approach here, I thought. 'Okay, I'm not going to ask any questions until we meet up and you can run through all your reasoning in detail,' I replied.

True to form, as well as telling us she'd found our father, Heather also thoughtfully emailed detailed parking advice, a recommendation that we bring lunch, and a quick rundown of the availability of coffee in the library's immediate vicinity. And she attached a photo so that we would recognise her. The photo showed a blonde woman happily patting a full-grown lioness. (She'd told me she travelled to

South Africa often.) By this point, nothing surprised me. I just forwarded it to Bec.

The few hours to Saturday seemed very long.

IT WAS RAINING, the start of winter. I met Bec under the stone arches of Sydney University's quadrangle. In one corner of the square, water dripped from a gnarled jacaranda onto the manicured lawn. Bec turned up with a black jacket, a scarf and a pram: inside, a tiny bundled-up Emily peeked out. She was very sweet and had an air of calm, as though dungeon grandfather reveals were her kind of normal.

I, on the other hand, was jumpy. So was Bec. We made a few nervous jokes, then headed to the Fisher. Down the stairs we walked, into the subterranean levels full of shadows and glass, until we came to a spot-lit cavern. There was a big table in the middle, carefully laid with paper: loose documents, full binders, a long, snaking family tree made of various sheets taped together. And behind the table, straightening some files, was Heather. A twinkly woman with shoulder-length blonde hair, bursting with secrets. We said some excited hellos, and then Heather got stuck into what she was clearly dying to share – the answer to who we were.

CHAPTER 33

HEATHER HAD SPENT hours putting together what she thought was our family tree from six generations ago right up until present day, setting out each branch, each marriage, each child. She'd even scoured the archives and printed out photos of as many of these individuals as possible. Everything was laid out on the table when the two of us walked right off the page, into the room.

Later, much later, Heather said she'd thought, when she saw Bec and me for the first time: '… Gee, there's a resemblance there. For both of you.'

Heather kept that thought inside as she began. Instead of giving us the name of our biological father and fielding a world of disjointed questions, we'd decided she was going to lay it out piece by piece through the generations, explaining her reasoning as she went. (The producers, quietly filming, liked this approach very much.) It was the logical and most efficient way of doing things. It was also killing me.

Heather started with James Moore, horse thief, Donegal native, and our personal Ground Zero. All three of us are related to Moore, who stole (and dyed) a horse, legend tells it, with a modicum of ingenuity but zero success. He was caught, convicted and deported to Australia.

James Moore arrived on the convict ship *Fergusson* in 1829. It was not a pleasure cruise. The 216 convicts were already 'in a low state of health, from deficient nourishment and the depressing passions' when they set off from Ireland, according to the surgeon superintendent on board.[1] Then came bad weather, terrible sea sickness, and a severe outbreak of scurvy, complicated with dysentery and 'affections of the lungs'. The ship docked in Sydney Cove with only two dead men: not a bad result for the time. A living James Moore was in the colony, ready to serve his life sentence. According to Heather, he was our great-great-great-great-grandfather.

'Right,' I said. It was very hard to think meaningfully about long-dead ancestors: I wanted the most recent one and was keeping everything else for later. Heather continued. The Moores had children, then grandchildren, then great-grandchildren. There was an ancestral connection to Charles Harpur, one of white Australia's first poets, which Heather was excited about. She showed us a sepia photo. The man had a long beard, hair striped like a badger, and he'd waxed his sideburns so that they stood out from his head like stubby wings. To Heather and Bec, I made what I hoped were suitably impressed noises about Harpur. Inside I was taking in almost none of it.

Heather had better luck with Sister Kenny. Elizabeth Kenny was born in 1880, in regional New South Wales. She was our first cousin several times removed, said Heather. I'm not usually thrilled by dim links to famous people – but she was *amazing*.

A SELF-TAUGHT BUSH nurse, Sister Kenny lived on her family's property on the Darling Downs. She used to ride out on horseback to treat patients for free. She nursed on troopships in WWI, where she was promoted to 'Sister'. Upon returning home, she designed and patented a new kind of stretcher for ambulances, but it was in the treatment of poliomyelitis that she made her name. Polio is a brutal, highly infectious disease which attacks its victims in early childhood and can cause permanent paralysis. There was no vaccine for polio back then, and there is no cure for it to this day. In the face of strong opposition from the medical establishment, Sister Kenny revolutionised treatment, and therefore ongoing quality of life, for polio patients.

In the 1930s, Sister Kenny established a clinic in Queensland to treat polio victims using the practical, careful techniques she'd been developing since her bush nursing: hot baths, foments, passive movements, the discarding of braces and callipers and the encouragement of active movements. She was massively ridiculed by both doctors and masseurs. 'The strong-willed Kenny … was opposed by a conservative medical profession whom she mercilessly slated and who considered her recommendation to discard immobilization to be criminal,' says the *Australian Dictionary of Biography*. I like this woman, I thought.

Sister Kenny took her groundbreaking methods of treating polio victims to England, then Brisbane. The medical superintendent noted that her patients recovered faster and that their limbs were more supple. Yet most of the Australian medical profession continued to ignore her. 'I was wholly unprepared for the extraordinary attitude of the medical world in its readiness to condemn anything that smacked of reform or that ran contrary to approved methods of practice,' she would say.[2]

So in 1940, Sister Kenny went to the US. She began treating patients in Minneapolis General Hospital, then started courses for doctors and physiotherapists from around the world. In 1942, Minneapolis became home to the first Elizabeth Kenny Clinic, later to become the Elizabeth Kenny Institute. Sister Kenny's methods became the foundation of what we know today as rehabilitation medicine.[3] She co-authored an autobiography called *And They Shall Walk*, published in New York, and a film was made about her life. In 1950, Congress bestowed on her the rare honour of free access to the United States without entry formalities.

To this day, the Courage Kenny Institute (and its Foundation) continues to treat people with disabilities and those with chronic conditions in the US. There is no such institute, or equivalent high-level recognition of her methods, in Australia. By all accounts, Sister Kenny might not have cared: 'It is better to be a lion for a day than a sheep all your life,' she reportedly once said.

Heather had brought along a book. It was titled *Sister Kenny, The Woman Who Challenged the Doctors*. Bec and I took a photo of us holding that book, grinning.

SISTER KENNY, FASCINATING though she was, was still a long way away from our own biological father.

Her story had, however, taken us into the twentieth century. Heather came back to our direct ancestors. So many families, so many surnames crashing into each other, with half the names subsumed and the other half emerging triumphant. Eventually, a female descendant of Charles Harpur married a man from a small country town in New South Wales. The couple had three children. One of those children was my grandmother.

Heather showed us a photo of her, and I stared. And stared. The photo was from the Australian War Memorial archives. My paternal grandmother was a sergeant in the Royal Australian Air Force, serving on the home front. She wore a shirt, tie, and blazer, with the RAAF eagle on one sleeve. On her head was a RAAF forage cap – a chic dark blue number, set at a ridiculously jaunty angle amid her curls.

The outfit was all very smart, but what got me was her face.

In her face was my face. And Bec's face too.

I can see my mother in me, no doubt. I am unquestionably Asian: the hair, the eyes, the build, the cheekbones. So I can see how I *am* my mother's daughter, but what I can't see is any actual resemblance, if that makes sense. I've spent a lifetime studying other Eurasian faces: seeing where the whiteness emerges, where the Asian genes dominate, trying to work out what happened in my case and never really understanding. But with this woman, I had my answer. I could be looking at a slightly rounder, whiter version of me in a RAAF uniform. Same face shape, same slightly pointy chin, same mouth and dimples. Given that she's an extra generation removed, I can't believe how easily we blend into each other. And Bec – you would never think, passing us on the street, that Bec and I were related. But with this sudden grandmother you could actually understand it. She's the bridge between us, the visual explanation.

It was the first time in my life I'd seen anyone from my own family who actually looked like me.

There was a pause while we stared. I can't remember if I voiced any of what I was thinking out loud; I was just stunned. This was the resemblance that Heather had seen the moment we walked into the room. 'I see her in both of you,' Heather told me later. 'Cheekbones, facial structure. Bec seems to have her nose.'

'She had two sons,' said Heather to us, while we studied the photo in silence. Both were born in the country. 'But only one of them was living in Sydney in the late '70s and early '80s, so I think he must've been the one that became a donor.'

And Heather had, of course, a photo of that son: the first colour photo she'd produced, a grainy profile shot from Facebook. If the photo of my apparent grandmother had cut me to the core, this one had the opposite effect. I was utterly nonplussed. It seemed to be a holiday snap. A probably fifty-something man in a pressed yellow polo shirt, with wire-framed glasses, brown hair and a handlebar moustache, standing in front of what appeared to be a German U-boat in dock at a naval base. I was baffled. This man looked nothing like me.

How on earth could he be my biological father? How on earth did I share half my DNA with him?

I knew Bec was thinking the same thing – this guy? After all these years, and a huge fight for answers … he turns out to look a little like Ned Flanders? There was absolutely nothing wrong with this man. He looked pleasant. He looked happy. That navy base tour must've been really fascinating. But he did not look like us. Staring at him, I felt nothing: zero connection. I'm not one for superstition, but shouldn't there be something, some spark, when you see your own biological parent for the first time? The only resemblance I could see between him and Bec was brown hair, and perhaps the length of the face (although I doubt she'd agree with me). The only resemblance I could see between him and me was that I also like yellow.

I understood, now, the importance of Heather going through all the steps in time, all the births, deaths and marriages. There was absolutely no way I would have believed her if she'd led with this photo. Even after the full explanation, I didn't think it was true. DNA doesn't lie, but maybe Heather had taken a wrong turn down the ages?

Yet poor Heather, standing there and watching our perplexed reactions ('I felt a bit dashed,' she told me later), was so unbelievably thorough. In typical, kind Heather fashion, she'd even prepared a folder for each of us to take home, which contained thirty-odd pages of research and calculations. And there was also that woman in the RAAF uniform: the uncanny sensation of looking at my own face.

I'll call the man in the polo shirt Steven McKenzie. He was, apparently, our father.

THE PRODUCERS DID interviews with Bec and I individually to record our reactions. In documentary, your reaction is what it is – I have no idea if the churn and the bafflement I was feeling on the inside made it out. I couldn't muster any instant delight and fulfilment, nor felt that I should have to. That's a reality TV cliché, not real life. In real life, when you discover something so fundamental which has long been denied to you, you can't process it straightaway. I had no idea how I felt. I needed time. And despite going on national television, despite publishing my story, despite being so exploited by strangers from the moment of my own conception – I was still, somehow, really quite a private person. A private person who was absolutely going to pieces inside.

There was another consideration, too. What if we made contact with Steven, and he later saw this footage at some point? *What if I said the wrong thing*? What if that, in turn, jeopardised any future relationship we might have? So much at stake. So many implications.

Compounding the whole situation was something we should by now have expected: Heather's conscientious approach to her research. She'd found us not only a name and a photo of this apparent biological father, but snippets of a life, including old addresses in Sydney and details of his education. He'd studied at Sydney University, as had Bec many years later. Heather had found his brother's name and the names of his nieces and nephews. And a final grenade: his contact details.

Neatly copied from the phone directory, on the last piece of paper that Heather had for us, was Steven McKenzie's name, full street address and telephone number.

CHILDREN OF A digital age, Bec and I stared at the contact details. Then we did what any of our contemporaries would do: we huddled over Heather's laptop and googled him. We found his home in Queensland. We located his Facebook profile. And we found many, many letters to the editor under his name, published in metropolitan dailies, community papers, journals and news sites. We knew it was him and no other because he'd signed off with his full name and his suburb. It seemed our dad was quite the correspondent, on everything from the state of the roads to federal politics. I started to wonder if we'd been fathered by a keyboard warrior. If so, he was an earlier, politer version: all his letters to the editor used courteous language, even the sarcastic bits. Especially the sarcastic bits. He wrote about: support for Australia becoming a republic. Something about bitumen. Praise for Malcolm Turnbull, at that time the prime minister. Brickbats for the Nationals, the traditional party of regional Australia. A strongly argued missive on how using the term 'guys' did not exclude women. There was, in short, a lot to go on.

Then we came to quite a rich vein of book reviews he'd written – referencing, in passing, everything from Machiavelli to Tacitus – and something caught my eye. It was a critique of Christos Tsiolkas, an Australian author most famous for his international bestseller *The Slap*. Tsiolkas has written a number of hits. He is also gay, and many of his characters are too. I read the Tsiolkas critique closely. Then, away from the producers, I pulled Heather aside.

'Heather,' I said. 'Just something I came across. I think he's gay.'

'I thought so too,' she said instantly. Heather had come across one or two other things in his social media profile which made her suspect. 'But I didn't want to say anything, I wanted you two to form your own opinions. Also, for someone of my generation, that's something that some people are still very private about.'

I shrugged. 'It makes no difference to me,' I said. I was thinking about something else. 'Maybe, if he's gay, he'll be more open to talking to us. Because he won't have a wife and kids of his own.'

She nodded. 'Yes, I think that's a possibility.'

I HAVE NO clear memory of the rest, what happened after I got home, or the ensuing weeks. I don't really know how I wandered through the days. But I do remember a very strong sense of peace. He was real: we were real. There was an explanation for how we came to be and everything that had gone before us. Suddenly, I was fully tethered to the human race. If you have never felt such dislocation, if you've always been comfortably ensconced in your family identity, I cannot possibly explain how reassuring that is or what it gives you. All I can say is the rest of that tight, dark knot of pain in my head came loose, unwound and straightened, and I breathed out.

Bec politely let me be for a few months. I'd told her that I didn't think cold calling him would be the best approach. Given that we had his address, I thought maybe a handwritten letter would be a nicer way of introducing ourselves, and more likely to be well received. If he didn't answer any such letter, then we could consider more immediate methods.

But I made no move to write or do anything. I was very happy to just float along, knowing that I possessed a piece of paper with his name on it. If this was the end of the search, it was fine by me. What I'd written in *Good Weekend* a few years back was true: I didn't need another father. I couldn't have asked for a better father than the man who raised me till I was fifteen. I'd been furious that a bunch of so-called professionals could make me, know who my own biological family was, and then deliberately deny me that same knowledge. The insult of that stuck in my craw. But I'd beaten them all – I'd found the name. I just wanted to bask in that for a while.

I think I was enjoying finally being happy. I had answers about myself. I was in a great relationship: Sam and I had just become engaged. And somehow, despite all my personal donor-conceived chaos, work was going well.

Bec, on the other hand, was crazy with impatience. She'd known she was donor conceived since the age of eleven, she finally had a name, and *you want to slow down now*?

Poor Bec. I put her off. I was in Germany, reporting. I was back home, scripting on a tight turnaround. A couple of months after that day at the Fisher Library, I emailed her with what now reads like infuriating nonchalance: 'I'm still just dealing with this whole Steven thing, have barely thought about any other family members, dunno about you.' She was probably out of her mind with frustration. Bec didn't want to move forward without me, and of the two of us, I was probably best placed to write any letter. Contacting strangers, after all, is my job.

If I'm honest, I think there was also a bit of fear in my reluctance to make contact with him. Not fear of any specific reaction on his behalf: more like fear of losing what I already had. If he turned out to be a complete arsehole, well, that would really ruin the moment. I didn't feel like descending into another heavy period of existential anguish. I'd just spent years in the last one.

But I could understand Bec's position; I could see her need to continue. And curiosity is my downfall.

While I was on a week's holiday in Tasmania with Sam, I decided I was ready. I'd had a break and filled my cup with happiness. I could now handle a bit more of the absolute insanity that being donor conceived brings. One morning, in a tiny but lovely Hobart cafe, I ordered an extremely large coffee and opened my laptop. While Sam read the paper, I bashed out a letter to Steven McKenzie. I would send the draft to Bec for her input, then handwrite the final version, with our email contacts at the bottom.

Dear Steven McKenzie,

Our names are Rebecca and Sarah, and we are seeking information regarding our family history, which we thought you may be able to help with. Apologies for approaching you out of the blue like this, but we thought it would be best to make contact with you via a letter.

We are both thirty-three years old, and we're half sisters – a fact which we've only just found out, and which makes us really happy. Sarah is a reporter and presenter at the ABC in Sydney. Rebecca is an Occupational Therapist, working in an acute hospital, also in Sydney. At first glance, we don't look much alike, apart from the general shape of our faces and appearance of our chins. Sarah is half Malaysian Chinese, and Rebecca is part Italian. But we're writing to you about the part that we have in common. We think we may share it with you too.

We were both conceived at the Royal North Shore Hospital in Sydney, as a result of sperm donated to both our mothers. We have the same biological father – the same sperm donor.

As a result of DNA testing, we've found out that we are half sisters. We also found a large number of distant cousins and their family trees. By tracing our new-found relatives and their family trees, we noticed that you were a common link for each of us, and believe you may be our donor. We also understand you were living in Sydney during the early '80s.

If you did indeed donate sperm to the Royal North Shore Clinic at that time, we'd like to thank you for your donation, because without it we wouldn't be here. We want to tell you that we both have wonderful, happy lives: Rebecca has a husband and two young children, and Sarah has just become engaged.

We would like to clarify at this point that we certainly aren't after any money, nor will we ever be, and neither is there any legal right to it. Apologies for being so crude, but we think it's worth being clear on that, because there's a lot of misunderstanding about that particular issue in the community. We would just like to know some basic family medical history so that we can plan our lives. Rebecca has two very young children, who would be your biological grandchildren, and this has become very important. Sarah has a chronic condition and would like to know more so that she can manage it.

The Royal North Shore Hospital can't provide us with any information, because they deliberately destroyed a number of medical records over several years. It is a shocking case of malpractice which has resulted in two investigations here in NSW. As a result, we don't have even non-identifying information about family – including the all-important basic family medical history. We both find this upsetting. We found each other only by luck. Once we'd met, and realised we were born around the same time at the same clinic, we realised a DNA test was the only way to find out if we were sisters – and it turned out to be true.

We would absolutely love to hear from you, and we would greatly appreciate any family medical history you can provide.

CHAPTER 34

One August afternoon in Brisbane, Steven McKenzie arrived home and pulled our envelope out of the squat mailbox which stood halfway up his driveway.

'It was quite puffy,' he recalled. 'And I thought I'd received another mad screed from a mad monarchist.'

He was in no rush to read said mad ramblings, and so didn't open the envelope straightaway. But when he did, it was quite clear that this was not going to be about defending a constitutional monarchy.

'I realised what it was, so I made myself a cup of coffee and sat down to read it,' he said. At the end, when he'd finished, 'I was very pleased, but also a bit nervy.'

At the end of that month, an email dropped for Bec and me. It was a reply to our letter from Steven McKenzie – a polite, curious mix of the mundane and the earth-shattering.

'Dear Rebecca and Sarah, Thank you for your recent letter. There was no need at all to apologise for approaching me out of the blue – I was delighted to receive it. I'd also be delighted to receive more letters from you, but in future please send anything to my postal address … Things put into the mailbox at home tend to get drenched whenever it rains.' He chose to begin with postal instructions? But wait – was that a good sign?

'Sarah, I've just read the piece about you in *Good Weekend* in August 2014, and was appalled. Not just at the loss of your father, but also at the runaround you got from RNSH. Since you're a reporter, I think you and I have a lot to talk about. I cannot agree with some of the things reported.' (My journalist brain immediately came to the fore. That piece was extensively fact-checked, I thought. A second later, my regular self surfaced: wait, did he mean what the clinic had done?)

'Now down to tin tacks. Sarah, the *Good Weekend* article says that you went to IVF Australia, and was told that the code on the relevant records was destroyed. After that, a personal contact from RNSH said that your donor was a medical student, and that his code was AFH. Neither of those details applies to me. I've never studied anything like Medicine, and I didn't look like your father (my hair was black, my teeth weren't so straight, my face was a different shape and so was my body).' Okay, I thought: but none of those were dealbreakers. And he wasn't finished. There were also, he said, some more 'positive' details, based on what I'd written in that article. He'd also studied German, and travelled to Germany; he shared my obsession with olives. 'And my code at RNSH was AKH. I hope that difference of one letter has not caused unnecessary heartache. I happen to know that IVF Australia has a file on me, with my photo in it and a letter which I wrote to all my donor children as long ago as 1997.'

It was him.

It had to be him. He was a donor. To the Royal North Shore Hospital in Sydney, no less, although he now lived in a different state. His donor code was almost the same as the one Diana Craven had dredged from a three-decade-old memory: AKH, not AFH. It had to be him. And – there was a letter? A photo? Supposedly waiting for us, for more than two decades, with IVF Australia? The outfit that had treated me so appallingly? What was that about?

'Sarah and Rebecca, I am willing to take a DNA test to determine whether I am your natural father. Because there is still some doubt about our connection, I'd rather not answer any of your questions yet, as I don't want to get your hopes up and then disappoint you. But if the test result is Yes, then I'll tell you everything you would like to know.

And I'd also be very, very glad of the amicable relationship mentioned in the *Good Weekend* article.'

All I could think was: holy shit.

THE ONLY THING that remained was to sort out the where and how of the final test. I emailed him about the various DNA options – the expensive, one-to-one labs used by the courts; the moderately pricey home paternity tests; and the cheapest option, the genealogy companies like Ancestry. Bec followed up with an email of her own, politely requesting we continue down the Ancestry route for reasons of familiarity and cost. Clever Bec. Ancestry was one-to-many: once tested, Steven would be on there for any other donor-conceived children to find. We all agreed that we were happy to wait for the outcome of any DNA test before chatting more in-depth, either in person or over the phone. I thought that was completely reasonable; I certainly didn't want to emotionally invest in the wrong person.

BEC AND I settled between us that we would pay for his Ancestry DNA test to be sent to him. I didn't feel we were in any way obliged to do that – children should not have to pay parents, or anyone, for the truth about themselves – but I thought the goodwill might be important. In the meantime, despite all his caution, he seemed to be growing increasingly confident, and even a bit excited. Bec had sent through a few pictures of herself. That seemed to confirm to him that we weren't just catfishing: he clearly wanted to show us what he saw in return.

'I'm working on a small portfolio of pix of me from 1980 through to now, with a few of my immediate family as well,' he wrote. 'I'm reluctant to send it to you before the test, but I may as well tell you now that I think the test result will be Yes.' (Whoa, I thought, there go all your careful boundaries.)

'I've looked at both Sarah's internet pix and your pix very closely, and right now I'm pretty confident about who your natural father was. The resemblances to some of my close relatives are very, very strong.'

We both knew that already. We were, thanks to Heather, way ahead of him. Steven McKenzie didn't even know some of the things we knew about his antecedents. He was aware of the Charles Harpur, face-winged-poet connection, but not some of the others. 'Being related to Sister Kenny would be delightful!' he said. (Privately, he would tell me which of my pictures he'd been struck by: an old Twitter profile shot of me in sunglasses. 'I saw that and I thought, oh yes,' he said. 'That looked like my mother in a bad mood.')

The Ancestry DNA kit arrived at Steven's post office box in mid-September. (They sent me a notification of arrival – another quiet perk of having ordered it at our end.) He emailed us, saying he'd spat in the tube and returned it immediately.

ONE MONTH LATER, he sent us an email – at half-past four in the morning.

'Hi Sarah and Rebecca,

The DNA test results have arrived. They confirm that I am your natural father.

Would you like to meet me? If so, I can come to Sydney and we can get together for as long or as short as you wish.'

HEATHER WAS RIGHT.

The circle closed: the last strands in the weave, flapping loose, found purchase and tightened. He was our biological father. We'd found him. It was five and a half years since my mother had told me that my dad was not my dad.

At the bottom of that email was an attachment. It was a copy of the letter Steven McKenzie had written more than two decades earlier, in 1997, to his donor-conceived children. To us.

Dear Child Who Was Made From Me,

Hello! How do you do? And congratulations on your decision to seek me out! I'm very happy that you've taken this step.

I have wondered about you from time to time over the years, and I wished you and your parents well, but until recently I hadn't thought that you might wonder about me. Thank you for doing just that ...

The letter was typed, with a handwritten salutation and sign-off. It was a letter he'd written knowing that its recipients might still be children, and as such, I thought, it struck a good balance, explaining the difficult without being overly simplistic. He'd left a photo of himself with the letter.

Yes, half of you came from me: your father wanted you but couldn't get you, and it was I who did him the favour he needed most. Yes, I will let you know where that half of you came from. Yes, I will gladly meet you if that's what you want. Yes, I will show you my life, and I will tell you about myself and my relatives. And I will always let you have any medical background information you may need ...

One by one, the dominoes fell: that promise of anonymity, so fiercely and maliciously protected by the fertility industry, collapsed. As far back as 1997, our biological father was happy to be identified. He was happy to meet us. He was happy to tell us about our ancestry, his life, our shared family medical history. He had explicitly consented to all this more than twenty years ago, and we had never been told.

The problem was not with our donor. The problem was with the gatekeepers, profiteering from our existence, keeping us apart from our own biological parent by dubious means – against both his wishes and ours.

... I hope this is the sort of greeting from me that you wanted, and that you will want to ask for the contact details which I have waiting for you ... I hope you'll go right ahead and get in touch with me. I'm looking forward to hearing from you. Warmest regards, The Man You Were Made From.

IN 2020, WHILE researching this book, I would discover that Steven McKenzie's letter to us had been hiding in plain sight. He had, it transpired, also provided a copy to the Donor Conception Support Group. They had used it as a resource. In 2010, the DCSG had included it in their lengthy submission to the Australian Senate inquiry into donor conception.[1]

My biological father's personal letter to me, about my own origins, had been on the website of the Parliament of Australia for years.

The rest of the goddamn country had received it before I had.

AS FAR AS Bec and I were concerned, once this letter was given to NSART (which later became IVF Australia) in 1997, it disappeared. We had never received it, nor been told of its existence. Presumably this was because clinic staff had destroyed our donor codes: but we will never really be sure at what point in time they did that, so who knows.

I, of course, wouldn't find out that Steven McKenzie was my biological parent until I was an adult, but Bec had known she was donor conceived since the age of eleven. And she could have done with that letter, growing up. 'I think I would have felt reassured and been glad to have received your letter,' she told Steven.

On his side, Steven was never told by anyone either at NSART or IVF Australia that donor codes had been destroyed – and that consequently there was no way of passing his letter on. He seemed shocked to discover that this was the case. I realised that he had full faith in the system, still, and the people who worked in it. He trusted what they told him and believed that all had been professional and aboveboard. That is, until he heard from us.

I asked IVF Australia and its parent company Virtus Health about Steven McKenzie's letter and photo, and why he wasn't told that donor code destruction would make them undeliverable: 'Why did NSART/IVF Australia not inform donors of code destruction, particularly donors who were specifically open to contact?'

'For reasons of privacy, we cannot make any comment on [Steven McKenzie's] specific case,' they replied. How unsurprising, I thought.

'I find the fact that IVF Aus had your photo and letter on file fascinating,' I wrote to Steven. 'First of all, I think it's really commendable that you wrote that letter and gave it to them. Secondly, one of the (many) mysterious things about code destruction at the RNSH is: we have never been able to establish with certainty at what point so many codes were destroyed. The RNSH conducted a somewhat weak investigation and concluded that they were destroyed before March 1984, I believe.

'Which would mean that at the time you gave them your letter, they would have known it could never reach anyone. Unless, of course, they're not being truthful about their timeline for code destruction.'

I knew which of those I considered more likely. Lies abound in donor conception, but the devastating lie of a major private clinic accepting such an important document, knowing it could never be delivered, seemed to me to be the most effortless.

'Thank you for being so decent about this, and so prompt with your reply,' I finished. 'Regardless of the DNA result, it gives me a lot of faith in other people.'

'Thanks for saying that my first answer to you gave you a lot of faith in other people,' he replied. 'That was one of the things I've hoped for over nearly twenty years. Back in 1997, IVF' – he meant donor conception – 'suddenly was topic-of-the-moment in newspapers and on TV. One of the things talked about was how shocked the children were at the discovery, and how they felt there was now a gap in their personal backgrounds which they yearned to fill. I decided that if any of my children found me, I would do what I could to close the gap smoothly and to make the children feel that at least something like their former self-image had been restored — to do anything less would be heartlessly cruel. The first step in this process was to write the letter and provide the photos; the rest I would have to make up as I went along, all the while bearing in mind that nobody ever needs another parent (I thought of that one long before you did). So now I am chuffed that my first answer to you generated such a positive reaction.'

We were on the same page, it seemed. That felt good.

THE THREE OF us arranged to meet in person for the first time in Sydney that November. At noon on a sunny spring day, I pulled up at Abbotsford Point, where the Sydney Rowing Club perches on the Parramatta River. The club itself is ripe with history, but my reasons for selecting that venue were firmly rooted in present-day considerations. 'If we have a nice day it should be very pretty. Also I think they're open all day, or their bar is anyway,' I wrote. If you're meeting your biological parent for the first time as an adult, having alcohol available is probably wise.

I walked into the main entrance, where light streamed in from the river beyond. In the foyer, a man stood up. He was formally dressed in a suit, still had that moustache, and was carrying a briefcase. It was Steven McKenzie. He had a longish, oval face and the wire glasses were perched on his nose. Despite all the photos, I still felt a jolt of disbelief; I saw nothing of me in him.

WE SAT AND made awkwardly pleasant conversation till Bec arrived. Part of me was operating like this was a work situation: I didn't want the talent to talk themselves out before we began the interview. So I tried to talk about anything but why we were there until my sister could hear it, with me, for the first time. It was difficult. Steven was definitely a talker. When Bec walked in, I heaved a sigh of relief: now I could stop trying to hold back the tide.

What followed, in fact, turned out to be a tsunami. I really didn't have to worry he'd talk himself out. Steven ricocheted from Brisbane property prices, to medieval history across several countries, to the Royal North Shore Hospital and back. It wasn't a free-ranging conversation: it was a free-ranging lecture. Bec and I sat. Around once every half hour or so, one of us would manage a word or two; that would set him off again. He didn't ask us anything about ourselves. I remember that very clearly. I saw no point trying to force it. If he wasn't interested, why would I talk over the top of him? I just waited for things to change. But they didn't. To my increasing astonishment, I began to realise that there was no shift coming. I started to get annoyed. Who, upon meeting two of their own children for the very first time, asks them zero questions? I thought. Who looks at two of their newly surfaced adult offspring – people who tracked him down by finding out more about his own ancestry than he knew himself – and decides there's nothing he needs to discover?

Seemingly, Steven McKenzie was one such person. We were his children, but we were adults. We felt ourselves equal. The conversation was anything but. An hour or two in, he'd started on family history:

white ancestor after white ancestor. I couldn't believe there had been so little give so far. So when Steven began the tale of yet another hardy early settler in the outback, who'd pluckily defended their remote holding from an uprising by the local Aboriginal people, I let go.

'She held them off all night,' Steven said proudly. 'Kept them at bay on her own with only a shotgun.'

I felt like it was time, in fact, to inject some reality into the whole afternoon. 'So she was a murderer?' I asked.

There was an awkward pause.

Then he kept going.

The only other slowing down that I recall was when I got a second question in and asked him, point-blank, if he was gay. I couldn't really find a good spot in the flow to ask him, so it must have come out of nowhere. I was being provocative, maybe: but I wanted something real, not an unrelenting stream of consciousness. The question made him stop and regard me for a second. Then he spoke more carefully than he had before. 'Yes,' he said. 'Why do you ask?'

'Well, you grew up in a country town,' I said. 'Was that difficult?'

He relaxed slightly. 'Yes,' he said. 'I wasn't really open about it until I left.' He told us more about that: about his relationship with his parents and his brother. About how he felt upon arrival in Sydney's Kings Cross, then a haven of hedonism, a place where nobody asked any questions. And it was good. It was really interesting. He spoke naturally. But gradually he got on to other subjects, the tide rose again, and soon we were riding another impenetrable wave of words.

After more than three hours of mostly listening, I made my excuses and left. Bec stayed. I walked away with a sense of breathing again for the first time. I went home and shook myself.

Later, that night, I spoke to Bec. 'How long did you stay for?' I asked.

'Oh, probably about eight hours,' she replied, in her pleasant way.

'Eight hours? What on earth did you talk about?'

Bec said there had been a potted history of France, among other things. I couldn't believe it. 'Did he ask you anything about yourself?'

'Not really,' she said lightly.

I decided that that was enough. I'd found him, met him, there had been no animosity. Mission accomplished. I didn't need any more.

I DON'T WRITE this to be deliberately nasty. I write it to explain, to be truthful – and in that truth-telling make space for what I think might be a common experience among donor-conceived people. Despite what some media will tell you, part of that truth is: this is no fairytale.

For me and Bec, and probably others, there was no sudden understanding when we met our biological parent for the first time. No dazzling ray of light. But that is real. That is what life, and other people, are like. Real people are imperfect. Instead of transcendental highs and crushing lows, the most likely reaction you'll have to meeting a stranger for the first time is somewhere in the middle. I didn't have any reason to dislike Steven. I'd just felt completely disconnected from the entire afternoon. Probably because he didn't, to me, appear to be interested in either of us. It was an afternoon I'd worked towards for years. Afterwards, the sense of anticlimax was extreme.

I maintained some distance for a while. I processed what had happened.

I began to see that maybe it had been a pretty intimidating experience for him, facing not one but two of us. And, sitting there, mired in disbelief, I probably gave off quite a stony vibe. I thought about that.

The more I thought about it, the more I realised it was probably true: I hadn't been so nice myself. Maybe he was feeling raw about the abrupt way in which I'd asked if he was gay. I could easily have been much nicer about it, more gentle. That was wrong of me. So I decided to say sorry. I wrote him another email.

'I asked if you were gay because I wanted to know more about you, but I didn't say the usual disclaimer that it means absolutely nothing to me whether you're gay, straight, a unicorn, etc. … So just so you know: it really doesn't matter to me … I'm proud to be related to someone who has contributed to a shift in attitudes throughout their life by being who they really are.'

He appreciated my note. He told me so in a reply the next day. It was a nice email, sincere and heartfelt: 'When you asked me whether I was gay, I immediately gave you an honest answer, and not only because in our joint situation, I couldn't tell you any lies (you'd both had quite enough of those already). I was also as confident of both of you as I had been of my family; regardless of how much or little time it might take, I never thought that either of you would end up any different from them.'

It felt good to read that email. We exchanged a few more over the new year. Each message was conversational, pleasant, something nice to see drop in your inbox. I started to think writing, not talking, might be the best foundation for our relationship.

After a few months, I had a sudden realisation. I knew what had been going on with Steven that day at the rowing club. I went back over everything. My god, I thought, he was nervous. He was probably nervous to begin with, and then I eyeballed him the whole time like a hostile seagull. So he talked more. He talked to cover the silence. And so it got worse. I'd made it worse.

The only way to test this, I thought, was to have another conversation with him. He'd said he was coming to town again for the Anzac Day long weekend; Bec and I couldn't meet up with him at the same time, but maybe that was for the best. Maybe we each needed to see him alone.

I met with him at a cafe. A few months earlier, my life had been upended again, but in a good way: I'd had my first baby. I brought her along. Steven performed admirably. He'd bought her a soft toy and bounced her on his knee. He'd met Bec's kids a few nights previously when he went to her house for dinner. He looked quite chuffed to hold my child. After all, he'd raised none of his own; perhaps being an instant grandparent was a good feeling. We ate lunch and chatted about any old thing. Steven still talked a lot, much more than me, but it was an exchange now; maybe, I thought, it would always be like that. Maybe he was naturally garrulous. Maybe I was still wary. That was okay.

My regular smartphone was broken, and all I had was a stand-in. Steven was a classic technophobe and hadn't even brought his phone, which he apparently loathed. All of which meant, at the end of the lunch, I had nothing but my ancient burner to record the moment. I took a photo which had a resolution of about six pixels.

It's a terrible, grainy shot of quite a nice meeting, but I sent it to him afterwards anyway: Steven in the cafe, holding his baby grandchild and a pink fluffy bunny on his knee. He's smiling.

PEOPLE EVOLVE IN their understanding of each other, and relationships don't form in an afternoon. I shouldn't have judged Steven so harshly that day. That was my fault. And perhaps, hopefully, he will forgive me for being honest about my first impressions and how they were later amended.

Today, I feel quite affectionate towards Steven. He's my bio dad, after all, although I suspect he might be horrified by that term, which is common parlance in donor-conceived circles. He still needs to feel that there are boundaries between my dad – the man who raised me – and himself. Which of course there are. My dad is, after this whole search and so many years gone, still my dad. He and no other holds that place in my heart. However, the truth is that I have two fathers of different kinds. To say otherwise – that one is not a father – feels wrong. It's simply incorrect.

I think Steven and I both understand (and like) each other perfectly well. I use the term 'father' and 'bio dad' to describe him, without excess sentimentality. I just prefer truth in labelling, and 'biological father' is too much of a mouthful.

These days, like any annoying kid, I like to shock Steven a bit. I find his lessened, but persistent, quest for boundaries kind of amusing. Once, I rang him on Father's Day to give him a mild heart attack. 'Well, well,' he sputtered, after I wished him a happy Father's Day, 'let's not get ahead of ourselves, shall we.' 'But Father's Day celebrates all kinds of fathers,' I responded sweetly. 'I thought, why shouldn't I give you a call?' 'Well, yes, uh,' he said. I think he was rather pleased. Then he hurriedly told me a long story about the last time he went to Turkey.

Once, he said to me on the phone, 'I will always be an optional extra in your life. If you want me, I'm there. If not, not.'

It was the best thing he could have come up with, and I know he meant it. If you are a donor reading this, bookmark this page. Copy those words. Here is the template for your relationships with your biological children.

CHAPTER 35

FINDING YOUR BIOLOGICAL father, in donor conception, is never just that. Other people get to worry about new lovers coming with emotional baggage, or with kids or exes in tow, or perhaps long-lost aunts or uncles turning up with a few skeletons in their closet.

In donor conception, your biological parent will come with both their own closet full of skeletons – and a long, snaking line of other people with history too. Your bio dad isn't just *your* bio dad. Or your bio mum, or whatever. You will probably share him or her with others – perhaps many others. Perhaps too many. It's unlikely you'll ever have an exact number. Each of these half-siblings will be a different person to hold in your head once you've met. Never finding any of them, never meeting them might seem easier, but I think in many ways the terror and uncertainty of that is far worse.

For me, finding Steven McKenzie also meant asking him for the answers that no-one else would give. How many half-siblings did I have? From when, from where? Why did he donate? What was he told? What were the rules of this game? Were there, in fact, rules?

After years of work, finally, I have some idea of what this jigsaw puzzle shows – but so many pieces are still missing. I will never find them all.

THIS IS WHAT Steven told me.

In the 1970s, when he was studying at the University of Sydney, he began donating blood. 'I thought it was a responsible thing to do and was certainly a way to help people without any complications,' he said. It's so like him to want to minimise complications: and yet so contradictory, given what he did next.

In 1981, says Steven, 'I heard an item on the ABC's AM' – a program which I would one day report for myself – 'about the sperm bank at the Royal Prince Alfred Hospital running out of stock. I thought I could donate and keep on donating for the same reasons as I had kept on giving blood.'

The RPAH is one of Sydney's major public hospitals. Steven donated sperm at the clinic at RPAH 'only for one cycle, so that would have been about six times'. Did they pay him? 'Yes, but I can't remember the amount.' It was a lump sum at the end of all donations. There was nothing friendly about the atmosphere. Instead, he says, it was all 'cold medical efficiency. Once I had finished their cycle of donations I was simply no longer required, not ever.' Steven says at RPAH he signed a donor consent agreement, he can't remember what it said, and he doesn't have a copy. He rang back 'a few weeks later', and RPAH told him that there had been no offspring from his sperm donations. (That seems rather early to be sure, but if this hospital wasn't freezing any of the donations – simply using them fresh on the day, with all the health risks that entails – it would be clear whether a woman had fallen pregnant or not.) On the phone, Steve asked whether he could donate again to RPAH. He was told they didn't need him anymore, 'but I could try at the Royal Hospital for Women and at the Royal North Shore Hospital if I liked'.

As it turned out, he did like.

Steven donated to the Royal Hospital for Women, another major public hospital in Sydney's inner east, for 'a few months' in 1981. They paid him, he thinks, '$10 a visit, for taxi fares'. (Around AUD$40 per visit in 2020 terms.) He can't remember how many times he did it over those few months. He can't remember if they took a blood sample for testing, or if they told him how long his donation would be kept for. He says he signed a donor consent agreement. He can't remember what it said, nor does he have a copy.

Prominent donor-conceived advocate Geraldine Hewitt (daughter of Leonie Hewitt of the DCSG) was born through the RHW clinic in the early '80s. She's the same age as me. She's spoken out about how she was told the public RHW also destroyed medical records of conception, including her own.

With Steven's donations in mind, I put a number of questions to the Health Department's South Eastern Sydney Local Health District, which oversees the RHW. Among other things, I asked them whether files at RHW were destroyed: if so, how many files and for what period, what were the reasons, when did that end, and why.

The response, from their media and communications officer, was: 'I've looked into this for you and unfortunately we're unable to help out on this occasion. Best of luck and take care.'[1]

STEVEN, WHO DONATED sperm to the RHW (but is not Geraldine's biological father), says that RHW never told him that they destroyed donor records. But Steven says RHW told him two other things that, if it were me, would have rung alarm bells. Firstly, he says, RHW told him that they would send some of his donations interstate. They didn't say where.

'The doctor interviewing me told me this to reassure me regarding any worries I might have about future unintentional incest between any of my natural relatives,' says Steven. Steven hadn't even considered this risk. 'Until then I had never given it a thought,' says Steven. 'It's well and truly in my mind now, though.'

You might think that sending sperm interstate seems like a reasonable measure to prevent accidental incest. But sending sperm away from the original donation site also increases the likelihood that many families will be born from the one man – perhaps far too many – as family limits become more difficult to keep track of between different clinics, different states and different regimes. And what conditions attended interstate deliveries? Were they selling sperm to medical colleagues for a profit? Banking professional favours?

In any case, I thought upon hearing this: I have sisters and brothers around the country. That the public RHW was allegedly already considering the prospect of accidental incest back then – while also destroying records of donor conception, which could prevent just such a problem – is deeply troubling.

In either the last quarter of 1981, or from early 1982, Steven stopped donating sperm at RHW and began donating sperm at his third and last donation site, the Royal North Shore Hospital and its Clinic 20. Steven was on a tour of the biggest taxpayer-funded institutions, it seems. He could be forgiven for assuming that his choice of large, reputable, public fertility clinics would prevent any major disasters.

Steven donated at the Royal North Shore Hospital for 'about two years', he told me. 'From 1981 to 1983 it would have been between 150 and 200 times.'

I was shocked.

My biological father had made up to 200 sperm donations at one fertility clinic alone? What had happened to all his caution?

Each donation of sperm, depending on its quality, can make between five and twenty straws.[2] Each straw is a potential baby. Clearly, Steven's donations were of reasonable quality, because here I am. However, let's be ultra-conservative, shall we? Let us assume that each of Steven's donations could produce only five straws, and that he donated a mere 150 times.

That still means the Royal North Shore fertility clinic could have made 750 straws from his donations. If every straw worked, I could have 749 half-siblings from a single one of his donation sites. And he donated sperm at two other public clinics, one of which sent sperm interstate. If we assume Steven donated sperm 200 times at the RNSH, and each donation produced twenty straws, and each straw worked, then there are literally 4000 of us from the RNSH fertility clinic alone. At which point my brain shuts down entirely.

But surely the rules surrounding family limits would keep the numbers down? As we've seen, so many rules have not been followed. Donor code destruction alone, let alone poor record-keeping in general meant it was impossible for a clinic to know exactly how many children every one of their donors produced. That may still be going on today. It lends itself to disaster.

Let us assume, conservatively once again, that of that lowest estimate of 750 straws donated by Steven to the RNSH, only one-fifth actually worked. That still means there are 150 of us half-siblings from the Royal North Shore alone. Me, Bec and 148 others.

For me, being part of a huge litter – probably most of us the same age – is something I can't look full in the face. It is too disturbing. It takes me to a dark place. Mass manufacture will do that to a human being.

Compounding that horror of scale are the payments made, and RNSH's risible 'regulation'.

'It was $15 every time, paid at the end of a cycle of six visits,' says Steven. 'The money was for taxi fares.' However, he also told me that he took the train to the RNSH: that was why it became his preferred donation site, because the RNSH was conveniently close to a train station.

I'm not interested in how Steven spent the money he was paid for his sperm donations. But if the money was for taxi fares, there should have been some basic measure to ensure that the donor was, in fact, taking taxis. Properly done, the money should've been paid direct to a taxi company, not cash handed out loosely for cabs.

Let's just think about what that sweetener adds up to. If Steven donated sperm only 150 times in the '80s, over two years he made $2250 – or in 2020 terms, around $9000. That's for catching a train once or twice a week, stopping off and having an orgasm. You can see why men do it.

None of this, it has to be said, leaves me feeling particularly good about my existence. But the baby business has never cared about its children.

I ASKED STEVEN if the Royal North Shore took a blood sample for testing when he donated. 'Only at the very beginning,' he said. A lab technician assured him, he said, that 'every donation was tested and analysed to the nth degree'. Steven began donating sperm to the RNSH before any AIDS media storm, in late 1981 or early 1982. He donated for two years. Then he went overseas. He came back to Australia after about a year, in 1984. When he returned, he went to the RNSH to donate again.

'I had very recently been in the USA, where AIDS was becoming a serious matter,' Steven said. 'I asked the lab technician if the possibility of the AIDS virus in donations was a problem. He said that all the heating and other treatments which donations were subjected to would kill any virus, so there was no need to worry.'

After his furlough overseas, Steven donated, he thinks, another four times at RNSH 'before both sperm banks and blood banks were closed down and all of their stocks were destroyed,' he says. This is, interestingly, similar to the notion of an industry-wide fertility clinic shutdown due to HIV transmission – the same one mentioned by John Tyler from Westmead Hospital, where Noelene Cliff contracted the fatal disease, but seemingly unheard-of by any government agency state or federal, or the medical director of IVF Australia, Peter Illingworth.

When the sperm and blood banks re-opened – which was at the same time, Steven said – he was no longer allowed to donate sperm or blood, because he was gay.

Half of that exclusion has persisted. In Australia today, a would-be male blood donor must wait three full months after having sex with another man (either with or without a condom) before they can be eligible to donate blood.[3] By contrast, that same would-be male donor can donate sperm.[4] Fertility clinics combat HIV transmission through a combination of techniques including blood testing for the disease and freezing and quarantining the sperm donation.

I asked Steven how he found donating sperm at the Royal North Shore Hospital's Clinic 20, before he was barred.

'The only staff members at RNSH I can remember talking to were a nurse called Sister Spring and a lab technician,' he said. Spring was Diana Craven's maiden name. 'I thought the atmosphere was a combination of clinical efficiency and slight furtiveness. I had to go into a small room, shut the door, produce my donation, then take it to the lab or Sister Spring's room,' he said. But that didn't last. 'This routine was abruptly changed after one visit,' Steven recalled, 'when I walked down the corridor carrying my sample jar as usual and found myself going past some (five? six? seven?) women who were obviously attending the clinic.' God forbid the women ever catch a glimpse of the man who would impregnate them. That was the end of any perambulations. 'Thereafter, I left the jar in the small room, and someone collected it … I always had the niggling feeling that my presence, even existence, was a slight embarrassment.'

I'm sure it was. If only donor conception could be done without the humans.

STEVEN MCKENZIE HAD some very firm ideas about who should benefit from what he left in that jar.

'I said flatly that I wanted my donations to go only to married couples,' he told me. Same-sex marriage would not be legalised in Australia for more than three decades. That meant no unmarried couples could use his donations, nor single women, nor anyone who wasn't heterosexual. Or at least pretending to be. 'RNSH was happy to agree to this.' Of course they were, given the alleged role of their ethics committee was to ensure that couples were married.

'I felt that what I was doing was to help people in a difficult situation,' he explained. 'If the wife of a sterile husband solved the problem by way of an affair or even just a one-night stand, that can have serious personal consequences, whether the husband has agreed or not … IVF in a cold, sterile clinic, however, is a very different thing from the intimacy involved in an affair or a one-night stand. So married couples were the only people I wanted to have my donations. Single women or lesbians do not have any such potential problem; they can make their own arrangements in the usual way.' Whatever that was.

I found his anxiety to protect heterosexual marriages – in which he himself would never partake – touching and strange, and completely misplaced. What Steven was doing was in line with the RNSH's rule, which shored up one of the biggest lies around donor conception: that it did not take place. The parents who can and do lie most successfully to the donor-conceived are heterosexuals.

In the end, though, it doesn't matter whether you are the donor-conceived child of heterosexuals, married or unmarried, or of a single mother, or any sort of LGBTIQ+ couple or individual. It doesn't matter who raises you, or how many of those people there are. The right to identity and to origins must be preserved. If you think deliberately and permanently severing a child from biological parent(s) and sibling(s) is fine as long as someone else takes their place, you are mistaken.

Fertility clinics, commissioning parents, and sperm, egg and embryo brokers need to stop taking something so fundamental from children, while simultaneously telling them that the theft does not matter. It is a self-serving lie. Every child should be guaranteed the right to know their own family – including all their siblings. They will form relationships as strong, or as weak, as they wish. They will tell you which of those bonds are important. It is their decision. It is their family. Not yours.

I CAN TELL you without hesitation that my sister Bec is important to me.

I asked Steven if the three public hospital fertility clinics where he donated ever gave him a total number of children conceived from his donations. One would have thought that would be the bare minimum they could do.

Steven had already told me that the RPAH had let him know within a few weeks that his donations had come to nothing. I'll pretend to believe this, and set the RPAH aside.

The RHW never told him how many donor-conceived children he'd fathered at their clinic, although they accepted the letter that Steven had written for any such children in 1997. They also said nothing to him about what had happened to the sperm sent interstate. They did not mention destroying files.

Steven also gave that letter and photo of himself to the RNSH fertility practice in 1997, as we know. 'They said it would be placed on the files of my donor children – and that was all they said,' Steven remembers. What a neat administrative picture that paints.

When he lodged the letter, the clinic told him only a handful of babies had been born from his donations.

'I was told that there was a total of seven: four boys and three girls,' he said.

Four boys, three girls. Far from the truth.

IT'S 2020, AND there are currently six of us that I'm aware of, but I don't think that's the final number by any means. We're now at one boy, five girls. Given what we know about heterosexuals and lying about donor conception, I can't help but feel that this small group represents, at a maximum, five or ten per cent of what's really out there waiting for me. I haven't even spoken to half of this little bunch of siblings.

Steven tells me that the first of his donor-conceived children to make contact with him surfaced in 2011. I'll call her Girl One.

Steven says Girl One approached him through IVF Australia. They exchanged a few emails but didn't meet in person until 2015. Steven says he offered each time he was in Sydney, but she wasn't ready. I can understand that. This girl is five months younger than me. She is in very sporadic contact with Steven. When Bec and I appeared on the scene, Steven says he told Girl One that we existed, but she said she didn't want to meet us. So that's that.

Girl One, however, was able to contact Steven through IVF Australia because her records were intact. The donor code was not destroyed. And yet she was born in the same year as Bec and I. She'd received Steven's letter and photo.

I've already speculated why some donor codes were destroyed – so that one donor's sperm could be used to create more than ten families. Repeat business, as it were. You hit the limit, and for any children thereafter you destroy the evidence. But at this point, I can't help feeling a bit of sibling jealousy towards Girl One: how lucky she was to have a code in her file.

Girl One may come round one day and want to meet me and Bec, or she may not. I'm comfortable with either.

At least Steven told me about Girl One. He also told me about Girl Two.

In 2012, Girl Two surfaced, also approaching Steven through IVF Australia. Which means that her file was intact as well. I have no idea how old she is. He was told of her existence and then IVF Australia said she'd changed her mind and didn't want to get in touch. That was it. Nothing he could do.

Girls Three and Four are me and Bec. Codes destroyed, a long fight, DNA legwork.

Girl Five surfaced in our lives around two years ago. She popped up as another 'first cousin' on Ancestry DNA for both Rebecca and I.

Girl Five politely emailed us both, asking to see our family trees and querying if we knew how she was related to us. She's about the same age as us.

The problem was, Girl Five clearly didn't know she was donor conceived. So it fell to poor Bec to tell Girl Five that we weren't cousins, we were half-sisters – and how that had come to be. In an email. Because there was no way Bec or I were going to lie to her. There is no way in hell, having been through so much to win the truth, that we would do so.

Unfortunately, the truth went down about as well as you'd expect. Bec is one of the nicest people I've ever met, and she was extremely cautious in how she phrased everything, but it was only ever going to be a terrible conversation. It is so unfair that in this 'system', we have to bear the burden of not only our own parents' lies, but also the lies of other people's parents. The result was a conflagration.

I logged in and responded to Girl Five too, to back up what Bec was telling her, because one of her immediate (and quite understandable) reactions had been absolute, furious denial. She can deny whatever she wants, of course, but it helps if two people tell you the truth, not one. I was brief. Unfairly, because Bec had been much nicer than me, I had a completely different exchange with her: it was civil and to the point. I think she'd had some time to process the shock and was ready to hear more.

Today, I still haven't met Girl Five in person – we've had some chats, and made plans several times, but life with kids is busy. However, she remains the only sibling that I've ever communicated with apart from Bec. And I'm glad we've spoken.

Which leaves the boy. My brother. Just as the world was first spiralling into the coronavirus pandemic, Steven received a letter from NSW Health's Voluntary Register. In it, a bureaucrat said that Steven had been matched to 'a donor offspring'. She noted that Steven had already 'expressly consented to the release or [sic] your identifying information and other information to your offspring'. Then she asked him to, once again, 'please confirm' that consent. Even when he'd gone out of his way to be found. In a brief, seemingly accidental way, the letter told him just one thing about this person: tucked away in a single sentence, the bureaucrat refers to 'the offspring' as 'he'.

Steven, of course, consented straightaway. He's heard nothing since. So in the next week, or month, or year, I may hear from Steven about this brother. Or I may even hear from the brother himself. Or this brother may vanish once more, never to be heard of again. Or maybe another ten brothers will suddenly surface. Or twenty. This will keep happening until I die – I will never know if the end has been reached. If ever the discovery of another sibling, or multiple siblings, sends me into a tailspin, either I deal with it or face going under. If more revelations about gross exploitation emerge, either I cope or I have a breakdown. That's the lifelong inheritance that the donor conception industry gives its babies.

Fortunately, I know by now that I am stronger than what was done to me.

EPILOGUE

I'M TUCKED INTO a corner of London's Heathrow Airport, dazed from travel. For the last couple of months, I've been putting together a story about the biggest refugee camp in the world, the Rohingya settlement at Cox's Bazar, Bangladesh. After returning to Sydney, we finished off the show in a last-minute rush and put it to air. Then I went home, stuffed some things in a suitcase and caught a cab back to the airport.

This second trip is both work, and holiday, and not quite either. I'm almost there: I'm waiting for my connecting flight. This is something I'm doing for me but also for other donor-conceived people. It may be one of the most important things I do in my life.

I'm on my way to Geneva, Switzerland, to join a group of donor-conceived and surrogacy-born people from around the world. In a few days, we'll be speaking at the United Nations.

This is no random jaunt: 2019 is the thirtieth anniversary of the Convention on the Rights of the Child, the most widely ratified human rights agreement in history. We're speaking at a three-day conference at the UN's Palais des Nations to mark that anniversary. Our session is the Working Group on Children's Rights in the Age of Biotechnology. And our group will tell governments around the world how the global baby business denies us the rights enshrined in that most successful of all Conventions.

Speaking at the UN is something that came up only a couple of months ago, and it's something I never thought I'd do. It never even occurred to me. After all, I'm a journalist by trade, and we're supposed to shine the spotlight on others. But there is a truth to be told, and despite a history of donor conception going back to Dr William Pancoast more than a century ago, this will be the first time the UN has heard from a group of people actually made by this industry.

We have seven areas of chief concern to put to the UN. I'm delivering the conclusion, with my friend Myf. It's only through the process of writing that conclusion with her that I've clarified in my mind what we're calling for.

We're going to tell them that this industry has to stop.

I have friends who have used donors. I know donors, including my own biological father. I have other friends who have been asked to be donors. I myself am a product of this. And yet I am going to tell them that it has to stop.

Sperm, egg or embryo donation, I think, should only happen under certain circumstances. Certain important, child-focused circumstances. Certain legislative protections and regulations which put the child's rights and best interests first. And the truth.

Myf and I have just six minutes to explain this.

A moratorium is what our group agreed on – and believe me, there's a spectrum of views out there. I'm not the most hardline donor-conceived person I know: at least I believe that donor conception may still happen – under certain conditions. I know a number of donor-conceived people who believe the practice can never be right and should be banned. They believe that their own conception was highly unethical and should not have occurred in the way it did – which means, should not have occurred. Some days, I feel the same.

It may seem a strange and difficult position to hold when you yourself are obviously a 'beneficiary' of these practices. But the end does not justify the means. Even being the end does not. I do not want what happened to me to be done to others.

Regarding my own situation, I think the circumstances surrounding my conception were nefarious, and the so-called professionals responsible have never been held to account. Obviously, I can't go back and change things. But I also cannot support the continuation of an opaque industry which has hurt so many, refuses to take responsibility and proceeds unchecked.

If you just want a donor-conceived baby, and all of this fills you with rage, before you send me hate mail, ask: why *doesn't* my government want to protect the rights of children? Why *won't* politicians enact laws to keep these kids safe and respect their fundamental dignity as human beings? And why does the baby business *still* trump the rights of the babies it makes, all around the world?

I FLEW INTO an amazingly sunny Swiss winter's day. From the airport I caught a train, then walked through the tiny, perfect village of Creux-du-Genthod, perched high on a bank overlooking Lake Geneva. On the horizon, the Alps were crystal clear. The streets underfoot were cobbled, and the village centre was simply a church and a restaurant with wine barrels out the front.

After several wrong turns, I found the right house and rang the bell.

The door opened to Myf, Dr Sonia Allan and Sonia's daughter Mahalia, all smiling at me. After a while Damian came down the stairs into the kitchen, grinning, and later that day Hayley arrived from Melbourne. With Myf, Damian and Hayley there, and visits from others in our presentation group, it was like living in a donor-conceived sharehouse for a week. I'd met some of these people only in the last few years – or even hours. Now we were all hanging out together in a picturesque Swiss hamlet.

Sonia Allan is a legal academic specialising in health law and ethics. She is, in my view, Australia's leading expert on the law and assisted reproductive technology, and by this point she was also a friend. That afternoon, we walked around the chilly lake, workshopping what was to come. It wasn't just the audience we were worried about. Our session at the UN was hosted by International Social Service, a global NGO working in child protection and welfare, which more recently has begun moving into the biotech space: that is, the manufacture of kids like us. Sonia told us she'd innocently inquired last year whether they had ever actually consulted with a group of human beings born of donor conception or surrogacy. They had not. One year on, they'd drafted some very concerning International Principles on Surrogacy – questioning, for instance, whether it was really necessary to always consider the best interests of the child – still without widespread consultation with the likes of us. At the last minute – just a few months before the anniversary conference – ISS asked Sonia if she knew any donor-conceived people in Australia, or anywhere else, who might be interested in speaking in their session at the UN.

Sonia asked us. The call went out online, through donor-conceived networks in Australia, Europe, the US, the UK. In the end, we assembled a UN presentation committee of donor-conceived people from around the world. All our speakers were adults and the nations represented skewed Western, where donor conception began, long ago. In time, I expect we will hear more from people who claim Indian, Nepalese or Thai heritage, where in more recent years gametes and wombs have become part of this trade. But first we have to wait for those kids to grow up and find us.

Our UN presentation committee had three donor-conceived speakers from the UK. One from the US. One from the US/Austria. One from Belgium. One from the Netherlands. One from New Zealand. One from Portugal/Angola. And nine Australians.

Australia seems to be home to one of the largest cohesive groups of donor-conceived people in the world. A lot has changed on the donor-conceived scene since I first found out about my origins. There's heaps of us, now, who know who we are; are open and vocal about it; and hang out in groups. I don't know why that is, but I'm proud, that's for sure.

THE NIGHT BEFORE our presentation I barely slept. The next morning, it was hard marshalling thoughts over muesli in a tiny, cold Swiss kitchen. We were all on edge, I think. Damian was wearing a suit jacket. In his buttonhole, he had a fabric flower pin: Myf had made a bunch of them, years ago, for us to wear at Rel's funeral. Rel had brought us all here too.

We piled the bowls in the sink, and I ran upstairs to get ready. I put on my dad's watch – the watch he bought for me as a child, a foundation present, an adult watch to last me all my life. As a result, of course, the watch became so special that I never wore it, but I'd brought it with me to the UN. I was also wearing something from my mother, a very

Mum-like thing: compression tights to get me through a long day of being on my feet. In my life, my dad gave me luck. My mother gave me the grit to continue.

At the station, waiting for the train, our group of Australians froze. It was minus 2 degrees Celsius but felt colder. The train stopped at Genève-Sécheron, and we got off and walked up the hill to the UN's Pregny Gate, growing in numbers as we went: Catarina (Portugal/Angola), Sebastiana (USA), Jo and her daughter Ceri (UK).

Then we collected our passes and entered the Palais des Nations.

TEN MINUTES, FIVE minutes, one minute, *now*. Our session began. The room, built to house hundreds of delegates, was maybe one-tenth full. I panicked. What was the good of coming all this way to the United Nations if no-one was there to hear us?

The problem was the difficulty with most large conferences: there were several working groups going on at any one time. Ours was scheduled for precisely the same slot as another session on children's environmental rights, and rumours were rife about the presence of teenage climate activist Greta Thunberg. Thunberg wasn't actually anywhere near us, nor in fact on land at all: she was sailing slowly to Europe, not flying, and not even Greta Thunberg is above the laws of physics. But the bulk of attendees were drifting towards a session which wasn't ours. It was devastating.

International Social Service, who were hosting our session, had decided to start with a quiz, to ease people into the complex-sounding (and complex in truth) topic of children in the age of biotechnology. While they did that, I had a chat with Katrien, a donor-conceived person from Belgium. Katrien had only found out she was donor conceived a matter of months ago, and to her enormous credit she was not only getting her head around it, she was doing so with the rest of us at the UN. Katrien wasn't booked to deliver the presentation with us. She was there to support, but her compatriot Stephanie Raeymaekers had brought along something clever. She'd brought multicoloured price tags.

Steph is the head of Donorkinderen, the national support group for donor-conceived people in Belgium, where to this day anonymous donation is still permitted (as it is in most countries around the world). Steph is also one of donor-conceived triplets. Steph is a veteran of these sorts of events; she'd already spent years talking to International Social Service and advocating for people like us across Europe. Her price tags each carried a message: what if you were bought and sold? What if you weren't allowed to know any of your siblings? We'd spent the morning hanging them on the walls of the Palais.

Now Katrien ran out with the rest of the tags and intercepted delegates in the halls, directing people towards our session: she worked fast. And hard. By the time the quiz was over, our room was full. I could see country placards: Israel, Ukraine, Brazil. Delegates unhooked the grey translation earpieces from their seats, put them on and looked at us expectantly. In the audience was also a long-serving member and former chair of the powerful UN Committee on the Rights of the Child, international children's rights expert Professor Jaap Doek.

We sat on a stage, in front of a row of microphones. Sonia and Steph walked to the lectern and began the introduction. Staring at the audience, trying to calm my nerves, I heard Sonia: 'Debates on how to regulate assisted reproduction and surrogacy are often absent of the voices of donor conceived or surrogacy born people, or only include them as an afterthought.'

That was why we were here. To change all that.

Then we put our seven questions to the audience, with one or two of us speaking briefly about each.

What if you know you're donor conceived, but don't know who your biological parent(s) or siblings are? What if the government is complicit in keeping your identity a secret and your birth certificate is a lie? What if you wonder if you're related to everyone who looks like you or the person you're dating? The audience listened intently. Albert described how, as a child in the US, his father expended his rage on him, sometimes leaving him unable to go to school for days: abuse which suddenly made a fraction of sense when he realised at age thirty that the man who raised him was not his biological parent. Matty and Beth spoke about how it felt to find out that they weren't full siblings, as they'd been led to believe, but instead had different fathers. Damian tore up a copy of his birth certificate.

It was a document that he had spent years trying to change through the courts in South Australia. Damian had petitioned for the right not to swap his social father's name for his biological father's – which would no doubt freak out sperm donors, recipient parents and fertility clinics across the country – but simply to be allowed to leave the spot blank or change it to 'unknown'. Once again: just to be allowed to tell the truth. Not even that could be tolerated. The state attorney-general's office sent a team of three lawyers to fight him, and Damian lost.

'Donor-conceived people are the only people who cannot challenge paternity,' he told the UN. Commissioning parents may squabble over a child and their birth certificate in the courts ad infinitum, and the media will cover every move (particularly if lesbians are involved, as we have seen). Yet donor-conceived people themselves do not have that right – to their own, undeniable, biological paternity – because it was sold off before they were born.

THEN IT WAS Joey Hoofdman's turn. Joey couldn't be with us on the day: there was a slight pause while the screen booted up, and then there was Joey on the screen, a man with close-cropped dark blond hair and blue eyes. Joey is from the Netherlands. He's in his early thirties, but only found out that he was donor conceived in 2017. On top of that, he lives with a terrible truth that, by now, may sadden but will not surprise you.

'I uncovered that the doctor who treated my parents due to fertility problems was actually my biological father,' the image of Joey told the room, in his precise, measured tones.

'When the news hit me for the first time, I was very angry but also sad. It made me realise that I am not the product of love. Instead, I am a product of lies and commercialisation.'

I could feel the pressure in the room increase.

Joey is one of the many biological offspring of the Netherlands fertility doctor Jan Karbaat. Right up until his death in 2017, Dr Karbaat denied all accusations of using his own sperm in his clinic and blocked any quests for answers by those who suspected they were his children. Two years later, in 2019, a group of twenty-two people including Joey won the right in court to have Dr Karbaat's DNA released. Turns out,

Joey's suspicions were well-founded, and so were many others'. DNA tests have so far shown that Karbaat has fathered dozens of children, but he may have treated more than 6000 women at his clinic. The final number of children Karbaat fathered at his own clinic remains unknown.[1]

'Between March 2017 and now I've found seventy-five half-siblings who live all over the world,' Joey told the United Nations. 'There could be more.'

'I feel like I am the result of a human mass production. Because we are so many, it is almost impossible to bond with all of them, or be able to provide enough support in processing this.'

Sitting there, thinking about my own situation, Joey's words cut me to the quick.

'I blame my biological father for having crossed a medical-ethical boundary by deciding to use his own sperm and conceiving so many offspring,' Joey said. Then came the bite: 'The reason why he was able to do so was because there was a lack in regulation, and insufficient supervision from the government. As a result, he thought he was untouchable.' The room was still.

'The past has shown us that we cannot rely on the so-called good intentions of the fertility industry, or even the good intentions of parents, nor governments,' Joey said. 'Please, try to ensure that from now on the interests and fundamental rights of children truly come first, and no longer are at the bottom of the priority list.'

IT WAS TIME for Myf and I to deliver the conclusion. We stepped up to the lectern.

'We are both donor conceived, created by science under ethically bankrupt guarantees of anonymity for the sperm donors,' Myf began.

'We note that despite decades of profiteering in the global trade in sperm, eggs, embryos and wombs,' I said, 'this is the first time the United Nations is hearing from a group of the human beings created by these practices. We are glad to be here. But we should have had a voice, and your attention, right from the start.'

I was angry. And it was the right time for it. 'There is no right to have a child under international law,' I said, emphasising each word.

'Children are not goods or services that the State, or businesses, can guarantee or provide. They are human beings with rights. The UN Special Rapporteur on the Sale of Children stated last year that commercial surrogacy usually results in the sale of children.' ('Usually': a weasel word.) 'Well, it's not just commercial surrogacy,' I continued. 'You have heard here today from donor-conceived people who were bought and sold.'

Myf picked up: 'So when we are considering donor conception and surrogacy, we must start from the position that these practices are not in the best interests of children where we know that if someone is conceived in this manner, their rights as stated under the Convention will be at the very least impacted – if not negated entirely.' She turned to me.

'Sarah, are there ever any circumstances in which donor conception and surrogacy can be allowed?'

It was a rhetorical flourish, but no less important for that. This was the question she and I had wrestled with. This is the big question about the unregulated, ad hoc system that made us and makes us to this day. This is what people like us struggle with around the world, and there is no universal consensus among us, but believe me when I say there are a hell of a lot of concerns. To this day, I'm not sure if I'm entirely satisfied with the answer that Myf and I gave. I only know that to me, it's better than any of the other answers currently out there.

'This can only happen if it is legislated like open adoption,' I replied. 'For donor conception and surrogacy to be ethical, all children must have a legal right to know their biological parents, all of their biological siblings, and also their birth mother, whether or not she is also a biological parent. They have a right to know that none of those parties were paid, compensated or otherwise rewarded.' I paused. 'This is non-negotiable.'

'There is no jurisdiction in the world which currently upholds and protects these rights,' Myf continued. 'Consequently, we say that wherever in the world a state allows donor conception and surrogacy today, it is unethical. It should be strictly regulated akin to an open adoption – or it should come to a halt.'

Ethical, legislated, regulated, or stop it right now. I have friends who have used an open-adoption model for donor conception in what would be classed as an ethical fashion, under that definition. And I'm glad for them. But a child's rights should not be utterly dependent on their parents being good people. They must be buttressed and protected by the state and the laws of the state.

'It is fundamentally offensive', said Myf, 'to think that many who sit here today and elsewhere do not take a strong stance to prohibit commercial practices that commodify and dehumanise us. And not only us, as the nature of these transactions often also involve disadvantaged gamete donors or surrogate mothers, some of whom are trafficked.'

'Children have a right to know their biological parents and siblings and to seek contact with them,' I added. 'Not through detective work when they're adults, but right from the start. Anything less than this serves doctors, commissioning parents, big business – everyone but the child.'

'Of course, the heartbreak of wanting a child is something we can all empathise with. However, supporting and allowing this international, commercial, exploitative industry to grow unheeded is at best misguided,' Myf said, in her clear voice. 'Expensive, quite often harmful and ineffective so-called fertility treatments are not the solution.'

We'd come to the end. I took a breath. 'Every child has the right under the UN Convention on the Rights of the Child, which we celebrate here today, to identity, to family, including biological family – and to not be bought or sold,' I said. 'Every child has the right to be heard. We are the products of this industry, and we have not been heard, or respected. If we are included at all, we are an afterthought – a tick-the-box exercise so that governments and business can progress with their documents and proposals.' As I spoke, I wondered how many of those listening had seen, or done, just that. 'But we are the voices of surrogacy-born and donor-conceived people. We are now grown, and our voices are stronger. We know what is in our best interests and what is not, and we hope you are listening.'

That was it. We all headed back to our seats.

After we'd sat down, the applause began. It deepened. Then people stood up, one by one. Hundreds, from around the world. The room gave us a standing ovation. I didn't know where to look.

For a few seconds, at the United Nations, we'd won.

THE UN, HOWEVER, is a rarefied environment: the outside world is somewhat different. As yet no government has delivered what we called for. If even one nation does curb a hugely powerful industry, with money to lobby them and pictures of happy families to dangle in front of politicians, I will be both pleased and surprised.

But we went there with nothing but our own stories, and we were heard. We met people from around the world and made them stop and think. Eight and a half years after learning that my father was not my father, I'd found out the truth about my origins. I'd found siblings. And I'd tried, in a whole variety of very unexpected ways, to rectify what I could about this massive mess of a practice.

I felt like I'd done the best I could with what I had. No-one can ask more than that. In the end, what I had was just my own self, nothing more, nothing less.

It was enough.

WHILE WRITING THESE last words, I had a call from a friend. Yet another friend who's considering getting involved in the baby business and having a child through donor conception. I have these conversations from time to time, and they're moderately upsetting for me, and probably for the other person too. They come to me to find a 'right' way to do it, which is commendable. But I always find myself struggling to articulate: there is no 'right' path through this industry.

One of the first concerns I usually mention, because it's the least considered but has greatest cut-through, is that their child will probably have half-siblings. Unknown ones. And lots. Perhaps the fact that this comes as a surprise speaks to our own self-absorption and willingness to be fooled: the fertility industry exists just for us, will deliver a baby just to us, in our own little cocoon, and we are good people paying good money, so everything will be fine.

I can't honestly tell those friends that everything is okay in the fertility industry now and they should go right ahead with donor conception. All I see is a minefield composed largely of mines.

If you already have donor-conceived children: please, if you haven't already done so, tell them the truth about their origins. And please, if you haven't already done so, tell them who their biological parent(s) are. And if you don't know, raise hell to find out. And if you don't know who all their siblings are, or even how many siblings there are, please, don't take no for an answer: your child needs that information. Whatever age your child is, you need to tell them that they may have unknown siblings out there. If your child is now over eighteen, they can consider a DNA test. If they are under eighteen, you need to talk through with them the possibility of a DNA test. If they're having sex, you need to tell them they should consider asking their sexual partners if they are also donor conceived, and if their sexual partners know who their biological parents are. You owe your child this. You owe them the ability to protect themselves.

You owe them, in essence, the same respect that you would desire for yourself.

It is better, much better, for the child to grow up knowing their donor(s), and all their siblings, and their surrogate if you used one. Not just knowing they exist, but knowing who they are, where they are, and quite literally being able to speak the same language. Your kids deserve the chance to be happy, and healthy, and whole. To grow with their family, not just have a print-out of their vital statistics. They deserve to not be part of a giant (and probably unknown) litter: they deserve the chance at genuine human relationships.

Most of the time, when I spell out my views, the other person comes back with obstacles. It's too hard to find a known donor. Or they can't spend the time doing so, it has to happen now. But there are no easy solutions in this. We're so used to wanting something and getting it, in a manner that suits us: we pay money and receive goods or a product. Even a child. If you come from the position of I-get-this-no-matter-what, the rights of the child will, inevitably, lose. And I know the chances are that my friend will compromise, on their own future child's rights, in favour of paying for the feeling of something happening right now.

I'm surprised, always, by how little some seemingly know, or want to hear; even if we've been friends for most of my life – and I'm quite open about my reservations – they still think that these days everything in donor conception is aboveboard. That all the problems have been fixed. That all donor-conceived children have rights. That they can trust the system. I don't know what that means they think of me. That I'm a damaged by-product, perhaps, but a comfortingly obsolete one.

That is one of the reasons I've written this book: because there are so many reasons not to trust the system, and even people who know me very well somehow miss them.

If you are considering having a donor-conceived child, there's one more thing to say.

In the months following Geneva, our group drew up International Principles for Donor Conception and Surrogacy – the first-ever such document drafted by the people actually made by the fertility industry. It's designed to show what all this would look like if it made a genuine attempt to put the rights of the child first.

These Principles are the bare minimum that we deserve. Things like: all donor-conceived people and surrogacy-born babies have the right to know how they were made. Truthful records of biological family must be kept in perpetuity. Inter-country sale of eggs, sperm and embryos should be prohibited. And no babies should be made from the dead.

The Principles are not meant to encourage either donor conception or surrogacy. They simply provide minimum standards for laws where surrogacy and/or donor conception already exist.

No country on earth currently complies with all these Principles.

APPENDIX

The International Principles for Donor Conception and Surrogacy:

Best Interests and Human Rights of the Child Paramount

1. The best interests and human rights of the child who will be or has been born as a result of donor conception and/or a surrogacy arrangement must be the paramount consideration in all relevant laws, policies and practices and in any judicial and administrative decisions relating to donor conception and surrogacy.

Pre-Conception Screening and Post-Birth Review

2. Pre-conception assessments and screening of donors, intended parents and potential surrogate mothers and post-birth review of the best interests and human rights of the child born as a result must occur in every case of surrogacy and donor conception.

The Right to Identity and to Preserve Relations

3. All donor-conceived and surrogacy-born people have an inalienable right to identifying information about all of their biological parents, regardless of when or where they were conceived or born.
4. All donor-conceived and surrogacy-born people have an inalienable right to identifying information about all of their biological siblings, be they half or full siblings, regardless of when or where they were conceived or born.
5. All surrogacy-born people have an inalienable right to identifying information about their surrogate mother, regardless of when or where they were conceived or born.
6. All donor-conceived and surrogacy-born people have the right to preserve relations with biological, social and gestational families, regardless of when or where they were conceived or born. Such relations should be able to be maintained if mutually agreeable.
7. Anonymous donation of gametes and embryos, and anonymous surrogacy must be prohibited.

Record Keeping, Birth Records and Access to Information

8. Comprehensive and complete records of the identity and familial medical history of all parties involved in the conception and birth of donor-conceived

and surrogacy-born people must be kept. Such records must be held by each Nation State in which the conception and birth is commissioned and/or occurs, in perpetuity and for future generations. Verification of the identity of donors, surrogate mothers, and intending parents must occur.

9. All children's births should be notified to and registered with the appropriate competent authority in the Nation State of birth. Truth in registration, noting the child is donor-conceived and/or surrogacy-born, must occur. Birth records must be maintained in perpetuity and for future generations that recognise biological, social, and birth parents.
10. All donor-conceived and surrogacy-born people have the right to be notified of their status and to access records pertaining to their identity, familial medical history, and birth registration.
11. Parents should be encouraged and supported to tell their children of their donor-conceived or surrogacy-born status as early as possible, and preferably from birth. This should be coupled with efforts to reduce stigma related to infertility.

Prohibitions on Commercialisation of Eggs, Sperm, Embryos, Children and Surrogacy

12. All forms of commercialisation of eggs, sperm, embryos, children, and surrogacy must be prohibited. This includes, but is not limited to any kind of consideration (payment or other consideration) for a) the recruitment of potential donors and/or surrogate mothers; b) gametes or embryos; c) 'services', time, effort, 'pain and suffering' related to the conception, pregnancy and/or birth of a child, or termination of pregnancy.
13. The sale and trafficking in persons and/or of gametes in the context of assisted reproduction and surrogacy must be prohibited.
14. The participation of paid intermediaries or agents in arranging surrogacy and/or recruiting or procuring women or donors of gametes for the purposes of surrogacy or gamete donation for profit, should be prohibited on the basis that their participation increases the risks of the sale and/or trafficking of women and children.

Prohibitions on Transnational Surrogacy and Donor Conception

15. It is not in the best interests of the child to be conceived or born in circumstances in which the 'intending parents' have circumvented or breached laws within their own country by engaging in cross-border assisted reproduction, including but not limited to donor-conception and/or surrogacy. States that prohibit such practices should include extraterritorial prohibitions in their laws. States that allow such practices should limit access to their own citizens. Extraterritorial prohibitions should be enforced.
16. It is not in the best interests of the child to be intentionally separated from their genetic families by geographical, linguistic or cultural barriers. As such, inter-country transfer of gametes should also be prohibited.

Family Limits

17. To avoid the risk of consanguineous relationships, and the psychological impact of an unlimited number of potential siblings, the number of families that may be created using one donor's gametes should be limited to five.

Requirement for Counselling and Legal Advice

18. Independent counselling and legal advice must be a requirement prior to entering into donor conception and surrogacy arrangements. All parties to donor conception and/or surrogacy must be able to give their informed consent after receiving information about the processes involved, material risks, legal and financial implications and their rights and responsibilities. All information must be delivered in a language the person receiving the counselling and advice can understand. All decisions must be made autonomously and free from duress, coercion, and/or exploitation.
19. The provision of counselling and legal advice must always uphold and convey the best interests and human rights of the child(ren) born to be the paramount consideration.

Transfer of Legal Parentage (Surrogacy)

20. Upon the birth of a child conceived as a result of a surrogacy arrangement, the child should share the birth mother's nationality to avoid the situation that a surrogacy-born child is 'stateless', and records to this effect must be kept.
21. Transfer of legal parentage in cases of surrogacy from a surrogate mother to 'intending parent(s)' should never be automatic nor based solely on intention. Intending parent(s) do not have a right to exclusive legal parentage or parental responsibility of a child born through surrogacy, regardless of any expenses they may have incurred through the process. The surrogate mother must never be compelled to relinquish the child(ren) she has given birth to.
22. Where a surrogate mother has carried the full genetic child of another couple and does not wish to relinquish the child, legal parentage of the child should be determined by a Court dependent on the best interests of the child.
23. Enforcement of contractual terms that purport to transfer legal parentage is not consistent with the best interests or human rights of a child.

Posthumous Use of Gametes

24. Gametes or embryos which a) have been retrieved posthumously from a person, or b) are stored by a clinic on behalf of a person who has since died must never be used in donor conception or surrogacy arrangements, regardless of whether any consent had been given by the person from whom those gametes were obtained prior to their death.

https://www.change.org/p/united-nations-making-humans-international-principles-for-donor-conception-and-surrogacy

Authors and members of the UN Presentation Committee 2019
Mr Damian Adams, donor-conceived person – Australia
Dr Sonia Allan, consultant, academic – Australia
Ms Caterina Almeida, donor-conceived person – Portugal/Angola
Ms Myfanwy Cummerford, donor-conceived person – Australia
Ms Sarah Dingle, donor-conceived person – Australia
Ms Courtney du Toit, donor-conceived person – Australia
Mr Albert Frantz, donor-conceived person – United States/Austria
Ms Sebastiana Gianci, donor-conceived person – United States
Ms Ceri Lloyd, daughter of donor-conceived person – United Kingdom
Mrs Joanne Lloyd, donor-conceived person – United Kingdom
Ms Giselle Newton, donor-conceived person – Australia
Ms Stephanie Raeymaekers, donor-conceived person – Belgium
Dr Joanna Rose, donor-conceived person – United Kingdom
Ms Hayley Smith-Williams, donor-conceived person – Australia
Ms Sharni Wilson, donor-conceived person – Australia
Ms Beth Wright, donor-conceived person – Australia
Mx Matty Wright, donor-conceived person – Australia

NOTES

Chapter 3

1 Frank, JB, 'Body Snatching: A Grave Medical Problem', *YJBM*, 49, pp. 399–410, 1976 http://europepmc.org/backend/ptpmcrender.fcgi?accid=PMC2595508&blobtype=pdf

2 Ellis, H, 'The Knife Man: The Extraordinary Life and Times of John Hunter, Father of Modern Surgery', *BMJ*, 330(7488), p. 425, 2005 https://europepmc.org/article/PMC/549129
Moore, W, 'John Hunter (1728–1793)', The James Lind Library, 2009 https://www.jameslindlibrary.org/articles/john-hunter-1728-93/
Wagoner, N, 'John Hunter (1728–1793)', The Embryo Project Encyclopedia, 2017 https://embryo.asu.edu/pages/john-hunter-1728–1793

3 Hard, AD, 'Artificial Impregnation', *Medical World*, 27, pp. 163–64, 1909 https://babel.hathitrust.org/cgi/pt?id=mdp.39015026093826&view=1up&seq=177

Chapter 4

1 *Encyclopaedia Britannica,* Ilya Ivanovich Ivanov, Soviet biologist https://www.britannica.com/biography/Ilya-Ivanovich-Ivanov

2 Foote, RH, 'The History of Artificial Insemination: Selected Notes and Notables', *Am Soc Animal Science*, 2002 https://www.asas.org/docs/default-source/midwest/mw2020/publications/footehist.pdf?sfvrsn=59da6c07_0

3 Verberckmoes, S, Van Soom, A and de Kruif, A, 'Intra-uterine Insemination in Farm Animals and Humans', *Reprod Domest Anim*, 39(3), pp. 195-204, 2004 https://doi.org/10.1111/j.1439-0531.2004.00512.x

4 Cohen, J et al., 'The Early Days of IVF Outside the UK' *Human Reprod Update*, 11(5), pp. 439–60, 2005 https://doi.org/10.1093/humupd/dmi016

5 Cox, LW, 'The Development of Infertility Treatment in Australia', *ANZJOG*, 31(3), pp. 254–59, 1991 https://doi.org/10.1111/j.1479-828X.1991.tb02793.x

6 Davis G, '"A Tragedy as Old as History": Medical Responses to Infertility and Artificial Insemination by Donor in 1950s Britain'. In: Davis G, Loughran T (Eds), *The Palgrave Handbook of Infertility in History*, 2017. London: Palgrave Macmillan https://doi.org/10.1057/978-1-137-52080-7_19

7 Lopata, A, 'IVF in Australia – An Introductory History by Dr Alex Lopata'. In Saunders, D, *Fertility Society of Australia A History: Its "precipitate" Birth & the Story of IVF – A History of In Vitro Fertilisation in Australia and the Founding of the Fertility Society of Australia*, 2013, Mosman, NSW

8 Danielson, A, 'Patrick Christopher Steptoe (1913-1988)', The Embryo Project Encyclopedia, 2009 https://embryo.asu.edu/pages/patrick-christopher-steptoe-1913-1988

9 Dunne, C, 'Donor Eggs for the Treatment of Infertility', *BCMJ*, 62(9), 2020, pp. 328–32 https://bcmj.org/articles/donor-eggs-treatment-infertility

10 Palermo GD et al., 'Intracytoplasmic Sperm Injection: State of the Art in Humans', *Reproduction*, 154(6), pp. 93–110, 2017 https://www.ncbi.nlm.nih.gov/pmc/articles/PMC5719728/

11 Arnold, C, 'Choosy Eggs May Pick Sperm for Their Genes, Defying Mendel's Law', *Quanta Magazine*, 2017 https://www.quantamagazine.org/choosy-eggs-may-pick-sperm-for-their-genes-defying-mendels-law-20171115/

12 Victorian Assisted Reproductive Treatment Authority, 'Is ICSI better than IVF? It depends', 2018 https://www.varta.org.au/resources/news-and-blogs/icsi-better-ivf-it-depends
Gregory, S, 'Expensive Form of IVF is Overused, Says Fertility Journal Editor', Bio News, 853, 31.05.2016 https://www.bionews.org.uk/page_95536

13 Li, Z et al., 'ICSI Does Not Increase the Cumulative Live Birth Rate in Non-male Factor Infertility', *Human Reprod*, 33(7), 2018, pp. 1322–30 https://doi.org/10.1093/humrep/dey118

Chapter 5

1 Email answers to questions posed to Northern Sydney Local Health District, NSW Health Department

2 Phone conversation with Margaret Saunders, May 2020

3 According to the IAB investigation report; ASIC lists the principal place of business for 1994–5 as Hunters Hill Private Hospital
4 Hawkins, B, 'Breaking the Code: Donor-conceived Children Search For Identity of Fathers and Their Biological Heritage', ABC News, 14.08.2014 https://www.abc.net.au/news/2014-08-18/code-breaking3a-abc-journalist-sarah-dingle/5676544
5 Virtus Health, 'Who We Are' https://www.virtushealth.com.au/who-we-are/our-history
6 Quadrant Private Equity, 'Virtus Float Breathes Life Into IPO Market', 14.03.2016 http://quadrantpe.com.au/Media-Centre/News/Virtus-Health-float-breathes-life-into-IPO-market.aspx
7 IBISWorld, *Fertility Clinics in Australia – Market Research Report*, 30.11.2020 https://www.ibisworld.com/au/industry/fertility-clinics/5091/
8 *The Economist,* 'The Fertility Business is Booming', 08.08.2019 https://www.economist.com/business/2019/08/08/the-fertility-business-is-booming

Chapter 6

1 NSW Health, *Medical Records in Hospitals and Community Care Centres,* 1976 https://www1.health.nsw.gov.au/pds/ArchivePDSDocuments/PD2005_004.pdf
2 NSW Government, *Assisted Reproductive Technology Amendment Act 2016 No 11*, pp. 11–12 https://beta.legislation.nsw.gov.au/view/pdf/asmade/act-2016-11
3 Parliament of Australia, Senate Inquiry Into Donor Conception in Australia – Submissions Received by the Committee, 2010 https://www.aph.gov.au/Parliamentary_Business/Committees/Senate/Legal_and_Constitutional_Affairs/Completed_inquiries/2010-13/donorconception/submissions.
Parliament of Australia, Interpretation of the External Affairs Power and Reform Proposals, 1996 https://www.aph.gov.au/parliamentary_business/committees/senate/legal_and_constitutional_affairs/completed_inquiries/pre1996/treaty/report/c05
4 IBISWorld, *Fertility Clinics in Australia – Market Research Report*, 30.11.2020 https://www.ibisworld.com/au/industry/fertility-clinics/5091/
5 Parenting SA, *Donor Conception: Telling Your Child* https://parenting.sa.gov.au/pegs/peg80.pdf
6 UNICEF, *United Nations Convention on the Rights of the Child* https://www.unicef.org.au/our-work/information-for-children/un-convention-on-the-rights-of-the-child
7 National Health and Medical Research Council, *Ethical Guidelines on the Use of Assisted Reproductive Technology in Clinical Practice and Research*, p. 38, 4.6.1, 2017 https://www.nhmrc.gov.au/sites/default/files/documents/reports/use-assisted-reproductive-technology.pdf
8 Parliament of Australia, *Donor Conception Practices in Australia*, Section 1.9, 2010 https://www.aph.gov.au/Parliamentary_Business/Committees/Senate/Legal_and_Constitutional_Affairs/Completed_inquiries/2010-13/donorconception/report/index
9 ibid. n7, p. 129

Chapter 7

1 Allan, S, *Donor Conception and the Search for Information: From Secrecy to Openness*, p. 224, 2017, Farnham: Ashgate
2 Adoptee Rights Australia, 'Powers to Seal Birth Records Forever – Comparison by State', 2018 https://adopteerightsaustralia.org.au/powers-to-seal-birth-records-forever-comparison-by-state/
3 Gass-Poore, J, 'Most American Adoptees Can't Access Their Birth Certificates. That Could Soon Change', *Mother Jones*, 13.03.2019 https://www.motherjones.com/politics/2019/03/most-american-adoptees-cant-access-their-birth-certificates-that-could-be-about-to-change/
4 Cuthbert, D & Fronek, P, 'Perfecting Adoption? Reflections on the Rise of Commercial Off-shore Surrogacy and Family Formation in Australia.' In *Families, Policy and the Law: Selected Essays on Contemporary Issues for Australia*, pp. 56, 2014, Australian Institute of Family Studies
5 ibid., p. 57
6 *Australian Story*, 'The Baby Maker', ABC, 10.05.2001
7 Parliament of Australia, Senate Inquiry Into Donor Conception in Australia – Submissions Received by the Committee, 'Donor Conception Support Group', 2010 https://www.aph.gov.au/Parliamentary_Business/Committees/Senate/Legal_and_Constitutional_Affairs/Completed_inquiries/2010-13/donorconception/submissions.

Chapter 8

1 Not even in Victoria: 'There is no provision within the Victorian legislation to contact donor-conceived people when they turn eighteen years old to let them know of their status. If they request a copy of their birth certificate as an adult, the Registry of Births Deaths and Marriages will provide an addendum to say that more information about this birth is available. The person will then be in a position to apply for information from the Central Register managed by VARTA.' Email communication from the Victorian Assisted Reproductive Treatment Authority, 02.09.2020

2 Sälevaara, M, 'Attitudes and Disclosure Decisions of Finnish Parents with Children Conceived Using Donor Sperm', *Human Reprod*, 28(10), 2013, pp. 2746–54 https://doi.org/10.1093/humrep/det313
3 Zadeh, S, 'Disclosure of Donor Conception in the Era of Non-anonymity: Safeguarding and Promoting the Interests of Donor-conceived Individuals?', *Human Reprod*, 31(11), 2016, pp. 2416–20 https://doi.org/10.1093/humrep/dew240
4 Jadva, V et al., 'The Experiences of Adolescents and Adults Conceived by Sperm Donation: Comparisons by Age of Disclosure and Family Type', *Human Reprod*, 24(8), pp. 1909–19, 2009 https://doi.org/10.1093/humrep/dep110
5 We Are Donor Conceived, '2020 We Are Donor Conceived Survey', 17.09.2020 https://www.wearedonorconceived.com/2020-survey-top/2020-we-are-donor-conceived-survey/

Chapter 10

1 Parliament of Australia, Senate Inquiry Into Donor Conception in Australia, Official Committee Hansard, Senate, Legal and Constitutional Affairs References Committee. Melbourne, 2010 https://www.aph.gov.au/Parliamentary_Business/Committees/Senate/Legal_and_Constitutional_Affairs/Completed_inquiries/2010-13/donorconception/hearings/index
2 Reproductive Technology Accreditation Committee, *Annual Report 2018/2019*, The Fertility Society of Australia https://www.fertilitysociety.com.au/rtac/rtac-annual-report-2018_2019/

Chapter 11

1 Saunders, D, 'Conversations with John Tyler – Risks of Donor Sperm and AIDS (HIV)' In Saunders, D, *Fertility Society of Australia A History: Its "precipitate" Birth & the Story of IVF – A History of In Vitro Fertilisation in Australia and the Founding of the Fertility Society of Australia*, 2013, Mosman, NSW
See also Clark, L, 'Professor Geoffrey Driscoll, Polio Victim who Became Pioneering IVF Surgeon', *SMH*, 17.11.2016 https://www.smh.com.au/national/professor-geoffrey-driscoll-polio-victim-who-became-pioneering-ivf-surgeon-20161108-gsk6ga.html
2 Kent, P, 'A Mother, Her Daughter and the Killer Virus That Separates Their Lives', *The Daily Telegraph*, 02.12.2010
3 Interview with Jessica, March 2020
ibid. n1(1), p. 69
4 Tyler, JPP, Crittenden, JA, 'Infertility and AIDS', In *AIDS and Obstetrics and Gynaecology*, 1988, Royal College of Obstetricians and Gynaecologists, Springer Verlag
5 UNICEF 'HIV and Infant Feeding' https://www.unicef.org/nutrition/index_24827.html
6 Morrison, P, 'Update on HIV and Breastfeeding', La Leche League, 04.04.2019 https://www.llli.org/update-on-hiv-and-breastfeeding-public/
7 NSW Parliament, Standing Committee on Social Issues, Inquiry Into Medically Acquired AIDS, 'George Cliff Evidence', 18.03.1991, pp. 2,3,4, 9, 11, 14, 15
NSW Parliament, Standing Committee on Social Issues, Inquiry Into Medically Acquired AIDS, 'George Cliff Evidence', 08.08.1991, pp. 3,4, 22, 23, 24
8 Davies, JA, 'AIDS Victims Paid At Last', *The Sun Herald*, 24.04.1994
9 ibid. n1(1), p. 69

Chapter 12

1 Leveton LB, Sox HC Jr. and Stoto MA (Eds), *HIV And The Blood Supply: An Analysis Of Crisis Decisionmaking*, Institute of Medicine (US) Committee to Study HIV Transmission Through Blood and Blood Products, 1995 Washington (DC): National Academies Press https://www.ncbi.nlm.nih.gov/books/NBK232419/
2 ibid. 3, History of the Controversy
3 ibid.
4 ibid.
5 Check, WA, 'Preventing AIDS Transmission: Should Blood Donors Be Screened?', *JAMA*, 249(5), pp. 567–70, 1983 doi:10.1001/jama.1983.03330290003001
Desforges, JF, 'AIDS and Preventive Treatment in Hemophilia', *N Engl J Med*, 308(2), pp. 94-5, 1983 doi: 10.1056/NEJM198301203080312
6 Bayer, R, 'Science, Politics, and the End of the Lifelong Gay Blood Donor Ban', The Millbank Quarterly, 93(2), pp. 230-33, 2015. doi: 10.1111/1468-0009.12114
7 ibid.
8 NSW Parliament, Standing Committee on Social Issues, Inquiry Into Medically Acquired AIDS. Martin Hatch, haemophiliac, NSW: given HIV through contaminated Factor VIII in March 1983 at RPA Camperdown. Noelene Cliff: given HIV from treatment with HIV-positive sperm in 1982/3. See Hansard 1820781676-57377. 17.10.1991. Legislative Council. Motion by the Hon Franca Arena.

9 Araneta MRG, Mascola L, Eller A, et al. 'HIV Transmission Through Donor Artificial Insemination', *JAMA*, 273(11), pp. 854–58, 1995 doi:10.1001/jama.1995.03520350036025
10 Feldman, EA, Bayer, R (Eds), *Blood Feuds – AIDS, Blood, and the Politics of Medical Disaster*, 1999, Oxford: Oxford University Press
11 Archer, M, 'A Key Figure in Protection of Blood Supplies', *SMH*, 15.10.2013 https://www.smh.com.au/national/a-key-figure-in-protection-of-blood-supplies-20131014-2vin6.html
12 NSW Parliament, Standing Committee on Social Issues, Inquiry Into Medically Acquired AIDS, 'Hatch Submission', 1991
See also Rev Nile remarks to George Cliff, in hearings of NSW Parliament, Standing Committee on Social Issues, Inquiry Into Medically Acquired AIDS, p. 10, 18.03.1991
13 NSW Parliament, Standing Committee on Social Issues, Inquiry Into Medically Acquired AIDS, 'Newcastle Herald, 24.06.1983, in Hatch Submission', 1991
14 Bowtell, W, 'Australia's Response to HIV/AIDS 1982-2005', Lowy Institute for International Policy https://archive.lowyinstitute.org/sites/default/files/pubfiles/Bowtell%2C_Australia%27s_Response_to_HIV_AIDS_logo_1.pdf
15 ibid. n9
16 'Acquired Immunodeficiency Syndrome – An Assessment of the Present Situation in the World: Memorandum From a WHO meeting', *Bull World Health Organ*, 62(3), pp. 419-432, 1984 https://www.ncbi.nlm.nih.gov/pmc/articles/PMC2536320/
17 Sendziuk, P, *Learning to Trust: Australian Responses to AIDS*, p. 40, 2003, Sydney: UNSW Press
18 Power, J, *Movement, Knowledge, Emotion: Gay Activism and HIV/AIDS in Australia*, 2011, Canberra: ANU University Press
19 Saunders, D, *Fertility Society of Australia A History: Its "precipitate" Birth & the Story of IVF – A History of In Vitro Fertilisation in Australia and the Founding of the Fertility Society of Australia*, 2013, Mosman, NSW
20 Cambridge Dictionary, 'precipitate' https://dictionary.cambridge.org/dictionary/english/precipitate
21 ibid. n19, pp. 69, 70
22 Email correspondence with John Tyler
23 NSW Government, Law Reform Commission, 'Discussion Paper 11: Artificial Conception: Human Artificial Insemination', November 1984, pp. v, 31, 42, 91
24 ibid. n9

Chapter 13

1 Saunders, D, *Fertility Society of Australia A History: Its "precipitate" Birth & the Story of IVF: A History of In Vitro Fertilisation in Australia and the Founding of the Fertility Society of Australia*, 2013, Mosman, NSW
2 Butt, C, 'Egg Donor Money: Fertility Clinic Offers Women $5000', *SMH*, 11.04.2015 https://www.smh.com.au/national/egg-donor-money-fertility-clinic-offers-women-5000-20150411-1miw9h.html
3 Harman, AE & Coslor, E, 'Earning While Giving: Rhetorical Strategies for Navigating Multiple Institutional Logics in Reproductive Commodification', *J Business Research*, 105, pp. 405-19, 2019 https://www.sciencedirect.com/science/article/abs/pii/S0148296319303121?via%3Dihub and here https://pursuit.unimelb.edu.au/articles/thinking-about-using-donated-eggs-to-start-a-family
4 World Health Organization, 'Voluntary Non-remunerated Blood Donation' https://www.who.int/bloodsafety/voluntary_donation/en/
5 Government of Australia, *Prohibition of Cloning for Reproduction Act 2002 No 144*, Section 21 https://www.legislation.gov.au/Details/C2017C00306
6 Australian Government, Australian Law Reform Commission, Amendment of the Human Tissue Acts, Art. 20.53, 28.07.2010 https://www.alrc.gov.au/publication/essentially-yours-the-protection-of-human-genetic-information-in-australia-alrc-report-96/20-ownership-of-samples-and-the-human-tissue-acts/amendment-of-the-human-tissue-acts/#_ftnref48
7 NSW Consolidated Acts, *Human Tissue Act 1983*, Section 32 http://www8.austlii.edu.au/cgi-bin/viewdoc/au/legis/nsw/consol_act/hta1983160/s32.html
8 Australian Government National Health and Medical Research Council, *Ethical Guidelines of the Use of Assisted Reproductive Technology in Clinical Practice and Research*, Section 5.4 'Provide Reimbursement of Verifiable Out-of-pocket Expenses', 2017 https://www.nhmrc.gov.au/sites/default/files/documents/reports/use-assisted-reproductive-technology.pdf
9 Parliament of Australia, 'Chapter 4 – Payments for Donors and Provision of Counselling Services', Section 4.11 https://www.aph.gov.au/Parliamentary_Business/Committees/Senate/Legal_and_Constitutional_Affairs/Completed_inquiries/2010-13/donorconception/report/c04
10 Beauchamp, P, 'Canadians Answer Sperm Call', *The Australian*, 09.07.2004, p. 19 https://journals.sagepub.com/doi/10.1177/0959353509342844
11 Email communication, March 2020

Chapter 14

1 Ministry of Health correspondence, May 2012
2 Notes of conversation with Ministry of Health, November 2014
3 Harper, JC, Kennett, D and Riesel, D, 'The End of Donor Anonymity: How Genetic Testing is Likely to Drive Anonymous Gamete Donation Out of Business', *Human Reprod*, 31(6), pp. 1135–40, 2015 https://academic.oup.com/humrep/article/31/6/1135/1749791
4 NSW Parliament, Inquiry Into Donor Conception Details on Birth Certificates. 'Submission No 1 – Managing Information Related to Donor Conception, Mr John Lindsay Mayger', 30.11.2012 https://www.parliament.nsw.gov.au/committees/DBAssets/InquirySubmission/Summary/48475/Submission%201%20-%20Mr%20John%20Lindsay%20Mayger.pdf

Chapter 15

1 Allan, S, *Donor Conception and the Search for Information: From Secrecy to Openness*, p. 86, 2017, Farnham: Ashgate
2 Victorian Assisted Reproductive Treatment Authority, 'Legislation and Guidelines', 2021 https://www.varta.org.au/regulation/legislation-and-guidelines
3 For e.g.: 'In Kidman, Justice Higgins recognised that retrospective laws are in most cases inexpedient and unjust. It is for this reason a Court will not interpret a law as having retrospective application unless the law's retrospective application is unambiguously clear. Nevertheless, the fact remains that there is no limitation upon the ability to enact a retrospective law, and they are used today in a number of areas.' In: Size, R, 'Retrospective Legislation and the Rule of Law', Rule of Law Education Centre, 30.09.2015 https://www.ruleoflaw.org.au/retrospective-legislation-and-the-rule-of-law
4 Gay, O, 'Retrospective Legislation', House of Commons Library, 2013 https://researchbriefings.files.parliament.uk/documents/SN06454/SN06454.pdf
5 ibid. n1, p. 90
6 Parliament of Victoria, Law Reform Committee, *Inquiry Into Access by Donor-Conceived People to Information about Donors*, p. 100, 2012 https://www.parliament.vic.gov.au/images/stories/committees/lawrefrom/iadcpiad/DCP_Final_Report.pdf
7 Australian Institute of Health and Welfare, *Adoptions Australia 2018–19*, 2019 https://www.aihw.gov.au/getmedia/d0c1e19c-881a-4176-829c-fa37d62f8bae/aihw-cws-71.pdf.aspx
8 ibid. n6, p. 120
9 Parliament of Victoria, Law Reform Committee, Inquiry Into Access by Donor-Conceived People to Information about Donors, 'Michael Linden evidence' , 2011 https://www.parliament.vic.gov.au/images/stories/committees/lawrefrom/iadcpiad/transcripts/2011-10-10_Smith_and_Linden.pdf
10 Parliament of Australia, Senate Inquiry Into Donor Conception in Australia – Submissions Received by the Committee, 'Miss Narelle Grech' 2010 https://www.aph.gov.au/Parliamentary_Business/Committees/Senate/Legal_and_Constitutional_Affairs/Completed_inquiries/2010-13/donorconception/submissions.
11 Parliament of Victoria, Law Reform Committee, Inquiry Into Access by Donor-Conceived People to Information about Donors, 'Submission by Narelle Grech', 2010 https://www.parliament.vic.gov.au/images/stories/committees/lawrefrom/iadcpiad/submissions/DCP18_Narelle_Grech.pdf
12 ibid., n10
13 ibid., n10
14 Parliament of Victoria, Law Reform Committee, Inquiry Into Access by Donor-Conceived People to Information about Donors, 'Submission by Narelle Grech', 2011 https://www.parliament.vic.gov.au/images/stories/committees/lawrefrom/iadcpiad/submissions/DCP67_-_Narelle_Grech.pdf
15 ibid.
16 NSW Parliament, Committee on Law and Safety, Inquiry Into Inclusion of Donor Details on the Register of Births, 'Narelle Grech submission', p. 4 https://www.parliament.nsw.gov.au/ladocs/submissions/43230/submission%2018.pdf
17 ibid. n14
18 Parliament of Victoria, Law Reform Committee, Inquiry Into Access by Donor-Conceived People to Information about Donors, 'Submission by Prof Gab Kovaca', 2011 https://www.parliament.vic.gov.au/images/stories/committees/lawrefrom/iadcpiad/submissions/DCP40_-_Prof_Gab_Kovacs.pdf
19 Fyfe, M, 'When Sperm-donor Children Come Calling', *SMH*, 02.09.2015 https://www.smh.com.au/lifestyle/when-spermdonor-children-come-calling-20150902-gjd76r.html
20 Dingle, S, 'Health Concerns Spark Call for Sperm Donor Revelations', ABC *7.30*, 28.03.2012 https://www.abc.net.au/7.30/health-concerns-spark-call-for-sperm-donor/3918868
21 Tomazin, F, '"Suddenly She's There": Daughter and Donor Dad United', *The Age*, 17.03.2013 https://www.theage.com.au/national/victoria/suddenly-shes-there-daughter-and-donor-dad-united-20130316-2g7mv.html

Chapter 16

1 NSW Parliament, Committee on Law and Safety, *Inclusion of Donor Details on the Register of Births*, Report 1/55, p. 5, October 2012 https://www.parliament.nsw.gov.au/ladocs/inquiries/2028/Inclusion%20of%20donor%20details%20on%20the%20register%20of%20birt.pdf
2 District Court of NSW, *AA v Registrar of Births Deaths and Marriages and BB* [2011] NSWDC 100, 17.08.2011 https://www.austlii.edu.au/cgi-bin/viewdoc/au/cases/nsw/NSWDC/2011/100.html
3 Lesbians and the Law, 'Birth Certificates' https://www.lesbiansandthelaw.com/birth-certificates
4 NSW Government, *Status of Children Act 1996 No 76*, Part 3, Division 1, Section 14 https://legislation.nsw.gov.au/#/view/act/1996/76/part3/div1/sec14
5 ibid. n1
6 NSW Parliament, 'Managing Information Related to Donor Conception - Terms of Reference', 2012 https://www.parliament.nsw.gov.au/committees/inquiries/Pages/inquiry-details.aspx?pk=2324
7 NSW Parliament, Law and Safety Committee, Inquiry Into Managing Information Related to Donor Conception, 'Submission by the Fertility Society of Australia', February 2013 https://www.parliament.nsw.gov.au/ladocs/submissions/43747/Submission%2014%20-%20Fertility%20Society%20of%20Australia.pdf
8 NSW Parliament, Law and Safety Committee, Inquiry Into Managing Information Related to Donor Conception, 'Submission by Fertility East', 2013 https://www.parliament.nsw.gov.au/ladocs/submissions/51115/submission%2023%20-%20Fertility%20East.pdf
9 NSW Parliament, Law and Safety Committee, Inquiry Into Managing Information Related to Donor Conception, 'Submission by Andrology Department, Concord Hospital', February 2013 https://www.parliament.nsw.gov.au/ladocs/submissions/47300/Submission%2025%20-%20Andrology%20Department,%20Concord%20Hospital.pdf
10 NSW Parliament, Committee on Law and Safety, *Managing Donor Conception Information*, Report 2/55, p. 13, October 2013 https://www.parliament.nsw.gov.au/ladocs/inquiries/2324/Final%20Report%20-%20Managing%20donor%20conception%20informati.PDF
11 NSW Government, 'Response to NSW Legislative Assembly Committee on Law and Safety Inquiries Into Donor Conception', April 2014 https://www.parliament.nsw.gov.au/ladocs/inquiries/2324/Government%20Response%20-%20inquiries%20into%20donor%20concept.pdf
12 NSW Government, *Assisted Reproductive Technology Amendment Act 2016 No 11*, p. 11, April, 2016 https://beta.legislation.nsw.gov.au/view/pdf/asmade/act-2016-11
13 Needham, K, 'Donor-conceived Children in NSW to Have Fewer Rights Than Victorian Peers, *SMH*, 12.03.2016 https://www.smh.com.au/national/nsw/donorconceived-children-in-nsw-to-have-fewer-rights-than-victorian-peers-20160312-gnhbpu.html

Chapter 17

1 Parliament of Victoria, Law Reform Committee, Inquiry Into Access by Donor-conceived People to Information About Donors, 'Dobby Oral Evidence', p. 4, September 2011 https://www.parliament.vic.gov.au/images/stories/committees/lawrefrom/iadcpiad/transcripts/2011-09-08_Kate_Dobby.pdf
2 ibid.
3 Parliament of Victoria, Law Reform Committee, Inquiry Into Access by Donor-conceived People to Information About Donors, 'Submission by Prof. Gab Kovacs', July 2011 https://www.parliament.vic.gov.au/images/stories/committees/lawrefrom/iadcpiad/submissions/DCP40_-_Prof_Gab_Kovacs.pdf
4 Parliament of Victoria, Law Reform Committee, Inquiry Into Access by Donor-conceived People to Information About Donors, 'Submission by the Australian Medical Association', August 2011 https://www.parliament.vic.gov.au/images/stories/committees/lawrefrom/iadcpiad/submissions/DCP71_-_Australian_Medical_Association.pdf
5 Parliament of Victoria, Law Reform Committee, Inquiry Into Access by Donor-conceived People to Information About Donors, 'Submission by Kate Dobby', p. 2, August 2010 https://www.parliament.vic.gov.au/images/stories/committees/lawrefrom/iadcpiad/submissions/DCP33_Kate_Dobby.pdf
6 NSW Parliament, Law and Safety Committee, Inquiry Into Managing Information Related to Donor Conception, 'Submission by the Fertility Society of Australia', p. 6, February 2013 https://www.parliament.nsw.gov.au/ladocs/submissions/43747/Submission%2014%20-%20Fertility%20Society%20of%20Australia.pdf
7 NSW Parliament, Law and Safety Committee, Inquiry Into Managing Information Related to Donor Conception, 'Submission by Andrology Department, Concord Hospital', p. 5, February 2013 https://www.parliament.nsw.gov.au/ladocs/submissions/47300/Submission%2025%20-%20Andrology%20Department,%20Concord%20Hospital.pdf
8 Adams, DH, Ullah, S and de Lacey, S, 'Does the Removal of Anonymity Reduce Sperm Donors in Australia?' *J Law and Medicine*, 23(3) pp. 628-36, 2016 https://europepmc.org/article/med/27323639
9 ibid.

10 ibid. n6
11 Premier of Victoria, 'Protecting Victorian Women Through Assisted Reproduction', April 2018 https://www.premier.vic.gov.au/protecting-victorian-women-through-assisted-reproduction/
12 Tuohy, W, 'Police Checks for IVF Patients to be Scrapped', *The Age*, 18.02.2020 https://www.theage.com.au/politics/victoria/police-checks-for-ivf-patients-to-be-scrapped-20200218-p541y2.html
13 Pownall, A, 'Victim of Baby Gammy's Father Speaks Out', *The West Australian*, 23.08.2014 https://thewest.com.au/news/australia/victim-of-baby-gammys-father-speaks-out-ng-ya-376290
Hawley, S, 'Two Australian Couples Stopped From Leaving Thailand With Surrogate Babies', ABN News, 15.08.2014 https://www.abc.net.au/news/2014-08-14/australian-couples-stopped-leaving-thailand-surrogate-babies/5672094?nw=0
'Baby Gammy: Australian David Farnell Says Twin Sister "100 per cent safe" Despite Child Sex Convictions', ABC News, 10.08.2014 https://www.abc.net.au/news/2014-08-10/baby-gammy-father-denies-threat-to-twin/5661242
Murdoch, M, 'Wendy Farnell Did Not Supply the Egg, Gammy's Thai Mother Says', *SMH*, 10.08.2014 https://www.smh.com.au/world/wendy-farnell-did-not-supply-the-egg-gammys-thai-mother-says-20140810-102joz.html
14 Hawley, S, 'Australian Charged With Sexually Abusing Twins He Fathered With Thai Surrogate', ABC News, 02.09.2014 https://www.abc.net.au/news/2014-09-01/australian-who-fathered-surrogate-twins-facing-abuse-charges/5710796

Chapter 18

1 Notes of phone conversation with HCCC, January 2015
2 Letter from HCCC, January 2015
3 Email to HCCC, February 2015
4 *Australian Story*, 'Searching for C11, Part 1', ABC, 11.08.2014 https://www.abc.net.au/austory/searching-for-c11---part-1/5777004
5 Dingle, S, 'Misconception', *SMH*, 16.08.2014 https://www.smh.com.au/lifestyle/misconception-20140811-3dha9.html

Chapter 19

1 Name since changed to 'Building Bridges in a Donor Conceived World' https://www.facebook.com/groups/503623156952692/
2 Email communication, September 2014

Chapter 20

1 Smith, T, 'Is Genetic Sexual Attraction a Real Thing?', 2020 https://www.e-counseling.com/relationships/is-genetic-sexual-attraction-real/
2 Cumbria County Council, *Genetic Sexual Attraction*, n.d. https://www.cumbria.gov.uk/eLibrary/Content/Internet//537/6379/6423/17162/42709145735.pdf
3 Alvarez, G, Quinteiro, C and Ceballos, FC, 'Inbreeding and Genetic Disorder'. In Dr Kenji Ikehara, *Advances in the Study of Genetic Disorders*, InTechOpen, 2011 http://www. doi.org.10.5772/18373
4 Australian Government, *Marriage Act 1961*, Section 23, Subsection 2 http://classic.austlii.edu.au/au/legis/cth/consol_act/ma196185/s23.html
5 Clark, R, 'The Incest Trap', *The Spectator*, 25.08.2018 https://www.spectator.co.uk/article/the-incest-trap
6 '17 British Sperm Donors Have Fathered 500 Children Figures Show', *The Telegraph*, 17.06.2018 https://www.telegraph.co.uk/science/2018/05/06/17-british-sperm-donors-have-fathered-500-children-figures-show/
7 Allan, S, *Donor Conception and the Search for Information: From Secrecy to Openness*, p. 119, 2017, Farnham: Ashgate
8 Human Fertilisation and Embryology Authority, 'Finding Out About Your Donor and Genetic Siblings', n.d. https://www.hfea.gov.uk/donation/donor-conceived-people-and-their-parents/finding-out-about-your-donor-and-genetic-siblings/
9 Parliament of Australia, Main Committee Constituency Statements, Mrs Gash https://parlinfo.aph.gov.au/parlInfo/search/display/display.w3p;query=Id%3A%22chamber%2Fhansardr%2F2010-10-25%2F0190%22
10 Hasham, N, 'Joanna Gash Concerned About Accidental Incest', *Illawarra Mercury*, 27.10.2010 https://www.illawarramercury.com.au/story/632439/joanna-gash-concerned-about-accidental-incest/
11 Conversation with Jemma Tribe, May 2020.
12 'Mums Shocked to Discover Children Have 43 Half Siblings', Kidspot, 12.04.2019 https://www.kidspot.com.au/news/mums-shocked-to-find-their-childrens-siblings-are-their-neighbours/news-story/6e748a5eb8355eef58a354ef6cf93f95
Ruiz, K, 'Lesbian Couple Who Conceived Five Kids by a Sperm Donor Discover Neighbour's Children Have The SAME "Blue-eyed Surfie" Dad Who Donated 48 Times', *Daily Mail Australia*, 06.04.2019 https://www.dailymail.co.uk/news/article-6891179/Same-sex-couple-warns-incest-dangers-learning-sperm-donor-fathered-48-children.html

13 ibid. n5
14 'New Thai Surrogacy Law Bans Foreigners', SBS News, 01.08.2015 https://www.sbs.com.au/news/new-thai-surrogacy-law-bans-foreigners

Chapter 21

1 Question to We Are Donor Conceived, March 2020
2 Joffe, E, 'My Wife Is My Sister', Dear Prudence, Slate, 19.02.2013 https://slate.com/human-interest/2013/02/dear-prudence-my-wife-and-i-came-from-the-same-sperm-donor.html?fbclid=IwAR2bX0pCDmvu3sDp2HShjySxDNHDr1-N-POOTmCxpmc7k9xfXDxa3Py9etY
3 Mroz, J, 'One Sperm Donor, 150 Offspring', *The New York Times*, 05.09.2011 https://www.nytimes.com/2011/09/06/health/06donor.html
4 Interview with Matt Doran, April 2020

Chapter 22

1 Women of Letters, All About Women Festival, Sydney March 2016
2 Email communication with Peter Illingworth, September–December 2014
3 Email communication with Belinda Hawkins, August 2014
4 *Australian Story* Part 1 broadcast 11.08.2014; files received from RNSH 12.08.2014
5 Email communication with RNSH and NSLHD, August–September 2014
6 IVF Australia, 'Ethics Committee' https://www.ivf.com.au/about-us/why-choose-ivfaustralia/ethics-committee
7 Email communication with NSLHD, October 2014
8 Email communication with Jamie Parker, October 2014
9 Parliament of NSW, 'Health Practitioner Regulation Legislation Amendment Bill 2014', Second Reading, Legislative Assembly Hansard, 14.10.2014 https://www.parliament.nsw.gov.au/Hansard/Pages/HansardResult.aspx#/docid/HANSARD-1323879322-58202/link/82
10 Email communication with RNSH, November 2014

Chapter 23

1 IAB meeting, 01.12.2014
2 Email communication with Peter Illingworth, February–March 2015
3 Email communication with Department of Health, March 2015
4 ibid. n2
5 ibid n3
6 Email communication with RNSH, April 2015
7 ibid. n6
8 ibid. n6
9 Kerin, L, 'Medical Documents of 88 IVF Patients Deliberately Changed', The World Today, ABC, 22.04.2015 https://www.abc.net.au/worldtoday/content/2015/s4221399.htm
See also NSW Health, 'Investigation Into Clinical Records of Royal North Shore Hospital's Former Assisted Reproductive Technology Clinic', 22.04.2015
10 ibid. n6

Chapter 24

1 IAB, *Investigation Report Into Possible Tampering of Clinical Records for Assisted Reproduction Technology*, IAB Job No: 2697, p. 1, April 2015
2 NSW Government, *Assisted Reproductive Technology Amendment Act 2016 No 11*, p. 12 https://beta.legislation.nsw.gov.au/view/pdf/asmade/act-2016-11
3 Australian Government National Health and Medical Research Council, *Ethical Guidelines of the Use of Assisted Reproductive Technology in Clinical Practice and Research*, Section 5.13 'Use of Gametes Collected Before 2004', p. 49, 2017 https://www.nhmrc.gov.au/sites/default/files/documents/reports/use-assisted-reproductive-technology.pdf
4 Email to Douglas Saunders, May 2020
5 Phone conversation with Margaret Saunders, May 2020
6 Letter from Medical Services, RNSH, May 2020

Chapter 25

1 Email communication from SESLHD, April 2020
2 We Are Donor Conceived, '2020 We Are Donor Conceived Survey', 17.09.2020 https://www.wearedonorconceived.com/2020-survey-top/2020-we-are-donor-conceived-survey/
3 *The Herald Sun*, 06.12.2012
The Advertiser 05.06.2011
4 Coronial investigation into Faith A Haugh, June 2015

5 Victorian Assisted Reproductive Treatment Authority, 'Becoming a Donor: Am I Eligible?' https://www.varta.org.au/understanding-donor-conception/becoming-donor#am-I-eligible
6 Merck Healthcare, 'Summary of Product Characteristics: GONAL-f 7', p. 13 https://hcp.merckgroup.com/content/dam/web/healthcare/fertility/h4b-content-2018/gonal-f/EU-SPC-LAB-PL-Follitropin-alfa-II-145-2019Dec-en.pdf
7 Merck Healthcare, 'Gonal-f' https://hcp.merckgroup.com/en/fertility/therapeutics/gonal-f.html
8 On OHSS, see Mayo Clinic, 'Ovarian Hyperstimulation Syndrome' https://www.mayoclinic.org/diseases-conditions/ovarian-hyperstimulation-syndrome-ohss/symptoms-causes/syc-20354697
On possible side effects of Gonal-f, see the Royal Women's Hospital, 'Ovulation Induction Program at the Women's', June 2018 https://thewomens.r.worldssl.net/images/uploads/fact-sheets/Ovulation-Induction-2018.pdf
9 Hall, L, 'Childless Couple Dedicate Lives to Helping Others Have Families', *SMH*, 30.03.2008, https://www.smh.com.au/national/childless-couple-dedicate-lives-to-helping-others-have-families-20080330-gds7d1.html
10 Better Health, 'Polycystic Ovarian Syndrome (PCOS)', Nov 2019 https://www.betterhealth.vic.gov.au/health/conditionsandtreatments/polycystic-ovarian-syndrome-pcos
11 Letter from the Coroner's Court of Victoria, June 2015
12 ibid. n9
13 Piper, M et al., 'Hepatocellular Adenoma (HCA)', Medscape, 03.12.2020 https://emedicine.medscape.com/article/170205-overview

Chapter 26

1 Interview with Natalie Parker, March 2020
2 Marriner, M, 'Plan to Encourage Embryo Donation', *SMH*, 20.01.2013 https://www.smh.com.au/national/plan-to-encourage-embryo-donation-20130119-2d08b.html
3 Embryo Donation Network http://www.embryodonation.org.au/default.aspx

Chapter 27

1 Letter from Minister Skinner to Natalie Parker, 16.05.2016
2 Email communication from Embryo Donation Network, May 2020
3 *Australian Story,* 'How I Met Your Father', ABC, 05.12.2017 https://www.abc.net.au/austory/how-i-met-your-father/5861470
4 *Australian Story*, 'Lexie's village', ABC, 28.09.2015 https://www.abc.net.au/austory/lexies-village/7202730
5 Murray, M et al., 'Donate or Discard? The Surplus Embryo Dilemma', ABC News, 04.11.2019 https://www.abc.net.au/news/2019-09-30/donate-or-discard-what-to-do-with-surplus-embryos/11377468?nw=0

Chapter 28

1 High Court of NSW, *Clark v Macourt*, 18.12.2013, pars 79 and 83
2 Supreme Court of NSW, *St George Fertility Centre Pty Ltd v Clark* [2011] NSWSC 1276 (25.10.2011), 13.12.2011 http://classic.austlii.edu.au/au/cases/nsw/NSWSC/2011/1276.html
3 ibid.
4 Riggall, L, 'Mother Takes Legal Action Against Sperm Bank for Her Child's Dwarfism', BioNews, 04.11.2019 https://www.bionews.org.uk/page_145966
'Sweden hit by Danish sperm bank scandal', *The Local*, 24.09.2012 https://www.thelocal.se/20120924/43416
Leidig, M, 'Child Killer on Books of World's No1 Sperm Bank', *The Telegraph*, 02.11.2003 https://www.telegraph.co.uk/news/worldnews/europe/denmark/1445756/Child-killer-on-books-of-worlds-No1-sperm-bank.html
5 Interland, J, 'Organ Trafficking is No Myth', *Newsweek*, 01.09.2009 https://www.newsweek.com/organ-trafficking-no-myth-78079
Scheper-Hughes, N, 'Opinion: The Market for Human Organs is Destroying Lives', *The Washington Post*, 06.01.2016 https://www.washingtonpost.com/news/in-theory/wp/2016/01/05/the-market-for-human-organs-is-destroying-lives/
6 The Royal College of Pathologists of Australasia, 'Ethical and Legal Issues in Relation to the Use of Human Tissue in Australia and New Zealand', April 2018 https://www.rcpa.edu.au/getattachment/ad0d4af1-901a-4056-af05-56bbc06167c1/Ethical-and-Legal-Issues-in-Relation-to-the-Use-of.aspx
7 NSW Government, *Human Tissue Act 1983 No 164*, Section 32: Trading in Tissue Prohibited, 27.10.2020 https://www.legislation.nsw.gov.au/#/view/act/1983/164/part6/sec32
8 Tonti-Filippini, N et al., 'Trade in Human Tissue Products', *MJA*, 194(5), pp. 263–65, 2011
9 'US Sperm Bank Xytex International is Offering Discounts on Vials of Sperm', news.com.au, 15.04.2009 https://www.news.com.au/finance/sperm-bank-offers-stimulus-deals/news-story/988d4ecde30593654f3ec1bd7b77a8a7

10 Van Dusen, C, 'A Georgia Sperm Bank, a Troubled Donor, and the Secretive Business of Babymaking', *Atlanta*, 13.02.2018 https://www.atlantamagazine.com/great-reads/georgia-sperm-bank-troubled-donor-secretive-business-babymaking/

11 NSW Court of Appeal, *Clark v Macourt* (S95/2013), 2013 https://cdn.hcourt.gov.au/assets/cases/s95-2013/S95-2013.pdf

12 Winterton, D, '*Clark v Macourt*: Defective Sperm and Performance Substitutes in the High Court of Australia: IV – An assessment of the High Court's decision', *Melb Univ Law Revue*, 38(2), 2014 http://www.austlii.edu.au/au/journals/MelbULawRw/2014/27.html#Heading128

Chapter 29

1 Phone conversation with Leonie Hewitt, May 2020

2 See The Royal Children's Hospital Melbourne, 'Beta Thalassaemia', July 2018 https://www.rch.org.au/kidsinfo/fact_sheets/Thalassaemia_an_overview/
Also Health Direct, 'Thalassaemia', February 2019 https://www.healthdirect.gov.au/thalassaemia

Chapter 30

1 Zhang, S, 'A decades-old Doctor's Secret Leads to New Fertility-fraud Law', *The Atlantic*, 08.05.2019 https://www.theatlantic.com/science/archive/2019/05/cline-fertility-fraud-law/588877/
Heisel, W, 'Doctors Behaving Badly: Connecticut Fertility Doctor Survives Despite Bombshell Accusation', Center for Health Journalism, 05.05.2010 https://www.centerforhealthjournalism.org/blogs/doctors-behaving-badly-connecticut-fertility-doctor-survives-despite-bombshell-accusation
Hogan, J, 'Former Idaho Falls Doctor Admits to Using His Own Sperm to Impregnate Patients', *Post Register*, 07.11.2019 https://www.postregister.com/news/crime_courts/former-idaho-falls-doctor-admits-to-using-his-own-sperm/article_1a130b1b-90df-53fb-9ca5-5d8ef32a1349.html
Blaisdell, E, 'More Motions Filed in Gynecologist Case', *Times Argus*, 13.08.2019 https://www.timesargus.com/news/local/more-motions-filed-in-gynecologist-case/article_95b602dd-6bfb-5547-819a-6b4cad95dd7b.html

2 Ettachfini, E, 'Doctors Can Legally Inseminate Patients With Their Own Sperm in Most States', *Vice*, 23.04.2019 https://www.vice.com/en_us/article/pajdn7/fertility-fraud-insemination-laws-donald-cline

3 Motluk, A, 'Insemination Fraud', HeyReprotech, 12.02.2020 https://heyreprotech.substack.com/p/insemination-fraud

4 California Code, Penal Code - PEN § 367g https://codes.findlaw.com/ca/penal-code/pen-sect-367g.html

5 Indiana in May 2019, Texas in June 2019: Trachman, E, '2 States Pass Laws to Reduce Donor Creepiness', Above the Law, 12.06.2019 https://abovethelaw.com/2019/06/2-states-pass-laws-to-reduce-doctor-creepiness/

6 Byrne, E, 'Texas House Passes Bill Classifying Fertility Fraud as Sexual Assault', *The Texas Tribune*, 16.05.2019 https://www.texastribune.org/2019/05/16/texas-house-bill-fertility-fraud-crime/

7 Phillips, K et al., 'Texas Woman Seeks to Change Law After DNA Test Reveals Shocking Truth About her Genetic Family Tree', ABC News, 04.05.2019 https://abcnews.go.com/US/texas-woman-seeks-change-law-dna-test-reveals/story?id=62809127

8 ibid.

9 Garrett, R, 'Dallas Woman's Push to Make Fertility Fraud a Crime Results in New Law on the Books in Texas', *The Dallas Morning News*, 05.06.2019 https://www.dallasnews.com/news/politics/2019/06/05/dallas-woman-s-push-to-make-fertility-fraud-a-crime-results-in-new-law-on-the-books-in-texas/

10 Christie, M, 'Texas Passes New Law After Woman Discovers Her Mom's Fertility Doctor is Her Father', ABC News, 06.06.2019 https://abcnews.go.com/US/texas-passes-law-woman-discovers-moms-fertility-doctor/story?id=63516936

11 Trachman, E, 'Reproductive Battery: a New Crime For a New World', Above the Law, 08.07.2020 https://abovethelaw.com/2020/07/reproductive-battery-a-new-crime-for-a-new-world/?rf=1

12 For e.g. see Pride Angel, 'Quarantining Frozen Sperm' https://www.prideangel.com/Information-Centre/Health-Screening/Quarantining-frozen-sperm.aspx

13 See Paddock, C, 'Frozen Sperm as Good as Fresh for IVF Treatment', Medical News Today, 08.08.2013 https://www.medicalnewstoday.com/articles/264550#1

14 'Fertility clinic founder may have fathered up to 600 children', *The Australian*, 08.04.2012 https://www.theaustralian.com.au/news/latest-news/fertility-clinic-founder-may-have-fathered-up-to-600-children/news-story/206a55eab0c404f14e2acf40cfcb6a3b

15 Trépanier, A, 'Class-action Lawsuit Against Disgraced Fertility Doctor Grows', CBC News, 15.06.2020 https://www.cbc.ca/news/canada/ottawa/norman-barwin-class-action-16-biological-children-1.5609426
Payne, E, 'Timeline: a Look at the Story of Dr. Norman Barwin', *Ottawa Citizen*, 03.03.2018 https://ottawacitizen.com/news/local-news/timeline-a-look-at-the-story-of-dr-norman-barwin

16 Broughton, T, 'Durban Sperm Doctor Fathered Five Children With His Patients', *Sunday Times*, 12.08.2018 https://www.timeslive.co.za/sunday-times/news/2018-08-11-durban-sperm-doctor-fathered-five-children-with-his-patients/

17 For e.g.: South Africa – total donor anonymity; https://journals.plos.org/plosone/article?id=10.1371/journal.pone.0226603
UK – identifying info only for those born after 2005
Australia – identifying info only for half of the eight states and territories
United States – no laws; depends on the clinic. Washington State is the only state that requires non-anonymous donation, for those born in 2011 or after; https://www.bionews.org.uk/page_95954
Canada – no laws banning anonymity, depends on clinic; https://ottawacitizen.com/news/local-news/dna-testing-has-virtually-brought-an-end-to-anonymous-sperm-donations-its-time-canadas-laws-caught-up-say-donor-offspring
Netherlands – no anonymity since 2004; https://www.researchgate.net/publication/7430930_A_new_Dutch_Law_regulating_provision_of_identifying_information_of_donors_to_offspring_background_content_and_impact

Chapter 31

1 Ancestry, 'Your Privacy', 23.09.2020 https://www.ancestry.com.au/cs/legal/privacystatement
2 Hautula, L, 'Ancestry Says Police Requested Access to its DNA Database', C Net, 04.02.2020 https://www.cnet.com/news/ancestry-says-police-requested-access-to-its-dna-database/
Whittaker, Z, ' Ancestry.com Rejected a Police Warrant to Access User DNA Records on a Technicality', Tech Crunch, 05.02.2020 https://techcrunch.com/2020/02/04/ancestry-warrant-dna-records/
3 'CentiMorgan', International Society of Genetic Genealogy Wiki, 22.06.2018 https://isogg.org/wiki/CentiMorgan/en
4 Buhrmester, D & Furman, W, 'Perceptions of Sibling Relationships During Middle Childhood and Adolescence', *Child Developm*, 61, pp. 1387–98, 1990
5 Brigham Young University, 'Sisters Protect Siblings from Depression, Study Shows', ScienceDaily, 02.08.2010 https://www.sciencedaily.com/releases/2010/08/100802125821.htm

Chapter 33

1 Willetts, J, 'Convict Ship *Ferguson* 1829', Free Settler or Felon https://www.jenwilletts.com/convict_ship_ferguson_1829.htm
2 Hansen, A, 'Sister Elizabeth Kenny – Pioneering Nurse Who Took on the Establishment', Australia's Science Channel, 30.04.2018 https://australiascience.tv/sister-elizabeth-kenny-pioneering-nurse-who-took-on-the-establishment/
3 Catrwright, R, 'Sister Kenny Institute', MNOpedia, 21.02.2017 https://www.mnopedia.org/thing/sister-kenny-institute

Chapter 34

1 Parliament of Australia, Senate Inquiry Into Donor Conception in Australia – Submissions Received by the Committee, 'The Donor Support Group of Australia Inc', p. 76, 2010 http://www.aph.gov.au/DocumentStore.ashx?id=4482af6c-a79d-46b1-90cb-3f65c1505f4c

Chapter 35

1 Email communication, April 2020
2 Concept Fertility Centre, 'Freezing and Storage of Sperm', 12.03.2010 https://www.conceptfertility.com.au/files/6915/6833/9452/Freezing_and_Storage_of_Sperm_12-3-10_UserTemp_12.pdf
3 'LGBTQI+ Donors', Australian Red Cross Lifeblood https://www.donateblood.com.au/lgbtqi-donors
4 Alexander, D, 'Wanted: Aussie Gay Sperm', *Star Observer*, 20.03.2015 https://www.starobserver.com.au/life-style/wanted-aussie-gay-sperm/134209

Epilogue

1 Tanner, C, 'I'm Still Working on Forgiving the Fertility Doctor Who Secretly Fathered Me and at Least 60 Children'", iNews, 27.03.2020 https://inews.co.uk/news/real-life/ivf-sperm-fertility-scandal-dutch-doctor-jan-karbaat-412100

ACKNOWLEDGEMENTS

When you come to speak out on a topic like this, you find you have no groups of established, natural allies. (In fact, quite the opposite.) So the following people are all the more special:

My publisher Arwen Summers, for believing in this from the very first, exciting conversation. My editor Kate Daniel, for being kind but ruthless with my wittering; Anna Collett and the rest of the team at Hardie Grant, for providing an amazing amount of support to a first-time author during a global pandemic. Deborah Bennett's team at the NSW State Archives, who perform a vital democratic service. The good brothers Hynd, and their better halves, Bianca and Sharon, for all their support. The fabulous COVID curry crew, in particular Dom, Amanda, Kirsty, Steve, Olly and Row, for countless neighbourhood kindnesses. Dans Bain, for continuing to stand with us. Damian Adams, Sonia Allan and Myf Cummerford, for their friendship, generous brains, and laughs. The whole UN contingent: we'll have another drink in a Swiss bar one day. Caroline Lorbach and Leonie Hewitt, for all their years of advocacy. Adriana Keating, Lucas Grogan and Lesley Lysaght, for their near-lifelong support. Patricia Fronek, Anna Noonan, Dans Bain and Marianne Leitch, for reading, advising, and unquestioning generosity with their time. My interviewees, especially those who trusted me with some of their more private thoughts, including my cousin Caroline. 'Steven McKenzie', for keeping his word and giving us answers. The indefatigable Heather Watkins, who's changed many more lives than just mine. The wonderful Zoë Wheeler. My absolute boss of a sister, Rebecca Ronan. My mother, for giving me leads at considerable personal cost, and providing invaluable help during a year-long writing process. The Olles – in particular Annette, Nina and Craig (honorary) – for supporting our little fam, patiently hearing out author anxieties and putting up with the abrupt finishing of a book while we were all packed into a single beach shack.

And finally: to Sam, my everything.

ABOUT THE AUTHOR

Sarah Dingle is a dual Walkley Award–winning investigative reporter and presenter with the ABC, working across radio and TV current affairs. As a journalist, her work for the ABC has also won the Walkley Foundation's Our Watch Award for reporting on violence against women and children, UN Media Peace Prizes, Amnesty Media Prizes, the Voiceless Media Prize and the Australian College of Educators Media Prize. In 2010, she was the ABC's Andrew Olle Scholar. *Brave New Humans* is her first book.